AF394476

# ANCIENT ROME

SENATVS
POPVLVSQVEROMANVS
DIVOTITODIVIVESPASIANIF
VESPASIANOAVGVSTO

# AN ILLUSTRATED GUIDE TO LIFE IN
# ANCIENT ROME

## SOCIETY · RELIGION · CULTURE

NIGEL RODGERS · CONSULTANT: DR HAZEL DODGE FSA

LORENZ BOOKS

# Contents

# ROME'S ENDURING LEGACY

*Above: This fresco of the Three Graces from the House of Titus Dentatus Panthera in Pompeii of c. AD79 epitomizes the brilliance of Roman art near the empire's zenith.*

*Below: The Forum Romanum, the ancient heart of the imperial city, was adorned over many centuries with temples and monuments.*

The Roman world lies all around us. Even this book is written in the Roman (or Latin) alphabet. Although the Roman empire in the West collapsed more than 1,500 years ago, Rome's fascination and relevance to the modern world are today as strong as ever.

## THE CULTURAL DEBT

Western culture is manifestly indebted to Rome and so too is that of Eastern Europe, through the Byzantine civilization which Russia perpetuated and, more indirectly, the Islamic world, conqueror of much of the former Roman world.

Although knowledge of Latin may no longer be common – few people now spice their speeches with Latin quotes – it remains very useful in the legal, medical and scientific worlds. Almost half the words in the English language derive from Latin, while Spanish, French and Italian are all Romance languages, the direct descendants of Latin. Similarly, the legal systems of most Romance-speaking countries, whether in continental Europe or Latin America, remain based on the majestic and logical edifice of Roman law. Symbolically, this was only finally summarized in the 6th century AD in Constantinople (Istanbul), the East Roman capital, after the fall of the Western empire. Rome's world survived the fall of its power.

In a more concrete sense, many of Europe's great cities – London, Paris, Lyons, Cologne, Milan, Seville, Vienna – were originally Roman, for Romans had a genius for choosing the right spot for cities that would thrive, endure and revive even after barbarians sacked them. Similarly, Europe's roads often follow or parallel routes pioneered by Roman road-builders. Roman brilliance as engineers, soldiers and as lawyers has never been disputed, but their literary and architectural achievements have sometimes been overlooked by those obsessed with Greece. Rome was never merely the channel through which Greek culture reached Western and Northern Europe: it provided its own unique input.

Observers looking at the Colosseum in Rome, the aqueduct of the Pont du Gard in France, the ruins of Ephesus in Turkey or of Lepcis Magna in Libya, may be awed by the splendour of Roman cities but they are seeing only the ruins of ruins. Rome's huge edifices were plundered by succeeding generations who saw in them only convenient quarries for marble, stone and brick. This applies even to the Colosseum. Revered as early as *c.* AD700 when Bede wrote of it as the epitome of *Christian* Rome's grandeur, its destruction continued until Pope Benedict XIV declared it a site sacred to Christian martyrs in 1749, so preserving what remained.

Our knowledge of the ancient world, while growing steadily as new archaeological findings supplement older literary sources, remains tantalizingly incomplete.

*Left: Rome's empire, while centred on the Mediterranean, spread Graeco-Roman civilization far to the north, west and south, founding cities and extending its language, religion and laws in a way that has proved almost indestructible.*

For half a millennium the Roman world united the lands of the Mediterranean basin (for the only time in their history) and pushed deep into northern Europe. It was in some ways very different from today's world, with different ideas about gods and the afterlife, the existence of slavery and social hierarchy, and yet it was a world whose inhabitants had many of the same aspirations, anxieties and dislikes as our own. Many aspects of everyday Roman life have been preserved at Pompeii, that urban time capsule buried by a volcano just as the empire neared its zenith. Its stunning wall paintings indicate just how much has been lost.

## THE FIRST WORLD CITY

Rome still fascinates as the first cosmopolis, the first truly global city. As its population surged past the one million mark, it drew in philosophers, merchants, slaves and adventurers from across the ancient world, from the borders of Scotland in the north to Iraq in the east. The first to offer the excitement and challenges of a world city, it also pioneered ways of supplying, entertaining and controlling such unprecedented numbers.

Every age, looking back afresh, can find aspects of Rome to admire and emulate, or to abhor and avoid. Some disapprovingly see obese senators, debauched emperors, Christian virgins eaten by lions, gladiators slaughtering each other and slaves toiling beneath the lash. Others glimpse white-colonnaded cities with libraries, theatres and baths, arrow-straight roads spreading prosperity from Britain to the Middle East, broad-minded governors ensuring religious tolerance and many centuries of political stability.

Napoleon Bonaparte modelled his short-lived militaristic empire on Rome's, emulating its eagles, triumphal arches and careers for all, irrespective of national or social backgrounds. In the 20th century, more vicious dictators notoriously copied his worst features. In the 18th century, many liberal Europeans saw in the balanced British political system some of the virtues of *Republican* Rome, which later inspired moderates and extremists in the French Revolution. However, the greatest, most obvious heir to Roman ideals is found in the United States, whose universalism and fusion of peoples echoes that of Rome.

*Above: The Library of Celsus in Ephesus, Asia Minor, testifies to that province's exuberant prosperity in the 2nd century AD.*

*Above: Christian martyrs thrown to the lions – the traditional but usually misleading view of the Roman world. Rome in fact was normally tolerant of almost all religions provided they did not disturb public order.*

*Below: The arched colonnades of the Theatre of Marcellus, dedicated by Augustus in 13BC in Rome, combine concrete arches and vaults with Greek-style columns to superb decorative effect.*

### GRAECO-ROMAN FUSION

*"Graecia capta ferum victorem cepit et artes intulit agresti Latio"* ("Greece, the captive, captured its conquerors and introduced the arts into backward Latium"), wrote Horace, one of Rome's greatest poets. He was stressing his own literary contribution while reiterating a point that was already a cliché. From the 3rd century BC, Romans found themselves ruling Greek cities and states more sophisticated and often wealthier than their own.

Although Rome soon siphoned off Greek wealth, it at first had to acknowledge Greek superiority in all intellectual and cultural fields, from technology to philosophy, from poetry to sculpture. Educated Romans became bilingual and knowledge of Greek precursors served to inspire their writers and architects. This produced an astonishingly fruitful Graeco-Roman synthesis.

While Greek writers originated many philosophical or political ideas, these have often come down to us through Roman writers such as Cicero, Seneca and Boethius. Catullus, one of the greatest among love poets, looked back to Sappho, the Greek poetess, when writing his searingly powerful lyric poetry; a generation later Virgil emulated Homer in *The Aeneid*, an epic fitting an imperial people but one touched with a new compassion for the conquered. Both, despite Greek influence, were deeply Latin poets.

This cultural fusion is nowhere more evident than in architecture. In its early days, under Etruscan influence, Roman architecture was colourful but provincial. Under Greek influence, however, it changed and blossomed. Greek architecture was mostly trabeated, using columns and beams to create buildings of sublime but rather static beauty. Roman architecture, by contrast, was arcuated, employing arches, vaults and finally domes to create a dynamic, exuberant and versatile classicism which has been frequently revived and adapted.

The Romans used new types of concrete to erect their monumental buildings. By the 1st century BC they had developed, in the Theatre of Marcellus, a way of building with brick-faced concrete where motifs such as columns, arches and architraves are used mainly for decorative effect. This theatre was built under Augustus (27BC–AD14) who sponsored a classical revival which looked back to classical Athens for its external forms. The solemn elegance this could achieve is still visible in the Maison Carrée at Nîmes, a flourishing Roman colony in Gaul. Perhaps the finest extant Roman building is the Pantheon, where a giant classical portico opens into a huge dome – the biggest in the world before 1800 – that owed absolutely nothing to Greek predecessors. (It owes its rare survival to its conversion into a church in AD608.) There are few Western cities that do not still reveal signs of this Roman classicism.

### SLAVES AND CITIZENS

Notoriously, Rome's world was built on slavery – as was that of almost every other ancient culture. Most captives from Rome's successful wars of conquest became slaves, a fate arguably better than human sacrifice. In the 1st century AD almost half of Rome's inhabitants were slaves, but this was exceptional. Across the whole empire, the proportion was about ten per cent. However, Roman slavery was not only often different from that of more recent times – slaves could hold positions of real importance – it was also mitigated by manumission, the formal freeing of slaves by their masters, in which Romans took real pride. Horace was the son of a freedman who had done well enough to buy the future poet a good education; Terence, one of Rome's chief playwrights, started life as a slave; Epictetus, one of the later Stoic philosophers, began life as a slave but ended it by corresponding with the emperor Hadrian. There was no racial prejudice in a modern sense under the Romans, to whom the term "barbarian" implied cultural rather than racial inferiority.

The Romans steadily extended the privileges of their citizenship until in AD212 almost all free inhabitants of the empire were granted Roman citizenship. Such universalism is most unusual historically.

**ATHENS, ROME, JERUSALEM…**
Rome's was an empire of many different cults and beliefs, adding to, rather than replacing, the original Roman gods, who were themselves given Greek forms and equivalents. Mystery religions such as those of Isis from Egypt and Mithras from Asia won adherents across the empire and the cult of the Unconquered Sun was adopted by some emperors. However, imperial favour finally fell on Christianity, which had earlier been intermittently persecuted, and it became the religion of the empire. The result was that Jerusalem joined Athens and Rome as one of the triple pillars of the Western world. From Jerusalem came the concept of a single personal god with all that that implies, while from Athens, standing for the whole Hellenic experience, came philosophy, drama and art. Although Greeks and Jews were often intellectual competitors and sometimes even literal opponents – ethnic clashes were common in the streets of the empire's cities – Rome's genius revealed itself in the way it managed to unite and transcend such divisions. Today, Rome lives on in our laws, language, art, architecture and in our religions.

*Above: Fructus being served a drink by his slave Myro, in a mosaic of the 3rd century AD from Uthina in North Africa, one of the empire's richest and most Romanized provinces. Much slavery was domestic in scale and nature.*

*Below: Vault mosaic showing cupids crushing grapes for wine, from Santa Constanza, Rome. This use of pagan motifs in a Christian building of the 4th century AD reveals an early fusion of Christianity and paganism.*

# TIMELINE

*Above: Julius Caesar.*

As this timeline of political and cultural events reveals, ancient Rome had a remarkably rich political and cultural history. As Rome's power grew across the Mediterranean, she adopted and adapted other cultures, notably Greece's, disseminating north and west the resulting culture, usually called Graeco-Roman. But Rome was never a mere conduit for Hellenic civilization. This is especially true in architecture and literature. In the late Republic (150–30BC), Greek culture seemed set to overwhelm that of Rome, but already Roman architects were making wholly original use of vaults and arches. Similarly Latin literature evolved its own distinctive voice. There is no exact equivalent in Greek literature of Virgil, ancient Rome's epic poet, nor of Petronius, the racy satirist. Roman women had far more freedom than Greek, if mainly within marriage, and many slaves were freed.

All dates given before 350BC are approximate. The Romans dated all events *ab urbe condita*, from the legendary foundation by Romulus of their city in 753BC. Only in the 5th century AD did the present Christian calendar supersede the old Roman calendar system.

## POLITICAL EVENTS: 753–101BC

**753** Legendary founding of the city of Rome by Romulus.

*c.***650–510** Etruscans dominant in Rome.

**509** Expulsion of the last king, Tarquinius Superbus; foundation of the Republic.

**496** Rome defeats Latins at the Battle of Lake Regillus.

**451** Twelve Tables of the Law published.

**405–396** Siege and capture of Veii.

*c.***390** Sack of Rome by Gauls.

**338** Defeat of the Latin League: Roman power extends into Campania.

**312** Censorship of Appius Claudius.

**298–290** Third Samnite War.

**275** Romans defeat Pyrrhus and conquer southern Italy.

**264–241** First Punic War.

**241** Sicily becomes first Roman province.

**218–202** Second Punic War.

**216** Roman army crushed at battle of Cannae by Hannibal.

**202** Scipio defeats Hannibal at Zama.

**200–196** Second Macedonian War.

**190** Seleucid king Antiochus III defeated at Magnesia: Rome arbiter of the east.

**167** Sack of Epirus: 150,000 Greeks enslaved.

**146** Sack of cities of Carthage and Corinth: Greece, Macedonia and Africa become Roman provinces.

**135–132** First Sicilian Slave War.

**133** Tiberius Gracchus, tribune, is killed; kingdom of Pergamum left to Rome.

*Above: The ruins of Carthage, once Rome's greatest enemy, then a thriving Roman city.*

## CULTURAL EVENTS: 753–101BC

*c.***620** Draining of Roman Forum.

*c.***540** *Ambush of Troilus by Achilles* wall painting from Tomb of the Bulls, Tarquinia; traditional date of building of first Curia (Senate House).

**510** Building of first Capitoline Temple.

**500** Capitoline Wolf bronze; Apollo of Veii.

**483** Building of Temple of Castor et Pollux.

*c.***390** Wounded Chimaera bronze.

**378** Building of Servian Wall.

**312** Building of first Roman road, Via Appia, and first aqueduct, Aqua Appia.

**300** Bronze bust of "Brutus the Liberator".

**275** Eratosthenes in Alexandria works out earth's circumference.

**264** First gladiatorial contest in Rome.

**254** Birth of Plautus.

**239** Birth of poet Ennius at Rudiae.

**234** Birth of Cato the Censor.

**220** Circus Flaminius built in Rome.

**212** Archimedes killed at Syracuse.

**204** *Miles Gloriosus* by Plautus staged.

**195** Birth of Terence in Africa.

**186** Senate issues edict against Bacchic rites.

**179** Basilica Aemilia and Pons Aemilius built.

**170** Basilica Sempronia built.

**169** Death of Ennius.

**166–159** Terence's major plays produced.

*c.***150** The "First Pompeian Style" of wall painting emerges.

**144** Construction of Aqua Marcia.

**106** Birth of Cicero.

*Above: Painting from the Tomb of the Bulls c.550BC, a fine example of Etruscan art.*

## POLITICAL EVENTS: 100BC–1BC

**107–100** Marius consul six times; reforms army; defeats Cimbri and Teutones.

**88** Sulla marches on Rome.

**82–80** Sulla dictator in Rome.

**73–71** Slave revolt of Spartacus crushed by Crassus and Pompey.

**66** Pompey given huge command in east.

**63** Consulship of Cicero; Pompey captures Jerusalem.

**60** First Triumvirate: Caesar, Pompey, Crassus.

**59** Caesar consul for the first time.

**58–51** Caesar's conquest of Gaul. Death of Crassus at Battle of Carrhae. Start of Civil War.

**48** Pompey defeated at Pharsalus: Caesar meets Cleopatra.

**44** Caesar becomes perpetual dictator; subsequently assassinated.

**42** Republicans defeated at Philippi: the empire is divided, Octavian taking the west and Mark Antony the east.

**40–38** Parthians invade Syria.

**36** Antony launches major offensive against the Parthians.

**31** Battle of Actium: Octavian defeats Antony and Cleopatra.

**30** Cleopatra and Antony commit suicide; annexation of Egypt; reunification of empire.

**27** "The Republic restored"; Octavian assumes title *Augustus*.

**18** Lex Julia: law against adultery.

**16–9** Alpine and Balkan areas annexed.

**12** Death of Agrippa.

*Above: Detail of the Ara Pacis (Altar of Peace), dedicated under Augustus in 9BC.*

## CULTURAL EVENTS: 100BC–1BC

**100** Temple of Neptune in Rome.

**96** Birth of Lucretius.

**84** Birth of Catullus.

**82–79** Building of *Tabularium* (Records Office).

*c.*80 Second Pompeian Style of painting develops.

**70** Birth of Virgil.

**65** Birth of Horace.

**60** Cicero published his *Catiline Orations*.

*c.* 55 Building of Theatre of Pompey.

**50s** Catullus writing greatest poems.

*c.*54 Birth of Propertius.

**46** Forum of Caesar and Basilica Julia begun.

**44–21** Strabo the geographer active.

*c.* 45 Cicero *Scipio's Dream*.

**43** Birth of Ovid; murder of Cicero.

**37** Temple of Mars Ultor in Augustus' Forum, Rome, begun (finished 2BC).

**29** Virgil's *Georgics*.

**23** Horace's *Odes* books 1–3.

**21** Agrippa marries Julia.

**20** Prima Porta statue of Augustus.

**19** Death of Virgil and Tibullus; publication of *The Aeneid*; building of the Aqua Julia; Start of Maison Carrée and Pont du Gard at Nîmes.

**13** Building of Theatre of Marcellus.

**9** First edition of Ovid's *Ars Amatoria*; Ara Pacis dedicated.

**4** Birth of philosopher and playwright Seneca near Cordova.

*Above: The Arch of Septimius Severus in the Forum Romanum, Rome.*

*Above: Augustus.*

*Above: Tiberius.*

*Above: Caligula.*

*Above: Claudius.*

*Above: Nero.*

*Above: Domitian.*

*Above: Trajan.*

*Above: Hadrian.*

*Above: Marcus Aurelius.*

*Above: Septimius Severus.*

## POLITICAL EVENTS: AD1–199

**6** Judaea becomes Roman province.

**9** Loss of three legions in Germany under Varus; withdrawal to Rhine frontier.

**14** Augustus dies; Tiberius becomes emperor.

**30/33** Crucifixion of Jesus.

**37** Death of Tiberius; accession of Caligula.

**41** Caligula assassinated: accession of Claudius.

**43** Invasion of Britain.

**54** Death of Claudius; accession of Nero; Seneca and Burrus chief ministers.

**62** Burrus dies and end of Seneca's influence; Nero becomes increasingly extravagant.

**64** Great Fire of Rome: Nero makes Christians scapegoats and begins rebuilding Rome.

**68–9** Suicide of Nero: Year of the Four Emperors.

**70** Capture and sack of Jerusalem by Titus.

**79** Pompeii and Herculaneum destroyed.

**81** Death of Titus; accession of Domitian.

**96** Assassination of Domitian; Nerva succeeds.

**98** Death of Nerva; accession of Trajan.

**101–6** Dacian wars.

**113–17** Parthian campaign ends in defeat.

**117** Death of Trajan; accession of Hadrian.

**121–2** Hadrian visits Britain.

**138** Death of Hadrian.

**161** Marcus Aurelius, Lucius Verus co-emperors.

**165–6** Plague brought back from Parthia by legionaries.

**167** Marcomanni and Quadi attack Italy.

**180** Death of Marcus on the Danube; accession of Commodus.

**192** Assassination of Commodus; civil war.

**193** Septimius Severus emperor in Rome.

*Above: Human body caught in the eruption of Vesuvius that destroyed Pompeii in AD79.*

## CULTURAL EVENTS AD1–199

**2** Forum of Augustus dedicated.

**8** Banishment of Ovid to Black Sea.

**18** Death of Ovid.

**27** Building of Tiberius' villa at Capri.

*c.* **40–3** Birth of Martial; Claudius builds new harbour near Ostia and Aqua Claudia.

**60** Birth of Juvenal; *De re rustica* by Columella.

**64–8** Nero builds the *Domus Aurea*.

**65** Deaths of Seneca and Lucan.

**66** Suicide of Petronius, author of *Satyricon*.

**79** Death of Pliny the Elder.

**80** Colosseum dedicated.

**82** Arch of Titus; start of construction of Palatine Palace; first of Martial's *Epigrams*.

**100** Pliny the Younger's *Panegyrics* on Trajan.

**100–10** Tacitus: *Histories and Annals*.

**103** Trajan's new inner harbour near Ostia.

**110** First of Juvenal's *Satires*.

**115** Arch of Trajan at Benevento.

**112–14** Dedication of Forum and Column of Trajan; death of Pliny the Younger in Bithynia.

**115** Library of Celsus in Ephesus.

**120–30s** Hadrian builds the Pantheon, Hadrian's Wall, Basilica at London, Villa at Tivoli.

*c.***127** Apuleius born in Africa.

**131** Hadrian establishes Panhellenion and completes Temple of Zeus in Athens.

**140–50s** Ptolemy active in Alexandria.

**150–60s** Galen active as doctor in Rome; Apuleius' *The Golden Ass*.

**174–80** *Meditations* of Marcus Aurelius, composed during wars on Danube.

**193** Column of Marcus Aurelius completed.

*Above: Arches of the Colosseum in Rome, dedicated in AD80 by the emperor Titus.*

*Above: Elagabalus.*

*Above: Diocletian.*

*Above: Constantine I.*

## POLITICAL EVENTS: AD200–540

**211** Severus dies; accession of Caracalla.

**212** *Constitutio Antoniniana*: Roman citizenship for all free men.

**222** Accession of Alexander Severus.

**235** Assassination of Alexander: beginning of the "years of anarchy".

**268** Assassination of Gallienus: Zenobia of Palmyra declares independent eastern empire.

**270** Accession of Aurelian.

**284** Accession of Diocletian: joint rule with Maximian from 286.

**303–11** "Great Persecution of Christians".

**312** Battle of Milvian Bridge: Constantine defeats Maxentius.

**313** Edict of Milan: religious tolerance.

**324–30** Foundation of Constantinople.

**325** Church Council of Nicaea.

**337** Death of Constantine; empire divided.

**363** Julian killed on Persian campaign.

**378** Battle of Adrianople: Valens killed.

**386** Removal of Altar of Victory from Senate House; campaign against pagans.

**395** Theodosius I dies, dividing empire between Honorius in west, Arcadius in east.

**410** Visigoths under Alaric sack Rome.

**439** Vandals capture Carthage.

**451** Battle of Châlons: Huns defeated by Romans and Visigoths.

**476** Last west Roman emperor, Romulus Augustulus, deposed by mercenary Odoacer.

**527** Accession of Justinian I in Constantinople.

**535** Belisarius begins (east) Roman reconquest of Italy.

*Above: Santo Stefano Rotondo, built AD468–83 to house the remains of St Stephen.*

## CULTURAL EVENTS AD200–540

**203** Arch of Septimius Severus; extensive building at Lepcis Magna.

**216** Baths of Caracalla dedicated.

**220s** Origen teaching in Alexandria.

**250–60s** Plotinus, Neoplatonist philosopher, teaching in Rome.

**270** Death of Plotinus.

**270s** Building of Temple of the Sun in Rome.

**295–300** Building of Basilica and the Kaiserthermem (imperial baths) at Trier.

**298** Construction of Baths of Diocletian starts.

**305–6** Diocletian's palace at Split, Croatia.

**307–12** Basilica Nova built by Maxentius, completed by Constantine.

*c.*310 Birth of poet Ausonius at Bordeaux.

**313–23** Building of first Christian basilicas in Rome and Piazza Armerina Villa in Sicily.

**350s** *Pervigilium veneris* (anon); Woodchester "Great Pavement" mosaic depicting Orpheus.

**354** Birth of Augustine, Christian philosopher.

**361–3** Julian's *Orations* and *Letters Against the Christians*.

**380s** Ausonius: *Mosella*.

**393** Last Olympic games held in Greece.

**413–16** Augustine: *The City of God*.

*c.*414 Namatianus writes panegyric of Rome.

**430** Death of Augustine in Carthage.

*c.*450 Mausoleum of Galla Placidia at Ravenna.

*c.*520 Boethius: *The Consolation of Philosophy*.

**528–39** Justinian's *Digest of Roman Law* compiled at Constantinople.

**529** Justinian closes the Academy at Athens.

**532–7** Hagia Sophia built in Constantinople.

*Above: A charioteer in his quadriga (four-horse chariot) in Rome c.AD300.*

*Above: Julian.*

*Above: Justinian I.*

# ROME: THE FIRST WORLD CITY

Rome was the first cosmopolis. By AD100 it had a population of over one million, unmatched by any other city. Greek was spoken almost as commonly in its streets as Latin for educated Romans were bilingual. The resulting Graeco-Roman cultural fusion was most marked in architecture. Greek classical architecture relied on columns and porticoes of stone and marble. The Romans, lacking such good stone, exploited concrete to create vaults, arches and domes. The Pantheon (built *c.* AD124–8) unites a sublime Greek portico with a brilliantly designed concrete Roman dome. The Romans, who never believed that form had to follow function, used classical columns less to support roofs or porticoes than for decorative purposes, humanizing massive, sometimes blank structures. Their columns employed a distinct classical language based ultimately on the human form.

Despite Rome's own vastness, humanity remained the measure and ideal of Roman classical culture. This classical style proved so flexible and inspirational that it influenced Byzantine, Romanesque (Norman), Renaissance, Baroque, Neoclassical and other styles well into the 20th century. Most great Western cities reveal this Roman influence, as the Capitol in Washington, St Paul's Cathedral in London and the Arc de Triomphe in Paris attest. The Romans built lavishly across their empire, founding or refounding cities. Some, since abandoned – Lepcis Magna in Libya, Palmyra in Syria, Pompeii in Italy – now vividly display the wonders of Roman architecture and city life, as does the city of Rome itself.

*Left: Rome's influence led to similar buildings across the empire such as the amphitheatre at Nimes, France, c AD80, inspired by the Colosseum.*

# CHAPTER I

# BUILDING THE CITY OF ROME

Rome, notoriously, was not built in a day, nor was it built following any clear-cut plan. Instead, its growth from a few huts above the river Tiber into the world's first giant city was often chaotic. The expanding city was short of space within its walls and spread upwards as well as outwards. Caesar, followed by the emperor Augustus and his successors, tried to plan the city along more rational lines. However, Rome, unlike ancient Alexandria or Antioch – or Paris or Washington today – was never a city of great avenues. Rather, it developed as an accumulation of tight-packed buildings and narrow streets punctuated by such immense monuments as the Colosseum or by noble colonnaded open spaces such as the Forum of Trajan.

Frequently ravaged by fires and serious floods, Rome was constantly rebuilt. The population probably peaked in the 2nd century AD, but emperors continued to adorn Rome lavishly until the time of Constantine. He founded a new centre in the East, Constantinople, which finally eclipsed the old metropolis. Rome's subsequent gradual decay – aggravated more by its inhabitants' tendency to use the ancient buildings as quarries than by barbarian attacks – was slowed by the remarkable skills of the Roman engineers who had built so well. Even the ruins of their ruins still impress.

*Left: The Forum Romanum today showing, left to right, the Temple of Castor and Pollux, the Arch of Septimius Severus and, far right, the Curia or Senate House.*

# BUILDING EARLY ROME:
## 753–200BC

*Above: This section of the Servian Wall on the Aventine, constructed after the sack of Rome by the Gauls in 390BC, shows the solidity of early Roman buildings.*

*Below: The impact of Greek classicism after 300BC, such as the early Doric Temple of Neptune in Paestum (built c.500BC and actually dedicated to Hera), was overwhelming in shaping Roman architecture.*

The Romans liked to consider themselves superior to their neighbours of central Italy. However, they were deeply influenced in architecture as in other matters by the Etruscans in their early years, whether or not Etruscan kings ever ruled in Rome. The simple shepherds' huts that supposedly sheltered Romulus and other early Romans were devoutly preserved as late as Augustus' time and still survive today. These gave way to larger buildings as Rome became an urban settlement in the 7th century BC.

### EARLY CIVIC STRUCTURES
Central to Roman life was the Forum Romanum (market/meeting place), which was first paved in the late 7th century BC. The digging of the *Cloaca Maxima*, the Great Drain or ditch, allowed the draining of the valley of the later Forum Romanum. When covered over, this became and long remained the world's greatest sewer. The first wooden bridge over the Tiber, the *Pons Sublicius*, was built c. 600BC, traditionally by the Etruscan king Ancus Marcius. This was the bridge held by Horatio against the Etruscan forces of Lars Porsena in c. 505BC, according to the historian Livy. The location of the city was partly dictated by the fact that it provided the lowest practical crossing point of the Tiber. These solidly practical measures sometimes also had a religious aspect, for the word *pontifex*, bridge-maker, came to mean high priest.

### ETRUSCAN INFLUENCE
The Etruscans' distinctive form of temple-building deeply influenced the Romans. The Etruscans were also influenced by the Greeks, but unlike Greek temples, whose columns ran all round the *cella* – the central chamber housing the deity's statue – Etruscan temples had their columns chiefly in front, with only a few on the side and none at the back. Etruscan temples also had a staircase at the front, as the temple stood on a high podium. This meant that they could be approached properly only from the front. This suited Etruscan religious practices, which were always much concerned with divination procedures that required their priests to be exactly positioned.

The temple superstructure was built mostly of mud brick, plus a timber or wattle and daub type of construction that was brightly stuccoed or painted, for the area adjacent to Rome lacked easily available attractive building stone. Yellow-grey volcanic *tufa* was the commonest local material, which was later supplemented by travertine stone. Adorning the temples' roofs were similarly colourful life-size terracotta statues of the gods. (Almost all ancient statues and many buildings, whether Greek, Etruscan or Roman, were vividly painted in a way which might strike modern eyes as garish.)

The greatest temple in Rome was that on the Capitoline Hill to Jupiter Optimus Maximus (Best and Greatest), traditionally built by the last Etruscan king Tarquinius Superbus (the Proud) just before his expulsion in 509BC. Raised on a podium about 13ft (4m) high, the huge edifice, 204ft (62m) long and 175ft (53m) long, was comparable in size to the biggest temples of the Greek world and presumably indicative of the wealth of Rome at the time. Only its podium remains intact. This shows the temple was generally Etruscan in style but that it had three *cellae*, with three rows of columns to the front and a single row of seven columns on either side. The central *cella* contained the cult statue of Jupiter – king of the gods and Rome's supreme deity – flanked by shrines to Juno, his wife, to the left, and Minerva (Athena in Greek), his daughter, on the right. The temple burnt down numerous times and was grandiosely rebuilt by Sulla in *c*. 80BC, actually using columns from the Athenian temple to Olympian Zeus but keeping its overall proportions. All private building on the Capitol was banned in 384BC.

Temples were also built around the Forum Romanum. These included the Temple of Saturn *c*. 498BC, the Temple of Castor and Pollux *c*. 483BC and the Temple of Concord of 366BC. A temple to the Greek healing-god Asculepius, whose worship was introduced in 291BC when a plague threatened, was built on the Tiber island. This was outside the *pomerium* or sacred city boundary, for the god, if essential to avert the plague, remained a foreigner.

Following the expulsion of the kings, Rome may for a time have become poorer but the newly republican city continued to grow, with civic life now more focused on the Forum. At first crowded with *tabernae* (shops or booths), the Forum became and remained the grand ceremonial and civic centre of Rome, especially after the cattle and sheep market was moved to the Forum Boarium and the vegetable market was similarly displaced to the Forum Holitorum. Porticoes and

balconies were added to the remaining shops on two sides of the Forum in 318BC, increasing the square's dignity and providing viewing facilities for the people. Many of the city's greatest buildings were rebuilt around the Forum Romanum: the Curia Hostilia (Senate House), the Rostra (Speakers' Platform) from which magistrates could address the people gathered in the *Comitium* (Assembly) and the *Regia* (the house of the Pontifex Maximus).

### THE SERVIAN WALL

Among the most imposing structures of early Rome was the Servian Wall, parts of whose massive tufa masonry survive. This was supposedly first built by the Etruscan King Servius in the 6th century BC but was in fact erected in haste only after the Gauls had sacked the nearly defenceless city in 390BC.

Seven miles (11km) long and about 30ft (20m) high, the wall enclosed an area of 1,000 acres (400 ha) and made the city, if properly defended, almost impregnable. It proved its worth against Hannibal, in the Second Punic War (218–202BC), who failed to capture the city.

*Above: The remains of the giant columns of the Temple of Vespasian. It was built at the same time (the AD80s) and in the same style as the Temple of Jupiter was rebuilt, but of this almost nothing remains.*

*Below: The outlet of the Cloaca Maxima, the Great Drain, dug before 600BC in the Etruscan period.*

# THE LATER REPUBLIC:
## 200–31BC

*Above: The austere Tabularium or Records Office dates from Sulla's dictatorship 82–79BC, but it has a Renaissance upper floor.*

*Below: Dating from c. 120BC, the Temple of Hercules Victor (or Vesta) was one of Rome's first temples to be built in the Greek style and of solid marble.*

As Rome conquered the Mediterranean, it gained numerous artworks looted from Greek cities, especially after 212BC when Syracuse, the greatest Greek city in the West, was captured. Roman generals soon saw other sophisticated Greek cities in the southern and east Mediterranean.

Rome itself now grew rapidly – its population had probably passed the half-million mark before 100BC – and its upper classes grew richer, developing a taste for Greek art, luxury and ostentation. Some Roman nobles began adorning their houses and, more strikingly, their city with statues and buildings that proclaimed their fame, power and wealth while revealing strong Greek influence.

Stone buildings with Ionic or Corinthian columns, such as the white marble Temple of Vesta (actually dedicated to Hercules Victor) of 120BC or the neighbouring Temple of Portunus, built of local stone, must have seemed shockingly innovative in a city still mostly filled with old-fashioned Etruscan-style mud brick and timber buildings.

### A DISTINCTIVE ROMAN STYLE

This Greek influence, which was probably at its peak by *c.* 100BC, never completely dominated all aspects of Roman architecture however. The first basilicas, great covered public meeting places such as the Basilica Aemilia of 179BC by the Forum, were essentially Roman buildings, despite their Greek origin and name. Even the Temple of Portunus differs from Greek models in having narrower proportions and a basically Etruscan plan. Most of its columns are massed in front and its side pillars are engaged – half-buried in the wall – a Roman device, decorative rather than structural, that proved very influential in architecture from the Renaissance on. About the same time, the Romans began to realize the potential of the true arch and vault through using *opus caementicum*, Roman concrete. While none of these was a Roman invention – the arch was known in pharaonic Egypt – Romans were to employ all three to unprecedentedly powerful effect.

Perhaps the most impressive surviving structure of the late Republic comes from Praeneste (Palestrina) just outside Rome. Now thought to date from *c.* 130BC, the remarkable complex of the Temple of Fortuna Primigenia, sited 600ft (196m) above the Latium plain, employs a vaulted substructure to support its upper terraces. Behind them the sanctuary of the oracle, novelly semicircular in shape, is cut deep into the hillside. It is approached by a series of criss-crossing ramps and colonnades up which worshippers would have had to walk in increasingly

breathless awe. The whole complex was built of limestone *opus incertum* and was probably originally covered with white stucco to create a marble-like effect which would have gleamed for miles. Such dramatic exploitation of the site suggests a brilliant if unknown architect.

In Rome itself, less radical buildings remained the norm. Of the many works of Sulla, the *Tabularium* (Records Office) of 78BC overlooking the Forum, is one of the few to survive intact (although Michelangelo added an upper floor in the 16th century). A massive, austerely dignified structure well suited to a dictator, it is built mainly of concrete. Its façade is of stone blocks, however, and has the arched opening flanked by columns which was to become a typical Roman feature.

Pompey's huge 55BC theatre in the Campus Martius, outside the ancient *pomerium* (sacred boundary) was the city's first permanent theatre. Theatres had previously been banned on the grounds that they promoted immorality and plays were performed in temporary wooden structures which were subsequently demolished. Pompey's theatre used concrete to support a stone-faced structure on a series of radial and curving vaults, so making a semi-circle 525ft (160m) in diameter that could seat an estimated 27,000 spectators. More than just a theatre, its spacious colonnaded gardens offered art galleries and new open spaces for the Roman public. Recent excavations have shown that a substantial amount of the substructures still survive.

### CAESAR'S GRAND PLANS

Never to be outshone by his defeated rival Pompey, Julius Caesar, in control of Rome from 49BC, drafted plans that would have transformed the city into a true rival of the great Hellenistic capitals such as Alexandria or Antioch in splendour as well as size. According to Suetonius, his projects included a "Temple to Mars, the biggest in the world, to build which he would have had to fill up and pave the lake where a naval mock-fight had been staged,

and an enormous theatre sloping down from the Tarpeian rock on the Capitoline Hill". (This almost suggests Caesar was planning to create a theatre exploiting a natural slope, on the Greek pattern.) He also planned "The finest possible public libraries", one for Latin, one for Greek literature, a new Curia Julia (Senate House) to replace the old one destroyed in a riot in 52BC, and a wholly new Forum and Basilica. He is also on record as apparently planning to change the course of the Tiber, probably to try to alleviate the flooding problem.

Caesar's assassination in 44BC prevented the full realization of such grand visions. (The land alone for the Basilica Julia in the Forum Romanum reputedly cost 100 million sesterces.) However, his heir Octavian later completed his restored Curia and the Forum and Basilica Julia became the first in a series of imperial basilicas and fora. Rebuilt after yet another fire under Diocletian and stripped of its medieval accretions, the Curia Julia still presents a proudly simple symmetry.

*Above: The new Curia, planned by Julius Caesar but built by his heir Octavian, still stands, although it was heavily restored c. AD300.*

*Below: The Temple of Portunus is Greek in its Ionic columns but reveals an Italian design in its high podium and narrow proportions.*

# AUGUSTUS AND HIS HEIRS:
## 30BC–AD53

*Above: The channels of the Aqua Claudia and Aqua Anio Novus, top right, were carried by the Porta Maggiore, with its rusticated masonry, across two roads. They were completed by Claudius in AD52 to bring water for Rome's growing population.*

*Below: The Theatre of Marcellus, Rome's largest surviving theatre, dedicated by Augustus in 13BC and named after his first son-in-law, Marcellus.*

According to Suetonius, Augustus claimed he had "found Rome of brick and left it in marble", boasting that he had restored 82 temples in 28BC alone. Even if this boast is exaggerated, it is certainly true that Augustus transformed the city during the half century that he ruled it after 36BC.

### CLASSICAL TRANSFORMATION

This Augustan transformation was classical, even conservative in style, at times looking back to 5th century BC Athens for ideas. What made Augustus' boast possible were the new supplies of marble from quarries at Carrara near Lucca. If not as finely translucent as Greek marble, Carrara marble was abundant and relatively cheap. For his grandest buildings, Augustus also imported coloured marble, setting the seal of approval on the use of coloured marble in public building. However, marble façades covered brick and concrete cores, while most housing, especially the

*Left: Known as the first Roman emperor, Augustus took pains to seem no more than princeps to his contemporaries.*

tall *insulae* (apartment blocks), lacked marble even to front their flimsy walls of rubble and mud brick. Rome remained extremely vulnerable to fire.

Augustus' first task was to fulfil the grand projects of his adopted father, Caesar, which had been halted by the renewed civil wars after 44BC. Among these was Caesar's Forum, designed to supplement the old Forum Romanum, Rome's ancient heart. Augustus completed this with fine colonnaded porticoes on three sides and the Temple of Venus Genetrix, the goddess from whom the Julian dynasty claimed descent, on its fourth. He enlarged and completed the great Basilica Julia (aisled hall) to the south of the Forum Romanum, and rebuilt the Curia (Senate House) on the north-east. This now austere building once had a stucco and marble front. Next to it Augustus also restored the Basilica Aemilia, lavishly decorating it with marble. A century later Pliny called it one of Rome's three most beautiful buildings. Augustus redesigned the whole jumbled Forum Romanum, moving the Rostra (Speakers' Platform) to a position at the west end. He built a second rostra at the east end of the Forum in front of the Temple of the Deified Julius Caesar, which he decorated with the ships' prows of Antony's defeated fleet from the Battle of Actium. At the other end was a temple to the now deified Julius and two arches, the Actian Arch (29BC) and the so-called Parthian Arch (19–18BC). This arrangement essentially shaped the Forum until the empire's end.

Greatest of Augustus' own projects was the Forum of Augustus north of the Forum Julium – the extra forum was needed by Rome's ever-growing population. Started in 37BC to celebrate victory over Caesar's assassins, it was only finished in 2BC. It had some markedly Greek features, notably the caryatids (columns like draped women) copied from the Athenian Erechtheum, supporting porticoes on either side on the upper level. Behind this lay *exedrae* (recesses) housing statues of ancient Roman heroes of the Republic, including legendary heroes like Romulus and Aeneas. The new temple of Mars Ultor (Mars the Avenger) was, by contrast, typically Italian. Resting on a high podium and intended to be seen only from the front, its eight tall columns at the front must have dominated the narrow Forum. Behind rose a huge wall built of tufa, which acted as a firewall and hid a slum area known as the Suburba. Augustus' fame as a peacebringer was honoured by the sublimely classical Ara Pacis (Altar of Peace), whose reliefs show Augustus, his family and friends in solemn but sociable procession. The last temple of Augustus' reign was the Temple of Concord, which again revealed Athenian influences and was probably part-built by Greek craftsmen. Augustus' own house was relatively modest. It consisted of the old house of Hortensius the Orator with other buildings added, such as the House of Livia. However, its location on the Palatine Hill was imperial: he had the mythical Romulus and the god Apollo as his neighbours.

### AUGUSTUS' SUCCESSORS

Agrippa, Augustus' right-hand man, inaugurated Rome's tradition of fine public baths with the Baths of Agrippa in the Campus Martius. If modest compared with later bathing palaces, they already had gardens for gymnastics. He built a new bridge, the Pons Agrippae, improved flood defences against the ever-turbulent Tiber and built new warehouses to store grain. Nearby he constructed the Pantheon (which was later replaced by Hadrian's more famous temple). To satisfy the city's growing water needs, Agrippa built two new aqueducts, the Aqua Julia in 33BC and the Aqua Virgo in 19BC. He did not neglect basics either, reportedly personally inspecting the Cloaca Maxima in a boat – the Great Drain was big enough for such voyages – and restoring it and other sewers.

By comparison, Augustus' successors built little. Tiberius concentrated the whole Praetorian Guard in Rome and necessitated the building of the large rectilinear camp that henceforth abutted the city to accommodate them. He also built himself a big square palace on the Palatine, the Domus Tiberiana.

Gaius Caligula's brief reign (AD37–41) was dominated by such abortive grandiose schemes as a planned new palace and bridge to the Temple of Jupiter from the Palatine Hill. Claudius looked to essentials, on the other hand. His new aqueducts, the Aqua Claudia and Aqua Anio Novus, entered the city on a monumental double arch, the modern Porta Maggiore, whose rusticated stone inspired Renaissance and Neoclassical architects. He also built the marble gates of the Circus Maximus, but his greatest work lay outside Rome, in the new harbour he created north of Ostia at Portus.

*Above: The Forum Romanum looking toward the temple of Julius Caesar. Augustus cleared the by then cluttered Forum and gave it what became its definitive shape.*

*Below: The remains of the Temple of Mars Ultor (Mars the Avenger), Augustus' greatest temple that crowned the Forum of Augustus.*

# NERO AND THE FLAVIANS:
## AD54–96

*Above: The Arch of Titus was dedicated to Domitian in AD81 to commemorate the sack of Jerusalem and the apotheosis of his brother Titus, the previous emperor.*

*Below: The arches of the Amphitheatrum Flavium or Colosseum, the great arena built by the Flavian dynasty and dedicated in AD80. It remains the biggest amphitheatre ever built.*

With the accession to the throne of the 16-year-old Nero in AD54 – an emperor passionate about most things Greek and with genuine artistic interests if not talents – Roman architecture entered what is often called its golden age. It lasted until the death of the emperor Hadrian in AD138, himself another noted philhellene (lover of Greek culture).

### BUILDING FOR A GOLDEN AGE

As the empire neared its zenith, architects emerged who could use concrete with daring new confidence on lavish imperial projects. Nero's new public baths were complexes which came to include gymnasia, gardens, libraries, restaurants and art galleries as well as swimming pools. Completed in AD62, they were praised by the poet Martial. (The baths were completely rebuilt in the 3rd century AD by the emperor Severus Alexander, along with a new market and a bridge across the Tiber.) However, Nero's real interest lay in extending and extravagantly rebuilding the imperial palace, which was still modest by the standards of the Hellenistic monarchies he admired.

Nero wanted to link the existing palace on the Palatine Hill with the lavish Gardens of Maecenas – already belonging to the emperors – on the Esquiline Hill about 600yds (660m) away. Around AD64 he began building the *Domus Transitoria* (literally Transit Palace) between them. Surviving fragments give some hints of the palace's lavish polychromatic marble, stucco and gilt decorations and also of its radical new architecture.

### EFFECTS OF THE GREAT FIRE

The fire that ravaged Rome in AD64 gave Nero the chance to build on a truly titanic scale. He began constructing his Domus Aurea (Golden Palace) on about 300 acres (120ha) of prime central land. This was laid out like a country estate, with extensive grounds and a lake, "like the sea, was surrounded by buildings that resembled cities, and by a landscaped park with ploughed fields, vineyards, pastures and woods," according to Suetonius. The palace amazed contemporaries with marvels such as a dining-room with a revolving ceiling fitted with pipes for sprinkling guests with perfumes. Architecturally, its octagonal room was revolutionary, for it not only broke with all the earlier conventional rectangular plans but exploited the resulting new spatial effects in ways that proved lastingly influential. The architects' concern with the building's interior was something quite new in the Graeco-Roman world.

Nero also issued sensible new building regulations for the ruined capital after the fire. These stipulated wider, straight streets in place of the previous narrow lanes, the building of porticoes to provide fire-fighting platforms, the use of

fire-resistant building materials and a height limit of 70ft (21m) for *insulae* (apartment blocks). These measures were intended to make Rome a safer, more salubrious city. However, they did nothing for Nero's plunging popularity and his reign ended in civil war.

**BUILDING FOR THE PEOPLE**

Vespasian, the victorious first Flavian emperor (ruled AD69–79), deliberately repudiated Neronian self-indulgence, building for the benefit of the whole Roman people. The wing of the Domus Aurea on the Palatine was incorporated, often at subterranean levels, into the Palatine palace of Domitian and the Esquiline wing of the palace was used by the Flavians as VIP accommodation. Its lake was drained to provide the site for one of the most famous of all Roman buildings: the Flavian Amphitheatre today known as the Colosseum.

The biggest amphitheatre in the empire, the Colosseum could seat up to 45–55,000 people. A vaulted ellipsoid mass rising 159ft (48.5m) to its upper cornice, the building posed unprecedented structural problems. These were solved by skilled engineering that made extensive use of a honeycomb of concrete barrel vaults, although much of the upper structure was of travertine and tufa masonry. The façade is of travertine blocks with purely decorative arches flanked by columns which rise in four successive tiers.

Vespasian also rebuilt the temple to Jupiter on the Capitol which had been destroyed in the civil wars, completed the temple to the deified emperor Claudius that had been left unfinished by Nero and constructed the Forum Pacis (Forum of Peace), to celebrate the return of peace to the empire and to house some of the spoils of the sack of Jerusalem.

Titus, Vespasian's heir, who inaugurated the Colosseum in AD80 with lavish games lasting 100 days, built new baths. According to a 16th-century sketch (for nothing remains) the modest building pioneered the imperial plan for baths with a central bathing block within a large symmetrical enclosure containing gardens and gymnasia. Built of brick-faced concrete, it offered ordinary Romans free or very cheap baths. Titus' brother Domitian (ruled AD81–96), built a fine marble arch in Titus' memory and constructed a vast palace on the Palatine Hill, the Domus Flavia (Flavian Palace). Approaching Nero's in splendour, it became the emperors' main palace from then on and has given us the word palace (from palatine). The palace was made up of a complex of buildings including state apartments, basilica, baths and private rooms. It exploited the use of vaults and was lavishly decorated with coloured and patterned marbles. Domitian, who had become paranoid and reclusive, was assassinated inside his creation in AD96.

*Above: The Palatine Palace seen rising above the Circus Maximus. The greatest creation of the despotic emperor Domitian, it became the chief palace of all subsequent Caesars and gave us our word palace.*

*Below: Nero's Domus Aurea (Golden Palace) was even more renowned for its lavish decorations than its daring architecture. This typical mythological decorative scene shows the birth of Adonis.*

# TRAJAN AND HADRIAN:
## AD98–138

The building of Rome reached its climax under the emperors Trajan (AD98–117) and Hadrian (AD117–38). As the empire neared its confident zenith, the *spolia* (booty) that Trajan gained from conquering Dacia (Romania) helped to pay for his grand projects. The reigns of Trajan and Hadrian also saw the culmination of the so-called Roman revolution in architecture, in which the use of concrete domes and vaults was fully mastered.

### TRAJAN'S ROME

Trajan took advantage of a fire that had destroyed the remains of Nero's Domus Aurea in AD104 to start building his baths on part of its site on the Esquiline Hill. Though not the first *thermae* (imperial baths), they were probably three times bigger than those built by Titus, and were almost certainly designed by Apollodorus of Damascus, who was arguably the greatest Roman architect. The baths were orientated to exploit the heat of the afternoon sun in an early form of solar heating and were built of brick-faced concrete. The great complex, which included gardens, lecture halls, libraries and other rooms for citizens' varied social activities, was dedicated in AD109.

Trajan spent even more money on his Forum and its adjoining Basilica, which were dedicated in AD113. For his Forum, which measured 220 by 130yds (220 by 120m), he cut away the high ground between the Quirinal and Capitoline hills. Flanked by porticoes with marble columns, with a great equestrian statue of Trajan in the centre and large *exedrae* (semicircular recesses) on either side, the Forum became one of the city's wonders. It also provided another much-needed open space for public life in a city whose population was still growing.

On the north-western side of the Forum and instead of the usual temple, Trajan built the Basilica Ulpia (commemorating his family). The largest such public basilica yet built in Rome, it was 185yds (170m) long, with five aisles and apses at either end. Its interior was richly decorated with a marble frieze and columns of grey Egyptian granite, suitably majestic for a building which often served as a law court. Beyond the basilica rose Trajan's Carrara marble column, 125ft (38m) high with a spiral staircase inside. It is carved with a continuous relief vividly illustrating scenes from the recent Dacian wars. Flanking the column were Trajan's two libraries, one for Latin, one for Greek literature, both damp-proofed to protect their vulnerable scrolls. It has been suggested the higher parts of the column's frieze would have been easily visible from the libraries' upper-floor windows, although they are not today.

Behind such obviously opulent buildings rose another more utilitarian but architecturally more radical structure. Trajan's Market was a covered complex built into the hill and remarkable for its

*Above: Built as a mausoleum for the emperor Hadrian and his dynasty, the Castel Sant'Angelo became a fort in the Middle Ages. The Ponte Sant'Angelo leading to it also has Hadrianic foundations.*

*Below: Among the most remarkable of Trajan's many buildings is his market. This covered complex of shops and offices rises above his Forum, with a vaulted hall at its core.*

semicircular shape which housed 150 shops and offices. Much of it is still extant, with a great vaulted hall and many booths. The entire market was built of the brick-faced concrete that was now becoming the norm in such complex edifices. Trajan also added a new inner harbour at Portus near Ostia. The hexagonal basin was excavated inland to shelter shipping from the storms that at times made Claudius' older outer harbour unsafe. Its waterfront was lined with warehouses and the basin was connected to the Tiber by a canal.

## TEMPLE OF ALL THE GODS

Hadrian, although a more cautious emperor politically (he abandoned Trajan's conquests east of the Euphrates), proved equally radical architecturally. His greatest building was the Pantheon or Temple of all the Gods. Consecrated in AD128, it is often considered the most sublime Roman temple. The temple was revolutionary, for unlike any earlier Roman or Greek temple, the Pantheon was intended to be looked at as much from the inside as the outside. Worshippers stood beneath a perfect hemisphere, its diameter exactly equalling its height, with an *oculus* opening to the heavens above lighting the whole building.

The coffered ceiling, which was originally gilded, was cut back in frame after frame, both a structural and a decorative device. The internal columns were, however, purely decorative, for the weight of the dome is carried by the drum's wall, which is supported by eight giant arches inside the brick-faced concrete walls. With a diameter of 142ft (43.2m) it remained the world's broadest unsupported span until the 19th century.

Hadrian also built the Temple of Venus and Roma to a bold, if perhaps not wholly successful, design. Consecrated in AD135, it was modelled closely on classical Greek precedents and was the first temple in the capital to be built to the cult of Roma. The structure was probably built to Hadrian's own designs. It had two *cellae* (inner chambers) which backed on to each other. Like Greek temples, it had columns all round, resting not on a Roman podium but merely on top of steps, which meant that it did not rise clear above its surroundings.

Hadrian also built a mausoleum for himself and his dynasty across the Tiber. This circular building of marble-faced tufa and concrete originally had earth piled high on it but has since become the Castel Sant'Angelo. Hadrian also built the bridge leading to it, the Pons Aelius.

# ROME IN THE LATER EMPIRE:
## AD138–312

*Above: Coin of Marcus Aurelius, emperor AD161–80 who built Rome's second great commemorative column.*

*Below: The Arch of Constantine, built AD315 by the emperor who started Rome's conversion to Christianity and founded a new capital in the east. His arch, however, is oddly conservative, stealing earlier edifices' decorative figures.*

The 60 years following Hadrian's death saw relatively little building in Rome. This was due in part to the exhausting wars that filled most of Marcus Aurelius' reign between AD161–80.

The emperor Antoninus Pius built a temple to the deified Hadrian and another to his wife Faustina (and later his deified self) in AD141 in the Forum Romanum. The temple, now embedded in a later building on the Campus Martius, owes its excellent state of preservation to its conversion into a church, a fate that saved it from being plundered for building materials but which relatively few ancient buildings experienced.

Marcus also began construction of a column commemorating his Danubian wars, which consciously echoed that of Trajan. Completed under his son Commodus, its carvings reveal the sea-change that was beginning to affect Graeco-Roman art. Classical realism had begun to give way to a more stylized portrayal of characters and to much starker and more realistic depictions of war.

With the advent of the new Severan dynasty in AD193 came new ambitions. Septimius Severus added a new wing to the Palatine palace and built more *thermae* (public baths), but these were soon utterly surpassed by those built by his son, Caracalla (ruled AD211–17), the bare ruins of which are still overwhelming today. The *Thermae Antoninianae* or Baths of Caracalla followed Trajan's Baths' layout of a century earlier but on a far larger scale. The whole complex with its gardens and gymnasia was nearly 500yds (460m) square and enclosed an area of almost 50 acres (20ha). Revealing the new priorities of Roman architects, the baths had luxuriously decorated interiors but rather plain exteriors.

### EASTERN INFLUENCE

The Severans also built temples, mainly to eastern deities – Caracalla to Serapis, Elagabalus (ruled AD218–22) to Baal and Alexander Severus (ruled AD222–35) to Isis, although this last was essentially a restoration. The influx of Eastern gods reflected the growth of new religions in the population as well as the emperors' own personal preferences. Elagabalus, for example, had been a priest of the cult of Baal in Syria. On a microscopic scale, a detailed map of Rome, known today as the *Forma Urbis Romae* and dated AD205–8, was carved on 151 pieces of marble, under Septimius Severus. The map's few surviving fragments are invaluable for our knowledge of the ancient city.

### ROME REWALLED

The catastrophes of the 3rd century AD, when more than 30 rival emperors fought each other in the 50 years after AD235, led to opportunistic barbarian invasions across the empire. This spelt a temporary end to massive but non-essential projects. Rome itself came under

threat of barbarian attack for the first time in almost 400 years. To counter this, new walls were constructed in great haste by the emperor Aurelian (ruled AD270–5), for the Servian walls had long since been allowed to decay. The new walls incorporated existing structures such as the aqueduct of Claudius (now the Porta Maggiore) and the Praetorian Guards' camp. Built of brick-faced concrete, 25ft (7.2m) high with 18 gates and 381 towers, they ran for 12 miles (19.3km) and covered an area of almost 3,500 acres (1,400ha), which was by then the extent of the city. Strengthened by both Maxentius and Valentinian I in the 4th century and Honorius in the early 5th, they protected Rome, often inadequately, up to 1870 when the city was incorporated into a reunited Italy. Aurelian also built a Temple to Sol Invictus (the Unconquered Sun).

**ORDER RESTORED**
Diocletian, founder of the tetrarchy system of four co-emperors, restored order to the empire during his reign (AD284–305). He rebuilt the Curia (Senate House), together with the two temples of Saturn and Vesta, reorganized the cluttered Forum Romanum and built another set of baths even grander than Caracalla's. Completed in AD305, the huge size of the baths – they measure 785 by 475ft (240 by 144m) – can be judged today by the 16th century church of Santa Maria degli Angeli that Michelangelo built in the *frigidarium* (cold bath). Diocletian and his fellow tetrarchs, however, no longer ruled the empire from Rome, but chose other cities closer to the endangered frontiers as their capitals.

Maxentius (ruled AD306–12) was the last effective emperor to make Rome his capital, although he ruled only part of the Western empire. Appropriately, he adorned the city with its grandest basilica, the Basilica Nova (which was actually completed by Constantine). The basilica's massive structure – rising to 115ft (35m) with a central nave of 260 by 80ft (80 by 25m) flanked by huge *exedrae* – recalls the greatest *thermae*. Maxentius also built a new palace or villa on the Via Appia, complete with a circus and race track.

After Maxentius' defeat, the victorious Constantine built a grand triple arch in AD315, plundering sculptures from earlier monuments for this age saw little new sculpture, and built Rome's last great *thermae* in AD320. Such buildings perpetuated Rome's proudly pagan imperial traditions but Constantine is chiefly noted for his patronage of Christianity.

*Above: Ruins of the Basilica Nova, Rome's largest basilica, started by the emperor Maxentius and completed by his victorious rival Constantine after AD312.*

*Below: Aerial view of the Baths of Caracalla, built AD211–17, which enclosed an area of 50 acres (20ha) with gardens, gymansia and restaurants besides the actual baths themselves.*

# ROME – THE CHRISTIAN CITY:
## AD312–609

*Right: The nave of the Basilica of Santa Maria Maggiore, built by Pope Sixtus III in the AD430s, is remarkable for its classicism. Its fine Ionic columns look back almost to Augustan styles.*

*Below: Santo Stefano Rotondo, built AD468–83, a church whose two concentric rings of columns recall those of pagan mausoleums. This was built as a martyrium to house the relics of Saint Stephen, an early martyr.*

The early Christians built little for several reasons: keen expectation of Christ's imminent Second Coming, which made all large-scale building seem rather futile; the relative poverty of many early Christians and, most important, the intermittent but sometimes savage persecution by the authorities that drove them underground. Nonetheless, Christianity gradually became the religion of the empire. This process began with Constantine's famous Edict of Milan of AD313, which granted freedom to all religions. A vast church-building programme began, in Rome as well as in Constantine's new capital on the Bosphorus, which was officially founded in AD330.

### FIRST CATHEDRAL OF ST PETER

Constantine gave land and money to Pope Sylvester I across the Tiber in the Vatican where, according to tradition, St Peter had been crucified. Here, the first cathedral of St Peter (it is often called "Old St Peter's" to distinguish it from the present church) was started in AD333. A basilica-style structure, its design owed nothing to pagan temples because it served a very different purpose from housing a god's image in mysterious obscurity. Instead, the church had to accommodate a congregation or assembly of worshippers – the Latin for church, *ecclesia*, comes from the Greek for assembly. (Christianity was another Eastern religion that had arrived in the capital speaking Greek.)

Architecturally, St Peter's was a simple if large basilica-style building, but with a flat timber-beamed ceiling instead of vaults, supported by a colonnaded nave and with a broad lateral transept. It also had a large courtyard in front with a fountain which was used for ritual washing. The whole building was meant to concentrate the attention of the increasing number of pilgrims on the tomb of the martyred apostle at the far end.

The mausoleum built *c.* AD340 on the outskirts of Rome for Constantine's daughter Constantia and since converted into the church of Santa Constanza, was a circular building. Internally, the wheel-like colonnade of double columns round the centre creates an impression of light and air, while its mosaics show delightful peacocks, vines and other fruitful details, all creating perhaps the most charming architecture of its age. The most resplendent of the 4th-century churches was the Basilica Constantinia, now San Giovanni in Laterano, which Constantine began in AD313. Rome's parish church, it is the seat of the bishop of Rome – the Pope. Built of brick-faced concrete, it originally had seven gold altars and glittering mosaics, but it has been much altered, most notably by Bernini in the 17th century and by a fire in the 19th century.

The city of Rome, usually shunned by Constantine's heirs, now became something of a backwater both politically and architecturally, compared to cities such as Milan and Constantinople, where the imperial courts' presence encouraged building. In any case, the imperial regime was increasingly hostile to Rome's overwhelmingly pagan heritage.

In AD382, the ardently Christian emperor Theodosius I ordered the closure of all the pagan temples and the removal of the statue of the goddess Victory from the Senate House. This step marked the consolidation of Christianity into its new intolerant guise. Most temples were not converted into Christian churches despite their central locations because of their associations with the pagan gods, whom early Christians considered not as charmingly poetic archaic vestiges but as maliciously demonic presences. Only a lucky few survived the thousand-plus years before the Renaissance revived appreciation of Rome's pagan past. The most famous of these was the Pantheon, which was consecrated as a church in AD609, just in time to preserve its glories almost completely.

## LONG DECAY

The barbarians who sacked Rome in the 5th century – the relatively restrained Visigoths in AD410 and the far more brutal Vandals in AD456 – merely hastened the decay of the city. Increasingly, Rome's inhabitants and government could no longer afford to maintain their huge inheritance. The long-drawn out war in the middle of the 6th century AD between the invading Byzantines and the Ostrogoths, who had established a kingdom in Italy, saw the aqueducts cut off in one of the

many sieges, an act which Italian historians traditionally regard as the beginning of the Middle Ages in Italy. Hadrian's mausoleum became a castle, for example, as did the Colosseum later. Within the great extent of the Aurelianic walls, large parts of Rome reverted to a rusticity that later charmed northern visitors.

Amid all these disasters, Pope Sixtus III (AD432–40) inaugurated a short-lived classical revival. The noble Ionic columns of the Church of Santa Maria Maggiore support a lintel in an almost Augustan style. Santa Sabina's great Corinthian columns provide another fine example of this surviving or reviving classicism, while Santo Stefano Rotondo (AD468–83), with its concentric rings of columns, again shows classicism flourishing at a remarkably late date.

Even in its long ruin, Rome somehow remained faithful to the classical tradition it had created, for buildings in the Gothic style were to be surprisingly rare in the Eternal City, as if memories of its imperial past discouraged them.

*Above: The Mausoleum of Santa Constanza in Rome, built c. AD340, was later converted into a church.*

*Below: The Church of Santa Sabina in Rome, built AD422–34, reuses grandiose Corinthian columns. It is a well-preserved example of the 5th-century classical revival that ignored all political crises.*

# Chapter II

# BUILDING TECHNIQUES AND STYLES

Roman buildings often seem to emulate classical Greek models, most notably in their use of classical columns. However, Roman architecture soon developed its own dynamic, versatile and highly practical form of classicism. This employed arches, vaults and domes, all made possible by the Romans' exploitation of concrete. The Romans developed types of *opus caementicum* (concrete) early on, due to a relative lack of attractive, readily accessible stone and also to their desire to build fast. They had abundant tufa, soft volcanic rock of varying densities and, further afield, travertine, a fine but brittle limestone. Only with the opening of marble quarries near Carrara in the 40s BC did relatively cheap white marble reach Rome. Most buildings were concrete structures, brick-faced then covered with marble, stucco or plaster.

Although classical columns or pediments in Roman buildings often had no load-bearing function, they were long thought essential to dignify and humanize buildings. However, in the 3rd century AD fashions changed. Although the exteriors of buildings still had some decoration, they became secondary as architects began concentrating mostly on interiors. As most such decorations have vanished, Roman buildings can look far more austere than they did when originally built.

*Left: The bridge at Alcantara, Spain, built under Trajan (AD98–117) and still in use, demonstrates Roman engineering skills at their most inspiring and durable.*

# BUILDING MATERIALS

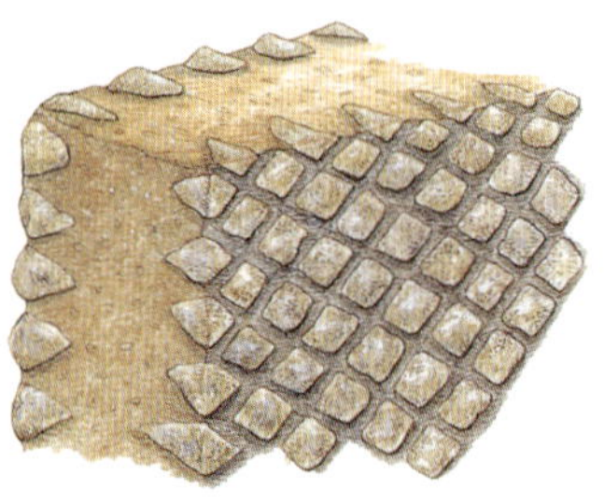

*Above:* Opus incertum, *the first type of facing for Roman concrete, consisted of irregular-shaped small stones placed on a concrete core.*

*Above:* Opus reticulatum, *the next type of facing for concrete, had small square-faced stones laid diagonally creating a network of interconnecting lozenge-shaped joints.*

*Above:* Opus testaceum, *the third sort of facing for concrete, had brick or tile facing over a rubble or concrete core.*

*Right: The main body of the Pantheon is of brick-faced concrete. The giant portico had 16 grey and red Egyptian granite columns weighing 84 tons each, and the pediment was of white marble.*

The earliest building materials used in the city of Rome were mud brick and timber-framing. However, soft volcanic tufa was used for some structures, most notably for the Servian Walls (built *c.* 378BC). Well-suited for the older type of *domus* (one-storied detached house), timber-framed mud brick continued as a common building material in the more jerry-built multi-storey *insulae* (apartment blocks) built from the end of the 3rd century BC. These were built, despite obvious structural weakness, at least until the great fire of AD64. This led to new, although not universally observed, building regulations that encouraged gradual improvements in the quality of *insulae*.

### ANCIENT CONCRETE

Using a characteristic trial and error approach, Romans learnt to exploit other materials, especially *opus caementicum*, their own type of concrete. At times this pragmatic approach worked wonders as at Praeneste, whose vaults still stand. Perhaps inspired by examples from Pompeii, the Romans in the 3rd century BC began building walls using mortar made of lime and *pozzolana* – black volcanic sand first found near Puteoli (Pozzuoli). The walls' cores were filled with smallish stones which produced a solid, cohesive mass when mortar was laid on top. Rome had abundant supplies of limestone which could be burnt to produce lime, essential to lime mortar. Vitruvius, the architect and theorist writing *c.* 30BC, recommended three parts of volcanic sand to one of mortar.

Roman concrete was seldom poured like modern concrete, but was normally laid by hand in roughly horizontal courses between timber frames. These were left in place and mortar added to produce a very strong monolithic whole.

In effect, Roman *opus caementicum* was an artificial stone, vastly cheaper and more malleable than any from a quarry. Initially Roman concrete used for building walls was faced with *opus incertum*, a surface of irregularly placed, small stones over the concrete core. The Porticus Aemilia, begun in 193BC, used this concrete on a large scale for its rows of barrel-vaults. *Opus reticulatum*, which succeeded this early concrete, had small stones with a square face laid diagonally to create a network of interconnected lozenge-shaped joints. This facing technique was developed in Rome and used to build the Theatre of Pompey. Completed in 55BC, this was Rome's first large permanent theatre. The third and final sort of concrete was *opus testaceum*, that had a brick or tile facing over its rubble and mortar core. By Augustus' reign, the Romans were increasingly using red *pozzolana* which produced a finer, stronger cement. (The Romans never made the mistake, common in the mid-20th century, of leaving bare concrete walls exposed to the elements, where rain could soon disfigure them.)

### STANDARDIZED BRICKS
When Augustus boasted that he had found Rome a city of brick and left it a city of marble, he may have been thinking of a city made of mud brick, but fired bricks were becoming more common as building materials. The Theatre of Marcellus – planned by Caesar and completed by Augustus by 13BC – is partly built of a reddish-yellow brick, lightly baked to absorb mortar porously.

Standardized bricks offer builders obvious advantages and Roman bricks came in four main sizes: *bessalis* eight Roman inches square (20cm); *pedalis* one Roman foot square (30cm); *sesquipedalis* 18 Roman inches square (45cm); and *bipedalis* two Roman feet square (60cm). These bricks were often cut into triangles to face walls and into rectangles to face arches. *Bessales* were the bricks most commonly used in the Principate; Domitian's giant Palatine Palace required a lot of *bipedales* for brick facing. *Bessales* were often used for the *pilae* of a hypocaust, and *bipedales* were used to span the distance between *pilae* as well as for bonding courses in concrete walls. Bricks were



*Right: The obelisk in the fountain in the Piazza Navona in Rome (by Bernini, c. 1650) was imported by Domitian for the Temple of Isis he built in the Campus Martius.*

made along the Tiber valley and transported by barge when possible. Roof tiles, which were hard-baked for waterproofing and darkish red in colour, sometimes had their flanges cut off for use for building purposes. Both tiles and bricks were occasionally stamped with the name of the *figulus* (brick-maker) and with the names of that year's consuls, a common Roman dating method. Travertine stone quarried near Tivoli was also used for structural purposes under the emperors, for example in the Colosseum.

### IMPERIAL IMPORTS
Rome imported both finished artworks and building materials on an increasingly large scale. Some victorious nobles in the last century of the Republic used Greek marble to adorn the temples proclaiming their own or their families' genius. Sulla the dictator went further, grabbing giant Corinthian columns from the unfinished Temple of the Olympian Zeus in Athens to rebuild the great Temple of Jupiter on the Capitol in 82BC. (The two gods were by then effectively identical, so the theft was less sacrilegious than it might seem.) Supplementing new supplies of white marble from Carrara, Augustus began importing coloured marbles from the Aegean, Asia Minor and North Africa for his buildings. Coloured marble had been thought decadent before, but there was nothing decadent about Augustus.

Egypt, his greatest conquest, provided another source of building materials and artefacts, notably obelisks. In 10BC Augustus erected Rome's first obelisk, a sundial in the Piazza di Montecitorio. Gaius Caligula imported another, larger, obelisk in a specially constructed ship. In the Piazza Navona today stands an obelisk originally brought to Rome by the emperor Domitian (ruled AD81–96) for the sanctuary of the Egyptian goddess Isis.

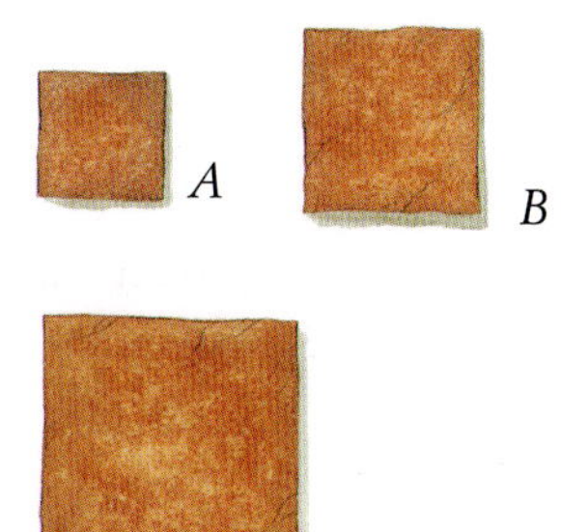

*Below: Four comparative Roman brick sizes.*
*A: bessalis, 8 Roman inches square (20cm). B: pedalis, 1 Roman foot square (30cm).*
*C: sesquipedalis, 18 Roman inches square (45cm).*
*D: bipedalis, two Roman feet square (60cm).*

# VAULTS, ARCHES, DOMEs

*Above: The Pantheon's perfect dome remained unsurpassed in span for 1700 years.*

*Below: In Trajan's Market the Romans made highly practical use of the arch and vault.*

The chief characteristic of Roman architecture from a relatively early date was its use of vaults, arches and domes. The buildings so created, especially during Nero's reign (AD54–68) and after, were still often adorned by classically proportioned columns, but they were not usually structurally dependent on such pillars. Instead, vaults, arches and domes transmitted their weight to the supporting walls.

## AN ARCHITECTURAL REVOLUTION

This development marked a true revolution in architecture, though one that was unplanned and untheoretical, for Roman architects and builders (there was little difference in practice) discovered the basic principles of engineering through trial and error. A vault is essentially an elongated arch covering a space. Built of brick, concrete, stone or any masonry building material, like an arch it depends on materials supporting each other under pressure.

The simplest vault is a barrel or tunnel vault, the continuation of the semicircular section covered by an arch. A cross- or groin vault is created when two barrel vaults intersect at right angles, producing what looks superficially like a dome. A cloister, domical or pavilion vault derives from the intersection of two barrel vaults, so that it rises from a square or polygonal base to create a dome-like structure. The Tabularium or Records Office (built 82–78BC to Sulla's orders) employs cross-vaults in its lower floors.

## ARCHES

A stone or brick arch consists of wedge-shaped blocks (called arch-stones or voussoirs) that stay in place because of the mutual pressure of one stone upon another. These are arranged in a curve to span an opening and to support the often vast weight on top, acting in place of a horizontal lintel (beam).

Stone is normally strong under pressure but weak under tension. This means lintels, lengths of extended stone, cannot span large distances while arches can. Each wedge-shaped voussoir, which is wider at its top than its bottom, cannot fall even if the arch is almost flat, as some are in the Colosseum, for example. However, arches need support until the keystone is in place, so construction of an arch usually requires a timber framework, called centring, to support it while it is being built.

The most distinctive Roman arches are their triumphal arches, which proclaim their engineers' skills as clearly as those of the emperors they commemorate. However, invisible interior arches support many Roman buildings.

## TRUE DOMES

A dome is a form of vault, composed of semicircular or segmental sections raised on a circular, elliptical, square or polygonal base. If built on a square base, an intermediate piece needs to be added for the transition between the square and the circle. It took Roman architects a long time to learn to build true domes. Even in the Baths of Caracalla, completed *c.* AD218, the architects were still experimenting.

Central to the dome's development is the extant Octagonal Room in Nero's Domus Aurea (Golden Palace), the grandiose palace he had constructed after the fire of AD64. Little is known about either Severus or Celer, the designer and engineer behind this great (and speedily executed) project. Whether their work represents a revolution or merely an evolution remains debatable, but their ingenuity, amounting almost to genius, in overcoming the problems in the Domus Aurea is indisputable. Standing on eight brick-faced concrete piers, which were originally lavishly covered in marble and stucco, this dome begins as an eight-sided domical vault but becomes a true dome towards the top. It has a wide *oculus* (central opening) to admit light, supplemented by other light wells.

With the Pantheon, built under Hadrian (ruled AD117–38), the problems of building a vast but perfect dome had finally been solved. This was perhaps due to the genius of its probable architect Apollodorus. Both the diameter and the height of its rotunda (cylinder-shaped building) of brick-faced concrete are identical at 140ft (43.2m). Eight piers support eight arches running right through the walls and help to buttress the walls against the outward thrust of the dome. The dome's weight was reduced by coffering (panels sunk in the dome),

*Right: The triple Arch of Septimius Severus reveals the Romans as masters of arch-building.*

producing an effect which is at once decorative and structural and one which has been much copied in recent centuries. The lightest forms of pumice were used along with concrete in the upper dome to reduce the overall weight.

To reduce the weight of the upper parts of vaults or domes further, *amphorae* (earthenware jars) were later used in the upper parts of some domes, such as the Mausoleum of Constantia (now the Church of Santa Constanza). This allowed windows to be inserted in the dome. The church, though still Roman, points towards Byzantine architecture, whose archetypal achievement would be the dome of the cathedral of Hagia Sophia. The dome of that great cathedral in Constantinople built by the Emperor Justinian in the 6th century AD, seems to sail effortlessly above its square basis, marking both the culmination and the last chapter of Roman architecture.

*Above: The barrel or tunnel vault is the simplest form of vault, continuing the semi-circular section of an arch.*

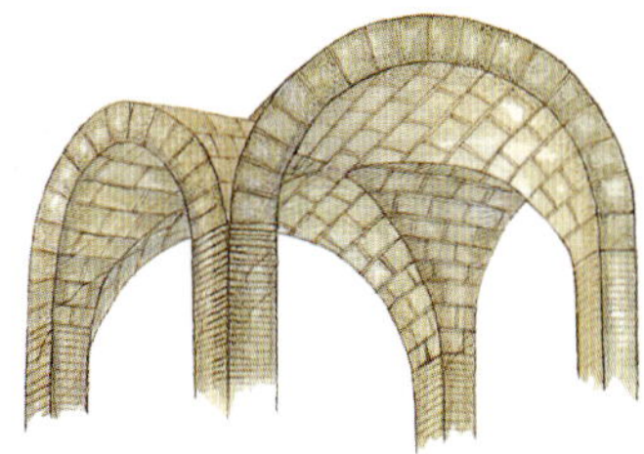

*Above: The groin vault, very popular with the Romans, is formed by two identical barrel vaults intersecting at 90 degrees.*

# BUILDING PRACTICES AND TECHNIQUES

The Roman genius at organizing and controlling huge numbers of men was as dramatically demonstrated in the ways they mobilized labour to erect vast public buildings as in their deployment of large standing armies.

## MASS MOBILIZATION

There was nothing original about mass mobilization in itself. All pre-industrial societies used huge numbers of labourers for their grand projects, from the Egyptian pyramids up to the 19th century.

What is remarkable about so many of the great imperial edifices, especially in Rome, is the *speed* with which they were erected. Nero's huge Domus Aurea (Golden Palace), for example, was built in only four years after the great fire of AD64. The Colosseum, a far more solidly built and enduring structure, took only a decade (AD70–80) to complete between its conception and its lavish inauguration (although its topmost tier may not have been completed until the reign of Domitian). The immense complex of the Baths of Caracalla apparently took only six years to build in its entirety from AD211. By comparison, some cathedrals in medieval Europe took literally centuries to conceive, design and build.

The Romans usually built fast but they seldom built shoddily, at least for public buildings. Indeed, they built to last. They also built without the aid of any mechanical power – without even the wheelbarrow, as far as we know. The closest they got to any mechanization was the treadmill illustrated in the funerary sculpture of the Haterii family from the late Flavian period (AD69–96). This shows five men turning a great "squirrel cage" at the bottom of a large crane to lift blocks up to a temple building site.

More typical of small-scale Roman building methods is the scene from the 4th-century AD Tomb of Trebius Justus in Ostia. This shows two men on scaffolding laying bricks, two men bringing mortar and bricks up the ladder and another mixing mortar on the ground with a hoe, a sight that must have been common across the empire.

## SKILLED LABOUR

Although Roman architects lacked the celebrity status some enjoy today, Vitruvius gave stringent requirements for the (ideal) architect. He was expected to be "literate, a skilled draughtsman and good at geometry, well-versed in history and philosophy, knowledgeable about music, medicine and law, with experience in astronomy". Although not every architect could have had these qualifications, almost all would have been able to draw and make accurate models. We know little about even the most famous Roman architects, such as Rabirius under Domitian and Apollodorus under Trajan.

Unknown master carpenters played an almost equally vital role in making the centring or framework essential in erecting domes, arches and vaults. They had to produce accurate models, for a dome or vault's centring required a continuous surface. This gave the dome its shape

*Above: The empire's largest amphitheatre, the Colosseum, took only 10 years to build (AD70–80) but still stands, in parts almost intact.*

*Below: The tomb of Trebius Justus from the 4th century AD shows a typical small firm of Roman builders at work, perhaps with slaves working alongside free labourers.*

while supporting the weight of the *opus caementicum* (concrete) that was laid on it. To reduce the huge amount of wood needed for *centring*, large roof tiles comparable in size to *bessales* or *bipedales* were later sometimes laid across timber scaffolding instead of solid timber planking. When the concrete had set, the timbers could be removed.

A big advantage of *opus caementicum* was that it required far less skilled labour than the masons who cut and laid stone. Even so, many Romans were employed in the building trade – possibly as many as 20,000 during the great imperial projects. The construction of the Baths of Caracalla is thought to have employed about 10,000 men at its peak, including about 700 marble workers and 500 decorators. Many of these would not have been slaves; the millionaire property-developer Crassus (died 53BC), who reputedly owned a team of 500 slave architects and labourers, was the exception rather than the norm.

Most building teams would have been made up of less than a dozen men: the boss, some free labourers and a handful of slaves. Building contractors normally belonged to a guild or trade union, the *collegium fabrum tignuariorum*, which had 1330 members in the 2nd century AD, mostly men of modest means. The *collegium* was divided with almost military precision into 60 *decuriae*, each with its own officials. When someone reputedly suggested a labour-saving device for the building trade to the emperor Vespasian (AD69–79), he rewarded the inventor but rejected his idea, saying he could not deprive the Roman people of work.

## SUPPLYING MATERIALS

Such huge projects required prodigious supplies of raw materials. By the end of the 1st century AD, huge amounts of marble, granite and porphyry were being imported into Rome. Exotic imports included Egyptian granite and Aegean coloured marble, but most material came from much closer to Rome. About 100,000 poles would have been needed for the scaffolding alone of

the Baths of Caracalla. Vast quantities of tufa or limestone were excavated; 100,000 cubic metres of material were needed for the Colosseum alone. Much of this was travertine for the façade and load-bearing piers, but a lot of concrete was also used, of which the chief source was the quarries near Tivoli.

As there was no waterway connecting these quarries with Rome, all the stone must have been transported in ox-carts. It has been suggested that one heavily laden cart must, on average, have left the Tivoli quarries every few minutes for 400 years. Sea transport could also have been used to ship stone from limestone quarries on the coast at Terracina. Increasingly under the empire, raw materials were stockpiled in warehouses by the Tiber for use in later projects.

*Above: The Tomb of the Haterii, a wealthy family of builders c. AD90, showing a crane being used to lift blocks of stone in a squirrel cage up a construction site. This simple, small-scale machine was typical of Roman technology, which advanced only very modestly. Most teams of builders were quite small, although the total work force employed in the great projects such as the imperial baths must have run to tens of thousands.*

# ARCHITECTURAL STYLES AND LANGUAGE

*Above: The Doric order, left, was the simplest and most rugged sort of column. The Ionic, right, was seen as more graceful and feminine.*

For all its innovatory arches, vaults and domes, the Roman architecture of the Republic and Principate (until *c.* AD275) still used the classical language of architecture to dignify and adorn its buildings. Classical details such as the use of columns both inside and outside major public buildings were thought to provide human relevance and scale, especially when statues surmounted pillars or otherwise decorated a building.

## THE SIGNIFICANCE OF COLUMNS

Among the most obvious classical features used were columns. These were derived from Greek originals and altered to suit emerging Roman tastes. Roman columns were often employed purely for decoration, in contrast to their use in Greek temples, where they had a load-bearing function, supporting the weight of the lintels. Arcuated Roman architecture generally used arches or vaults rather than columns and lintels. The proportions and decorations of these columns were based on five different "orders" or styles. (Many archaeologists now believe that the Tuscan and Doric orders were not really separate orders for the Romans, although they have become so since the Renaissance.)

The correct proportions for columns were first fully explained by the architect and writer Vitruvius in his book *De Architectura* (On Architecture), written *c.* 35BC and dedicated to the future emperor Augustus. His ideas, enthusiastically rediscovered and reapplied at the Renaissance, have had such an immense influence on Western architecture over the last 600 years that the orders have been called Vitruvian.

## THE CLASSICAL ORDERS

Pragmatic and busy Roman architects and engineers did not plan buildings with Vitruvius' book in their pockets, but they scarcely needed to. Examples of classical Greek architecture or buildings influenced by them were all around them and by the mid-2nd century BC many were being built in Rome itself. In Greek cities in southern Italy and especially in Sicily, the conquering Romans could see sublime Greek architecture.

In steadily increasing order of ornateness or luxury, the four major orders were Doric, Ionic, Corinthian and Composite. (The last was a wholly Roman innovation

*Left: The Corinthian capitals of the Maison Carrée at Nimes, France. One of the finest and most obviously classical temples of the Augustan period, it looks back to Athenian precursors while using the classical orders in a distinctly Roman manner.*

or development.) Roman Doric, the simplest order, differs from Greek Doric in that its column sits on a base, its proportions are more slender and its capital (the decorated head of the column) is simple and angular. The column can be either smooth or fluted. An early example is the Temple at Cori.

Ionic columns have volutes or spiral scrolls at their capitals' corners and are longer and more slender than Doric. An early example is the Temple of Portunus, rebuilt c. 120BC. Corinthian columns have longer proportions and are still more ornate, with two rows of acanthus leaves and other complex decorations. The most luxurious Roman order of all is the Composite, a development of the Corinthian order. Examples appear in the interior of the Baths of Caracalla (AD211–17) and on the Arch of Titus.

According to Vitruvius, the Doric order expressed rugged strength and virility, while the Ionic was graceful and almost feminine. Corinthian columns displayed lavish splendour and Composite columns rejoiced in unabashed luxury and power. In the Colosseum, the decorative columns flanking the arches in the lowest circle are Doric, those in the middle circle are Ionic, those around the top line of arches are Corinthian, while at the very top of the building the Composite order appears.

Besides columns, other key elements in classical architecture include:

*pilasters*, engaged piers or rectangular columns attached to a wall and only half-emerging from it.

*architraves*, the horizontal beam resting directly on and linking the capitals of columns.

*pediments*, the triangular gabled end of a ridged roof.

*Right: Roman buildings had an immense influence on later Western architecture, as demonstrated in the Circus of Bath, England, built by John Wood after 1754. It repeats the Colosseum's design, with a development of linked houses with tiers of engaged columns.*

*entablature*, the whole horizontal superstructure carried over a colonnade.

*colonnade*, a long row of columns at regular intervals normally supporting a covered structure along a street or around a piazza.

*exedrae*, large, sometimes semicircular recesses often housing statues.

CLASSICAL REVIVALS

Although these classical elements became less important in some great buildings of the later empire (AD284–476), whose exteriors were often relatively austere, they were revived again and again after Rome's fall. These revivals or renascences started with the Carolingian Renaissance of the 8th century AD and continued with the Ottonian Renaissance of the 10th century, until the Italian Renaissance of the 15th century triumphantly and permanently resurrected Rome's classical architectural language in its entirety. This language was to govern most of Western architecture in varying forms until the mid-20th century.

*Above: The Corinthian order, left, was used to convey an air of splendour, and the Composite order, right, had an air of opulent luxury.*

# CHAPTER III

# PUBLIC BUILDINGS

Although most people in the Roman empire lived and worked on the land, city life was considered the only really civilized life, ideally passed in Rome itself. Emperors decorated the imperial city with ever more monuments and buildings – baths, arches, fountains, temples, palaces, libraries, basilicas, fora – until Rome itself became the greatest wonder of the ancient world. The emperor Constantius II, visiting Rome for the first time in AD357, was "thunder-struck" to see "baths built like provinces, the great solid mass of the amphitheatre ... so tall that human sight can scarcely reach its top".

Such majestic buildings were replicated in hundreds of cities around the empire that were built or partly rebuilt in the Roman style by their inhabitants. Urban life, which was mostly lived in the open, focused on the Forum (market/meeting place). This was a key public space in any Roman city and it was copied across the empire. Life in the open suited a Mediterranean people whose homes were often cramped. However, as Rome became richer, more spacious buildings – most notably the grand imperial baths, along with libraries and basilicas – provided covered, sometimes heated shelter for commercial and legal activities. This was appreciated not only in more northerly cities of the empire such as Lyons, London or Trier but also in Rome itself, where winters can be chilly and wet.

*Left: The Forum Romanum in the 19th century. The heart of Rome from very early days, the Forum was replicated in almost every city founded by the Romans across the empire.*

# THE FORUM ROMANUM

*Above: Under Julius Caesar, who ruled Rome for five years after 49BC, the Forum Romanum was extensively replanned, although little was actually built.*

*Below: To accommodate Rome's swelling population, Augustus constructed a Forum bearing his name just to the north of the Forum Romanum. It was dominated by the Temple of Mars Ultor, three of whose columns still stand.*

For the Romans, the word forum meant a meeting place, a public area and a market place. The original Forum Romanum, a marshy area between the Capitoline and Palatine Hills, was drained and paved by the 6th century BC. Long before the expulsion of the kings, traditionally in 509BC, this area became the centre of the city's social and political life.

**LIFE IN THE FORUM**

On the north-west side of the Forum stood the old Senate House, the Curia Hostilia. In the roughly circular space in front of the Curia the people met in the Comitia (Assembly) to exercise their (strictly limited) powers of voting. From the Rostra, the platform adorned with the prows of galleys captured at the Battle of Antium in 338BC, magistrates and candidates for magistracy orated and harangued the people. So, more rarely, did some of the less autocratic emperors later.

In the Forum Romanum, great nobles met their *clientalia*, supporters or hangers-on. Business (*negotium*) and other deals were made among more general socializing. The custom was that business was conducted in the Forum Romanum in the morning. Meetings for pleasure took place later in the day and elsewhere in the city. Augustus tried to enforce the wearing of the traditional, rather cumbersome formal toga in the Forum, instead of the more casual Greek-style *chiton*, in order to preserve the Forum's special dignity.

Initially, shops or booths (*tabernae*) lined the Forum's north-east and south-west sides, leaving only two sides for public buildings. As Rome grew explosively through the late Republic and early Principate – its population, at least 200,000 in 200BC, more than doubled in the following century before doubling again in the next – other fora became necessary. Rome's emperors provided these with increasing lavishness.

In the early Republic (500–250BC) the Forum Romanum must have still seemed half-rustic with its cattle and vegetable markets. Only a few temples such as those of Saturn or Castor and Pollux added a note of Roman *dignitas* (dignity). This was not inappropriate in what was still predominantly a city of farmer-citizens. (In 458BC, for example, Regulus was called from his plough to save the city in a moment of acute danger but then happily returned to his fields.) However, when the markets were removed in 318BC and porticoes added to the shops, the Forum began to acquire the majesty better suited to the city which was fast becoming the greatest in Italy.

Chief among Rome's new ennobling edifices were the basilicas. These large, aisled buildings were used for both commercial and legal affairs. The Basilica Aemilia, which was built on the north-east side of the Forum and completed by *c.* 170BC, had three aisles and three floors. To the north-west of the Forum, Sulla, dictator from 82 to 79BC, built the grimly

imposing Tabularium (Records Office) on the slopes of the Capitoline, rebuilt the Curia and raised the overall level of the Forum by about 3ft (1m), paving it with marble and tidying up its edges. However, none of these works increased the area of the now overcrowded Forum itself and indeed, they tended to reduce it.

### CAESAR AND AUGUSTUS

Julius Caesar's plans for reorganizing the Forum Romanum were typically ambitious and, equally typically, were left unfulfilled at the time of his assassination in 44BC. He ordered the rebuilding of the Curia (Senate House) that had been burnt down again in a riot in 52BC. Henceforth, the Senate House was always known as the Curia Julia. In place of the old Basilica Sempronia, Caesar built a new larger basilica, the Basilica Julia.

Although he settled a reported 80,000 Roman citizens in colonies outside Italy, Caesar realized that radical measures were needed to deal with Rome's growing demand for public space. He therefore spent 100 million sesterces on new land for a brand new centre for Rome: the Forum of Julius Caesar to the north-east of the Forum Romanum. He did not live to see the completion of any of his plans.

Caesar's heir Octavian, later Augustus, had the time, money and authority to fulfil them all and gave the Forum Romanum the shape it retained for most of the rest of the empire. Besides completing the Basilica Julia and the new Curia, Augustus tidied up the whole Forum, which had become encumbered with many monuments over the years, erected by the city's great nobles. He moved the Rostra to the north-west end of the open area of the Forum to provide an axial focus and built a temple to his now deified predecessor at the opposite end. This was dedicated in 29BC, with another rostra in front of it, decorated with prows from his victory over Antony and Cleopatra at Actium.

Beside the new rostra were Augustus' own triumphal arches; the Actian Arch (erected in 29BC) and the Parthian Arch (erected in 19–18BC), which listed all the triumphs celebrated, from Romulus down to the last to be celebrated by a general not of the imperial family, that of Cornelius Balbus in 19BC. When the Basilica Aemilia burnt down after a fire in 14BC, Augustus had it rebuilt in a much more lavish style.

*Above: Much the grandest new forum built by any of the emperors was that of Trajan who, flushed with victory over the Dacians and unprecedentedly wealthy, in AD107 ordered the construction of an enormous piazza 220 by 130 yds (200 by 120m), flanked by two semi-circular exedra. There was a resplendent equestrian (mounted) statue of the emperor in the middle of the court. To the right lay the Forum of Augustus and, below it, the smaller Forum of Julius Caesar. Trajan's Column still rises up on the left between what were his two libraries, one for Greek and one for Latin literature.*

# THE IMPERIAL FORUM

*Above: Coin of Augustus, whose officially acknowledged reign started in 27BC but who had already started remodelling Rome by carrying out some of Caesar's grand projects in honour of his adopted and deified father.*

*Below: The commercial activities that had once taken place in the Forum Romanum found a new home in the covered Markets of Trajan that curved dramatically above Trajan's Forum.*

In no other building project did Caesar show himself so boldly radical as in proposing a wholly new forum for Rome, but it was arguably a long overdue decision. The original Forum, while adequate for a relatively small citizen body, was not big enough for the huge numbers who now crowded the imperial city. An Augustan census counted 350,000 male citizens in Rome. Although it is not likely all of them were resident in the city itself and that this number included boys over the age of ten, this was still a huge population. The series of imperial fora that came to supplement (never to displace) the old Forum gave the metropolis vital extra public space, besides allowing emperors and their architects opportunities to shine.

## LEGENDARY STANDING

Caesar's Forum had colonnades round three sides. At one end was a temple to the goddess Venus Genetrix, the mother of Aeneas, the legendary ancestor of Romulus and Remus who founded Rome and from whom the Julian family claimed descent. Augustus followed this pattern

for his own Forum just to the north-east. Begun in 37BC, it was only completed in 2BC, an unusually long time for normally speedy Roman builders, as Augustus liked to joke. It was dominated by the Temple of Mars Ultor (Mars the Avenger) which celebrates the victory over Caesar's assassins at Philippi in 42BC.

Inside the temple were statues of Mars, Venus and the deified Caesar, with the standards of the legions lost to the Parthians at Carrhae but restored after the eastern settlement of 19BC. The temple rises abruptly from the Forum's rather narrow space. According to Suetonius, Augustus had wanted to buy more land than he finally did and, perhaps as a result, the Forum is not wholly symmetrical. This was disguised by the flanking porticoes. Massive walls of tufa 115ft (35m) high served as a firebreak and shielded the complex from the crowded *insulae* area of Suburba just beyond. The temple shows Hellenistic classicism in the decorations mingled with Italian architectural traditions. Greek craftsmen probably carved the caryatids (stone female figures supporting an entablature) on the upper floor of the porticoes and the capitals of the columns and pilasters but the plan is very Roman. On each side, semicircular *exedrae* (recesses) housed statues of legendary and historical figures including Romulus and Aeneas and earlier Julians and emphasized the legitimacy of the Augustan settlement. The years of building the Forum also saw the appearance of Virgil's epic poem *The Aeneid*, which gave the new regime the legendary justification which it craved.

No other Julio-Claudian emperor added a forum. However, Vespasian, first of the succeeding Flavians, added the Forum Pacis (Forum of Peace), which was built just to the east between AD71–9. Dominated by its Temple of Peace, it was

meant to emphasize the blessings of peace restored after the horrors of civil war – which were very real, including fighting in Rome itself – and to celebrate the capture of Jerusalem in AD70 by Titus, Vespasian's son.

A rectangle 120 by 150yds (110 by 135m), laid out on the same alignment as Augustus', the forum was occupied mostly by a formal garden which was enclosed on three sides with porticoes whose columns were of red Egyptian granite. The fourth side had a colonnade of large marble columns. The temple façade's six columns were in line with the surrounding columns, so the temple did not dominate the complex. It contained famous trophies such as the Seven-branched Candlestick and Ark of the Covenant from Jerusalem (spoils of war), as well as fine Greek paintings and sculptures. Pliny praised it as one of the three most beautiful buildings in Rome; the others were the Basilica Aemilia and the Forum of Augustus. The short reign of Nerva (AD96–98) saw the completion of the small Forum Transitorium which had been started by Domitian. This linked up the previously disparate series of fora.

### TRAJAN'S FORUM

The last and grandest imperial forum was that of Trajan, the greatest imperial builder since Augustus. Flush with gold from his conquest of Dacia, Trajan in AD107 ordered the construction of a vast piazza 220 by 130yds (200 by 120m), flanked by two semicircular *exedrae*. To allow this, the high ground between the Esquiline and Capitoline Hills had to be cut back to a depth of up to 125ft (38m). Inspired by Augustus' Forum and entered through a colonnaded sunken atrium, the Forum had at its centre a huge gilded equestrian statue of Trajan. The upper floors of the colonnades, lined with gigantic

*Right: This map reveals the intense concentration of public buildings in a relatively small area around the ancient Forum Romanum.*

marble columns, had statues of captive Dacians and horses. The entrance side of the Forum was gently curved. At the far end, instead of a temple, rose the huge Basilica Ulpia with libraries beyond, and beyond that, Trajan's column, which is still intact. The covered complex of booths called Trajan's Markets, which rises up the hill behind in a series of vaulted galleys and halls, also survives.

*Above: Despite the many new imperial fora, the Forum Romanum continued to be adorned with new and restored temples including that of the posthumously deified Vespasian. His reign (AD69–79) marked the start of the new Flavian dynasty who proved dramatic builders.*

# ROME'S BASILICAS AND THE SENATE HOUSE

*Above: Constantine I (AD306–37) was the last emperor to erect great buildings in Rome, although he finally founded a new capital on the Bosphorus.*

*Below: Some of the ruins of the enormous Basilica Julia. Once one of Rome's grandest basilicas, it was actually built by Augustus and was the place where law courts sat.*

The largest public buildings in Rome, except for the grand imperial baths, were the basilicas. Oblong halls on one or two floors, they sometimes had clerestory lighting and some of the larger basilicas had double colonnades and apses (semi-circular recesses) at the end. They were originally used as covered extensions to the forum and later became law courts, exchanges and assembly halls. The word "basilica" may derive from the Greek for royal hall, but the concept was typically adopted and developed by the Romans and later exported across the empire.

### A NEW PUBLIC SPACE

The first basilica was built on land bought by Cato the Censor after one of Rome's many fires had destroyed buildings round the north-east of the Forum Romanum *c.* 180BC. This basilica, the Basilica Aemilia, named after Aemilius Lepidus who helped supervise its construction, soon faced another, the Basilica Sempronia which was built in 169BC by Tiberius Sempronius Gracchus, the father of the radical Gracchi brothers. Houses belonging to nobles like the Scipios were demolished to make way for it. Both halls were surrounded by porticoes, from which spectators could watch both the Forum's civic life and the gladiatorial games sometimes staged there, and by *tabernae.* Very little remains of them, but they were probably built of local tufa stone. Their function was initially to shelter businessmen and the general public. Only gradually did the proceedings of law courts move inside them, when the halls were subdivided by curtains.

Caesar planned a larger and more splendid basilica, the Basilica Julia, to replace the Sempronia. His plan was executed by Augustus. This basilica was 345ft long by 150ft wide (105 by 46m). It was open on three sides, with a double ambulatory portico and gallery surrounding its central hall, supported mostly on travertine stone piers rather than columns. The arcades of its two main façades were framed between half columns, like the Theatre of Marcellus. The courts of the Centumviri, the "hundred men", and the Chancery Court sat inside the grand building to judge suitably important cases. Augustus also rebuilt the Basilica Aemilia in 14BC after another fire, mainly on pre-existing lines. (It was damaged by yet another fire in 12BC.) It had a long narrow central hall about 295 by 90ft (90 by 27m) with an extra row of columns on its north-east side, which were probably decorative rather than structural. Indisputably decorative were the Doric columns supporting a luxuriant frieze on the side opening on to the Forum. The interior was paved with marble and lavishly decorated.

Trajan's Basilica Ulpia, which commemorated his family name and dominated his new Forum, was even larger and more luxurious, as befit a ruler who expanded Rome's frontiers to their widest extent.

Built across the Forum's north side, it measured about 560ft long by 200ft wide (170 by 60m). Its central nave, about 60ft (20m) wide, had two aisles on each side, divided off by giant columns of grey Egyptian granite. It probably had a flat beamed roof with galleries above the inner aisles that would have allowed a view of Trajan's column and a clerestory to provide light. It was dedicated along with his Forum in AD113. Despite its splendour and size, it is thought to have been relatively conservative in style.

Two centuries later, more radical elements in Roman architecture emerged in the huge Basilica Nova (New Basilica). Started by Maxentius, the last emperor actually to rule from Rome (AD306–12), it was finished by Constantine. In place of earlier columnar designs, its huge vaults copied those of the Baths of Caracalla and Diocletian. Also like them, its design concentrated on a very lavish interior at the expense of the plain exterior. Its central nave measured 260 by 80ft (80 by 25m), while its three cross-vaulted bays rose to a giddy 115ft (35m) from eight gigantic marble Corinthian columns. The concrete vaulted ceiling was decorated with painted sunken coffers. Constantine changed the axis of the building by building another entrance with a staircase. In the apse he placed a gigantic seated marble and gilt statue of himself, staring out over his subjects. Even the surviving fragments – head and hands – still impress, as does all that remains of the basilica, the side vaults.

### THE CURIA

Traditionally built by the Etruscan king Tullus Hostilius in the 6th century BC, the original Curia (Senate House) was the Curia Hostilia. Burnt down several times, it was replanned by Caesar in 44BC, completed by Augustus and henceforth called the Curia Julia. A tall gabled building, it was 69ft (21m) high by 88ft (27m) long and 59ft (18m) wide – the exact proportions recommended by Vitruvius – with three oblong windows above a shallow porch. A raised platform opposite the door inside seated the presiding magistrates, and senators sat facing each other on benches. From Augustus' time there were often 1,000 senators, more than the Curia could seat, so younger senators stood at the back. A statue of the winged goddess Victory, presented to the house by Augustus, probably stood by the dais. Diocletian restored the Curia after another fire in AD283.

*Above: The Curia was burnt down again in 52BC and replanned by Julius Caesar in what became its final form.*

*Below: The arches of the Basilica Nova, started by Maxentius but finished and refurbished by Constantine, whose giant statue once dominated the interior.*

# TEMPLES: THE REPUBLIC AND THE EARLY PRINCIPATE

*Above: The remains of the terrace of the temple of Claudius, completed under Vespasian long after his death.*

*Below: The Temple of Venus Genetrix, the mythical ancestress of the Julians, dominated Caesar's Forum.*

As Roman temples evolved in later republican and early imperial Rome, they revealed the intermingling of native Italic traditions, derived ultimately from the Etruscans, with imported Greek styles. By the time of Augustus (30BC–AD14) something of a classical synthesis had been achieved. Although Roman architects continued to develop new ways of building temples, culminating in the Pantheon in the early 2nd century AD, this temple's novel form marked an effective end rather than a beginning to grand temple-building in Rome itself. In the provinces, however, especially in the east, new styles of temple building continued to emerge with often exuberant inventiveness.

The first large temple in Rome, and one that was always deeply revered, was that of Jupiter on the Capitoline Hill.

Traditionally started by the last monarch Tarquinius Superbus before 509BC, it was typically Etruscan in design. It stood on a podium made of tufa blocks about 13ft (4m) high and measured 203ft long by 174ft (62 by 53m), making it comparable in size to the biggest contemporary Greek temples. It had three *cellae* (inner chambers), with Jupiter in the central one flanked by his wife Juno and daughter Minerva. The temple's emphasis is very much on its front, where steps led to a portico of 18 columns, probably of stuccoed wood, with only three on the flanks and none at the rear. (Greek temples had columns all round.) Its overhanging roof was decorated with bright-painted terracotta ornaments and statues, some full-size. Etruscan statues, like the famous Apollo of Veii, could be remarkably fine.

## GRAECO-ROMAN FUSION

The early Republic's temples, such as those of Saturn or Castor and Pollux, followed this Etruscan pattern in the 5th and 4th centuries BC, giving the city a colourful if scarcely classical air. However, by 200BC increasing contacts with the Hellenistic world had opened Roman eyes to far more sophisticated styles, while wealth from conquests enabled them to import Greek marble and craftsmen. The resulting temples show Greek detail based on a Roman plan.

The Greek architect Hermodorus built the first all-marble Temple of Jupiter Stator in 146BC. The slightly later Temple of Portunus, which is still almost intact, exemplifies the emerging Graeco-Roman synthesis: classically Greek Ionic columns rest on a raised Roman podium, the approach stairs and portico are at the front and the side pillar is engaged in the wall of the *cella* (inner chamber). This fusion is also apparent at the Temple of Hercules at Cori (*c.* 100BC). Here, the

ground-plan looks Italic, a style closely related to the Etruscans, but the fine Doric columns copy the current fashions of Hellenistic cities such as Pergamum.

Few temples were as wholly Greek in inspiration as the circular Temple of Hercules Victor (formerly called the Temple of Vesta) built soon after 100BC in the Forum Boarium. Made of Pentelic marble from Athens and probably the work of an Athenian architect (the names of most architects in Rome have not survived), its circular form is very Greek, as are the steps wholly surrounding it and the Corinthian capitals. Its construction marks the peak of the Hellenizing influence in Rome. A notable early exception (*c.* 150BC) to this Greek trend was the Temple of Fortuna Primigenia at Praeneste (Palestrina), whose dramatic use of vaulting and circular shapes anticipate the architectural revolution sometimes held to have started two centuries later with Nero's Domus Aurea (AD64–8).

### AUGUSTUS' PROGRAMME

Augustus claimed in his autobiographical *Res Gestae* to have restored 82 temples in Rome in 28BC. Augustus' was certainly the biggest temple construction programme ever seen in Rome. His temples reveal his generally classical tastes. Although generally not large – central Rome was now densely populated and space was at a premium – they were usually magnificently decorated. They were still set on tall podiums, often against a rear wall, with their columns grouped towards the front.

The emperor's grandest temple, that of Mars Ultor in his new Forum, was almost square, backed by a huge, slum-excluding firewall. Its giant Corinthian columns were set on a lofty podium of 17 steps which could only be approached from the front. Augustus' temple to his patron deity Apollo on the Palatine was built of solid Carrara marble between 36BC and 28BC and adorned with famous Greek statues.

The century after Augustus' death in AD14 saw little development in temple-building, as attention was devoted chiefly to secular structures. In his 23-year-long reign, Tiberius did not even manage to complete the temple to the deified Augustus. Caligula finally finished it in the Ionic style. Nero started to build a temple to his deified stepfather Claudius, who had probably been poisoned by Agrippina, Nero's mother and Claudius' last wife. The emperor Vespasian, who admired Claudius, completed it in AD75. The enormous platform of the large structure still survives today.

*Above: The Temple of Fortuna Primigenia at Praeneste (c.150BC) was a radically daring building in its use of vaults and circular shapes, anticipating much later styles.*

*Below: The Temple of Portunus typifies the Graeco-Roman fusion at its finest: classical Greek Ionic columns on an elevated Roman-style podium.*

*Above: The Pantheon's visionary union of portico and dome influenced many later buildings, such as the Church of St Mary in Mostal, Malta.*

*Below: A partial cutaway of the dome of the Pantheon, revealing the coffering that lightened its weight. Its mathematically perfect proportions help explain its remarkable appeal.*

# TEMPLES: THE PANTHEON AND AFTER

Often considered not just the most perfect Roman temple but the apogee of Roman architecture, the Pantheon, the temple to all the gods, was the emperor Hadrian's supreme architectural achievement in Rome. Its fame derives in part from its unusually well-preserved state (it was converted into the Church of Santa Maria ad Martyres in AD608) but it is indisputably merited as one of the most sublime of Roman buildings.

### STRUCTURE OF THE PANTHEON

Two earlier temples had been built on the same site, one by Agrippa in 27BC and one by Domitian when Agrippa's temple burned down in AD80. Built between AD118–25, the Pantheon is composed of three rather disparate elements: a huge colonnaded porch, a tall middle block, and the rotunda that forms the temple's *cella* and supports its dome. The porch has 16 giant columns of the Composite order. These are made of grey and red Egyptian granite, with bases and capitals of white Carrara or Greek marble. With

an eagle on top of its pediment, the porch originally dominated a colonnaded piazza in front, looking higher than it does now (the surrounding ground has risen, as it has in most of Rome). The intermediary block, like the rotunda, was built of brick-faced concrete covered in marble. The rotunda's diameter and height are exactly the same, 142ft (43.2m), making it larger than any dome built in the next 1800 years. The dome springs 71ft (21.6m) above the floor. This means that a sphere of 142ft (43.2m) diameter would fit exactly inside the temple.

The rotunda rests on an immensely solid travertine and concrete ring 24ft (7.3m) wide and 15ft (4.5m) deep. It has eight load-bearing piers that form the building's framework, between which are curved or rectangular *exedrae* (recesses), each screened by two yellow Numidian marble columns, that may have once housed gods' statues. The piers support eight arches which run through the wall's core from inside out, part of a complex system of relieving arches that buttress the upper walls against the outward thrust of the dome.

The dome itself is built of concrete with an *oculus* (eye) opening 27ft (8.3m) at the top that gently illuminates the whole temple, drawing the eye up past the coffered roof to the sky, abode of the gods, far above. The upper parts of the dome are made of progressively lighter materials, with very light porous pumice stone being used at the top around the oculum. The 140 coffers of progressively diminishing size, arranged in five tiers of 28, also help to reduce the dome's weight while adorning its interior.

Like the roof tiles of the dome, these coffers were probably once gilded. Other interior decorations, surviving at least in part, are slabs of porphyry and dark green marble, while the floor was also paved

with marble. Only a small section of the original décor has been restored, but the Pantheon has retained more of its original decoration than any other Roman temple and the overall effect is still very lavish. The Pantheon impresses not only as a tremendous feat of engineering but also because it gives us a vivid idea of what a Roman temple may have been like. Its mathematically perfect proportions also elevate the spirit of visitors as they look up into the huge airy dome of this temple to all the gods.

## EMPEROR AND ARCHITECT

Hadrian's other great temple, the Temple of Venus and Roma, stands on a high piece of ground between the Colosseum and Vespasian's Forum Pacis. It is also remarkable for a Roman temple for its very Greek design. Instead of standing on the usual Roman podium, it is set, like the Athenian Parthenon, in the centre of a rectangular platform on low steps that encircle it in Greek style. Hadrian was such a notorious philhellene that his enemies dubbed him *Graeculus* (Greekling).

Even more unusually, instead of having a single *cella*, the temple has two, back to back, both with apses, one for each goddess. (Roma Dea was the goddess of Rome itself.) These apses date from a rebuild under Maxentius. The original design had rectangular *cellae* back to back.

The temple was huge, 217ft wide by 348ft long (66 by 136m), with ten columns of grey Egyptian granite on its ends and 20 along its sides. Apollodorus, the brilliant architect of Trajan's great projects, who may also have been involved in designing the Pantheon, criticized the design, which was apparently Hadrian's own. Apollodorus claimed the temple was too wide for its height. Reputedly, the emperor had the

*Right: G.P. Panini's 18th-century painting of the Pantheon's interior. The temple's perfectly proportioned dome rising to an oculus (central opening) makes it among the world's most magical buildings. It is also luckily the best preserved of Rome's temples.*

architect exiled and then killed in AD129 for such impertinence, which suggests a prickly artistic pride in the emperor. The temple, dedicated in AD135, was rebuilt by Maxentius in the early 4th century AD. After Hadrian, Rome was no longer the one vital centre of great temple-building projects. Other cities across the empire competed with it increasingly and often showed more innovatory flair.

The Temple of Antoninus Pius and Faustina begun in AD141 in the Forum Romanum, which later became a church, was an unexciting rectangle. The Severans built temples to their favourite gods which were notable chiefly for their immense size and restored many older temples.

Before the days of Roman temple building drew to a close, the emperor Aurelian (AD270–5) built a temple to Sol Invictus (the Unconquered Sun), his favourite deity. This was apparently an unusual circular edifice within a large rectangular enclosure, that strongly suggests a Syrian influence.

*Above: The Temple of Antoninus Pius and Faustina, Hadrian's successor, is a plain, even dull rectangular structure, preserved by being made into a church.*

# BUILDING THE THEATRES

*Right: The theatre at Sabratha, Libya, is among the best-preserved of all Roman theatres. Its scaenae frons (built-up backcloth) has been reconstructed with 96 marble columns on three storeys.*

*Below: An actor wears a mask in a 3rd-century AD carving from the theatre at Sabratha, Libya. All actors in Greek and Roman theatres wore such masks.*

The Greeks developed the world's very first permanent theatres; stone-built open-air structures where plays could be performed in front of huge audiences. However in their usual way, the Romans adapted the Hellenic model to make something distinctively Roman out of it. Whereas Greek theatres usually exploited natural sites to stunning advantage and retained a religious link with the god Dionysus, in whose worship dramas and comedies were originally staged, by the end of the Republic the Romans increasingly regarded theatre more as an entertainment than as a religious festival.

## SUPPLY AND DEMAND

The Roman method of building massive structures raised on concrete vaults dispensed with the need for a suitable slope into which the hemicycle of a Greek theatre could be fitted. This meant Roman theatres could be built wherever there was a demand for them, principally in cities. Despite the huge success of early Roman comic playwrights such as Plautus (254–184BC) and Terence (195–159BC), Roman public taste tended increasingly to prefer mime or pantomime to plays proper. Changes in theatre design included making the theatre completely semicircular and turning the *orchestra* into seating for important officials rather than using it for performers. These changes can be seen clearly at the theatre of Taormina in Sicily. Here, the original Greek structure offered stunning views of Mount Etna behind until the Romans constructed a heavy *scaenae frons* (built-up backcloth). This obscured the view until its partial collapse!

Remarkably, there were no permanent theatres in Rome itself until very near the end of the Republic. Instead, temporary timber structures were built for each set of performances and then demolished.

(These temporary buildings could be grand, nonetheless. According to Pliny, Marcus Scaurus raised a structure in 58BC which, if timber-framed, was covered in glass and marble and could seat 80,000 people.) This lack was due mainly to the Senate's conservative puritanism, for it distrusted the loose morals that were then associated with the stage.

### POMPEY'S THEATRE

It was only under the effective domination of the state by Pompey in the 50s BC that the first permanent stone theatre was built in Rome. It was completed in 55BC, just outside the old sacred *pomerium* (city boundary) in the flat Campus Martius. What Pompey built was not just a theatre, but a grand complex, with gardens and porticoes sheltering art galleries and other shops. As a sop to conservative sentiment, he described his theatre as a monumental stairway to the Temple of Venus Victrix (the Victory-bringer) sited at the top of the *cavea* (tiers of stepped seating). The theatre was made of concrete, which permitted the architects to support the seating on a series of radial and curving vaults, rather than having to seek a site on a hillside. Substantial parts of the substructures survive in cellars. Its *cavea* was 525ft (160m) in diameter and could seat about 27,000 spectators.

One of the oldest surviving theatres in Rome is that of Marcellus, which Augustus dedicated to the memory of his son-in-law in 13BC, fulfilling one of Caesar's grand projects. Still mostly extant, although partly converted into a hotel (it has also been a fortress and a palace in its time), it gives a good idea of an early Roman theatre. Built mainly of travertine stone with stone or concrete barrel-vaults, it closed the audience off from the hubbub of city life outside and so rendered the actors' dialogue audible on even the highest levels. There would have been retractable awnings against the sun to protect the spectators. The *scaenae frons* was as high as the *cavea* but seems to have been simple in design. The travertine façade had at least two series of ornamental arches framed by pillars, Doric on the ground floor and Ionic on the first. A third floor may have had Corinthian pillars or have been a simple attic floor. The theatre seated about 11,000 people.

### THEATRES IN THE PROVINCES

To see further developments in Roman theatres we need to turn to other cities. At Lyons (Lugdunum), long the chief city of Gaul, a fine theatre was built under Hadrian (ruled AD117–38), enlarging and replacing an earlier building. Here pragmatic Roman architects showed that they were not averse to exploiting hillsides where they could. Next to this large theatre was a much smaller *odeum*, which was originally roofed and used for poetry recitals, lectures and musical performances. At Vienne, across the river Rhône, and even more notably at Orange in Provence, what became the standard type of theatre is still visible. Both theatres have a central *exedra* (recess) matched by two flanking ones in their monumental *scaenae frontes*. The full effect of a Roman theatre is best seen at Sabratha in modern Libya, where the *scaenae frons* has been reconstructed on all its three storeys with 96 marble columns.

*Above: Arches flanked by columns from the Theatre of Marcellus. Dedicated by Augustus in 13BC and Rome's largest extant theatre, today part of it is a hotel.*

*Below: Masks epitomizing tragedy (left) and comedy (right). The Romans preferred the latter but also enjoyed violent melodramatic shows.*

# AMPHITHEATRES AND THE COLOSSEUM

No type of building is more closely associated today with the Roman empire than the amphitheatre. However, there was no permanent amphitheatre in Rome until the giant Flavian Amphitheatre, or Colosseum, was constructed. Built between AD70 and 80, its top storey may not have been completed until after the emperor Titus' sudden death in AD81.

### THE GAMES AND PUBLIC ORDER
Rome's lack of amphitheatres was due less to the Senate's disapproval of gladiatorial activities *per se*, than to well-founded fears of public disorder and as riots had been known to occur after games in other cities. There had been full-scale riots at the Pompeii amphitheatre during games there in AD59, for example. (Pompeii has one of the empire's earliest and best-preserved arenas, dating from the 1st century BC.) Rome, however, was a much more heavily policed city.

Many games in the city took place not in amphitheatres but in the immense Circus Maximus, in theatres or even, in Rome's early days, in the Forum Romanum itself, when gladiatorial combat took place in the context of aristocratic funerals. Conversely, amphitheatres in the provinces such as Britain could seldom afford full gladiatorial fights, so amphitheatres were used instead for sporting contests or for military tattoos. Even so, the grand elliptical shape of amphitheatres, especially of the colossal archetype in Rome itself, remains justifiably linked with gladiatorial games.

### A CROWD-PLEASING PROJECT
The emperors Gaius Caligula and Nero had loved gladiatorial games. These had been performed in temporary if lavishly decorated timber structures which were destroyed in the great fire of AD64. (A small stone amphitheatre built by Statilius Taurus, one of Augustus' generals, in 29BC was destroyed in the same fire.)

In a stroke of political genius, Vespasian decided to use the drained lake of Nero's Domus Aurea (Golden Palace) – which was detested less for its ostentation than for the huge area it ate up in the heart of Rome – for a great crowd-pleasing project: Rome's first, and the empire's greatest, permanent amphitheatre. Well-drained, with good clay subsoil for such a heavy building, in the very centre of the city, it was the perfect site. Work began early in Vespasian's reign (AD69–79) and Titus held typically splendid inauguratory games in AD80.

The Colosseum fully deserves its name, given by the historian Bede in the early Middle Ages either because of the colossal gold statue of Nero nearby, or because of its colossal size. A substantial part of the amphitheatre survives today. It was constantly pillaged for building materials over the centuries until Pope Benedict XIV pronounced it sanctified by the blood of martyrs in 1749, safeguarding the remainder. The Colosseum is still the most impressive extant building in Rome and a

*Above: Detail of a model of the Colosseum, Rome's largest amphitheatre, built AD70–80, showing the statues that once adorned its arches.*

*Below: A view of the Colosseum as it appears today from the Via Sacra. Human depredations, not time, have ravaged the huge structure.*

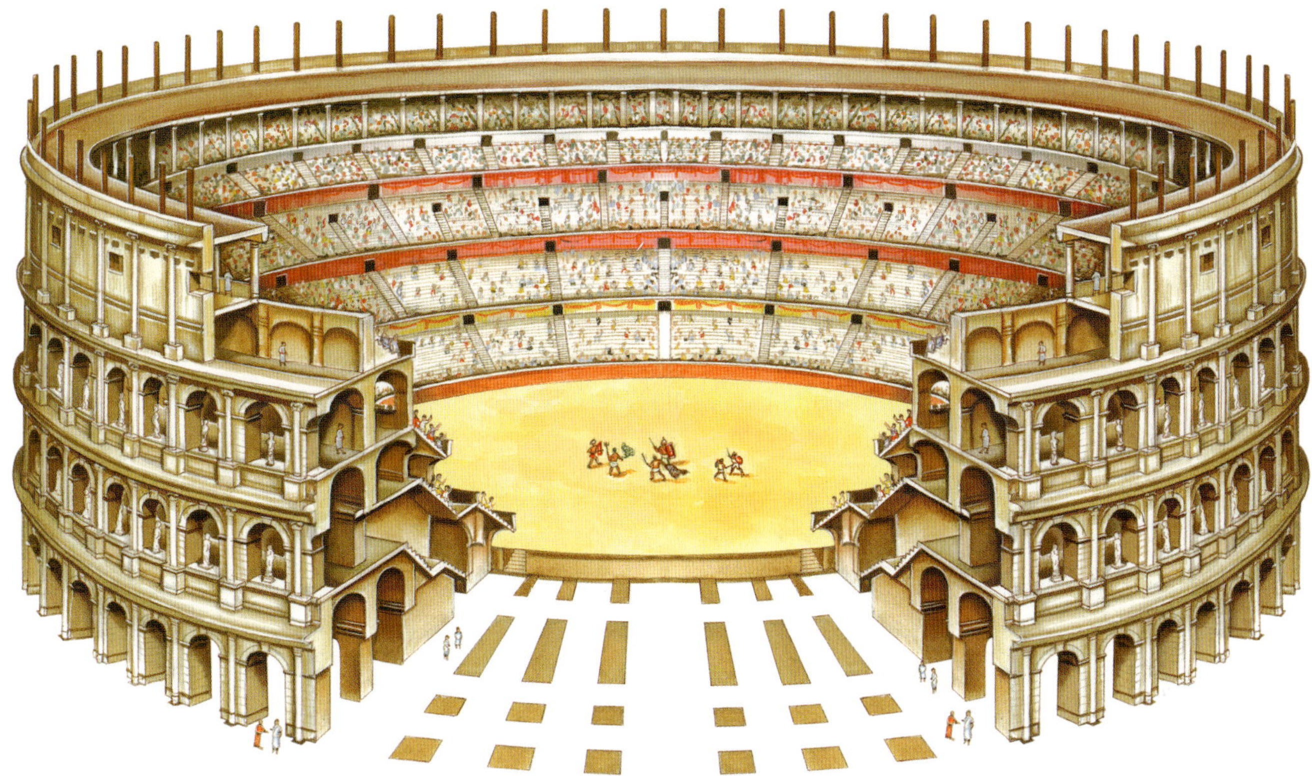

massive testament to the enduring skills of Roman engineers. Its typically elliptical outer shape measures 615 by 510ft (188 by 156m). The arena inside measures 282 by 177ft (86 by 54m) and its outer wall once rose to 171ft (52m), making it the tallest building in the city. It could accommodate an estimated 45–55,000 spectators.

To support the Colosseum's huge *cavea* (stepped seating), a vast ring of concrete 170ft (51m) wide and 40ft (12m) deep was laid. The lower part of about 20ft (6m) was cut into a trench while the upper, equal-sized part was contained inside a huge circle of brick-faced concrete above ground. These foundations supported a framework of loadbearing piers of travertine specially quarried near Tivoli. Between the piers ran radial walls of squared tufa up to the second floor. Almost all the vaults are barrel-vaults made of concrete, but some have brick ribs. About ten million cubic feet (100,000 cubic metres) of travertine were needed to build the façade alone and 300 tons of iron were used just for the nails. The façade has three

tiers of low arches framed respectively by Doric, Ionic and Corinthian columns, all semi-engaged (half columns) and purely decorative. The arches probably once had statues of gods or heroes in them, judging by depictions on coins. The top storey had tall Corinthian pilasters and originally had huge shields of gilded bronze, alternating with large windows, that would have gleamed impressively. Although this storey looks the most solid, it is in fact the lightest-built section.

The Romans erected this gigantic, complex structure with impressive speed, helped by their quasi-military organization of the process. Each material used in the building was handled by different groups of craftsmen, so that travertine could be added to the concrete core in one area while the final marble coatings were being laid in another. The whole structure was so massively built it withstood a lightning strike in AD217 – though it was closed for some years for repairs – and other assaults by recurrent earthquakes and the elements. Only human quarrying has done lasting damage.

*Above: A cutaway section of the Colosseum in its prime, revealing the tiers of concrete barrel vaults and arches, suppported on load-bearing walls mostly of travertine stone buttressed by radial walls of tufa stone running between the piers.*

*Below: To Titus in AD80 fell the honour of inaugurating the amphitheatre that bears his dynasty's name, the Flavian Ampitheatre, with spectacularly lavish games.*

*Above: The amphitheatre at Arles in southern France is one of the finest extant outside Italy. Probably built in the late 1st century AD, its architect Crispus Reburrus also designed the amphitheatre at Nimes nearby.*

*Below: The emperor Vespasian (AD69–79), in whose reign the building of the immense Flavian Amphitheatre or Colosseum began.*

## SEATING BY RANK

The imperial box, richly decorated with coloured marbles, occupied the prime position on the short axis. Elsewhere, seating was allocated according to class or status. Augustus, as part of his attempted restoration of public morality, had tried to stipulate exactly who should sit where while watching performances in theatres, to reduce the opportunities for chatting up girls that Ovid so fondly described, and this seems to have applied in the Colosseum as well.

In the Colosseum, women were relegated to the topmost tiers – where they would have had the worst view but protection from the sun – except for the Vestal Virgins, whose high religious status overrode their lowly sexual status. They joined senators, equestrians (knights) and other dignitaries, often including ambassadors, in the smart seats in the lowest tier. Immediately above them was the first row for the general public, the *maenianum primum*, followed by the *maenianum secundum immum*, the *maenianum secundum summum* and finally the *maenianum secundum in ligneis*, with a gallery around that where ordinary spectators had to stand.

Some tickets were reserved in block-bookings for *collegia* (guilds) or for particular groups such as the citizens of Cadiz, privileges tenaciously preserved down the centuries. Tokens for all types of seats except the very best were given out free for the games by the emperors on various occasions. This made admission to the games something of a lottery.

All seats were made of marble, another weight carried on the vaulted masonry substructure, except for the topmost tier, where they were made of wood to reduce the weight pressing down on the upper walls. No complete seats survive but fragments found in excavation have been pieced together to give an idea of what seating in the *maenianum secundum immum*, middling rank seats, were like. They were 17in (44cm) high by 21in (61cm) wide. Lower seats may have been more generous in size. Spectators reached their seats by climbing up or down rows of steps half the size of the seats. These led from the points where the inner stairs emerged into the *cavea* (stepped seating) from the myriad stairs and corridors below.

## EXITS AND ENTRANCES

There were 76 public entrances, some of whose Roman numbers can still be seen. The emperor's monumental entrance, surmounted by a *quadriga* (four-horse chariot), was in the south, between entrances I (1) and LXXVI (76), a part of the amphitheatre that has been almost completely destroyed. Surviving far better is the next most important entrance, that of the consuls at the other end of the short axis. Renaissance drawings and remnants of stucco show that the vaulted entrance was originally richly decorated with stucco and other ornaments and probably topped by a pediment. The performers reached the arena directly by entrances at the long ends of the axis. The east entrance connected directly via a tunnel with the Ludus Magnus, the main imperial gladiatorial school nearby.

Ordinary spectators would have entered by their relevantly numbered arch and then climbed up stairs that connected the rings of circuit corridors, all of which were plastered and painted, until they reached their particular *vomitorium* (exit ramp) as the Romans punningly called the entrances. To protect the people from the 10ft (3m) drop from the seats into the stairwells, stone balustrades were provided. These were carved with animals such as dogs hunting deer or dolphins or mythological beasts such as sphinxes or griffins. Outside, barriers were erected around the travertine pavements that encircled the arena to control the eager crowds. Surviving stone posts suggest that chains were stretched between them.

## ABOVE AND BELOW

The Roman audience was protected from the sun – and sudden rain showers – by a *velarium*, a huge canvas awning that covered the whole of the *cavea* and left only the arena open. Around the top of the amphitheatre are 240 stone brackets. These presumably once supported the rigging masts which held up this giant sunshade. (An alternative would have been long poles, as shown in a painting of Pompeii's amphitheatre, but the Colosseum may have been too vast for this simpler approach.) The whole system was operated by a special team of about 1,000 marines from the fleets at Misenum or Ravenna, who could also have acted as an auxiliary police force if needed. It has been tentatively calculated that the 240 ropes and the canvas would have weighed more than 24 tons.

Beneath the floor of the arena was an even more impressive network of subterranean passages and chambers which accommodated the wild beasts and the human performers before the games. About 246ft long by 144ft wide (75 by 44m) and 20ft (6m) deep, this seeming labyrinth was in fact organized with characteristic Roman efficiency, although later alterations and additions make the original structure hard to discern. It had five parallel corridors down the centre and three elliptical corridors along the sides. Beyond the outermost and narrowest corridor were 32 vaulted chambers which were used to cage the animals. Lifts operated by man-cranked windlasses lifted the animals up in their cages to trapdoors through which they sprang, bedazzled,

into the sunlit arena. The exact dimensions of their cages and the means by which the largest animals – elephants and hippopotami, for example – reached the arena remains under investigation. However, there were at least 30 lifts and many more trapdoors, so beneath the arena's floor a positive machine operated during the games.

The floor itself was probably of wood, although parts may have been made of stone slabs. It was covered with sand during the games to absorb the blood. The floor of the arena was probably not fully flooded to permit the large-scale *naumachiae* (re-enacted sea battles) historians describe and it is likely these took place elsewhere. However, early on there may have been a shallow pool for aquatic displays.

## OTHER ARENAS

The Colosseum had few permanently built precursors but many imitators outside Rome, as an amphitheatre became an essential requirement for any self-respecting city. Most follow the same elliptical pattern and some have similar decorations on their exteriors, of arches flanked by columns. The amphitheatre at Verona, which held about 25,000 spectators, is *relatively* much larger than the Colosseum, as Verona was never one of the empire's biggest cities. The amphitheatres at Arles and Nîmes are particularly fine, as are many in Africa such as Thysdrus or Sabratha in Libya.

*Above: The amphitheatre of Thysdrus (El Djem) in the fertile province of Africa (Tunisia) was built c. AD238. In its arena Gordian I was proclaimed emperor and later it became a refuge for the local inhabitants. It shows the still overwhelming influence of the Colosseum in Rome.*

*Below: Amphitheatres were relatively rare in most of the Eastern provinces, but theatres such as this at Pergamum in Asia Minor were sometimes adapted for combats or animal displays.*

# AQUEDUCTS AND SEWERS

*Above: The Trevi Fountain in Rome is still supplied by the Acqua Vergine (Aqua Virgo), the only Roman aqueduct still functioning.*

*Below: These arches once carried the Aqua Claudia and the Aqua Anio Novus, the two aqueducts completed by Claudius in AD52.*

The Romans were proud of their aqueducts and sewers, two essential aspects of civilization. As the geographer Strabo wrote early in the 1st century AD, "The Romans had foresight in matters about which the Greeks hardly cared, such as the construction of roads and aqueducts and of sewers that flush the filth of the city down to the Tiber… Water is brought to the city through aqueducts so copiously that positive rivers flow through the city and its sewers". At the end of the same century Frontinus declared, "Compare if you like the Pyramids or the useless if famous monuments of the Greeks with such a display of essential structures carrying so much water".

## IMPERIAL CONFIDENCE

Sextus Julius Frontinus, who assumed the important post of *curator aquarum* (Water Commissioner) in AD96, wrote a book on Rome's water supply *De aquis urbis Romae* (On Rome's Aqueducts), that forms the basis of our knowledge. Classical Athens, among other cities, had piped fresh water to its citizens but Rome, the world's first giant city, needed water on an unprecedented scale, especially for its lavish *thermae* (imperial baths). Rome was also the first city to dig huge sewers to remove its waste waters. The aqueducts' giant arcades testify to something else: Roman confidence in its own power. Such highly visible and easily disrupted (or poisoned) water supplies were only feasible when no enemies closely threatened Rome. Ten major aqueducts built over six centuries finally supplied the city. The cutting of its aqueducts in AD537 during the Byzantine-Gothic wars symbolized the final end of ancient Rome.

## PRACTICAL ENGINEERING

Rome's first aqueduct, the Aqua Appia, was built in 312BC by the censor Appius Claudius to supply water for the city's growing population. It had previously been supplied by springs or by the dubious water of the Tiber. Fed by springs near Albano, the aqueduct ran underground for 10 miles (16km); water was only carried above ground on arcades for about 100 yards inside the city. The Romans were far too practical to waste money building grandly arcaded aqueducts except when really needed.

Lead pipes were only used inside the city. For the most part, the aqueducts were stone-lined channels carrying water underground or just above it. As the Romans had no power to pump water uphill they had to ensure that the water always flowed downhill. The gradient of most aqueducts was surprisingly modest: about a 3ft drop per 1000, enough to keep the water flowing steadily.

Further aqueducts followed, at first slowly. The Anio Vetus in 272–269BC, which was almost four times as long as the Aqua Appia, took its water from the river Anio. The Aqua Marcia was

started in 144BC and paid for by booty from the sack of Corinth. It ran for 56 miles (91km) and was famed both for the purity of its waters and for the 6 miles (10km) of its length that ran on arcades, at some stages 95ft (29m) high.

The next two aqueducts were the Aqua Tepula started in 125BC and the Aqua Julia, with a capacity double that of the Tepula, built in 33BC. Both had similar lengths raised on arcades.

The Aqua Tepula was the work of Marcus Agrippa, Augustus' chief minister, who undertook a total restoration of all Rome's waterworks. In 19BC Agrippa also built the Aqua Virgo, the only aqueduct to enter the city from the north and the only one still functioning (as the Acqua Vergine, which supplies the Fontana di Trevi). Agrippa left his team of 240 slaves to Augustus. The latter made them public property and set up a permanent commission to oversee water supplies. The office of *procurator aquarum* was created by Claudius.

### DEMAND FOR WATER INCREASES

Claudius built two aqueducts, the Aqua Claudia and the Aqua Anio Novus. Both had been started by the capricious emperor Caligula in AD38, partly to supply water for his *naumachiae* (re-enactments of sea-battles). Claudius completed them by AD52. The aqueducts' combined arcade marches for 6 miles (10km) across the Roman campagna before entering the city at what is now the Porta Maggiore.

The last great aqueduct, the Aqua Traiana, was built by Trajan in AD109. It brought good spring water from the hills north of Rome to the west bank (Trastevere), a region of the city that had been undersupplied. However, its elevation meant it could supply all the city's regions, which not every aqueduct could.

By this time the water supply to Rome had increased greatly. Since the building of the Aqua Claudia it had increased perhaps 15-fold to around 200 million gallons per day (900 million litres). This increase was

less a reflection of population growth than of the huge demands of the *thermae*. The aqueducts usually had settling tanks, to allow the sediment picked up en route to fall from the water. Water was also stored in *castella aquae* (reservoirs) or *stagna* (tanks) at the *thermae*.

### GREAT SEWERS

Understandably, sewers were less widely lauded than aqueducts – Vitruvius discreetly ignores them. However, since the 6th century BC when the Cloaca Maxima (Great Drain) was dug as a drainage ditch, the Romans had built spacious, durable sewers made of well-crafted masonry.

Most Roman dwellings did not connect with the sewage system, however. This was chiefly because its reliance upon a constant, uninterrupted flow of water to flush it clear made it very expensive. Instead, many poorer Romans used chamber pots or the city's 144 recorded public latrines. Often lavishly decorated, these latrines provided facilities in which citizens could chat while seated in rows above the ever-flowing waters. Meanwhile, ever-flowing fountains flushed street litter into the drains. Down river from Rome, the Tiber cannot have been a salubrious stream.

*Above: The Pont du Gard near Nîmes in France forms the most famous part of all Roman aqueducts, partly because it has survived so well. Built by Agrippa between 20–16BC, this arched section rises 160ft (49m) above the river.*

*Below: The exit of the Cloaca Maxima (Great Drain), an unglamorous but vital aspect of public health. Started in the 6th century BC and restored by Agrippa, it bears testimony to the enduring skills of Roman engineers.*

# IMPERIAL BATHS

*Above: In the 16th century Michelangelo created the vast Church of Santa Maria degli Angeli out of the frigidarium (cold bath), one section of the extant Baths of Diocletian.*

*Right: The frigidarium of the baths of Diocletian inspired the magnificent waiting room of Union Station, Washington DC. Designed by D.H. Burnham and completed in 1907, it has since been demolished.*

The largest and architecturally most adventurous structures in Rome were the *thermae*, the imperial baths, of which 11 were finally built. By far the grandest and best-preserved are the four erected by the emperors Trajan (AD98–117), Caracalla (AD211–17), Diocletian (AD284–305) and Constantine (AD306–37).

**BATHS AS A WAY OF LIFE**

Roman *thermae* were far more than just baths. Their immense, lavishly decorated complexes – the largest enclosed spaces in the world before the 20th century – included libraries, gardens, art galleries, gymnasia, restaurants, meeting places and bordellos or rooms for sexual dalliance. For many Roman men, long, leisurely baths became a necessity, socially even more than hygienically, and occupied much of the afternoon. From the outset, the *thermae* used concrete vaulting for their construction. This material was ideally suited to such innovative and enormous buildings.

The first public baths appeared in the 2nd century BC. Pompeii had four large and many smaller public baths by the eruption in AD79. All showed the basic division into *frigidarium* (cold bath), *tepidarium* (warm) and *caldarium* (hot), the last heated by hypocausts, the piped hot-air floor and wall heating that became standard in baths throughout the empire.

The first full-scale Roman *thermae* were built by Agrippa in the Campus Martius, probably after 19BC, as they were supplied by the Aqua Virgo aqueduct which was completed that year. Little of Agrippa's original *thermae* remains – they were rebuilt in the 3rd century AD – but they probably had gardens and a gymnasium. For half a century they were the city's only *thermae*. Nero then built baths praised by the poet Martial: "What worse than Nero? What better than Nero's baths?" These were presumably more luxurious but they too were totally rebuilt between 222 and 227AD. Only with the *thermae* of the emperor Titus, inaugurated

in AD80, can we begin to glimpse imperial baths in their full splendour. Even here very little survives and we have to rely on the not necessarily accurate drawings made by the Renaissance architect Palladio. These suggest that the baths, built next to the Colosseum, were symmetrically planned with a terraced rectangular enclosure and the baths themselves placed on the north side, a layout broadly similar to the later, far better preserved baths of Trajan and Caracalla.

## THE BATHS OF TRAJAN

Trajan was the most munificent of emperors and the one – after Augustus – with the most money (acquired in his Dacian conquests). He began Rome's first really grand *thermae* in AD104 after fire had damaged much of the Esquiline Wing of Nero's Domus Aurea (Golden Palace). Its wrecked upper floors were completely demolished, leaving only the vaulted ground floor, whose rooms and courtyards were joined together by vaulted roofs to raise the whole area to 154ft (47m) above sea level. The remainder of the hill was then levelled off to create a huge platform 1,115 by 1,083ft (340 by 330m). Almost certainly designed by Apollodorus of Damascus, Trajan's great architect, the *thermae* were three times as big as Titus' baths just south-west of them. They occupied 23 acres (9ha) and were able to accommodate many thousands of bathers at one time.

The *frigidarium* (cold bath), the tallest part of the building, was in the very centre of the baths. This was a large rectangular room with giant monolithic columns of red and grey granite placed in its corners. These seemed to carry the building's soaring roof but were in fact wholly decorative, as the piers behind them really supported the cross-vaulted ceiling. Like the rest of the interior of the baths, the *frigidarium* would have been richly decorated and probably coffered. There were four cold plunge pools. On either side were large colonnaded areas open to the sky and closed off by big

half-domed *exedrae* (recesses) called *palaestrae*, where bathers would exercise before entering the hot rooms. A fraternity of athletes was based there for approximately two centuries.

To the north-east of the baths lay the big *natatio* (swimming pool), open to the sky and flanked by a colonnade. On the other side of the *frigidarium* lay the small *tepidarium* (warm bath), which was maintained at an intermediate temperature to acclimatize bathers to the heat to come.

On the south-west front of the building, carefully sited to capture the heat of the afternoon sun, was the *caldarium*, the (very) hot bath. Its curved bay windows were possibly double-glazed, an example of solar heating. Glass had become more widely available by this time but the row of tall windows along the south side was still startlingly innovatory. The *caldarium* had apses on three sides, each containing a hot plunge pool. The whole vast room, and the similar but smaller hot chambers adjacent, was heated by hypocausts not only in the floor – which might have been almost uncomfortably hot to walk on – but also in the walls and even the ceilings. The heat for both the hypocausts and the hot water came from a series of *praefurniae* (furnaces) beneath, stoked by slaves

*Above: One of the great hemicycles of the Baths of Trajan on the Esquiline Hill in Rome, on the north-east side of the baths. Completed in AD109, they surpassed all preceding baths in their grandeur and lavishness.*

*Below: Mosaic floor decorations such as this were common in the imperial baths.*

*Above: A fanciful recreation of the Baths of Caracalla by the Victorian painter Lawrence Alma-Tadema captures the atmosphere of luxury, even licentiousness, often associated with the great imperial baths that was much attacked by the early Christians.*

1,000 years later sometimes corroborate and sometimes contradict the Marble Plan.) To the enclosure's north-west and north-east ends were other *exedrae*. Each contained a *nymphaeum* (ornamental fountain). The open spaces between the baths and the perimeter buildings were planted out as gardens. The whole complex was made of brick-faced concrete, covered in plain stucco on the outside but lavishly decorated in coloured marble with pillars, pilasters and marble floors throughout the interior.

Water for the baths was supplied partly by Trajan's new aqueduct, the Aqua Traiana, carried in pipes over bridges from its debauchment on the west bank, and partly from the neighbouring reservoir known as the Sette Salle, a two-storeyed building with a capacity of about 1½ million gallons (7 million litres). This was probably supplied by the Aqua Claudia, rather than the Aqua Traiana. The whole complex was inaugurated in AD109 and immediately eclipsed all its predecessors in grandeur and luxury.

who worked in abominably smoke-filled confinement out of sight of the bathers who sweated so contentedly in their magnificent marble halls.

The buildings around the perimeter included two hexagonal half-domed *exedrae*, about 95ft (29m) in diameter, on the south-west and south-east corners. These were probably Latin and Greek libraries respectively, for the Romans tried to cater for the mind as well as the body. Their brick-faced concrete skeletons survive, although most of Trajan's *thermae* have not. (We rely for information about the baths on two written records, the *Forma Urbis Romae* (the Marble Map of Rome) from the Severan period and the unknown medieval architect called the Anonymous Destailler, whose works

### THE BATHS OF CARACALLA

Although Rome's population probably did not grow appreciably in the century after Trajan built his *thermae* – in fact, it probably shrank after the great plague of AD164–5 – its citizens' expectations continued to increase, despite mounting problems on the empire's frontiers. To meet these expectations and to boost his own rather shaky popularity, the emperor Caracalla (ruled AD211–17) decided to build a grand new complex of baths to the south of the Forum Romanum.

In the century since Trajan's rule, architecture in Rome itself had not progressed much but in the provinces it had. Caracalla's dynasty, the Severans, came from Africa. This perhaps partly explains the daring size and shape of his *thermae*, dedicated in AD216 and among the most impressive ruins in Rome. Although they follow the general pattern of Trajan's baths, the central block is detached from its surrounding enclosure. This is nearly

500yds (460m) square and encloses an area of almost 50 acres (20ha). Here water could be stored and the subsidiary amenities now expected of a great *thermae* be provided. The main bath block itself was a simple rectangle 712ft long by 360ft wide (214 by 110m), except for the massive semicircular projecting *caldarium* (hot bath). Its huge circular, elliptical or oblong rooms open logically into each other along two axes that intersect at the great three-bay *frigidarium* in the centre. Its three cross-vaults rose above the level of the adjacent rooms, lighting it by eight lunettes (semicircular openings). Connecting but insulating the *caldarium* and *frigidarium* was the *tepidarium*, a room whose markedly small doors prevented heat entering or escaping from it.

While only four doorways pierced the complex's blank north-east front, the south-west front had a long line of great windows to absorb the sun's rays into the series of hot rooms. Dominating these was the huge circular *caldarium*, a domed hall whose span of 115ft (35m) approached that of the dome of the Pantheon and whose height exceeded it. Beneath each of the eight huge windows that bravely pierced the dome's drum – a feat that no earlier Roman architect had attempted because of the structural problems – was a hot plunge bath.

On the north side of the building was the *natatio* (swimming pool), shielded from the north by a high wall and protected from the sun's rays by the bulk of the *frigidarium*. At either end of the long axis was a *palaestra* (exercise yard) surrounded by terraced porticos. Built of the now standard brick-faced concrete and presenting a blank face to the outer world except on its many-windowed south–western front, the Baths of Caracalla were decorated on the inside with unprecedented lavishness, with multi-coloured marbles and mosaics and a profusion of ornaments. Roman taste may have abandoned the restraint of Augustan classicism but the subtle contrast of differently shaped rooms, the alternation of light and shadow as bathers moved into and out of the sunlight, above all the soaring height of the vaults above, demonstrated a new technical mastery.

### THE LAST *THERMAE*

The political chaos of the mid-3rd century precluded much further lavish building apart from the Baths of Decius on the Aventine and the Palace of the Gordians on the Via Praenestina. However, although Rome was no longer the only capital city of the empire, it retained its imperial mystique. Once Diocletian (ruled AD284–305) had restored order and instituted the new Tetrarchy (four-ruler system), he decided to build another massive set of baths as part of his overall renovation of Rome. In AD298 he began building his *thermae*, broadly following Caracalla's design but with greater simplicity and less daring. It was even larger, its central block being 785ft long by 475ft wide (240 by 144m). Its central axis from east to west allowed a view right through the resulting alternation of light and shadow. Again, the *caldarium* was a curved room on the south-west side, with other elliptical or polygonal rooms, but the overall effect was less dramatic. The exterior was rather stark, the interior imperially magnificent.

Constantine I, the last emperor to build significantly in Rome, erected his own *thermae* closer to Rome's centre. Against the rather severely rectilinear plan of Diocletian's baths, this made great use of curves, circles and semicircles, at least according to the drawings made by Palladio in the 16th century. However, it probably still followed the essentially symmetrical pattern pioneered by the Baths of Titus over 200 years before. The imperial *thermae* were prodigious users of fuel as well as water and could not long survive the general collapse of the Western empire in the 5th century. Early Christians generally disapproved of over-lavish baths, with all their sensual connotations, and they were abandoned in the West. In Byzantium, however, *thermae* survived.

*Above: Parts of the massive, brick-faced concrete walls of the Baths of Caracalla still stand, but the internal splendour of the building has long since vanished.*

*Below: The Thermal Baths, as the Antonine Baths in Carthage are known (built AD146–62), which rivalled those of Caracalla in size.*

# CIRCUSES

*Above: A 4th-century AD relief showing the races in full frenzy in the Circus Maximus conveys the heady mixture of glamour and danger that so captivated the Roman populace.*

*Below: A Roman charioteer on a* quadriga *(four-horse chariot), a dangerous yet common form of racing chariot, with the outer horses attached to the chariot only by loose reins.*

Chariot-racing was immensely popular with Romans from a very early date. By 500BC, races were being held in the Circus Maximus (biggest or grandest circus). This was located in an area in the valley between the Palatine and Aventine Hills connected with the gods that the races originally honoured.

## ORIGINS OF THE CIRCUS MAXIMUS

For a long time the Circus Maximus was only a track with temporary wooden stands and a simple central barrier round which chariots raced. Rulers from Julius Caesar onwards added or made improvements to create an increasingly grand, permanent structure and it was entirely redeveloped by the emperor Trajan. Other circuses were smaller and used mainly for ceremonial displays.

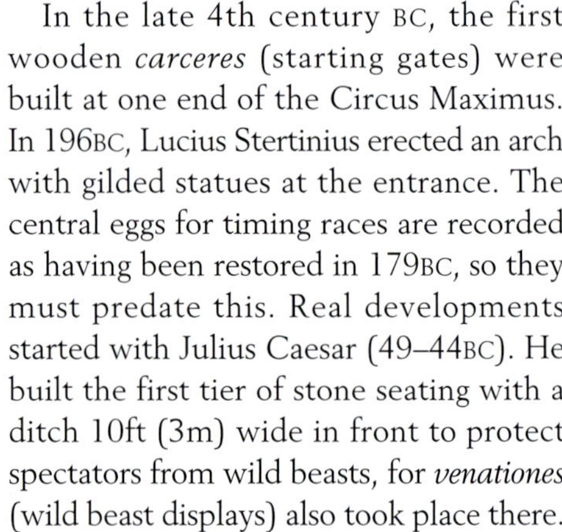

In the late 4th century BC, the first wooden *carceres* (starting gates) were built at one end of the Circus Maximus. In 196BC, Lucius Stertinius erected an arch with gilded statues at the entrance. The central eggs for timing races are recorded as having been restored in 179BC, so they must predate this. Real developments started with Julius Caesar (49–44BC). He built the first tier of stone seating with a ditch 10ft (3m) wide in front to protect spectators from wild beasts, for *venationes* (wild beast displays) also took place there.

Augustus created the *pulvinar*, the imperial box, from which emperors could majestically look down on the races. It later connected directly with the grand Domus Flavia (Imperial Palace), completed by Domitian in AD92. Augustus transformed the *spina* (central barrier) by adding a 13th-century BC obelisk brought from Heliopolis, centre of the Egyptian sun-cult.

Augustus' general Agrippa added bronze dolphins as a second lap counter device. Claudius built monumental stone gates but the rest of the Circus, still built of timber, burnt down in the great fire of AD64. Titus added a triumphal entrance arch to celebrate his sack of Jerusalem. Finally, Trajan transformed the structure into a massive monument. Built mostly of brick-faced concrete covered in marble, stone or stucco, the Circus could now seat an estimated 300,000 people, about a quarter of the city's population, making it the largest single structure for public entertainment in the world. (Ancient sources give even higher figures for spectators.)

In Diocletian's reign (AD284–305) the top part of the seating collapsed killing 13,000 spectators. Constantius II erected Rome's tallest obelisk at 112ft (32.5m) in it on his visit in AD357. The site remains but only fragments of the building survive, including the curved end, for it has been plundered for building materials.

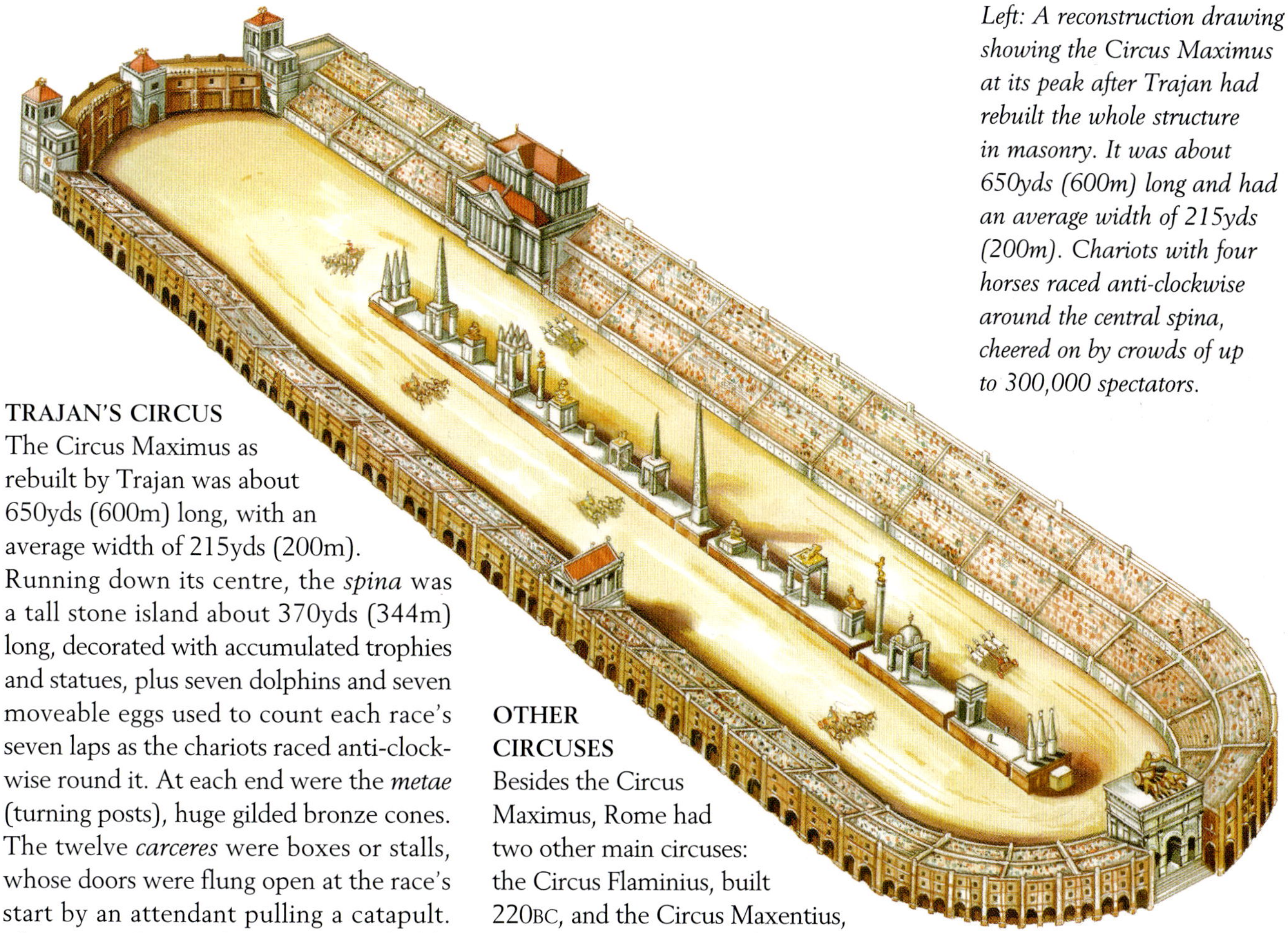

*Left: A reconstruction drawing showing the Circus Maximus at its peak after Trajan had rebuilt the whole structure in masonry. It was about 650yds (600m) long and had an average width of 215yds (200m). Chariots with four horses raced anti-clockwise around the central spina, cheered on by crowds of up to 300,000 spectators.*

**TRAJAN'S CIRCUS**

The Circus Maximus as rebuilt by Trajan was about 650yds (600m) long, with an average width of 215yds (200m). Running down its centre, the *spina* was a tall stone island about 370yds (344m) long, decorated with accumulated trophies and statues, plus seven dolphins and seven moveable eggs used to count each race's seven laps as the chariots raced anti-clockwise round it. At each end were the *metae* (turning posts), huge gilded bronze cones. The twelve *carceres* were boxes or stalls, whose doors were flung open at the race's start by an attendant pulling a catapult. The *cavea* (stepped seating), probably about 115ft (35m) high, rested almost completely on vaulted substructures. Externally, it had three storeys, with arcades on the ground floor and engaged (buried) pilasters on the floor above.

The Circus was not used solely for chariot racing. *Venationes* were staged in it – far more people could see wild beast shows there than in the Colosseum – and especially odious criminals, including early Christians, suffered the horrendous fate of *damnatio ad bestias* there: they were tied to a stake and savaged to death by goaded carnivores. In AD204, the emperor Septimius Severus staged special games in which a massive, specially built ship fell apart in a mock *naufragium* (shipwreck) to disgorge 700 wild animals, who then fought each other. At other less sanguinary times, the huge arena filled with stall-holders, fortune-tellers and buskers who turned it into a lively market.

**OTHER CIRCUSES**

Besides the Circus Maximus, Rome had two other main circuses: the Circus Flaminius, built 220BC, and the Circus Maxentius, built AD306–12. The Circus Flaminius was located in the Campus Martius, outside the city's sacred *pomerium* (boundary), because it was used for games connected with the *dei inferni* (gods of the underworld), as well as for assemblies and displaying booty. In 2BC Augustus flooded it for the display and slaughter of 36 crocodiles, so it clearly had a retaining wall, but it was never monumentalized into a stone structure and was later overshadowed by the Theatres of Pompey and Balbus nearby.

The Circus Maxentius, built outside the city on the Via Appia as part of Maxentius' complex of villa and mausoleum, is large – about 570 by 100 yds (520 x 92m) – but having a low *cavea*, it could accommodate only 15,000 spectators, members of Maxentius' court and hangers-on. It shows interesting architectural developments. The *spina*, for example, is placed off-axis to allow for the crowding of chariots at the start.

*Below: A view across the site of the Circus Maximus towards the Imperial Palace built by Domitian on the Palatine Hill. Emperors could enter the Circus directly from their palace.*

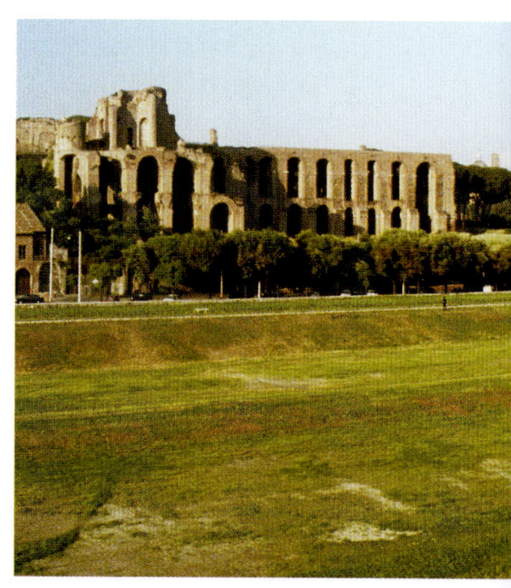

# TRIUMPHAL ARCHES

*Above: One of the first triple triumphal arches, the Arch of Tiberius was built in Orange, France to commemorate the defeat of the rebel Julius Sacrovir in AD21. Its large central arch is flanked by Corinthian columns and smaller side arches.*

Few monuments are more characteristically Roman than the freestanding monumental triumphal arches that they built, usually to celebrate military or political triumphs. Although the Romans did not invent the arch, they were the first to use it to commemorate such events ceremonially. Cities around the Roman empire and, after the Renaissance, across the world, also built triumphal arches, showing how deeply this monument has caught the Western imagination.

## COMMEMORATING VICTORY

In its essence a triumphal arch is a vaulted passageway apparently, but not in reality, supported on pilasters with a decorated frieze (sculpted entablature) and an attic carrying statues, trophies and, in ancient Rome, inscriptions.

The first *fornices*, honorific arches with statues, were built in Rome in the 2nd century BC by nobles commemorating their exploits. These include those of Lucius Stertinius in the Circus Maximus and in the Forum Boarium in 196BC and of Scipio Africanus on the road up to the Capitoline in 190BC. No arches of the Republican period remain, chiefly because Augustus so radically reordered the Forum that few monuments unconnected with his family or faction survived.

Augustus built his Actian Arch, commemorating victory over Mark Antony, next to the temple of his adopted father, the deified Julius Caesar, in 29BC. After his Parthian "victory" of 19BC – actually just a notably successful diplomatic settlement – he either rebuilt it more grandly or built a new arch on the other side of the temple.

In its final form it was, unusually, a triple gateway, the central grand arch flanked by two smaller, attached openings that were not arched but simple flat, pedimented gateways. Above the central arch was a statue of Augustus in a *quadriga* (four-horse chariot). On the sides of the arch, marble inscriptions listed the names of *triumphatores* (generals granted triumphs) from the time of Romulus, Rome's mythical founder, thus linking Augustus with his predecessors. Augustus also built a smaller arch to Gaius and

*Right: The last great arch in Rome was the triple arch of Constantine built AD315. It looks back to earlier arches, most notably in its plundering of older material. These panels show Marcus Aurelius' head awkwardly reworked to resemble Constantine.*

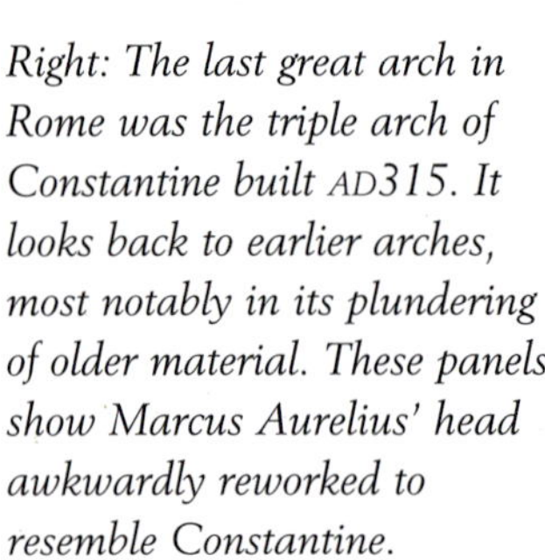

Lucius, his grandsons and intended heirs who both died young. This was probably located on the temple's other side. Arches were built around the Forum for some later victorious generals, all of them descendants of Augustus, such as that of Germanicus in AD16 and of the younger Drusus in AD19. A half-ruined arch to Germanicus survives at Pompeii.

Perhaps the finest arch to survive extant in Rome is that of Titus (ruled AD79–81), the Flavian emperor who was so generous to the Roman people and so merciless to his enemies. Built at the top of the Via Sacra (Sacred Way), it was finished after his death by his brother Domitian. Fine white Pentelic marble from Greece covered its concrete core (it was restored in 1821), but it impresses chiefly through the calm dignity of its lines. Slightly taller than it is wide, its single opening is flanked by massive piers with eight half columns of the Composite order – a favourite in Flavian architecture – standing on a high podium and supporting an architrave and frieze. This depicts Titus' triumphal procession in Rome after sacking the temple in Jerusalem. The eloquent simplicity of the arch marks a peak of Roman classicism. The fine arch to Trajan at Benevento in southern Italy is so similar in design that it could be by the same architect.

The next great arch extant is that of Septimius Severus built in AD203 right over the Via Sacra. A grand triple monument, it is 68ft high by 76ft wide (21m by 23m). It was originally surmounted by a *quadriga* bearing the emperor and his two sons Caracalla and Geta. Besides its size, it is notable for the four great panels depicting Severus' victorious eastern campaign, in which he had won the new province of (northern) Mesopotamia. Rejecting the classical three-dimensional realism that had so long been the rule, the flattened style of its carvings anticipates that of the later empire. By contrast, an austere yet classically proportioned arch erected by Gallienus (ruled AD253–68) survives but is squashed between later buildings on the Esquiline Hill.

## THE LAST ARCH

Constantine I was the last of arch-building emperors in Rome whose work survives. His triple arch, completed in AD315, celebrates his victory over Maxentius. Although it is the biggest in Rome and generally imitates Severus' closely in design, it is hardly the most elegant. Longer than it is wide, it looks rather earth-bound compared to earlier arches. Its finest carvings were lifted from other monuments – of the Flavian, Trajanic and Antonine periods – while the original carvings are poorly modelled. The tradition of carving sculptural reliefs in stone had almost died out in Rome 50 years earlier. Tastes were changing anyway. Newer buildings, such as the Basilica Nova and the Baths of Diocletian relied on coloured marble, stucco and mosaic to embellish their interiors, leaving the exterior relatively austere. Constantine's arch was in fact antiquarian, looking back to an age that had already ended.

*Above: The noble dignity of the Arch of Trajan at Benevento, dedicated in AD114, stems from its fine proportions and its Parian marble covering.*

*Below: The Arc de Triomphe, Paris, is the largest modern arch emulating Rome's arches.*

# TRIUMPHAL COLUMNS

Commemorative or triumphal columns celebrated great individuals, especially military men. The Romans, like the Greeks or Egyptians, were passionate about perpetuating their fame by the most durable means available, but the idea of erecting marble columns topped by bronze or marble statues seems to have been a wholly Roman one. The practice was revived in the Renaissance and has long continued: one of London's most famous landmarks is Nelson's Column, which dominates Trafalgar Square.

Columns known as *columnae rostratae* were erected from the 3rd century BC. One of the earliest is the Column of Gaius Duilius, a column with ships' prows dating from 260BC. By the 2nd century BC, relatively small columns celebrating successful Republican nobles' exploits were being erected in and around the Forum Romanum. (An ancient pillar, the Maenian Column, originally stood near the old prison to the west of the Curia Hostilia, the first Senate House, but it was a landmark helping officials tell the time of day, not a memorial.) The Forum, however, soon became so cluttered with monuments of various sorts, including statues, arches and columns, that in 158BC the censors ordered that space be cleared to let citizens move around easily.

### TRAJAN'S COLUMN

The truly great triumphal columns of Rome were built not in the still half-Republican Forum Romanum but in the grand new complexes of the emperors. Trajan, perhaps the most grandiose of Rome's imperial builders, crowned his resplendent new basilica with a triumphal column rising just beyond its tall roof. This

*Left: Trajan's great column soars 131ft (40m) into the sky, the grandest in Rome. In front are the columns of the Basilica Ulpia.*

*Above: A river god, personifying the River Danube, looks up at the Roman soldiers triumphantly crossing the Danube during Trajan's Dacian campaign.*

became the unsurpassed archetype of such monuments. Built in AD112–13, probably by Trajan's famous architect Apollodorus of Damascus, it is truly prodigious. The column is 125ft (38m) high including its base and composed of 19 giant drums of Carrara marble, each weighing about 40 tons. It is both classical, comprising a single gigantic Doric column in form, and radical in its design, with a hollow interior up which a spiral staircase of 185 steps winds to a balcony.

The column is also remarkable for its carvings. These form a continuous frieze which coils around the column like a gigantic illustrated marble scroll about 600ft (180m) long. The carvings depict in amazingly graphic detail the story of Trajan's recent conquest of Dacia (Romania) and give us an impression of the Roman army in its conquering prime.

Scenes of the emperor addressing his troops, of legionaries crossing rivers, marching, building and fighting, and of the wounded being tended, are punctuated halfway up by a figure of the goddess Victory. She is flanked by trophies that form a link with the sculptures at the column's base which show captured barbarian equipment. The columns' higher parts would have been more visible than they are today, as the upper storeys of the adjacent libraries and basilica would have allowed people to view them halfway up. The frieze is one of the finest examples of Roman low relief. Brimming with artistic energy, it had a great influence on carvings around the empire in the following century.

Within this colossal monument to self-glorification was a tomb-chamber for Trajan himself. This was almost certainly not part of the original plan in view of the spiral staircase within the column. Trajan's ashes were laid there after he had died in Tarsus in Asia Minor in AD117 on his way home from his disastrous Parthian war.

The column owes its unusually good state of preservation to Pope Gregory the Great (ruled AD590–604). Reputedly, Gregory was so moved by a relief showing Trajan helping a grieving woman that he prayed to God to release the emperor's soul from hell. According to the story, God agreed, Trajan became the only pagan ruler thus spared and the land around his column was declared sacred.

The gilded bronze statue of the emperor that once topped the column was replaced in 1587 by a statue of St Peter. Restored for Rome's millennial jubilee in 2000, it now gleams with almost pristine freshness.

### IMITATING TRAJAN

Trajan's superb column was hard to match but Marcus Aurelius (ruled AD161–80), who fought even longer if less victorious wars on the Danube, had a column erected to him after his death by Commodus, his son. About 100ft (30m) high, it is composed of 28 drums of marble. It also has an internal staircase and a spiral relief depicting Marcus' wars. The relief's overall tone, however, is very different. In place of Trajanic triumphalism, there is a sense of exhaustion and despair and it is carved in a manner which indicates that the tradition of classical realism was approaching its end. The tradition of self-glorification did not die so easily, however. In Constantinople, the emperors Theodosius I (AD378–95) and Arcadius (AD395–408) both raised similar columns to themselves, of which little survives.

One of the strangest uses for such columns in the now Christian empire was as ostentatiously uncomfortable retreats for saints or hermits, who clambered up, dislodged the pagan statue on top and then squatted between heaven and earth, to be admired by the faithful below. St Simeon Stylites, the Syrian saint (AD387–459) was only the first of many such holy exhibitionists.

*Above: The Roman obsession with perpetuating their fame posthumously depended partly on a literate posterity that could read such fine inscriptions as this one, which was dedicated to the deified emperor Titus.*

*Below: The figures on Marcus Aurelius' column (c. AD180) seem exhausted by their years of bitter war on the Danube.*

# CHURCHES

*Above: The Basilica of Sant' Apollinare in Classe, near Ravenna, was begun in AD490 and finished under the Byzantines.*

*Below: The simple rectangular form of the Basilica of Old St Peter's, Rome, begun c. AD333.*

Poverty, persecution and expectations of the imminent end of the world meant the first Christians built little. However, when Constantine became the first Christian emperor after AD313, he inaugurated a vigorous programme of church building that continued throughout the vicissitudes of the next two centuries.

## A NEW ARCHITECTURE

Christian worship differed radically from pagan cults. In the latter, the image of the god was often secluded in a small, mysteriously dark shrine inside a temple's *cella* (inner chamber) and only taken out on special festivals, with most worshippers remaining in the outer court. Some old temples did become churches, as the Pantheon did in AD608, but its shape and size were both exceptional. Christian worship required the presence of the whole body of the faithful for prayers, responses and sermons and much larger, more open buildings were needed. Architects turned to the great basilicas that now dominated many cities across the empire for inspiration. Trajan's grand but architecturally simple basilica, with its colonnaded aisles, high beamed roof and apses at each end well suited for altars, with lighting provided by clerestories above, provided a model for many churches in the 4th and 5th centuries AD.

## BUILDING THE BASILICAS

Across the River Tiber on the Campus Vaticanus, the site of St Peter's martyrdom in AD64 in the Circus of Nero, Constantine donated land to Pope Sylvester I to build Old St Peter's, the foremost church in Western Christendom. Started in AD333 (the present domed church dates only from the 16th century), it was a simple rectangular building with a flat, timber-beamed ceiling supported by colonnaded naves. The basilica had a broad lateral transept placed, exceptionally, between the apse and the nave to allow the circulation of pilgrims who came to venerate St Peter's tomb. Above the tomb, a marble *baldachino* (canopy) with spiral fluted columns was erected. The basilica's colonnaded nave and aisles were used both as the prototypical covered cemetery – many saints and popes are buried there, but there had never been burials within pagan temples – and as a banqueting and funeral hall. Outside, a central fountain was provided for religious ablutions, the only type of washing that ascetic early Christians admired. The whole complex was completed by AD344.

In Rome proper, a grand example of early basilicas was the Basilica Constantinia on the Lateran Hill. This is known today as San Giovanni in Laterano

(St John's in the Lateran). Begun by Constantine in AD313, he gave the basilica and its adjacent land to the pope. Until 1309, when the papacy left Rome for its exile in Avignon, the adjoining Lateran palace was the official papal residence.

Today's basilica retains the original groundplan but has been destroyed by fire twice and rebuilt many times, most notably by Borromini in 1646. The Constantinian church, built of brick-faced concrete, was reputedly very splendid, with seven gold altars, 100 chandeliers and 60 gold candlesticks to illuminate its mosaics. Contrasting with this imperial grandeur is the church of Santa Costanza, built as a mausoleum for Constantine's canonized daughter Constantia in AD340. Its dome is supported by a circular arcade resting on 12 pairs of fine columns, while its barrel-vaulted ceiling has marvellous extant mosaics showing flora and fauna and the grape harvest.

Church-building continued, if more slowly, after Constantine's move east. San Paolo fuori le Mura (St Paul's Outside the Walls), begun in AD385, has columns supported by arches while a giant arch divides its nave from the apse. Unfortunately, the church was drably restored after a fire in 1823. Surviving much better is Santa Maria Maggiore (Great St Mary's). It originated in a dream Pope Liberius had in AD356 in which the Virgin Mary told him to found a church on the spot where snow fell in August. It was actually built under Pope Sixtus III (AD432–40). Its imposing, classical giant Ionic columns line the colonnaded nave. Santa Sabina on the Aventine is another elegant, well-preserved example of this short-lived but remarkable classical revival.

### BYZANTINE ARCHITECTURE

Late Roman styles developed into Byzantine mainly outside Rome. At Ravenna, which was the capital of the Western empire from AD402, then of Ostrogothic kings and finally of Byzantine *exarchs* (governors), the empress Galla Placidia constructed a mausoleum for

herself and her brother Honorius in AD425. Its mosaics reveal a joyfully pastoral vision of Christianity. Grander but heavier are the mosaics in the Basilica of Sant'Apollinare in Classe outside Ravenna. Begun in AD490 under the Ostrogoths and finished in AD549 by the Byzantines, it is still a basilica-type church, as most churches in the West were always to be.

However, in the East a new architecture was emerging in the radical designs of the cathedral of Hagia Sophia in Constantinople, built under the emperor Justinian I (ruled AD527–65). A centrally planned church whose 180ft (55m) dome seems to float without visible support – "Marvellous in its grace but terrifying because of its seemingly insecure composition", as the writer Procopius put it – it satisfied Byzantine needs for a cruciform church and must have later inspired Islamic builders. However, its construction marks an effective end to the period of truly Roman architecture.

*Above: The mausoleum of Galla Placidia in Ravenna, one of the finest buildings of the 5th century AD in Ravenna, was renowned for its mosaics.*

*Below: The high point of Byzantine architecture is the cathedral of Hagia Sophia. Its simple, seemingly unsupported dome was hugely influential.*

# Chapter IV

# IMPERIAL PALACES

The English word palace comes from Latin, from *palatium*, the hill that gave its name to the imperial residence on the Palatine Hill. This majestic complex of courtyards, halls, basilica, stadium and private apartments, built by Domitian (AD 81–96), became the palace of all subsequent emperors, some of whom enlarged it. The official wing was called the Domus Flavia (Flavian Palace) and its private section was the Domus Augustana (Palace of Augustus), so the whole building became known as the *palatium* and the word passed into almost all West European languages (*palais, palacio, palazzo, palast*).

The house on the Palatine overlooking the Circus Maximus was not the first great imperial residence, for Nero's Domus Aurea (Golden Palace) had anticipated and in some ways exceeded it in extent and grandeur. Nor was it to be the last word in Roman palace architecture. As the tetrarchs and other rulers of the later empire set up their own administrative capitals – at Trier, Milan, Arles, Thessalonica, Nicomedia and finally Constantinople – they built palaces to match their grand pretensions, complete with baths and circuses. Most remarkable of all was Diocletian's massive retirement home to which he retreated in AD 306: a palace-fortress at Split on the Dalmatian coast. The building of these imperial palaces both incorporated and accelerated some of Rome's greatest achievements in architecture, especially the use of vaults and domes.

*Left: The ruins of the imperial palace complex built on the Palatine Hill, as seen from the Circus Maximus.*

# THE PALACES OF AUGUSTUS AND HIS HEIRS

*Above: An aureus (gold coin) of Augustus, first and most successful of emperors, whose own house was deliberately modest and unregal in its size and appearance.*

*Below: The infant Hercules killing snakes. A fresco from the House of the Vettii at Pompeii, typical of the sort of decorations the earlier imperial palaces would have had.*

Augustus, the first and most revered Roman emperor, lived in an almost ostentatiously modest house, not in a palace. On his return to Rome in 29BC after defeating Antony and Cleopatra, Octavian (as he was called until 27BC) did not build himself anything remotely regal.

### A HOUSE FOR THE *PRINCEPS*

Republican Rome had never had proper palaces, although Octavian had seen, indeed probably slept in, the palaces of Hellenistic monarchs such as the Ptolemies in Egypt. However, this was not the image he wanted to project in Rome, a city still proud of its Republican traditions. Instead, in line with his attempts to appear only as the *princeps*, the first among (almost) equals of the Roman nobility, he chose to live in the house that had once belonged to the orator Hortensius, a rival of Cicero.

This was a dignified, good-sized but not exceptional *domus* (detached house) on the Palatine Hill, a favoured location for wealthy nobles.

Some nobles in the Republic's later decades had built themselves very large and luxurious houses, on the Palatine among other hilly – and healthier – areas, but usually near the Forum, the heart of Roman life. The house of Aemilus Scaurus on the Palatine, for example, was sold in 53BC for 14,800,000 sesterces, an immense sum. Augustus' house probably still had an old-fashioned atrium, centred on its *compluvium* (pool). This was traditionally where business was conducted, especially where a patron dealt with *clientalia*, his clients or dependants. However, a wealthy noble's *domus* now normally also had extensive *peristyles* (colonnaded courtyards) and proper gardens, that together would have given the space for the social and official activities that even such a modest emperor needed. The best-preserved and halfway comparable villas are at Pompeii and include the House of the Faun or House of the Vettii.

Augustus' *domus* was probably larger than these, with its own libraries. It was right next to the marble temple of Apollo that he had just had built and also near the ancient but carefully preserved hut in which Romulus and Remus had traditionally grown up, so it had a truly imperial location. The so-called House of Livia, which may have belonged to Augustus' wife (who long survived him), was nearby. Later building covered these structures, but they are all visible today.

Tiberius, Augustus' morose successor in AD14, built the Domus Tiberiana before he finally retired to his cliff-top hermitage on Capri in AD27. This was a large rectangular palace 200 by 130yds (180 by 120m) on the north-west side of the Palatine. Built around a vast *peristyle*

court with an oval fishpond, it now lies inaccessible beneath 16th-century gardens. Caligula is thought to have harboured grand designs for extending this palace towards the Forum Romanum but was assassinated before anything was built. His successor Claudius was content to live almost as modestly as Augustus.

### NERO'S FIRST PALACE

Almost from the start of his reign in AD54, Nero, still only 16 years old, wanted to emulate the Hellenistic monarchies' love of culture and regal splendour. As he shed the early inhibitions imbued in him by his tutor, the philosopher-playwright Seneca, he began to build. Nero decided to connect the Domus Tiberiana and other imperial properties on the Palatine and Oppian Hills with a house inherited from his father by a series of linking buildings across the low saddle of land now crowned by the Arch of Titus. This Domus Transitoria (literally Palace of the Passageway) was destroyed in the great fire of AD64, but some of it has survived to reveal Nero's love of opulent materials, refined if lavish taste and his architects' bold inventiveness.

Traces of his Nymphaeum (Fountain Court) beneath the later Flavian Palace show this was an elongated rectangular building whose open courtyard had ornate shell-shaped fountains along all of one wall. On the other side was a square, raised platform topped by a colonnaded pavilion. Opening off this were suites of rooms – presumably intended for intimate outdoor dinner parties as opposed to the grand public dinners at which emperors often officiated – decorated with marble panellings and vaulted ceilings covered with semi-precious stones, white and gilded stucco and paintings.

Many of the raw materials for this building came from Greece, Asia Minor, Africa and Egypt. Its decorations make very fine examples of what is known (from excavations at Pompeii, buried in AD79) as the Fourth Style, with a few still in the earlier Third Style.

*Above: The atrium of the House of Menander at Pompeii. Its murals are very similar to those in the first imperial palaces.*

More remarkable architecturally, and still surviving beneath the platform of Hadrian's later Temple to Venus and Roma, is the domed intersection of two barrel-vaulted corridors, supported on four huge piers and probably lit by an *oculus* (central opening). Such a design anticipates many later buildings, most famously the Pantheon. There were marble pools behind screens of columns in two of the arms and the whole area was opulently decorated, partly in coloured marbles, partly in geometric patterns of semi-transparent glass paste. Nero's extravagance on such wholly personal apartments, as opposed to the public buildings on which Augustus had lavished his wealth, was however only just beginning and prefigured the opulence he would eventually create in his Domus Aurea (Golden Palace).

*Above: Coin of Nero (ruled AD54–68), the extravagant yet creative emperor.*

# NERO'S GOLDEN PALACE

*Above: The octagonal dining-room lies in the middle of the markedly symmetrical Esquiline Wing, with other rooms radiating off it. Its domed design was strikingly novel.*

*Below: A gouache copy of a Domus Aurea wall-painting. The style influenced Renaissance artists such as Raphael and 18th-century architects.*

The fire that broke out in the Circus Maximus in June AD64 raged for several days, gutting the Domus Transitoria, Nero's first palace, and three of the city's 14 regions, leaving only four regions untouched. It was one of the greatest of all the recurrent fires in the ancient city's history, but it also provided Nero with an unprecedented opportunity.

While there is no truth in the old stories that he started the fire and then "fiddled while Rome burned" – he was actually at Antium some 30 miles away at the time but hurried back to oversee the fire fighting – Nero could now plan on a scale and with a scope normally reserved for the founders of cities.

Dominating the new Rome was to be Nero's own palace, with immense grounds extending some 300 acres (120ha). He called it the Domus Aurea (Golden Palace). In its design, scale and building techniques, most notably in its use of concrete domes and vaults, it is considered to mark a revolution in Roman architecture.

## A BRIEF FLOWERING

Most of the palace had a very brief existence. It was built over or incorporated into later structures such as the Baths of Trajan or the Flavian Amphitheatre by Nero's less extravagant successors. Only some lower rooms survived in the Esquiline wing, which was incorporated into the platform of the Baths of Trajan, to be rediscovered in the Renaissance and influence artists such as Raphael and Giulio Romano, who crawled in to admire and copy them.

These subterranean chambers today appear damp and dark and provide a poor impression of how they must have appeared in their short-lived prime. While the more luxurious types of decoration such as mosaics, marble and stucco veneer have long since vanished, the rooms still have fine wall-paintings with delicate landscapes and architectural motifs. These are mostly executed in the Fourth Style, which is best seen in the well-preserved villas at Pompeii.

The architects of this remarkable complex, which was built in under four years, were Severus and Celer, who had already started, but not completed cutting a canal from Lake Avernus to the Tiber. According to Suetonius, writing about the Domus Aureus early in the 2nd century AD (when it had already mostly vanished), "Its entrance hall was large enough to contain a colossal statue of Nero himself, 120ft high, while its whole area was so great that it had a triple colonnade a mile long. An enormous pool, like the sea, was surrounded by buildings that resembled cities, and by a landscaped park with ploughed fields, vineyards, pastures and woods, where all sorts of domestic and

wild animals roamed. Everything in the rest of the palace was inlaid with gold and highlighted with precious stones and mother-of-pearl. The dining-rooms had ceilings with rotating ivory panels which could sprinkle flowers or perfume on guests below. The most remarkable dining-room was circular, its roof rotating day and night like the sky. Sea water or sulphurous water flowed through the baths. When the whole palace had been completed, Nero dedicated it but only remarked, 'At last I can begin to live like a human being.'"

## A PALACE IN THE HEART OF A CITY

Nero's walled urban park – about the size of Hyde Park in London, or one third the size of Central Park in New York – was approached from the Forum Romanum along the Via Sacra (Sacred Way), which was straightened and lined with colonnaded porticoes in line with the new regulations for rebuilding all Rome. What angered the Roman people about the new palace was less its ostentatious luxury than the fact that it used so much prime property in the very heart of the city simply for one man's private luxury. A contemporary joke ran, "Rome will become one huge palace, so migrate to Veii [ten miles distant], citizens, until the palace reaches Veii too!" Such open extravagance inside the city contributed to Nero's unpopularity and his downfall within months of the palace's completion in AD68.

Perhaps because the palace was built at breakneck speed – made possible by using brick-faced concrete which was then covered in decorative marble or stucco – the plan of the Domus Aurea is oddly asymmetrical, sometimes even jumbled. The most innovatory of the rooms, which was later incorporated into the platform of the Baths of Trajan, was the octagonal dining-room with rooms radiating off it. The dome had an *oculus* (central opening), while slits let light into the radiating rooms. (This may have been the remarkable dining-room described by Suetonius.) Behind the octagonal room was a jumble of lesser rooms. To the west, at the heart of the palace, was a large pentagonal courtyard which was open to the south and surrounded by a series of major rooms that was flanked by smaller chambers.

As with the rooms opening on to the main courtyard, the architects grouped alternating rectangular rooms, such as the large vaulted dining-room which had screens of columns at both ends, with rooms with apses (semicircular spaces). Of particular note is a barrel-vaulted room off the dining-room, which had a fountain at one end and a mosaic frieze running around the walls made mostly of polychrome glass. The Domus Aurea lived on in public memory as the epitome of extravagant luxury but it also marked a significant development in Roman architecture.

*Above: Part of Nero's Domus Aurea, the lavish new palace he built after the Great Fire, with its splendid courts, gardens and colonnades, ate up 300 acres (120ha) of prime urban space in central Rome.*

*Below: The self-indulgent vanity of this most extravagant of emperors is evident in this bust of Nero.*

# THE PALATINE: PALACE OF THE EMPERORS

*Above: A coloured marble floor from the* nymphaeum *of the Domus Transitoria, on the Palatine Hill.*

*Below: The courtyard of the* nymphaeum *(fountain) in the Domus Flavia, looking towards the basilica from the west side of the main* peristyle.

Vespasian, Nero's successor and founder of the Flavian dynasty, chose the Gardens of Sallust as his house with deliberate modesty; his son Titus (ruled AD79–81) occupied the Domus Tiberiana.

Titus' successor Domitian (ruled AD81–96) was commonly remembered as a tyrant – at least by the Senate and the equestrians, though the army loved him. Undoubtedly, he built grandly in a style befitting the absolute monarchy that the Principate was now becoming.

Domitian's greatest achievement was the palace on the Palatine Hill. This became the emperor's residence for the next three centuries. Praised by the poet Martial for its splendour and size, it was dedicated in AD92. Various repairs were made by several emperors and Septimius Severus added bulky extensions to the eastern and south-western extremities of the palace early in the 3rd century AD. Nonetheless, it remains very much Domitian's monument.

## PALACE BUILDINGS

The Domus Aurea had become impractical as an imperial residence for the Flavian dynasty, partly because it was the former palace of the despot Nero and also because, once the Colosseum and Baths of Titus had been built in its park, it was cut off from the main Palatine buildings. Domitian chose Rabirius, a great Roman architect about whose life, typically, nothing is known but who was clearly an inventive genius fond of octagonal and semicircular shapes, to build a completely new palace on the Palatine. The western side of this hill, hallowed by its links with Augustus and Romulus, was already occupied by ancient temples and other venerable buildings, so Rabirius cut a huge terrace in the east ridge which sloped away both south-east and south-west. With the material this produced, he created a flat platform at a higher level to the north.

The palace had two distinct parts: the public audience halls, known as the Domus Flavia, and the private apartments, known as the Domus Augustana. It also had a pleasure garden in the guise of a race track, referred to as a stadium or *hippodromos*, and baths.

There were two main approaches. The official route from the north-east led up the Via Sacra (Sacred Way) and under the arch of Titus into a large paved area, the Area Palatina, which the Domus Flavia overlooked. It was from this approach that the massive bulk of the palace must have looked most imposing. The other route was from the Forum Romanum through a vaulted vestibule. The official wing of the palace, the Domus Flavia, was built on a large platform on top of the hill with a colonnade round

its edge. Behind this colonnade lay three grand state rooms: the Lararium (Chapel to the Lares or household gods); the Aulia Regia (Throne Room) and an apsed basilica.

The Aulia Regia was the largest state room, measuring 98 by 120ft wide (30 by 37m) and very high. Visitors entering by the official, north-east approach would have seen the emperor majestically enthroned beneath a shallow apse at the far end, ready to receive ambassadors and other dignitaries, including Roman senators. This last group regarded being summoned like mere ambassadors as a grievous insult, for they were accustomed to having the emperor come to the Curia (Senate House) to speak to them. Domitian, moreover, insisted on being addressed as *"dominus et deus"* (lord and god), in keeping with his new splendour. This, too, was bitterly resented.

The walls of the throne room were covered with multi-coloured marble while twelve niches held giant statues in black basalt. Free-standing columns of Phrygian marble on tall plinths supported projecting entablatures. The roof, like those elsewhere in the palace, was probably not vaulted but had timber beams. (Whether or not most rooms in the palace had vaulted concrete or straight timber roofs remains a matter of furious debate.) Alongside the throne room there was another grand hall, the basilica, where the emperor heard law cases. It was divided into three by two rows of columns of Numidian yellow marble, which stood forward about 7ft (2m) from the walls, perhaps to allow those waiting to sit on benches. Soon after its construction, the basilica's outer wall began to show signs of subsidence and needed massive buttressing under Hadrian (ruled AD117–38).

### THE *TRICLINIUM*

From the throne room visitors passed into the large *peristyle* courtyard. This had a big octagonal pool with a fountain in its centre. Its pink columns of Cappadocian marble, along with its walls

of shining white marble were, according to Suetonius, polished like mirrors to let Domitian see any lurking assassins. (The precaution proved useless, for the emperor, who grew increasingly paranoid, was indeed assassinated in the palace.)

A series of semicircular rooms, perhaps official guest bedrooms, lay on the north side of this court, while on the opposite, west side stood the grand *triclinium*, or banqueting hall, called without undue modesty the *Cenatio Iovis* (Jupiter's dining-room). At the far end, a raised apse held the emperor's dining-table, where privileged guests might join him, while spaces for other dining-couches were marked out on the floor. The floor was paved with coloured marble *opus sectile* of purple and green porphyry from Egypt and Greece, *portasanta* from Chios in the Aegean and *giallo antico* from Numidia. The *triclinium* opened on to the courtyard behind a screen of six huge columns of grey Egyptian granite and had five huge windows on each side.

*Above: The ruins of the huge columns in the grand* triclinium *(dining-room) of the Domus Flavia that Domitian proudly called "Jupiter's dining-room".*

*Below: Some of the surviving coloured marble floors of the Domus Flavia, whose lavishness was noted at the time.*

*Above: Arches from the heavy Severan additions made to the Domus Flavia in the early 3rd century AD.*

*Below: Although only the brick-faced concrete core of the Domus Flavia has survived, its arches and vaults still rise imposingly on its hill.*

### THE DOMUS AUGUSTANA

The south-east section of the palace, the domestic wing called the Domus Augustana, was conceived almost as a separate building. Although it covered about twice the area of the Domus Flavia and had three *peristyles* instead of one, for example, it must have seemed less massive from an external viewpoint, except on the side that faced the Circus Maximus. This architectural understatement was perhaps deliberate, for Domitian wanted to advertise public imperial grandeur rather than lavish personal consumption. The Domus Augustana was, in effect, a private villa on a grand scale. In all probability it was very luxurious, but only its lower part has survived to provide clues to its grandeur.

The Domus Augustana was approached from the Area Palatina through a monumental entrance which gave on to a large rectangular *peristyle*, corresponding to that of the Domus Flavia. This led to another *peristyle* with a sunken pool in its centre, whose walls were decorated in Fourth Style paintings. To the south-west lay a maze of small rooms in many different shapes, heights and sizes. Here Rabirius seems to have given his imagination free rein and, far from the public gaze, his imperial patron may have dallied with his harem of concubines, whom he reputedly depilated personally. The puritanism which Domitian tried to enforce in public, most notoriously by reviving the ancient punishment of burial alive for Vestal Virgins who broke their vows of chastity, did not apply inside the palace. Some of these rooms have niches and two are perfect octagons lined with round-headed niches.

A single staircase led from this suite of rooms down to the lower parts of the palace. The staircase was lit by a light-well, at the bottom of which a pool lined with polychrome glass mosaic would have both reflected and coloured the incoming light. Two other light-wells – again over pools whose waters would have reflected and increased the light – lit the surrounding rooms, which included a fine marble-lined *nymphaeum* (fountain room) and another, more intimate *triclinium* (dining-room). Most of these rooms had concrete vaulted ceilings and many were polygonal in shape, reflecting the contemporary prejudice against rectangular shapes. Services such as latrines were hidden discreetly beneath the staircase.

Throughout the Domus Augustana, as in the Domus Flavia, the decorations seem to have been exceptionally rich, with columns, paving and wall veneers of imported, coloured marbles. The few fragments that survive, such as the *opus sectile* floors of the *triclinium*, were made of differently shaped and coloured marbles and formed geometric patterns or pictures. On the walls, mosaics and wall paintings repeated and reinforced the overall impression of sumptuousness. According to Suetonius, however, Domitian was by no means a great gourmet. He normally ate heavily at midday – which was not the usual Roman custom – and contented himself with an apple and a glass of wine in the evening.

### OVERLOOKING THE CIRCUS

A passage led from this second *peristyle* into the *hippodromos* or stadium, a sunken garden about 160 by 700ft (50 by 184m) on the palace's south-eastern flank. Lined by a continuous pillared arcade round its two long sides and curved end, it playfully imitated a real circus with mock *carceres* (starting boxes). Trees and pools adorned this most secluded of imperial gardens, with elaborate semicircular fountains at either end.

On the Domus Augustana's south-western façade, overlooking the valley of the Circus Maximus, Rabirius revealed his genius most clearly, for the towering façade curved gently inward with an intercolumnated screen to produce a truly majestic effect, surpassing in external grandeur anything in the Domus Aurea.

If Nero's architects had begun the Roman revolution in architecture by skilfully employing concrete, Rabirius carried it much further. Incorporated in this façade was a *loggia* or imperial box, which the emperor and his entourage could reach directly from the palace. This innovative convenience was subsequently much copied in the later empire.

*Above: The ruins of the lower part of the Domus Flavia, with its elaborate, sunken peristyle, courtyard garden. It was built over earlier structures such as Nero's Domus Transitoria, inadvertently preserving them.*

*Above: A coin of Domitian (ruled AD81–96), the emperor responsible for building most of the palace on the Palatine.*

# CHAPTER V

# HOUSING FOR RICH AND POOR

As Rome grew richer in the late Republic (from *c.*150BC), the gap between rich and poor was reflected in increasingly divergent standards of housing. Originally most Romans lived in modest *domus* (detached houses). But while the rich inhabited ever more elaborate, spacious *domus*, decorated by artworks and with large gardens adorned with fountains and trees, the not so wealthy increasingly found themselves living, at times precariously, in *insulae*.

*Insulae* (literally islands) – large, many-storeyed apartment buildings that often took up a whole block – have been called the world's first skyscrapers. A few earlier cities, such as Phoenician Tyre, had had very tall buildings, but *insulae* became the first high buildings to house most of a great city's population and the first to reach (and sometimes breach) height limits of up to 70ft (20m). Initially, these blocks of flats were built very quickly and were in constant danger of fire or collapse. Nero's sensible regulations after the great fire of AD64 helped to improve them, and by AD100 not all *insulae* were slums. Both *domus* and *insulae* were eclipsed by the splendours of the great country villas built by emperors, magnates and other wealthy men across the empire. These have survived better than more modest villas, but are not really typical.

*Left: A view of the* peristyle *courtyard of the Villa di Poppaea, Oplontis, preserved by Vesuvius in* AD79. *Its size and splendour are typical of the grander villas of Pompeii.*

# THE DOMUS: HOUSES OF THE RICH

*Above: The interior of a typical Roman house at Herculaneum, showing how the atrium receives light from above and how the* impluvium, *a small reflecting pool, catches the rainwater.*

*Below: The* peristyle *of the House of the Vettii at Pompeii, the house of a wealthy man, showing its recreated gardens surrounded by typical colonnades.*

The early Roman *domus* (house, from which we derive our word domestic) was a simple, one- or two-storeyed building with rooms set around an *atrium*, a central hall open to the sky. An *impluvium* (pool) in its centre caught rainwater. This type of *domus*, called the Italic house, was derived partly from Etruscan originals. Another larger courtyard, the *peristyle*, was increasingly added to the *domus* in the later Republic. Although both courts grew more grandly colonnaded and decorated, a *domus* typically had mere slits for windows. Often wholly windowless rooms opened off the *atrium* to the outer world, for security rather than privacy.

In Rome, up to the First Punic War (264–241BC), although such houses were the commonest form of dwelling, the *domus* of great patricians were far grander than plebeians' houses. As early as 509BC, the traditional date of the founding of the Republic, there were large houses on the Palatine Hill, with several rooms on more than one floor. Although Roman puritanism, which was strong in the early Republic, long discouraged ostentatious displays of luxury and wealth, houses were nonetheless prized in fashionable areas, preferably close to or in the Forum Romanum, the centre of political life. Bitter rivals among the nobility often had to live side-by-side.

## A SOURCE OF DYNASTIC PRIDE

Despite a surprisingly brisk market in Roman property, a *domus* could remain in the same family for generations, sometimes centuries. The patrician Clodius Pulcher, for example, mocked his rival Cicero in 58BC as a "*novus homo*" (literally, new man, one without ancestors in the Senate) for having bought, rather than inherited, his house.

When Cicero was temporarily exiled soon after, his house was pulled down to underline his disgrace. By contrast, when the great general Pompey's house passed into Mark Antony's possession after his fall, his trophies were allowed to remain proudly on its walls. The architect Vitruvius, writing *c.* 35BC, observed that, "Distinguished men, required to fulfil their duty by holding public office, must build lofty vestibules in regal style, with spacious atria and peristyles …also libraries and basilicas comparable with magnificent public buildings, because public meetings and private trials take place inside their houses."

Many nobles' houses, with their revered busts of their ancestors, remained intact up to the great fire of AD64 which destroyed much of central Rome. After this, nobles tended to move further from the centre, as life ceased to focus on the Forum Romanum.

The *domus* was therefore never merely a home; it was also a repository of dynastic pride. In addition, its public rooms provided a place for transacting social

and political, rather than commercial, business. Tacitus, writing more than a century after the Republic had ended, still observed that, "The more impressive a man's wealth, house and clothing, the more his name and *clientela* (supporters) become famous". As the nobility's wealth grew, so did the splendours of their *domus*. According to Pliny, the house of Domitius Lepidus, considered the finest in Rome in 78BC, did not even make it into the top 100 only 35 years later.

A visitor to a typical *domus* of the late Republic or early empire would first enter the *atrium*, which was often a room of majestic height. The water in the central *impluvium* helped to diffuse incoming light and to ventilate the surrounding rooms (although it may also have bred malarial mosquitoes). The surrounding rooms were generally simple bedrooms, offices, store-rooms and *alae*, recesses used to store hallowed masks or the busts of family ancestors.

A curtain or wooden screen separated the *atrium* from the *tablinium* (main reception room/office). Beyond lay the *peristyle*, the colonnaded garden around which other rooms were grouped, including open-fronted *exedrae* and often the *triclinium* (dining-room). Only the grander *domus* had proper bathrooms, as many were not connected to mains water and relied instead on rainwater from the *impluvium* or from public fountains. However, the richest displayed their aquatic wealth with elaborate fountains in huge *peristyles*.

The volcanic eruption at Pompeii in AD79 preserved useful physical evidence for all this. However, the *Forma Urbis Romae* (the Severan Marble Map of Rome) also shows a good number of *domus* in the region of the Esquiline and elsewhere.

## DECORATIONS

The walls of a *domus* were often brightly painted and the floors covered in mosaics. Thanks to their usually axial layout, which created a vista from the entrance passage through to the *peristyle*, entering visitors would have been dazzled by strong

Mediterranean sunlight alternating with deep shadow. In summer, a *domus* must have been pleasantly cool and airy. In winter, it might have been dark and chilly, with oil lamps shedding feeble light and the only heat provided by smoky braziers. Hypocaust central heating was uncommon except in bathrooms and among the very rich. Glass for windows was also initially uncommon, as it was relatively expensive before the 1st century AD.

The House of the Faun, built *c.* 120BC, in Pompeii is a well-preserved and exceptionally large house of the late Republic. A truly grand *domus*, larger than the contemporary royal palace of Pergamum in Asia Minor, it has a double *atrium* and remarkable mosaics, most famously one showing Alexander the Great's victory at the Issus in 333BC. The subject indicates that Hellenistic influences – which included the *peristyle* itself – had now fused with Italic traditions to create complex, luxurious houses. However, even in Pompeii, which was less heavily populated than Rome, houses were being subdivided by AD79 and the atrium/peristyle house was becoming confined to the very rich.

*Above: The atrium in the House of the Mosaic Atrium at Herculaneum shows both the typically fine black-and-white mosaic floor that gave the house its name and the alternation of light and shade through the axis of the house.*

*Above: Detail of mosaic of Alexander the Great, from the House of the Faun, Pompeii.*

# INSULAE: THE FIRST APARTMENTS

*Above: Brick-faced concrete was the normal building material used in Rome and, as here, in Ostia for both* insulae, *the apartment blocks, and shopping markets.*

*Below: While many earlier* insulae *were jerry-built, by the 2nd century* AD *solidly constructed apartment blocks with internal courtyards or gardens were becoming common in Ostia, Rome and other cities. They have lasted impressively well.*

By *c.* AD150, as Rome's population peaked at probably more than one million, many of its inhabitants were living in *insulae*. This translates literally as islands, although not all actually occupied a whole block of their own. According to the mid-4th century catalogue, there were 46,600 *insulae* in Rome and only 1,790 *domus*. These blocks of flats rose to five, six, even at times seven storeys. Augustus and later Trajan tried to limit their height to 60 and then to 70 ft, but the reiteration of such regulations suggests that such laws had only a limited effect.

## LIFE IN AN *INSULA*

Juvenal, the satirical poet, provides a vivid, unflattering but not impartial portrayal of life in an *insula*. "We live in a city supported mostly by slender props, which is how the bailiff patches cracks in old walls, telling the residents to sleep peacefully under roofs ready to fall down around them. No, no I have to live somewhere where there are no fires or alarms every night … if the alarm is sounded on the ground floor the last man to be burnt alive will be the one with nothing to shelter him from the rain but the roof tiles."

Some *insula* blocks survive in Rome, but most evidence comes from Ostia, whose remains show that in fact, many apartments on lower floors were very habitable, even comfortable. Some first-floor apartments had running water and large, possibly glazed windows.

Spacious apartments, with separate rooms for dining and sleeping, were inhabited by wealthy citizens, including some equestrians (knights) and even senators, perhaps as friends of the usually aristocratic owner. Often such wealthier tenants paid rent annually and had some security of tenure. In contrast, garrets under the tiles up many flights of stairs must have been cramped, hot in summer, cold in winter, insalubrious without toilets or water and dangerous because of the fires that repeatedly ravaged Rome. Here tenants paid by the week or even day and faced the constant threat of eviction. However, all lived in the same building, the rich beneath the poor, in a pattern repeated in many great cities before the advent of lifts.

*Insulae* are first recorded surprisingly early – in 218BC an ox climbed two floors up one before falling, according to Livy – but they really developed in the last century of the Republic (from 133BC) as the city's population exploded. At first they were mainly jerry-built, with thin walls of mud-brick and upper floors made mostly of wood. Crassus, notoriously the richest man in mid-1st century BC Rome, made his fortune in property speculation. He would turn up with his gang of fire-fighting slaves when an *insula* caught

fire, commiserate with the bereft owner and buy up the smouldering site cheap for redevelopment at greater density. However, even the high-minded Cicero owned *insulae* which he admitted were unsafe but which brought him the sizeable income of 80,000 sesterces. Rome was less a city of owner-occupiers than one of a few great landlords, with their dependants and friends, and of many harassed, poorer tenants. This hierarchy was typical of Roman society.

## TYPICAL *INSULAE*

After the great fire of AD64, new building regulations – which were not universally enforced but which still provide a useful guide – stipulated that *insulae* be built of brick-faced concrete, with balconies or arcades for fire-fighters.

One of the few substantially surviving *insulae* in Rome is on the Via Giulio Romano (named after the Renaissance painter) at the foot of the Capitoline Hill. It is a typical *insula* with shops on the ground floor and residential mezzanines (half floors) above. The first floor proper was occupied by two decent-sized apartments, and its second and third floors by flats with smaller rooms, most with concrete vaults. There are traces of at least two more floors above (the Capitoline Museum now above it precludes further

archaeological investigation), which probably became progressively more cramped. Another *insula* built under Hadrian (ruled AD117–38) has been discovered beneath the Galleria Colonna with shops, some with back rooms, on all four sides on the ground floor. On the west side, facing the ancient Via Lata, was an arcade which reached to the adjoining buildings, obeying Nero's fire regulations. Separate flats occupied its upper floors and were reached by their own staircases. One *insula*, the Felicula built in the 2nd century AD, was so imposing that it became one of the famous sights of Rome, alongside the Colosseum and Trajan's Forum.

However, the best-preserved *insulae* are in Ostia. This city grew into a boom-town after Trajan constructed a new harbour at nearby Portus but was later completely abandoned to the river silt. Here, solid buildings of brick-faced concrete with fine depressed brick arches often faced on to courtyards or communal gardens, with shops on the street side and light-wells on the other. Staircases rose up to apartments above, some of which had balconies and fine wall paintings, as in the House of Diana. This complex of shops and living areas was at least three storeys high, with a communal toilet for nine or ten people. The overall effect is surprisingly modern.

*Above: A reconstruction of a typical block of flats in Ostia, probably built soon after AD100. The ground floor would have contained shops with mezzanines above, and the first floor above that could have held spacious, even comfortable apartments.*

*Below: Ostia boomed after Trajan built a new harbour at Portus, but the Romans always built to last, as the state today of these massive brick-faced piers attests.*

# TIBERIUS' VILLA AT CAPRI

*Above: Tiberius, Augustus' charmless successor, inherited his power but not his tact, and finally withdrew to Capri.*

*Below: Tiberius chose a markedly inaccessible site 1,000ft (300m) above the sea for his main villa on Capri.*

Outside the city of Rome, emperors could build more grandly and freely. Augustus acquired the small island of Capri, which retained some of its original Greek-speaking inhabitants, and built a relatively modest seaside villa there, the Palazzo a Mare. Tiberius (ruled AD14–37) was Augustus' uncontested successor, but his was a hard act to follow.

## RETREAT FROM ROME

While Augustus had mellowed into a tactful, deeply revered *pater patriae* (father of his country), Tiberius became embittered by the perceived repeated snub of being passed over in the succession in favour first of Augustus' son-in-law and then of his grandsons. By the time Tiberius assumed power, he was in his fifties. He had a fine military record, great dynastic pride – his family, the Claudii, were grander than the Julii – but also a morose, cynical temperament that gradually emerged from beneath a hypocritical veneer of Republican virtue (or so wrote Tacitus a century later).

Tiberius came to hate living in Rome where his position was awkwardly anomalous: in theory he was *primus inter pares* (first among equals) in a Republic, in practice he was absolute monarch. In AD22, after the death of his only son Drusus, he moved to a villa on the Campanian coast, and in AD27 finally withdrew to Capri. Roman officials now had to go to this relatively inaccessible if beautiful island in the Bay of Naples to consult their emperor. Their journey was made worse by the security precautions that Sejanus, Tiberius' Praetorian Prefect, erected around his master. (Sejanus' own imperial ambitions – he wanted to marry into the imperial family and create his own dynasty – led to his downfall in AD31.)

Tiberius owned 12 properties on Capri, of which by far the most important was the Villa Jovis (Villa of Jupiter), vertiginously sited on the island's eastern promontory 1,000ft (300m) above the Tyrrhenian Sea. It was not a spacious site and, being so high, the water supply was a major problem, but it satisfied the ageing emperor's two main desires for security and privacy. Capri was noted for having few beaches suitable for landing and very high cliffs.

At the heart of the villa was a rectangular courtyard around 100ft (30m) square, probably covered with mosaics and surrounded by colonnades. Beneath it was a network of massive vaulted cisterns that collected every drop of water from Capri's infrequent but heavy rainfall. Built around this were four separate wings at different levels. These were linked by staircases and ramps. At the south-west corner lay the entrance vestibule with the guard house; along the south side was a suite of baths; along the west side, built up against the sheer outer face of the cistern block, were rooms for the courtiers and officials on three floors. On the east was a large semicircular state hall flanked by similar reception rooms and on the north flank, accessible only by a single, well-guarded corridor and almost separate from the rest of the palace, lay the relatively modest quarters of the emperor himself.

Richly decorated, the emperor's quarters opened on to a sheltered loggia below, with steps leading up to a belvedere with stunning views over the Bay of Naples. Here the emperor would walk after his evening meals in the *triclinium* (dining-room), which had coloured marble floors. The unknown architect exploited the site to magnificent effect, allowing the emperor to withdraw from the world to a waterless cliff-top and yet still enjoy his luxurious Roman baths.

## UNQUIET SECLUSION

Approaching not on the meandering, tree-lined track that the modern tourist takes, but by a herring-bone brick paved road ascending abruptly from the west, a Roman visitor would have seen the palace rising an impressive 60ft (18m) above the hilly ground. Tiberius seldom welcomed visitors, however, and grew increasingly paranoid in his later years.

Such seclusion fuelled ugly rumours that Suetonius later happily collated and reported as historical facts. Among these was the story of the fisherman who climbed up the cliffs to present the emperor with an exceptional mullet he had caught. This so alarmed the security-mad Tiberius that he ordered his guards to rub the scaly fish in the man's face until he bled. Tiberius also delighted in having victims thrown off the cliffs from his palace, while sailors waited at the bottom with boat hooks to finish off survivors. Although in his seventies, Tiberius, wrote Suetonius, became sex-

ually depraved in his old age: "Collecting bevies of boys and girls from all over the empire, adepts in unnatural practices, to copulate in front of him in threesomes to stimulate his jaded appetites. Many rooms were filled with obscene pictures … he further had boys and girls dress up as Pan and nymphs to prostitute themselves in front of caves or grottoes".

One man whom Tiberius continued to trust was Thrasyllus, his chief astrologer, for astrology, along with Greek literature and mythology, was one of Tiberius' life-long interests. Symbolically, a light house on Capri that Tiberius used to signal to the mainland was struck by lightning and destroyed shortly before the emperor's death (probably from natural causes) in AD37. News of the reclusive ruler's demise was rapturously received in Rome and his villa at Capri was soon abandoned.

*Above: The walkway from the Great Hall in the Villa Jovis, showing construction in concrete with opus incertum facing and brick course.*

*Below: Part of the massive wall of the substructure of Tiberius' villa, made of reticulate facing with fired brick bands.*

# HADRIAN'S VILLA AT TIVOLI

*Above: Portrait bust of the emperor Hadrian. The most peripatetic, cultured and cosmopolitan of emperors, Hadrian created at Tivoli a villa of unparalleled size and luxury where he could both recall his travels and summon the empire's ruling classes.*

*Below: Model of the villa-complex at Tivoli, showing the Piazza d'Oro at its centre. The grandest of imperial residences, the villa in many ways witnessed the climax of Roman architecture with its boldly, even astonishingly innovatory, curved shapes.*

Hadrian followed Nero in being a great builder and a passionate philhellene (admirer of Greek culture), but similarities end there. While Nero was an increasingly debauched playboy and would-be artist who neglected affairs of state, Hadrian was an excellent soldier and tireless administrator, traversing the empire and founding cities or fortifications from Egypt to Britain, where he built his renowned Wall.

## A MUCH FAVOURED SPOT

Although Hadrian was among the finest emperors Rome ever had, paradoxically, he did not much like the city of Rome itself. He got on badly with the Senate, four of whose most senior members were summarily executed at the start of Hadrian's reign on dubious charges of treachery, possibly on his orders. Nor was he popular with the Roman people, who preferred their emperors less openly cultured. (He was contemptuously nick-named *Graeculus*, "Little Greek", by the upper classes.) However, his reputation with the army, administration (including the equestrian order) and the provinces – with troubled Palestine perhaps the one exception – remained unshakeable.

The huge villa-palace Hadrian built at Tivoli (Tibur) some 20 miles (32km) east of Rome, where he spent most of his last years, did not rouse the same disapproval as Nero's Golden Palace precisely because it was *outside* the city. The area had long been a favourite beauty spot and the poets Catullus and Horace and the emperor Trajan had owned villas there, but for Hadrian it marked no hermit-like retreat from public life to the *campagna* (countryside). Instead, the highest members of Rome's increasingly cosmopolitan governing class came to his villa-palace both to discuss affairs of state and to be imperially entertained. Tivoli remains the most radical, intriguing and grandiose of Roman villas. Its buildings cover an area of around 300 acres (120ha) and stretch nearly half a mile (800m) along a plateau.

## AN ARCHITECTURAL CLIMAX

The period of the villa's probably intermittent construction (*c.* AD118–33) is sometimes considered to mark the climax of the Roman revolution in architecture, when the design of a building's interior came to dictate its overall shape. It certainly shows the keen interest of Roman architects at the time in curvilinear forms, which produced some of the most remarkable of all Roman buildings.

The villa, which was some distance from Rome, had to be big enough to accommodate the emperor's entourage – soldiers, servants, bureaucrats and courtiers – but it also provided Hadrian with the opportunity to recreate, imaginatively rather than exactly, some parts of the empire that had appealed to him. In this he was following Roman precedents but on a much grander scale. The layout, which deliberately juxtaposed conflicting axes to follow the lie of the ground, was influenced by earlier villas' landscaped gardens. This produced what initially seems a haphazard appearance but one that worked well with, rather than against, the contours of the land. The palace and its gardens were unwalled although guarded, for Hadrian was no recluse.

Construction of the complex probably began around the Republican-era villa owned by the Empress Sabina, Hadrian's unloved wife. A pre-existing grotto with fountain and *cryptoporticus* (basement or subterranean vaulted corridor) was incorporated into the new villa around what became the library court and Hadrian's private suite.

Among the main structures was the *poikile*, a huge *peristyle* courtyard measuring about 250 by 110yds (230 by 100m) with a large pool in its centre. Substantial buttressing with rows of concrete barrel vaults was needed at its west end to produce the required flat area. These vaults then provided rooms for guards or servants. All four sides are lined with colonnades and the two shorter ends are curved like Trajan's Forum, which had been built only a few years before.

It was once thought that the *poikile* was a careful reproduction of the *stoa poikile*, (painted colonnade) in Athens, which gave its name to the Stoic school of philosophers who met there. However, the recently excavated Athenian Stoa does not really resemble it and the complex was more probably an imitation of either Aristotle's Lyceum or Plato's Academy.

The central part of the *poikile* was arranged as a *dromos* (race-track). From the east of this *dromos*, visitors could pass through an apsed library into the Island Villa, the so-called Teatro Marittimo (Maritime theatre) set within a circular moat, crossed by bridges, around which ran a barrel-vaulted passage supported by white Ionic columns. This is perhaps the most original building in the whole highly original palace, without a single straight line in it. Instead, an amazing mixture of convex and concave chambers face on to a

miniature courtyard with a small fountain, whose conch-shaped plan echoes that of the surrounding rooms, which are themselves arranged in four curved groups. Here the emperor could retreat from the state business of the rest of his palace and devote himself to literature (he was a poet) or to other relaxations, soothed by the sound of running waters and by their sparkling in the sunlight which they reflected into the shaded rooms around. A small bath house and latrines were secreted within the building, along with a suite of bedrooms.

## PUMPKIN VAULTS

The motif of curve and counter-curve is repeated in the Piazza d'Oro (Golden Square), as the richly decorated *peristyle* court is now known because of the surviving gold-yellow mosaics on the floor of its colonnades. It was entered from the north through an octagonal vestibule with niches on seven of its sides. The whole room was covered by an eight-sided umbrella vault, the famous "pumpkin vaults" supposedly criticized by Trajan's great architect Apollodorus. Opposite, on the south-east side, stands a larger pavilion or *nymphaeum*, that was octagonal with alternately concave and convex sides.

*Above: The Maritime Theatre, or Island Villa, offered the busy emperor a retreat from affairs of state.*

*Below: Floor mosaics retain some of the gold that explains the name Piazza d'Oro.*

*Above: Caryatids, modelled on Greek originals, line the Canopus, a waterway recalling the canal near Alexandria in Egypt. They are a typical example of Hadrian's highly original, even capricious, eclecticism.*

The four convex sides gave on to four remarkably shaped rooms, each of which ended in a semicircular *exedra*. Two of the concave sides open on to small summer rooms with fountains in their centres, while one formed the entrance. On the opposite side, the other wall led into a large semi-circular *nymphaeum* whose dramatically curving back wall was lined with alternately round and square fountain niches. The whole pavilion must have been filled with the sound of jetting waters and lit up by the sunlight reflected off them.

(Second-century AD Roman architecture has sometimes been called baroque because of such complex and dynamic shapes.) The Corinthian columns of this building and courtyard were of white marble and some have been re-erected. In the centre of the *peristyle* was another long pool.

## THE IMPERIAL APARTMENTS

The largest group of buildings at Tivoli lay south-west of the Piazza d'Oro. This included the *triclinium* (state dining-room), stadium (or hippodrome) and what were probably the main imperial apartments, which were approached by a single staircase. These combined to form a single, imposing block.

The rooms west of the secluded court have the villa's best views – St Peter's in Rome is now visible from them – and the only hypocaust heating of the villa, suggesting they were inhabited by the emperor himself.

The *triclinium* on the far side of the stadium is half open with three *exedrae*, each with a semicircular garden, while the fourth side has a large ornate fountain whose roar must have soothed diners. Domitian's palace in Rome was the obvious inspiration for this. The *triclinium*'s walls were covered in white Proconnesian marble with remarkably elaborate columns. Beyond were two sets of baths: the Small Baths were probably for the emperor's personal use and their design was again curvilinear to suit the site. The Large Baths are more conventional but have an impressive vaulted *frigidarium* (cold bath) with Ionic columns. To their west is a circular room, the *heliocaminus* or sun room, whose tall windows faced south-west to capture the sun's heat.

## MEMENTOES OF TRAVELS

The Canopus/Serapeum complex directly north of the baths most obviously recalls Hadrian's travels in Egypt. The lake, 130yds (119m) long, resembles in miniature the canal from Canopus to Alexandria and is lined with copies of Greek and Egyptian statues, while the

*Above: A figure of a river or sea god reclining near the Canopus. One of the numerous Greek statues copied at Tivoli.*

semicircular half-domed *nymphaeum* at its end recreates, again in miniature, the Serapeum, the temple to Serapis in Alexandria. A special aqueduct supplied the whole villa. Beyond the Serapeum lay the Academy, a mainly open-air, octagonally shaped building. An exact copy of the Temple of Venus on the Greek island of Cnidos is among the other buildings which adorn the grounds.

### STATUES AND PAINTINGS

If the villa Hadrian built at Tivoli was architecturally radical, the sculptures and paintings he chose to decorate it were artistically conservative or nostalgic. The caryatids lining the Canopus look back –

beyond Augustus' own neoclassical use of them for his Forum over a century before – to the 5th century BC originals of the Erechtheum on the Athenian Acropolis. Other statues at Hadrian's villa are also copies of famous Greek originals and some of the mosaics are copies of famous classical Greek artworks. For example, the *Centauromachia* (Battle of the Centaurs) imitates a painting by Zeuxis of almost 500 years earlier.

Such emulation, common among Romans of many classes, was especially marked in Hadrian's reign, which witnessed the movement called the Second Sophistic. This, one of many neoclassical revivals in Rome's history, was a deliberate attempt to recreate the styles, manners and even debates of classical Greece in its 5th-century BC heyday.

The villa at Tivoli shows the resources of the whole empire devoted to realizing the grand vision of a man of exceptional talent and originality – this was probably the emperor himself, who is thought to have quarrelled with and exiled Apollodorus – using the latest techniques of Roman concrete and vaulting. Plundered repeatedly after the collapse of the empire, its marble stolen or burnt to make lime for cement, the Villa has been partially restored in recent decades to recall a few of its former wonders.

*Above: The Baths of the Heliocaminus, a circular sun room whose tall south-west-facing windows would have caught the afternoon sun and so helped to heat the chamber.*

*Below: Intersecting vaulted corridors with skylights. These ran beneath the villa complex and gave access to the rooms built into the substructure where the emperor's many guards and other attendants were quartered.*

# VILLAS OF THE RICH IN ITALY

*Above: Typical of the many opulent villas built on the shores of the Bay of Naples in the 1st centuries BC and AD is the Villa di Poppaea at Oplontis, near Herculaneum. It was preserved for posterity by the eruption of Vesuvius.*

*Below: This landscape fresco imaginatively but not perhaps unrealistically depicts villas with fine colonnades, porticoes and gardens looking out over the Bay of Naples.*

If no other villa approached Hadrian's in lavish inventiveness or size, many wealthy nobles built themselves remarkably fine villas across the empire, most especially in Italy. A villa in the Republic meant a country house, increasingly comfortable perhaps, but still the centre of a working agricultural estate with farm buildings often attached, as they were with Palladio's Renaissance "villas" in the Veneto much later. They were not mere pleasure pavilions, as the writings of Cato and Varro attest. By the 1st century AD, however, elaborate villas were being built solely for the relaxation of wealthy Romans. Seaside villas – for wealthy but not necessarily noble owners – were common around the Bay of Naples, the Roman "Riviera". Such villas often had slender, elongated pillars, broken pediments and elaborate sun terraces and colonnades looking out to sea. These were depicted in the murals in the House of Lucretius Fronto of the mid-1st century AD. These murals are now thought to depict actual houses, if perhaps imaginatively. This Roman love of the seaside was not to recur before 18th-century England invented seabathing and it testifies to the peacefulness of the Mediterranean, the empire's inland sea. The greatest Roman villas in Italy were mostly built further north. These very large, luxurious structures are the exception rather than the rule. Many villas in Italy were much smaller and far less luxurious, but still relatively opulent and well-appointed.

**THE VILLA OF PLINY THE YOUNGER**
Few villas had such an interesting owner as Pliny the Younger (*c.* AD61–112), the genial man of letters, senator, consul and friend of the emperor Trajan, who ended his career as proconsul (governor) of Bithynia in Asia Minor.

Pliny had two villas which he used as retreats from urban business, one near Rome at Laurentum, the other, larger one in Tuscany at Tifernum. As he confessed in one letter, beautiful surroundings were the first thing Pliny looked for in a villa, although he was also a conscientious landowner, overseeing his mostly tenanted farms. (They brought him in a huge 400,000 sesterces a year.)

Pliny's writings about his villa, with its large glazed windows, heated bath houses, formal gardens filled with statues and topiary, *triclinia* (dining-rooms), libraries and picturesque site, later influenced houses from the Renaissance on, especially in Georgian England. In it, Pliny could enjoy *otium cum dignitate*, the cultured, dignified leisure that was the Roman ideal. His villa was conservative in style, however, for it retained, on an expanded scale, the *atrium/peristyle* plan *"ex more veterum"* (in the old manner) as he expressed it.

More radical architecturally was the so-called Grotte di Catulle (Grottoes of Catullus), although the great poet had nothing to do with the building erected long after his death except for the fact that he, too, had once owned a villa on Lake Garda. The huge villa, built for an unknown but wealthy Roman on the northern tip of the peninsula of Sirmione, which juts into the lake, probably dates from the early 2nd century AD. It exploits concrete in a way which suggests that the architect was aware of recent developments in Rome, which included Domitian's Domus Flavia.

A huge platform was built over massive concrete vaults at the villa's northern end, offering superb views of the lake and mountains. Its plan was severely rectilinear, consisting of a great central block 590ft long and 345ft wide (180 by 105m). Roughly symmetrical, it had rectangular, almost block-like *exedrae* at each end. The rooms were grouped around the vast *peristyle* court, although the *tricilinia* probably looked out over the lake to allow diners to enjoy the views. Roman appreciation of such dramatic natural beauty anticipates that of the Romantics by almost 17 centuries.

### A LUXURY SURBURBAN VILLA

Many Roman nobles preferred to build their luxurious villas closer to Rome. Typical of these is the Villa of Sette Bassi, only 6 miles (10km) south of Rome on the Via Latina and therefore almost suburban in location.

The villa seems to be the result of three separate phases of construction, carried out with typically Roman speed between AD140 and 160. In the first phase its plan was conventional enough, with a modest residential section ranged along the south side of a large *peristyle*. This first villa was mostly single-storeyed, with a simple exterior. Not long after its completion, a second wing was added on the west of the entrance *peristyle*. This required the construction of terraces on concrete substructures, a rather more adventurous

project, if on a smaller scale. On the southern side of the new west façade projected a semicircular veranda with a fountain in the centre of a colonnade courtyard. The surface of the supporting terrace was topped by shallow segmental arches on brackets of travertine stone similar to contemporary *maeniana* (balconies) in Trajan's Market in Rome.

In the third and most complex phase of building, a wing was built across the north end of the area west of the older buildings and a huge *cryptoporticus* (underground vaulted corridor) about 1,000ft (300m) long enclosed the whole complex as a formal terraced garden. A massive new north wing, built on terraced vaults, rose at least three storeys, with two immense, tall reception halls with triple windows and gabled roofs. These halls were lit from above in a way developed by later Roman architects.

Buildings of such scale must have been hugely expensive, affordable only to the wealthiest of aristocrats. It is possible that the villa was built by a senator who wanted to keep a safe distance from the imperial court, but this was exactly the sort of lavish suburban villa the debauched emperor Commodus (AD180–92) later expropriated for orgies.

*Above: The Grotte di Catulle is a splendid villa of c. AD120 at Sirmione, but it is not connected with Catullus.*

*Below: The House of Marcus Loreius Tiburtinus at Pompeii. Some of the fine and elaborate decorations that once covered the building still survive.*

# PIAZZA ARMERINA

*Above: One of the villa's fanciful and colourful mosaics shows a* putto *or cupid in the god Neptune's entourage riding a sea monster.*

*Below: A huge* peristyle, *with a fountain, gardens and paths decorated with mosaics, lay at the heart of the villa.*

In the centre of Sicily, once one of the empire's most fertile provinces, lie the ruins of one of the grandest Roman villas. Now listed as a UNESCO World Heritage Site, the villa dates from the early 4th century AD, a period when the empire had partly recovered from the turmoil of the 3rd century under the iron leadership of Diocletian (ruled AD284–305).

Luxurious and complex, the villa boasts such remarkably fine and extensive mosaics – they cover nearly 400,000sq ft (35,000sq m) – that it was long thought to have belonged to Maximian, Diocletian's co-emperor, who retired to Sicily. It was called the Villa Imperiale.

Today, the imperial connection is doubted and the owner is thought to have been a very wealthy member of the Roman aristocracy. It is thought possible that he had estates in North Africa – the greatest Roman families had estates in many parts of the empire – for the villa's plan suggests African influences. Whoever the owner was, he clearly enjoyed a life unclouded by threats from barbarians, for the villa is rambling and unwalled, unlike Diocletian's compact fortress-palace at Split of slightly earlier origin. It seems that the owner was also unconcerned by the rise of Christianity, for the scenes in the mosaics are sensually and exuberantly pagan, revelling in hunting, mythological and bathing scenes.

## LOOKING INWARD

The villa is made up of four connected groups of buildings, probably constructed between AD310 and 330 on the site of a modest 2nd-century AD villa. The overall irregularity of its plan in some ways recalls the planned informality of Hadrian's Tivoli villa, but at Piazza Armerina there is no attempt to relate the buildings to the landscape. This suggests that its owner preferred to look in on his own elaborate decorations rather than out at the natural world beyond.

Piazza Armerina is typical of late Roman buildings in the way that the design of the interiors dominates that of the exteriors. The suite of bath houses, for example, was planned as a series of inter-connected interiors and creates a jumbled effect from outside. However, the overall plan reveals a unity of design which suggests that a single mind may have been behind the entire project.

The villa may have been inhabited as late as AD900 – Sicily was reconquered by the Byzantines in AD535 and remained in their hands for more than 400 years. In the 12th century the whole area was covered by an immense mudslide. This destroyed most of its walls but preserved the mosaics both from the elements and from vandalism. Excavations only began in 1881 and are still continuing. Some of the pillars have been restored and, in a few areas, walls rise high enough to reveal the layout very clearly.

*Left: Part of the Great Hunt Mosaic in the ambulatory or hall of the villa. These mosaics, which are very well preserved, are Piazza Armerina's crowning glory and rejoice in exuberant scenes of life and death. Here, a lion kills a deer.*

Approaching through a monumental triple arch into a horseshoe-shaped entrance courtyard to the west, Roman visitors would have turned right into the main part of the villa. This consisted of an enfilade of rooms: a vestibule gave on to a massive *peristyle* with living quarters around it. Beyond this, approached by a small staircase, lay a transverse corridor about 200ft (63m) long, now known as the Ambulatory of the Great Hunt Scene.

Beyond the walkway was a large hall with an apse at its far end. At the south end lay the private wing with a tiny semi-circular *sigma* (courtyard). This had two bedroom suites and a small *triclinium* (dining-room). South of this was another ceremonial wing with a large trilobed *triclinium*. The substantial baths complex projected obliquely to the north-west of the *peristyle*. The nearby latrine was typically elegant, with a brick drain, marble wash basin and lavish mosaics.

## GLOWING WITH COLOUR

The greatest glory of the Piazza Armerina lies underfoot in its superb mosaics, which still glow with colour after their centuries under 30ft (9m) of preserving mud. Probably the work of craftsmen from Africa, they give an extraordinarily vivid picture of life in the later empire, at least as enjoyed by the very rich. The transverse corridor is also more poetically called the Ambulatory of the Great Hunt Scene because it has the finest mosaics. These show figures in imperial-looking capes watching a remarkable scene in which all sorts of animals – leopards, tigers, elephants, ostriches, antelopes and a rhino – are being caught and loaded on to a ship, presumably for transport to Rome to be slaughtered in the games.

West of the main *peristyle* in the *palaestra* (gymnasium), mosaics show detailed and informative scenes of games in the Circus Maximus in Rome. The owner probably sponsored these games in a typical form of aristocratic patronage. A smaller room to the *peristyle*'s south is the aptly named Room of the Ten Girls. Here, colourful mosaics depict girls wearing what may be the world's first bikinis. The mosaics in total are a splendid manifestation of the still vibrant and sensual pagan world, although their rather flattened style points to the emergence of a new, late Roman-early Byzantine art.

*Below: The world's first bikinis? These mosaics, in the well-named Room of the Ten Girls, show girls wearing jewellery but not much else, dancing, exercising and swimming in bathing costumes that look surprisingly modern.*

# DIOCLETIAN'S PALACE AT SPLIT

*Above: The steely resolution of Diocletian, who established the tetrarchy and, uniquely among Roman emperors, retired peacefully.*

*Below: The Golden Gate, the main entrance to Diocletian's fortress-palace, was ornamental and functional. Its statues in niches hint at Syrian influences.*

Diocletian (ruled AD284–305) was unique among Roman emperors in retiring peace-fully – traditionally to grow cabbages in his garden – before dying in bed six years later. Equally unusual was his retirement home. Far from being a luxurious villa in Italy, it was a massive fort enclosing a palace on the Adriatic coast at Split (Spalato), now in Croatia. Its military plan testifies not just to Diocletian's life in the army – in fact, he was more an administra-tive reformer than a brilliant soldier – but to the general insecurity of the age.

While Split was far enough from any frontier, barbarians had, within living memory, penetrated even into central Italy, the heart of the empire. Diocletian may not have completely trusted his successors in the tetrarchy, his carefully designed system of four emperors, either.

As it was, his retirement was disturbed only by calls for him to mediate between his quarrelling heirs, which he did only once, in AD308, without success. It is possible the huge walls he constructed helped to deter would-be aggressors. They later sheltered the whole of the small town's population for many centuries and still stand substantially intact today.

**DOMESTIC MEETS MILITARY STYLE**

Built AD300–6, the palace is halfway between a self-contained, fortified coun-try residence of a type becoming common across the increasingly troubled empire, and a small town. Its overall plan, how-ever, recalls a typical Roman army camp. It is rectangular – 590 by 710ft (180 by 216m) – with square towers in each cor-ner, six further square towers along the walls and octagonal towers flanking the three land entrances. Two intersecting colonnaded streets divide the palace into four sections. On the seaward side, the wall was surmounted by a gallery of arches flanked by columns, the whole facade unbroken apart from one small postern gate giving access to the quays. That part of the Dalmatian coast is relatively inaccessible by land, and Diocletian must have relied on ships to supply him with the news and other necessaries that were required for his imperial retirement.

The palace's northern parts formed barracks for the imperial guard that Diocletian retained, while the southern two sections, built out on terraces over lower ground, formed the palace's residential and state apartments. These have not yet been fully excavated. The southern end of the street forms the so-called *Peristyle* and is flanked by still impressive arched colonnades with a huge broken-pedimented end wall. To the west of this street lay a small temple and to the east an octagonal mausoleum, that was circular inside. The *Peristyle* led to a circular vestibule, beyond which was a large rectangular hall, presumably a state reception room. This gave on to the corridor flanked by the line of arches overlooking the sea, and was itself flanked by two further state rooms.

Although in retirement, Diocletian maintained much of the almost hieratic splendour with which he had surrounded the throne. The western hall had an apse at one end and was probably a throne room; the eastern hall was probably the *triclinium* (dining-room). Beyond these halls on each side lay domestic suites with bedrooms and bath houses.

### THE PALACE'S PRECEDENTS

It has been suggested that the palace's layout derives partly from Diocletian's palace at Antioch – which he had built on the other side of the River Orontes on a site first occupied by the emperor Valerian in AD259 – and partly from the city-palace of Philippopolis in southern

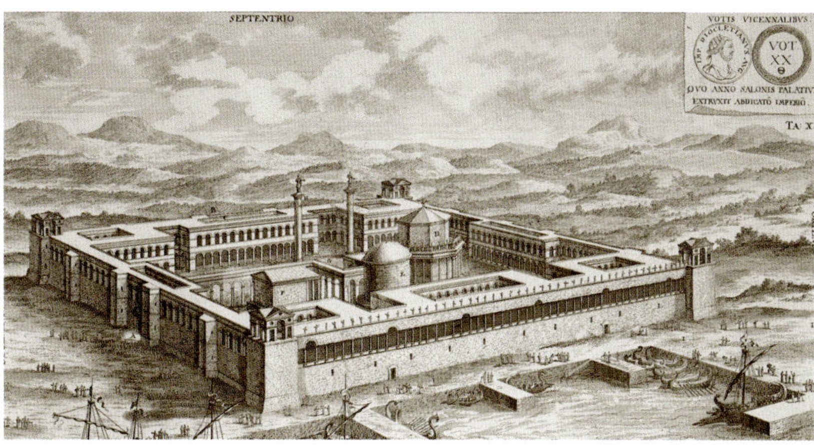

*Above: An imaginative reconstruction of how the palace looked in its prime, c. AD306. It was mainly supplied by sea.*

Syria, the birthplace of the emperor Philip the Arab (ruled AD244–9). Diocletian, although born in the Balkans, had spent most of his reign governing the East and would have had the opportunity to see and even to occupy both. The extreme regularity of the plan more obviously recalls the roughly contemporary Baths of Diocletian in Rome.

Architects and craftsmen from Syria and other Eastern provinces were probably employed in building Split. Typical of this Syrian influence are the arcuated lintel – an arched entablature over the centre of a classical façade – and the arcaded columns of the *Peristyle*. The main entrance, the Porta Aurea (Golden Gate), also reveals Eastern influences. Its open arch with horizontal lintel and its decorative front with statues in niches were probably inspired by the Temple of Bacchus at Baalbek, built 150 years before. However, more recent, Western influences are apparent too, such as the circular vestibule and the framing of the seafront gallery's arches between decorative half-columns, a device also employed in the Mausoleum of Maxentius outside Rome and the grand Porta Nigra at Trier.

The palace's thick walls enclose courtyard gardens where the elderly emperor could have strolled and done some gardening. But the monumental architecture, while undoubtedly palatially opulent, is distinctly heavy. The final effect is both impressive and oppressive, rather like Diocletian's imperial regime itself.

*Below: Diocletian built an elaborate mausoleum for himself that was later turned into a cathedral, while his palace became a town.*

# VILLAS OF BRITAIN

*Above: The larger and more luxurious Roman villas made great use of hypocausts (underfloor) and intramural hot-air heating, as in this villa at Chedworth. This was the first and almost the last form of central heating in Britain until the 20th century.*

*Below: Cupid rides a dolphin in a fine mid-2nd-century AD floor mosaic from Fishbourne Palace. Built c. AD75, the Sussex villa was palatial in size and luxury if not in name.*

Britain, part of the Roman empire for nearly four centuries, soon became far more than a mere frontier province, and today is recognized as having been wealthier and more Romanized than was once thought. Unlike villas nearer the Mediterranean, British villas were not usually built around a *peristyle* but tended to be "winged corridor" types, with wings of rooms added incrementally, almost accidentally and sometimes forming courts. If most Roman villas in Britain (as elsewhere) remained modestly rustic, a few developed into grand houses of a scale and complexity not seen again in Britain until at least the 16th century.

**THE PALACE AT FISHBOURNE**

The first great villa – in every way atypically grandiose because of its royal and imperial links – is the palace at Fishbourne on the Sussex coast. It may have belonged to the client king Cogidubnus, king of the Regnenses. Alternatively, it could have been the residence of a Roman governor in the Flavian period (AD69–98). However, almost no evidence survives to link the villa with specific individuals. A substantial villa was built on the site under Nero (AD54–68) with baths, colonnaded garden and mosaic-decorated rooms. These were all luxuries then unique in Britain. Ten years later this was demolished to make way for a truly palatial complex.

Visitors approached from the east through a grand porticoed entrance hall that led into landscaped gardens. The main official buildings lay to the west, with an apsed audience hall for the king/governor. The residential wing lay to the north. The palace interior was richly decorated with mosaics in the black-and-white style of the time, with fine marble and stucco-work on the walls. In the 2nd century further buildings, including a bath house, were added, but in AD296 Fishbourne was abandoned after a fire.

Most villas in Britain in the century after the conquests of AD43–84 remained simple. When Tacitus wrote that his father-in-law Agricola, Britain's most farsighted governor (*c.* AD77–84), persuaded British nobles to build themselves Roman houses, he meant town houses, northern versions of the *domus*. Rural villas developed slowly, sometimes on top of round Iron Age farmsteads – perhaps owned by important Britons Romanizing themselves in the Agricolan way – into rectangular houses of several rooms fronted by a veranda. These corridor villas were often built of timber, which was then abundant in the British Isles. However, the small, late 1st century Villa of Quinton in Northamptonshire was of rectilinear stone built over a round house. At Brixworth nearby, the villa's development can be traced from Celtic round house through successive stages of Roman construction. These developed from the first rectangular house, built AD70–100,

which boasted painted walls, to the grandest 4th-century phase, when a bath house was added. However, the villa remained haphazard in design throughout and was built for use rather than for ostentation.

More impressive is Lullingstone Villa in Kent beside the River Darenth. It was first built (AD80–90) on a terrace cut into the hill on the winged-corridor pattern. In the 2nd century AD, the "deep room" in the centre, once a grain store, was seemingly turned into a shrine, complete with a painting of nymphs adorning a niche and two fine portrait busts. In the 4th century AD, the central room was reconstructed, with an apse and a mausoleum built to the north. A Christian chapel seems to have been built in one chamber, judging by wall paintings bearing the chi-ro Christian symbol, making the villa one of the few Christian sites in Roman Britain. The villa was burnt down and abandoned early in the 5th century AD.

### A GOLDEN AGE

In AD306, Constantius Chlorus, Augustus (senior emperor) of the West, died in York. He had just returned from a northern campaign that, while only half successful, had restored Roman prestige throughout an island which a decade before had appeared to be slipping out of the Roman orbit under rebel rulers. The half century that followed has been called the golden age of British villas. While towns built themselves ever thicker walls against possible barbarian attacks, villas in southern Britain expanded to sometimes majestic size, apparently unworried by Saxon raiders. Some fertile areas, such as the Fens, have few villas, indicating probably huge imperial estates that precluded private ownership.

Woodchester Villa in Gloucestershire exemplifies the building of the golden age. Started c. AD100 with a line of buildings on the north side of what became the central courtyard, it was extended southwards around this court in the next 150 years. The villa reached its climax after AD300 with a grand second northern

courtyard and bath houses. It is famed for its Orpheus mosaic. At 2,500sq ft (225sq m) this was the largest and most ornate mosaic in Britain, showing the mythical Greek poet charming the beasts. Other rooms in this and comparable villas were similarly decorated.

Chedworth Villa in a secluded valley near Cirencester was among Roman Britain's finest. Started in the late 2nd century AD as two houses with a bath suite, it developed in the 3rd and 4th centuries into a single building with two parallel wings connected by a veranda. The north range had elaborate bath suites, beyond which was a small temple with an octagonal pool, possibly devoted to the healing god Lenus-Mars (the Romans assimilated local deities whenever they could). Another villa which was occupied over many centuries is Gadebridge Park, Hertfordshire. Originally built of wood c. AD100, it grew into a large house of the winged-corridor type in the 4th century. It had a bath suite with a sizeable swimming pool and towers at either end. It was demolished c. AD350. No Roman villa long survived the collapse of Roman power after AD400.

*Above: Mosaic at Lullingstone Villa, early 4th century AD, showing the Rape of Europa.*

*Below: Among the greatest Romano-British villas was that at Chedworth in Gloucestershire.*

# CHAPTER VI

# CITIES OF THE EMPIRE

Rome's empire has been called a "confederation of cities". City to the Romans meant a self-governing polity, with its own *curia* (council) of annually elected magistrates. There were more than 1,000 such cities in the empire by AD200, ranging from metropoli such as Carthage to tiny but proud Gloucester. Some were former city-states of great antiquity like Ephesus, prospering again in the long Roman peace. Other cities, especially in the unurbanized West, were new foundations. Trier in Germany, Paris, Nîmes and Arles in France, London and Bath in Britain are cities founded by Romans and still flourishing. Other cities, such as Timgad in North Africa, blossomed and died with the empire, leaving only ruins as eloquent reminders of former wealth. Corinth and Carthage were refounded to boom under the empire after being deleted under the Republic.

As the empire grew, so did its cities, many building theatres, amphitheatres, baths, basilicas and fora, in expensive competition. At times older local traditions – Punic (African), Syrian, Celtic – influenced the classic Graeco-Roman mould. A few cities were seen as emulating Rome: Carthage was called Rome-in-Africa by its inhabitants, and Trier the Rome-of-the-North. Any survey of the empire's cities must start with the two that suffered the singular fate of being preserved for posterity by the eruption of Vesuvius: Pompeii and Herculaneum.

*Left: Aerial view of the ruins of Pompeii with Vesuvius in the background, the volcano that both destroyed the city in its eruption of AD79 and preserved it in ash.*

# POMPEII AND HERCULANEUM

*Above: A view of the atrium of the House of the Faun, Pompeii, a typical atrium-style house of a wealthy citizen just before the eruption of AD79 that has so well preserved it.*

*Below: A map of Pompeii just before the eruption of AD79, showing the major public buildings and the mainly rectilinear street plan. The grey areas on the map are as yet unexcavated.*

The eruption that began about midday on 24 August AD79 was a catastrophe for the people of the small cities who had lived for centuries in the fertile lands under Mount Vesuvius – a mountain no one had ever suspected of being a potential volcano. That vast eruption blew the top off the mountain and killed thousands of people. Not realizing their danger, many had remained in the city until too late, although others escaped. The eruption covered Pompeii in 17ft (5m) of volcanic matter and Herculaneum in very hot ash, dust and stones to a depth of up to 70ft (21m), which hardened to form an excellent preservative.

Much of central Italy was powdered in dust, prompting the ever-generous emperor Titus in Rome to promise all the aid he could. It proved of little use and the cities were never reoccupied. They were forgotten until chance discoveries fuelled passionate if destructive excavations from 1748 on. However, Vesuvius' eruption has proved an immense blessing to posterity, for it has preserved – almost ghoulishly – intact the houses, artefacts and corpses of two prosperous, fashionable towns as the Roman empire neared its zenith. Bread has been left preserved in ovens, meals left ready on tables, scurrilous election notices for the forthcoming *curia* (council) elections – "Thieves support Vatius for aedile!" – survive on the walls. Inside the houses the bodies of lovers have been found entwined in doomed embrace, while in the streets looters were overwhelmed with their booty. Without that terrible day, our knowledge of ordinary Roman life would be far less vivid.

## LIFE BEFORE THE ERUPTION

Pompeii was a city long before it came under Roman rule. First inhabited in the 8th century BC, by 500BC it had acquired solid walls made of local tufa and limestone which ran for 2 miles (3.2km). The urban area of some 165 acres (66ha) was not built over completely at first, for there are signs of orchards or gardens within the walls, but by AD79 Pompeii's population was approaching an estimated 15,000. Greek and Etruscan influences, along with the local Samnites', are apparent in the early city. (In the 6th century BC a temple to Apollo, the archetypally Greek deity, was built, but Etruscans also worshipped Apollo.) By the 3rd century BC, Pompeii was under Roman control but Hellenistic influences still predominated artistically, as is most evident in the city's wall paintings.

In 80BC, the dictator Sulla settled about 5,000 Roman veterans with their families in Pompeii, renaming it Colonia Cornelia Veneria Pompeianorum. Local inhabitants must have been displaced but many important public buildings date from soon after this date. However, a major earthquake struck the city in AD62 and at the time of the eruption in AD79, many of the city's buildings were being rebuilt.

In the last century before its end, the Forum acquired notable temples to most Roman gods, indicating that Pompeii was an official religious centre.

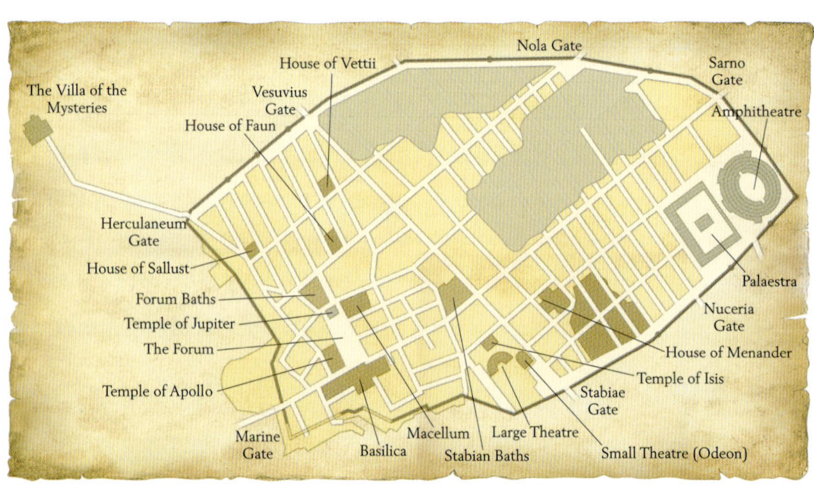

*Left: Under the shadow of Vesuvius at dusk, a plaster-of-paris cast captures a Pompeian at the moment of death, caught in the violent pyroclastic flow from the volcano in* AD79. *The bodies of those who died, overwhelmed by ash and rock, left hollows or "moulds" from which these poignant casts were made.*

*Below: A street crossing showing the stepping stones in what is now called the Via dell'Abbondanza in Pompeii. The city, if small, had all the amenities of a Roman city, including proper paved streets.*

## THE TEMPLES OF POMPEII

Approaching from the seaward side, the first temple the visitor saw before entering the Forum would have been the Temple of Venus – the divine mother of Aeneas and so, according to later imperial propaganda, of the Julian dynasty. This rose impressively on the right and was probably built by Sulla's colonists. Typically Italian in form, the temple stood inside a wide precinct on a tall platform with a deep colonnaded front porch.

The Temple of Apollo dates to the 6th century BC and, with the Temple on the Triangular Forum, is the oldest building in Pompeii. It stood on the west side of the Forum at a slight angle, suggesting it was planned to align with an earlier Forum. It was much expanded and decorated under Augustus.

The Temple of Jupiter or the Capitolinum was the grandest of Pompeii's temples, in whose ruins a colossal torso of a seated male figure, presumably the king of the gods, has been found. A temple to the recently deified emperor Vespasian (AD69–79), with a wide colonnaded porch, was under construction on the east of the Forum, while next to it the Lararium, a temple to the Lares, the city's guardian gods and intended to ward off further catastrophes, had just been completed. Another temple, that of Isis, had also been swiftly restored. Built originally *c.* 120BC and dedicated to the popular Egyptian goddess – if one whose cult had been half-Hellenized – this had elaborate exterior stucco decorations covering plain brick walls. Interestingly, its restoration was paid for by Numerius Popidius Celsinus, the son of a freedman (former slave), indicating that upward mobility was not uncommon.

Other buildings in the centre added in the city's last century include the vegetable market, the *macellum*, the meat and fish market, and the vast Eumachia, the guild headquarters of the cloth fullers, named after their rich patroness. A large basilica, built 130–120BC – before the city became a Roman colony – had three aisles and fine Ionic columns. The Forum itself was in the process of being rebuilt more grandly with paving in travertine stone when the volcano woke.

*Above: The fine Ionic columns of the city's large basilica, built 130–120BC, before Pompeii became a Roman colony.*

*Below: Fresco still life of a rabbit and figs from the House of the Stags, Herculaneum.*

## BATHS, THEATRES, AMPHITHEATRES

Pompeii, though it was only a modest provincial city, had public baths and a stone theatre and amphitheatre well before Rome. It boasted five different public bath houses. The largest, the Stabian Baths, dates back to the 4th century BC and came to cover an area of 40,000sq ft (4,000sq m). It is possible that later the Romans were inspired to build public baths with three rooms at progressively higher temperatures by Pompeian examples.

The Pompeians made extensive use of brick from Augustus' time, notably in the façade of the Central Baths, where half-columns alternate with large windows. A big theatre, built partly in stone and more Greek than Roman in plan, predates Rome's first permanent Theatre of Pompey of 55BC by a century.

Pompeii also had one of the first stone amphitheatres (earlier arenas were wooden). Built in the south-east corner of the city against the city walls, which reduced the need for massive earth banks to support its tiers, it probably catered initially for Sulla's veterans. An inscription dates it to about 70BC. With an estimated capacity of 20,000 spectators, it drew crowds from the surrounding area, sometimes with unpredictable consequences. In AD59, an argument over one gladiator led to a full-scale riot between the citizens of Pompeii and those of neighbouring Nuceria, anticipating more recent problems with football hooligans by almost two millennia. The Roman authorities reacted strongly, however, and the Pompeians were banned from holding any further gladiatorial events for ten years.

## VILLAS AND HOUSES

Pompeii is famed for its houses which, if not the largest in the empire, are now among the most interesting because they survive in such quantity. Their design shows increasingly strong Hellenistic influences, revealing the city's links to the Greek East.

Early houses like the House of the Surgeon, built before 200BC, which centred round the *atrium*, gave way to more luxurious houses in which the *peristyle* and gardens gained ever greater importance. The House of the Gilded Cupids, built *c.* 150BC, had a huge *peristyle*, which was effectively a colonnaded garden. The House of the Faun, among the largest in Pompeii, covers about 1 acre (0.4 ha). Decorated throughout in the elegant, rather austere First Style, it progresses from an entrance passage through the *atrium* with bedrooms only on the left, to another bigger *atrium* opening to the right, which has two Ionic columns of tufa. Beyond this lies the room which contains the Alexander the Great mosaic. Perhaps the most famous mosaic in Pompeii, it was copied from a Greek painting. Beyond lies a large garden.

Increasingly, wealthier citizens tended to move out of town. About 400 yards out of Pompeii stands the famous Villa of the Mysteries. Built on an artificial earth platform, it is entered by the *peristyle*. Beyond this is a large *atrium* on the far side of which is a *tablinium* (central room) overlooking the sea. The house, which dates from the 2nd century BC with later alterations, is vast; it has 60 rooms and covers 1.4 acres (0.56 ha). Its famous murals show in dramatic detail scenes of a mystery religion, probably that of the god Dionysus.

A bedroom in a villa at Boscoreale outside Pompeii was decorated with murals showing gardens, fountains and bowls of fruits in frescoes. The murals are expressive of the superb illusionistic skills of the Second Style of the mid-1st century BC. Here too the inspiration was Greek.

By AD79, in luxurious houses like that of Loreius Tiburtinus, which was being extended at the time of the eruption, the *peristyle* had shrunk. The still spacious *atrium* was flanked by two-storeyed buildings, but the *peristyle* simply led into the long formal garden on to which many rooms, including the luxurious *triclinium*, opened. With its pergolas, statues and fountains, the garden was clearly the villa's real focus, from which a view of the mountains could be enjoyed.

## HERCULANEUM

Smaller and far less extensively excavated than Pompeii, due to the hard, compacted volcanic material, which buried it, and the busy modern town above it, Roman Herculaneum boasts fine villas overlooking the sea. The Bay of Naples was considered to have some of the finest scenery in Italy, as well as the best climate.

Here the *peristyle* was replacing the *atrium*, as is evident in two adjoining villas built on terraces over the city walls, the House of the Stag and the House of the Mosaic Atrium. In the latter, built in the mid-1st century AD, the traditional pattern was partly followed in the north wing. It had an *atrium* minus its side

rooms and then a large central garden surrounded by rooms on two floors with a *triclinium* at the far end. Two small living rooms flanked a long narrow terrace, in the centre of which were the main reception rooms.

In the House of the Stags the *atrium* is only an entrance lobby with rooms arranged symmetrically around the garden courtyard. The inner *triclinium* faces on to this courtyard. Villas such as these had magnificent decorations. These often took the form of vividly realistic murals such as that of the Tragic Actor and show Graeco-Roman painting at its zenith.

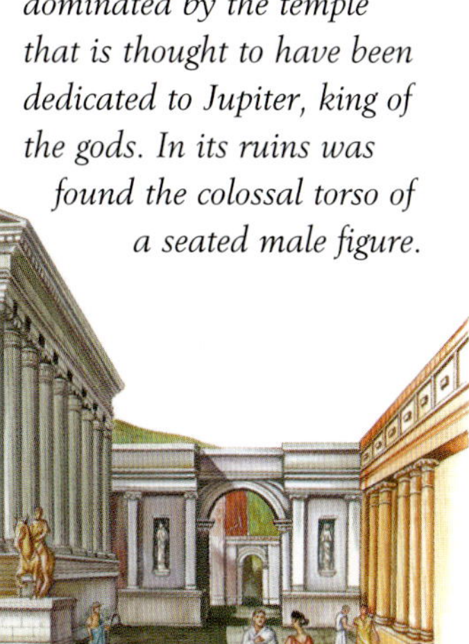

*Above: This fresco shows the riot in the amphitheatre between the people of Pompeii and those of nearby Nuceria in AD59. The amphitheatre at Pompeii is the earliest dated example of a permanent amphitheatre.*

*Below: Pompeii's Forum was dominated by the temple that is thought to have been dedicated to Jupiter, king of the gods. In its ruins was found the colossal torso of a seated male figure.*

# OSTIA AND PORTUS

*Above: The ruins of the Baths of the Charioteers, one of 18 such baths in Ostia.*

*Below: A portico in Ostia decorated c. AD120 in the fashionable black and white style with ships, the symbols of Ostia's then booming trade.*

Ostia, situated at the mouth of the Tiber, was one of Rome's first colonies. Founded *c.* 350BC as a base against pirates, its walls covered only five acres (2 ha). Later it became one of the colonies Sulla took for his veterans, expanding its walled area to around 160 acres (64ha). Ostia was early Rome's main port, but its harbour was open to storms and plagued by sandbars, and never ideal because it was a river port and could not cope with big ships. As Rome became crucially dependent on imported grain, Pozzuoli (Puteoli) near Naples became the deep water harbour for Rome. There, goods were transhipped to barges which crawled along the coast to Ostia. The latter was still Rome's outlet to the sea. This was expensive and risky, so in AD42 Claudius, reviving one of Julius Caesar's grand projects, decided to build an artificial harbour on the coast two miles north of Ostia, called Portus.

## THE BUILDING OF PORTUS

A gigantic ship with a displacement of 7,400 tons, used by Caligula to transport an obelisk from Egypt, was sunk to provide the base for a large *pharos* (lighthouse). Breakwaters were built to make a harbour 1,200yds (1,100m) across., but storms still wrecked ships sheltering inside the wide harbour – Tacitus records 200 sunk in AD62 alone – and most grain fleets still avoided Ostia in favour of Pozzuoli.

Trajan (ruled AD98–117) solved the problem by excavating an octagonal inner basin about 770yds (700m) across, with a canal link to the Tiber. Flanked by large warehouses, the new quays at Portus had numbered columns corresponding to mooring berths. More than 100 ships could dock in its inner basin at the same time, while the outer harbour was used as a holding area for arriving ships.

Ostia boomed thanks to Portus' new dock and for two centuries the places' fortunes intertwined. Many merchants, chandlers and others associated with Rome's import trade – Rome *exported* nothing except edicts, administrators and refuse – lived in Ostia, although they presumably worked in Portus. Their joint population approached an estimated 100,000 at their 2nd-century peak.

Ostia declined in the 4th century and its buildings were abandoned to the river silt that finally blocked up its harbour. The river silt also, however, preserved Ostia's buildings, to provide evidence of how ordinary Romans lived.

Private houses initially remained mostly simple *domus* (individual house) types, some half-timbered, although they began to unite their porticoes to create colonnades

like those of Eastern cities. The rebuild-ing of Ostia began under Domitian, and, with Trajan's new docks, Ostia was rapidly transformed into a showcase of contem-porary Roman building techniques.

## REBUILDING OSTIA

The western quarter was rebuilt first with *insulae* (apartment blocks) in brick-faced concrete. Although not covered in stucco, this was meant to be seen, as arched door-ways and balconies broke up its otherwise plain façades. The *insulae* rivalled those of the capital but at a lower density – they seldom rose more than four floors – and are today much better preserved.

The House of Diana is a typical *insula*. Its south and west sides had large win-dows facing the street but the other sides, which adjoined neighbouring houses, lacked windows. To give them light, the architect put a courtyard in the centre, along with a water cistern for all residents to use, as piped water was a luxury restricted to the first floor at best.

Fronting the streets were *tabernae* – single-roomed shops with a mezzanine above where the shopkeepers often lived. Staircases between the shops led to the upper floors. Many *insulae* looked impressive and some, with inner gardens, were spacious and comfortable.

Even the city's warehouses were impos-ingly built. The Horra Epagathiania of *c.* AD150 had an arched entrance made of brick but flanked by proper Corinthian columns with pediments.

Among the major public buildings was the Capitolium (Temple to Jupiter, Juno and Minerva). Built on the Forum's north side *c.* AD120–30, it stood at the end of a broad street which led down to the river and was flanked by brick porticoes. Built of brick-faced concrete sumptuously covered in marble, it was raised on a high podium to dominate surrounding buildings and measured about 70ft (22m) tall. A temple to Roma and Augustus, also covered in marble, dates from Tiberius' reign (AD14–37), but Ostia's many temples to more exotic gods reveal foreign influences. The city also had at least 18 public baths, reflecting Roman priorities. Of these, the Forum Baths (*c.* AD150) is the finest, its octagonal west-facing room recalling the sun rooms in Hadrian's Villa at Tivoli.

This surge of building activity faded after AD160. In the 4th century AD, as Ostia's population fell to make more space available for bigger houses, some fine new *domus* were built, such as the House of Cupid and Psyche.

By the 4th century AD Ostia was in decline as Portus supplanted it. Although far smaller, Portus had notable buildings of its own, including the Imperial Palace, which lay on the western quay of the new basin looking out over Claudius' harbour. Built of fine brick-faced con-crete with a bath house, it was probably connected with the administration or it may have been the Forum. Portus was to remain Rome's port for centuries.

*Above: Ships laden with amphorae (earthenware jars) sailing past the lighthouse at Ostia. This 3rd-century* AD *relief is rather unusual as it comes from a Christian tomb in the Catacombs of Praetextatus.*

*Below: The House of Diana in Ostia. A typical insula (apartment block), with large windows facing the street and a light-well and courtyard behind it, it dates from the early 2nd century* AD.

# CONTRASTING CITIES: CARTHAGE AND TIMGAD

*Above: Corinthian capitals of the Antonine Baths, Carthage.*

*Below: Ruins of the Punic district of ancient Carthage.*

Founded by the Phoenicians in 814BC, Carthage swiftly became the most powerful city in the western Mediterranean, with an extensive commercial network, and later Rome's most feared opponent. Hannibal, its great general, devastated Italy in the Second Punic War (218–202BC) and even threatened Rome itself, so Carthage's total destruction by Rome in 146BC was an act of delayed revenge. Yet Carthage's superb site, with fine harbours and fertile hinterland, led Romans such as the reformer Gaius Gracchus in 122BC and later Julius Caesar to propose a colony there. Under Augustus, these plans were realized in 29BC with the foundation of Colonia Julia Concordia Karthago. Three thousand colonists were settled on what became one of the empire's largest cities and the magnificent capital of one of Rome's richest provinces.

## ROMAN MEETS PUNIC CULTURE

If the Romans had tried to delete all traces of the Punic city in 146BC, the suburbs of modern Tunis today cover the Roman city very effectively. However, enough has been excavated to show that Augustus' surveyors created a typical grid pattern for the new city.

The old Punic citadel of Byrsa was levelled to make a rectangular platform of about 10 acres (4ha) on which the usual public buildings – forum, basilica, temples – were erected. Local topography meant, however, that the Roman city followed the general alignment of its Punic predecessor, while its inhabitants themselves became a mixture of Roman newcomers and slowly Romanized Punic inhabitants. An altar to the *gens Augusta* (family of Augustus) deliberately recalled the Ara Pacis (Altar of Peace) in Rome. The Capitoline triad was worshipped but local Punic gods were also tolerated and assimilated into the Roman pantheon. Only Moloch with his reputation for human sacrifice was excluded.

Punic Carthage had been renowned for its rectangular outer harbour and an inner, circular harbour reputedly able to shelter and launch 200 galleys. Carthage now became the chief port as well as capital of the Roman province of Africa. As the province became Rome's main source of wheat and olive oil, the harbours were rebuilt for more peaceful traffic. A large

amphitheatre was built in the west of the city around the time of Augustus, along with a circus 1,700ft (516m) long, able to seat up to 55,000 people. Only the Circus Maximus in Rome itself was larger. Under Hadrian (ruled AD117–38) a luxurious theatre, decorated in marble, onyx, granite and porphyry, was constructed. Finally, the immense Antonine Baths were built in AD143–62, the largest baths outside Rome itself at the time. With an ingeniously planned ring of interlocking hexagonal *caldaria* (hot baths), these were enormous – 650ft (200m) long, covering 192,000sq ft (17,850sq m) – and richly decorated with mosaics and imported marbles. An aqueduct, substantial parts of which survive, brought water from 35 miles (56km) away, supplying an estimated 7 million gallons (32 million litres) a day to the city.

From Carthage came Apuleius, the novelist of the 2nd century AD and a short-lived dynasty of emperors, the Gordiani (AD238–4). St Augustine, the great theologian, lived there AD370–83 (Carthage was an important centre of early Christianity) and praised its tree-lined avenues and many churches. Despite conquest by the Vandals in the 5th century, the city remained a bastion of Roman culture and provided loyal support to the Byzantine empire after it was restored to the empire in AD535. Carthage only fell to Arab invaders after prolonged sieges in AD698, a fall that marked the end, after seven centuries, of Rome in Africa.

### TIMGAD: A VETERANS' COLONY

Almost 200 miles (320km) south-west of Carthage, on a low and then fertile plateau, stand the ruins of a very different city, Timgad (Thamugadi) in modern Algeria. Founded by Trajan in AD100 as a colony for veterans, it was planned exactly like a large legionary camp, forming a square of 1,200 Roman feet (1,165 ft/355m) subdivided into 12 equal blocks, each 100 Roman feet square. The two main streets – the *cardo* and *decumanus* – intersect at the exact centre, where lay the forum with a basilica,

a *curia* (local senate house), temple and public lavatory – this last a building of some elegance, with marble arm rests in the shape of dolphins. Just to the north was the 4,000-seat theatre.

Intended to provide homes for retired legionaries and to help Romanize a still half-wild region, Timgad grew into a town with a population of around 15,000 people by AD200. It spread rather chaotically beyond its original plan as more baths, temples and a library were built. At first its houses were simple if solid single-storey buildings made of local limestone and timber – the mountains nearby were then well wooded – but with continuous colonnades in the Eastern style.

Before the city of Timgad was totally abandoned in the 7th century AD, a small Byzantine fort was built to the south. Most spectacular of the surviving ruins is the triple Arch of Trajan – which was actually built *c.* AD190, and so commemorates the city's famous founder – with pediments above the side arches, at the end of a colonnaded street.

*Above: A servant offering a diner wine in a mosaic from Carthage of the early 4th century AD. Carthage soon became second only to Rome in the Western empire in its size and wealth.*

*Below: The triple Arch of Trajan standing at the end of a colonnaded street in Timgad. It was built about AD190 to commemorate the city's imperial founder.*

# LEPCIS MAGNA: AN EMPEROR'S BIRTHPLACE

*Above: A bust of Septimius Severus (AD146–211), Lepcis' most famous son who became emperor in AD193 and richly adorned the city.*

*Below: One of the central pavilions of the* macellum *(market) in Lepcis. It was built c. 8BC of the fine local limestone as the city grew under the Augustan peace.*

Lepcis Magna in Tripolitania (western Libya) was founded by the Phoenicians or Carthaginians *c.* 600BC. A Punic (Carthaginian) city long before it became part of the Roman empire after 100BC, under the Pax Augusta, the 250-year-long peace established by Augustus in 30BC, it became steadily more prosperous. It was opulently adorned by its greatest native son Septimius Severus, emperor AD193–211. Later totally abandoned, its surviving ruins are among the finest of any Roman city.

Little remains of pre-Roman Lepcis, although many of its inhabitants long spoke Punic as well as Latin. Under Augustus, the Old Forum by the sea was laid out on standard rectangular lines, except in the north-east where an earlier temple survived. The three new temples are typically Italian in style, with high podiums and frontal emphasis. The central temple to the goddess Roma and Augustus was dedicated *c.* AD18. A *macellum* (market) with two central octagonal pavilions was built inside a rectangular courtyard in 8BC, with shops sheltering from the harsh African sun under its porticoes. A private citizen, Annobal Rufus built the theatre in AD1–2, which had an auditorium 300ft (90m) across. Partly resting on a natural slope, it had a splendid *scaenae frons* (stage wall), with three tiers of curving columns (some later rebuilt in marble) and a slot in the floor into which the curtain was lowered before performances.

## GROWING PROSPERITY

Under Hadrian, magnificent new baths modelled on those of Trajan in Rome were erected in AD126–7. They made novel use of expensive marbles that were imported from Greece or Asia Minor even in their well-appointed communal lavatories, which could seat 60 people. The baths had the usual *natatio* (swimming pool), *tepidarium* (warm room) and *caldarium* (hot room) sequence, with the addition of *sudatoria* (sweat rooms), ancestors of the Turkish bath. They reveal Lepcis Magna's growing prosperity, as careful dry farming techniques, capturing and conserving every drop of rain, pushed back the desert to give Tripolitania its golden age.

Many public buildings were now opulently remodelled in marble. The Hunting Baths, externally unadorned concrete vaulted structures on the beach, are notable architecturally. They may have been used by wealthy local huntsmen, but the name comes from the hunting scenes painted on the vaults inside. It is thought they might have served as the baths of a guild or as private baths which could be hired by groups. By the 2nd century AD, Lepcis was one of the empire's richest cities, but its best was yet to come.

Above: The resplendent macellum (market) at Lepcis Magna was built c.8BC, during the Pax Augusta, the peace established by Augustus, the first emperor. A large colonnaded peristyle measuring 73 by 43m (80 by 47yds) surrounds the market. Two circular market-halls, rather than the usual single hall, stood in the centre, crowded with market stalls. Its size shows Lepcis was already a wealthy city.

Below: The citizens of Lepcis erected a four-sided triumphal arch in gratitude to their emperor Severus for his visit in AD203. It was exuberantly decorated with winged victories holding wreaths.

## SEVERAN HEYDAY

Septimius Severus was a senator (of Rome) and commander of the Danubian legions when he launched his bid for the imperial throne in AD193, but he always remained faithful to his home town. Indeed, his family was so obviously Libyan that it is reported that he had to send his sister back home because her marked Lepcis accent made her ridiculous at court. Septimius endowed his native city with a new monumental quarter, including an enclosed harbour, temple, new forum and basilica and a piazza dominated by a huge *nymphaeum* (fountain building) – buildings that would have looked impressive even in Rome.

The harbour was a circular basin about 400yds (365m) in diameter with a lighthouse and warehouses. From the waterfront a colonnaded street about 450yds (411m) long and 70ft (21m) wide, flanked by porticoes, led up to the piazza near the Hadrianic baths. North of this Severus built a new forum, 200 by 330ft (60 by 100m).

On the forum's south-west side was a vast temple to the Severan family. Standing on a double-height podium on a tall flight of steps, it had eight red Egyptian granite columns in front, with columns of green *cipollino* marble with white Pentelic marble capitals on either side. It resembled but surpassed in grandeur Augustus' Temple of Mars Ultor in Rome. On the other side of the forum rose a huge new basilica, over 100ft (30m) high, with apses at both ends flanked by two pairs of white marble pilasters. The galleries over the double height lateral aisles were supported by Corinthian columns of red Egyptian granite. The timber roof had a span of 62ft (19m). Elaborate coloured marbles were used throughout Severus' projects. The raw materials and the craftsmen were imported; even the unknown architect probably came from the Aegean world.

The Forum was surrounded by a high masonry wall – it became a fortress under the Byzantines – but inside ran an opulent arcaded portico with alternating Medusa and Nereid heads. The *nymphaeum* had a big semicircular fountain basin, which was richly decorated with niches and columns of red granite.

In gratitude for this imperial largesse, the citizens of Lepcis erected a triumphal arch to their emperor for his visit in AD203. Four-sided, it has exuberant decorations, with columns, winged Victories holding wreaths and reliefs showing Severus and his triumphant armies. Lepcis was finally covered by sand as the collapse of Roman farming methods allowed the Sahara to push north to the coast.

# ATHENS: A GLORIOUS PAST

*Above: Tiers of marble seats in the Theatre of Dionysus in Athens, refurbished and restored under the Romans.*

*Below: The School of Plato, traditionally the greatest of Greek philosophers, shown in a 1st century AD mosaic.*

Athens lost its last political importance after Sulla brutally sacked it in 86BC for supporting Mithradates' war against Rome. However, it retained a unique status in the empire broadly comparable to that of Florence or Venice today, under which it was revered for its past artistic and intellectual glories. Illustrious Romans, from the great orator Cicero in 80BC to the last pagan emperor Julian in AD354, studied in Athens, while emperors endowed it with new buildings or special privileges. Far smaller than Hellenistic cities such as Alexandria, Athens was still recognized as the cultural capital of Greece and its craftsmen's skills were much appreciated in Rome. It even regained its position as the chief centre of philosophy. It did not, however, regain its democracy, for emperors were also making a political point through their buildings, emphasizing Rome's power over Greece. Roman imperial monuments filled up the old *agora* (forum), which had once been the centre of Athenian democratic life. Most Athenians, who had suffered in Rome's civil wars, were too impoverished to object to the wealthy new masters who gave them work.

### PROCLAIMING ROMAN POWER

Julius Caesar had provided money for a new *agora* that was built under Augustus and dedicated in 10BC. A rectangular court 270 by 225ft (82 by 69m), it was enclosed by Ionic porticoes and entered by a monumental gateway whose style revived Athenian 5th-century BC classicism. (Augustus chiefly admired Greek classicism for its air of dignity and authority.) Greek cities in the East used brick, stone and mortared rubble rather than Roman concrete. The Temple of Ares (Mars), originally 5th century BC and erected elsewhere in Attica, was moved block by block into the Agora and linked with Augustus' temple of Mars Ultor in Rome.

In 15BC Agrippa, Augustus' chief minister, built an *odeion* (roofed theatre), a lofty rectangular gabled hall to seat about 1,000. Its carved marble ornaments again copied classical examples but its giant scale – its interior was 76ft (23m) high and 82ft (25m) square – was new in Athens. A small circular temple to Rome and Augustus was built on the Acropolis. This was artistically influenced by the nearby classical Erechtheion but politically it proclaimed the power of Rome.

The flamboyantly philhellenic emperor Nero refurbished the old Theatre of Dionysus beneath the Acropolis between AD54 and 61, erecting a Roman-style stage building. This had seen the first performances of most of the great Greek tragedies by Aeschylus, Sophocles and

Euripides. It now also witnessed gladiatorial games. The games themselves apparently became popular with some Athenians after an initial period of disgust. Meanwhile, wealthy young Romans came to Athens to study at one of the competing schools of philosophy: Stoic, Platonist, Epicurean or Cynic.

## THE CITY OF HADRIAN

By the early 2nd century AD, Athens had regained a modest prosperity through the export of its fine Pentelic marble and skilled craftsmen. The emperor Hadrian, whose philhellenism ran deep, spent some of his happiest years in the city he first visited in AD124–5.

Hadrian became *archon* (mayor) of Athens and made the city head of his new Panhellenion League (an essentially honorific title). He also completed the temple of Olympian Zeus (Jupiter) whose building was started by the tyrant Peisistratus in the 6th century BC and revived in 174BC by the Seleucid king Antiochus IV. Antiochus' Roman architects, the Cossutius brothers, had opted for the Corinthian order for the 60ft (18m) high columns, but the huge temple had suffered when Sulla removed many columns to Rome. Hadrian dedicated it in AD132, placing a chryselephantine (gold and ivory) statue of Zeus inside the building.

Hadrian also provided a new aqueduct, a library whose plan recalled the Forum Pacis in Rome, a *stoa* (portico) with symmetrical gardens and baths. To commemorate his work, Hadrian erected an arch at the boundary between the original city and the new quarter he had founded in AD131. This was not in the usual triumphant Roman style but linked him to Theseus, Athens' legendary founder. The inscriptions on one side read, "This is the city of Theseus, not Hadrian", and on the other, "This is the city of Hadrian, not Theseus."

In AD143, Herodes Atticus, a wealthy aristocrat, restored the Hellenistic stadium (which was used for the Panathenaic games) in Pentelic marble. The stadium

was also used for gladiatorial games after this restoration. He built a new marble *odeion*, but there was little further construction. Third-century troubles saw Athens sacked in AD256 by marauding barbarians and, like so many cities at this time, it rewalled itself. More damagingly, the Visigoths under Alaric ravaged all Greece in AD398, attacking pagan temples in particular. (The Visigoths were keen, if heretical, Christians, but the remaining temple treasures were the chief attraction.) Despite this, Plato's Academy continued to flourish as the centre of Neoplatonism, the last great philosophical movement of antiquity. Proclus (*c.* AD410–85), who lectured in Athens, was its supreme systematizer. He extended the thinking of its founder, Plotinus, to stress the interconnectedness of all things, arguing that time itself is a circular dance.

However, Christian intolerance was growing. In AD529 the Byzantine emperor Justinian ordered the closure of all the schools of philosophy, so ending a thousand years of intellectual freedom and ancient Athens itself.

*Above: The gigantic Temple of Olympian Zeus was completed by Hadrian in AD132, some 650 years after it was started.*

*Below: The Tower of the Winds, which housed an elaborate monumental clock dating from c. 50BC.*

# TRIER: THE ROME OF THE NORTH

*Above: The now plain interior of the huge Basilica was once decorated with glowing mosaics that surrounded the emperor enthroned in majesty in the apse at the far end.*

*Below: The Porta Nigra (Black Gate), the northern gateway, rises 100ft (30m) and dates from c. AD300. Its unusually fine state of preservation is due to its conversion into a chapel in the Middle Ages.*

Three days' march up the Moselle valley from the Rhine frontier, Trier (Augusta Treverorum) had a superb strategic position. When Postumus proclaimed his separatist Gallic empire in AD260, he made Trier his capital, but in the ensuing civil war and invasions the city was sacked. It recovered, however, to become the leading city in the Western empire in the 4th century AD. Politically, economically and culturally it supplanted Lyons (Lugdunum), which never recovered from being sacked by Septimius Severus in the civil wars of AD195.

### ORIGINS OF A CITY

There was no pre-Roman settlement at Trier when Agrippa, Augustus' general, chose the site for a military camp. This attracted the local Celts and a township grew up around it. (The Treveri had been a warlike people, supplying Caesar with cavalry, but had not previously been city dwellers.) Under Claudius (ruled AD43–54) Trier gained the important status of *colonia* and a charter. It developed rapidly thanks to its position on the major trade routes that ran north–south and east–west and to the stone bridge which Claudius had constructed. Its piers still support the modern bridge. Trier became the seat of the procurator (governor) of the province of Gallia Belgica. There are traces of houses with stone foundations and a large rectangular hall from the 1st century AD.

Soon after AD100, the grand St Barbara Baths were constructed. Elaborately decorated, with marble statues in semi-circular niches around an open-air *natatio* (swimming pool), they also had several heated rooms, essential in a city so far north. Along with a stone amphitheatre that could seat up to 20,000 people, private houses were now constructed that boasted fine mosaic floors. The Forum, about 1,300 by 500ft (400 by 150m), was built around this time, as was the *curia* (council room). The monumental northern gateway known as the Porta Nigra (Black Gate – age has weathered it) is an early 4th-century building in a deliberately archaic style. At 100ft (30m) high and 120ft (36m) long, it was intended to impress visitors or invaders with the majesty of Rome, with its many tiered arches flanked by pillars. It may have been left unfinished, which accounts for the rough, even crude quality of its stonework. Its survival is due to its conversion into a chapel in the Middle Ages.

### A GOLDEN AGE

In AD293 Constantius Chlorus became Caesar (junior emperor) of the West from Morocco to the Tyne, and Augustus (senior emperor) in AD305. Like the other tetrarchs, he chose a permanent new capital, in his case Trier, and adorned it lavishly. Among his new structures was the Basilica, although it was probably completed by his son Constantine I who held court at Trier from AD306–312. Built of solid red brick, the Basilica is a

huge bare hall, measuring around 95 by 220ft (29 by 67m) and almost 100ft (30m) high. Part of the imperial palace, it was not then a free-standing building. Today it is a completely plain Lutheran church, lit by two rows of round-headed windows, which continue around the apse. The upper windows of the apse are lower and shorter than those in the nave, producing the illusion that the apse is larger than it is. This effect was intended to magnify the power of the emperor who sat enthroned in its mosaic-covered apse. The floor was originally covered in black and white marble and heated by hypocausts, which were themselves veneered in marble. The exterior of the building would not originally have seemed as austere as it does now, because it was probably stuccoed and had two rows of wooden balconies around it.

Equally imposing buildings formed the Kaiserthermen (Imperial Baths) erected after AD293 at the southern end of the palace complex, probably for courtiers' sole use. Their main bathing-block (450 by 400ft/ 137 by 122m) occupied half the rectangular site, facing the large porticoed court and surrounding buildings. They may not have been completed when Constantine finally left Trier in AD316, and only parts were used as baths by later emperors. Other parts were probably used as offices.

### A CENTRE OF CULTURE
Trier continued to enjoy imperial favour. Constantine II and later Valentinian I (AD364–75) and his son Gratian (AD375–83) all chose to rule from it. Constantine I had started its polygonal cathedral, the first in northern Europe, which now forms part of Trier Cathedral.

Two massive limestone warehouses were built near the river, each 230ft long by 65ft wide (70 by 120m). About AD300 city walls, 20ft high and 10ft thick (6m by 3m), with 75 towers, were built to enclose an area of 700 acres (280ha).

In the 4th century AD, Trier was a centre of culture as well as power, with its own university. Ausonius, the poet and courtier who tutored the young Gratian,

famously praised the beautiful Moselle valley and its terraced vineyards in his poems. Other intellectually distinguished visitors included St Augustine, St Jerome – both key Church fathers – and Lactantius, a noted Christian orator. Trier deserved its title *Roma Transalpina*, Rome north of the Alps, but it did not survive the calamitous 5th century. Finally abandoned by the imperial court in AD395, it was sacked by German invaders in AD406.

*Above: A carving on a tombstone of the 2nd century AD showing a tavern scene (top) and a wine barrel being transported by ox cart (beneath). The Moselle valley was already famed for its wines under the Romans.*

# EPHESUS: WONDER OF THE WORLD

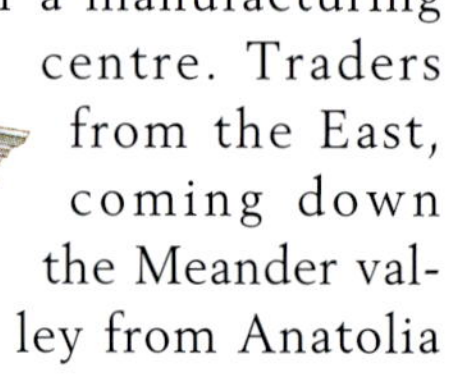

*Above: Artemis (Diana), the great goddess of the Ephesians, portrayed as a fertility goddess with many breasts in this statue of the 2nd century AD. Her huge temple was one of the seven wonders of the world.*

Ephesus was a very ancient city dating back to Mycenaean times when the Romans made it the capital of their new province of Asia (western Anatolia) in *c.* 129BC. Like Athens, Ephesus had long been an important intellectual and religious as well as commercial centre. However, unlike Athens, it boomed under the Pax Romana, becoming one of the wealthiest cities in the empire, with a population of perhaps 200,000 people. Large areas of the central city have been excavated and many buildings testify to this long prosperity. While remaining firmly Greek in spirit, Ephesus' architecture was more innovative than Athens', reflecting its citizens' greater wealth and self-confidence.

Up to *c.* 180BC, Ephesus had thrived, sometimes as the Western capital of the vast Seleucid empire, more often as an independent city state. However, Rome's wars – especially its civil wars – half-ruined the Greek cities of Asia Minor and Ephesus only recovered after Augustus had restored peace in 30BC. The city grew rich primarily from trade, as it was never a manufacturing centre. Traders from the East, coming down the Meander valley from Anatolia and points east as far as China, which was then the world's only source of silk, offloaded their valuable cargoes in the port at Ephesus on to ships bound for Rome.

## DIANA OF THE EPHESIANS

Ephesus' gigantic temple of Artemis (Diana) – traditionally built with money provided by the wealthy King Croesus of Lydia *c.* 550BC and certainly dating to before 500BC – was another, if smaller, source of wealth and a great source of civic pride. It was among the first Greek temples to use the Ionic order throughout, rather than the Doric or Aeolian orders. Many times restored or rebuilt to the same design after fires (one of them started deliberately), the temple was constructed mostly of marble and considered one of the seven wonders of the ancient world, chiefly because of its size. It measured 374ft by 180ft (114 by 55m). With its huge Ionic columns 65ft (20m) high, it was the largest temple of the classic rectilinear column and lintel type ever constructed. Within its *cella* (central chamber) was a giant statue of Artemis, depicted not as the usual chaste huntress-goddess of Graeco-Roman mythology but as a many-breasted deity, pointing to the Asian origin of her cult at Ephesus.

Around the temple precincts swarmed peddlers of locally made religious trinkets. Theirs was the highly profitable trade that St Paul tried to disrupt on his mission, causing local craftsmen to riot shouting, "Great is Diana (Artemis) of the Ephesians!" After Constantine had made Christianity fashionable, however, Ephesus became an important Christian city and the seat of a bishop.

*Left: The Library of Celsus, Ephesus, built c. AD110. It is remarkable for its undulating façade with projecting pavilions topped by curved and triangular pediments.*

## THE ARKADIANE

Ephesus had reasonably abundant building materials and most of its public buildings in the Roman period were of solid masonry. This applied to the colonnaded street, running 650yds (600m) from the harbour to the theatre – superbly sited at the foot of Mount Pion – called the Arkadiane. Along this 36ft (11m) broad avenue lay most of the important buildings of the Roman era.

The Library of Celsus was among the most striking of the buildings of Ephesus. Dating from about AD110–35, it stands at the bottom of Euretes Street. It was built by the son and grandson of a rich and illustrious citizen, Caius Julius Celsus Polemeanus, who had become a consul in Rome – the highest honour a normal citizen could attain – and who was, most unusually, buried inside the Library beneath its apse. A tall rectangular hall, 55ft wide by 36ft long (16.7 by 10.9m), it had a small central apse with a statue of Celsus. Round three sides ran three rows of recesses to house the books or scrolls. Two orders of columns carried the two tiers of balustraded galleries to give access to the upper bookcases. Its richly carved façade has been re-erected, revealing that pairs of upper columns were staggered over the lower columns and alternated with curved and triangular pediments. This has shown that Ephesian architects could play sparkling new variations on old classical themes. The nearby Temple to Hadrian – which was erected by a private citizen and is therefore relatively small – is remarkable for its Syrian arch where the central span of the façade is arched up into the pediment. Like the colonnaded Arkadiane, this may also have been Syrian-inspired.

The most innovatory buildings of Roman Ephesus were its numerous resplendent baths. Largest of these were

the Harbour Baths of the late 1st century AD. In the centre of this bulky complex lay the two *Marmorsaalen* (Marble Rooms), opulently decorated marble halls on either side of a *peristyle* court, with the baths themselves in between. The Greek preference for gymnasia with covered running tracks distinguishes these baths from those in the Romanized Western empire. Such very Greek taste for athletics and classical architecture survived until the advent of Christianity in the 4th century.

*Above: Detail of a garland from a sarcophagus, probably from the 2nd century AD, when Ephesus was booming under Roman rule. The dynamic exuberance of this relief illustrates the self-confidence and wealth of the city at the time.*

*Right: The Temple of Hadrian, built AD130–8, has an ornate frieze across its façade rising up into an arch resting on two Corinthian columns.*

# VANISHED CITIES OF THE EAST

*Above: The Temple of Bel in Palmyra, dedicated in AD32, is Hellenistic in its tall Corinthian columns, but its entrance by a grand side doorway is not at all classical.*

*Below: Reconstruction of the markedly Graeco-Roman theatre in Palmyra. Here its most famous ruler, Queen Zenobia, reputedly liked to watch Greek dramas after her victories.*

Pompey had added western Asia from the Caucasus to the Red Sea to the Roman sphere of influence in the 60s BC, but it was centuries before Rome directly controlled all this area, home of many ancient civilizations. While most cities gained a Hellenistic veneer after Alexander the Great's conquests (334–323BC) – and metropoli like Antioch in Syria or Seleucia-on-the-Tigris were totally new Greek-speaking foundations – the population remained mainly Aramaic-speaking (Semitic). This made for a fertile mixture of styles. Meanwhile, the Pax Romana allowed long-distance trade to flourish even beyond Rome's eastern frontier.

## PALMYRA

Located in the Syrian desert, Palmyra, long a semi-independent client state, was well situated to benefit from this peace. The city was an oasis midway between the Euphrates and the Mediterranean ports. Its excellent cavalry – it included heavy armoured cataphracts besides mounted archers – protected caravans carrying the spices and other exotic goods so valued in Rome and it became a major caravan city on the trade routes with the East. (The "protection" may not have been entirely voluntary, but it helped rather than hindered trade.) Visiting Palmyra in AD128, Hadrian granted it the status of "free city", allowing it to set its own taxes and dues. It consequently prospered even more, while moving closer into the Roman orbit. The Palmyrene Tariff is a list of taxes charged for goods coming and going and for the use of the springs.

## AN AUDACIOUS QUEEN

When the Persians over-ran Rome's eastern provinces and captured the emperor Valerian in AD260, Odenatheus, ruler of Palmyra, rode to Rome's rescue. His cavalry drove the Persians out of Syria and Anatolia and he won himself the title *Dux Orientis* (Duke of the East), before he was assassinated in AD267. His widow Zenobia, noted alike for her dark-haired beauty and for her audacity, inherited his power.

Zenobia claimed descent from Cleopatra, the last Ptolemaic queen of Egypt, and rivalled her in ambition. The great historian Edward Gibbon, admittedly writing 1,500 years later, called her, "The most lovely as well as the most heroic of her sex...Her large black eyes sparkled with an uncommon fire, tempered by the most attractive sweetness".

Proclaiming her son Augustus and herself Augusta, Zenobia rejected Roman suzerainty and invaded Egypt in AD270. Finally provoked, the emperor Aurelian marched east and crushed her in a series of battles, capturing Palmyra in AD271. After these defeats the city became a

Roman frontier fort – an ignominious fate that, paradoxically, has preserved it well. The most striking aspect of Palmyra today is its long colonnaded streets. The main colonnaded street, dating from the early 2nd century AD and three-quarters of a mile (1.2km) long and 35ft (11m) wide, ran from the Grove Temple in the west to the Temple of Bel, intersecting similarly colonnaded streets.

The great temple of Bel, the city's chief deity of Babylonian origin, was dedicated in AD32. From the outside it appears to follow classical canons fairly closely, with six columns at either end on a low platform, like many Hellenistic temples. However, it is far from classical in layout. It is entered not from the front but through an elaborate doorway at the head of a grand staircase on the west side. Inside are two cult chambers. It was possibly topped by a parapet of crowstepped merlons and its roof, behind its classical pediments, had flat terraces. Parthian influences are also apparent in many of its statues, which are stiffly stylized. However, architecturally Palmyra became more Graeco-Roman in the following centuries, with the construction of an *agora* (forum), a theatre – where Zenobia reputedly watched Greek dramas after her victories – and a bath house.

### THE ROSE RED CITY

Almost impregnable in its remote valley among the Edom mountains in the south Jordanian desert, Petra is another city abandoned after a brief period of glory. Described by Strabo early in the 1st century AD as peaceful and well-governed, with caravans converging on it from the south or east, its great days as a trading city were already fading when Trajan annexed it in AD106, but it had once surpassed Palmyra. Debate continues about the exact date of its most famous monuments, the rockcut façades – some scholars date them before the Roman occupation, others after it – but their architecture is remarkably original. Situated in the Siq gorge between towering

mountain, Petra is built of the local reddish sandstone – hence its nickname "the Rose Red City". The visitor today first sees the Khasneh, or Treasury, with a remarkable central kiosk in the middle of its broken pediment. The same design is seen in Petra's most majestic building, the mausoleum called the Deir. Its façade is massive – 150ft long by 125ft high (46 by 38m) – larger than the west front of Westminster Abbey. However, it remains only a façade with a style that deserves the name baroque. Lost completely in its valley after its decline, Petra was only rediscovered in the 19th century.

*Above: Façade of the Khasneh or Treasury at Petra, which has a circular kiosk in the middle of its broken pediment, an architectural extravagance typical of a style sometimes called Roman baroque. It was never a treasury, but was later thought to contain treasure by tomb robbers.*

# NÎMES AND ARLES: CITIES OF ROMAN GAUL

*Above: The Tour Magne, Nîmes, an octagonal tower 130ft (40m) high above the walls built by Augustus.*

*Below: Perhaps the most striking section of all aqueducts, the Pont du Gard crosses the gorge of the Gardon River.*

Julius Caesar called Gallia Transalpina *nostra provincia* (our province), because southern Gaul (today Languedoc and Provence) had been Roman since 121BC, and had long been influenced by Greek colonies such as Marseilles and Nice. Narbonne, which gave the province its later name Gallia Narbonensis, was Rome's first colony outside Italy, founded in 118BC. Under Augustus, the province thrived, becoming almost a second Italy and so peaceful it could be governed by a senator without an army. Meanwhile Roman civilization spread up the Rhône valley into central Gaul, transforming the region, with Lyons (Lugdunum) as its central city. Lyons' theatre, odeum, aqueducts and amphitheatre are all well-preserved.

Nîmes (Nemausus) was founded as a legionary veterans' colony in 35BC on the site of an earlier tribal capital and shrine to Nemausus, Gallic god of the local spring. In 16BC Augustus endowed his new city with walls nearly four miles (6.4km) long, enclosing an area of about 500 acres (200ha). These walls, by then as much status symbol as military requirement, were 8ft wide (2.5m) and had 19 towers, of which the highest is the Tour Magne, a 130ft (40m) octagonal tower. A fine gateway has survived with two arches for wheeled traffic and two smaller side arches for pedestrians.

## CLASSICISM IN THE PROVINCES

One of the best-preserved and most elegant of all Roman temples is the Maison Carrée (literally square house), which was begun in 19BC and dedicated to Augustus and his *gens* (family) – the imperial cult flourished outside Italy even while Augustus was still alive. Influenced by contemporary buildings in Rome, especially the Temple of Mars Ultor and the Ara Pacis (Altar of Peace), this is a superb example of Augustan classicism transplanted to the provinces, indeed possibly even built by the same craftsmen, with mathematically perfect proportions: its podium, columns and entablature are related in the ratio of 2:5:2. Nîmes' amphitheatre, dating from the late 1st century AD, has survived well. Its creators were clearly inspired by the Colosseum (Flavian Amphitheatre) built shortly before in Rome, as well as by the older Theatre of Marcellus, for they used the now standard motifs: arches framed by pilasters on the ground tier and by engaged columns in the second.

The Romans had realized very early on that Nîmes' spring waters would be inadequate for the growing colony. An aqueduct built by Agrippa or in the later 1st century AD brought water from near Uzès 31 miles (50km) away. Mostly this flowed in a channel buried underground or carried on a low wall, at a gentle 1:3,000 slope, but where the line crosses

*Right: The calm elegance of the Maison Carrée at Nîmes shows how successfully Augustan classical ideals were transplanted to southern Gaul.*

the gorge of the river Gardon, the most celebrated Roman aqueduct bridge was constructed: the Pont du Gard. Built entirely of squared stone, without clamps or mortar but with some individual stones weighing six tons, it is 295yds (269m) long and carries the water over the valley at a height of 160ft (49m) above the stream. Its proportions are simple yet aesthetically satisfying: four units for the central arch, three for the lateral arches, one for the upper tier of arches and six for the height of the whole structure. Its many projecting bosses were left to support scaffolding when repairs were needed. Inside the city the water flowed into large circular settling tanks from which outlets carried the water throughout the city. At its peak *c.* AD100, Nimes had a population of possibly 50,000, so a copious water supply was needed.

**THE LAST CAPITAL OF ROMAN GAUL**
On the banks of the Rhône, which became an important trade route, Arles (Arelate) rivalled Nîmes as a wealthy, increasingly sophisticated city under the Principate (30BC–AD285), but it was also important in the empire's last days. The first legionary colony was founded in 46BC by Caesar after his Gallic conquests. Arles' two outstanding earlier Roman monuments still extant are its amphitheatre and its theatre. The amphitheatre is probably contemporary with that of its rival in Nîmes (AD80–100). The same architect, Crispius Reburrus, is thought to have designed both in the same essentially classic style. The theatre nearby resembles that of Aosta just across the Alps in northern Italy, in that the outer extremes of its *scaenae frons* (stage backdrop) was straight, not curved and its central door stands in a porch at the back of a shallow curved *exedra*, suggesting transalpine links.

The vaulted remains of a double portico lie beneath what must have been the Forum. Arles' town walls, again initially more ornamental than functional, resembled those of some Italian cities. They were strengthened in the 4th century AD when Arles was becoming increasingly important. The site of the first imperially sanctioned Church Council in AD314, Arles became the military headquarters of the westernmost empire after Trier was abandoned in AD395. It was briefly the capital of the pretender Constantine from Britain in AD407–9. Much grander imperial-style baths survive from this period. Arles was one of the last Gallic cities to remain in Roman control as the Western empire finally disintegrated in the AD450s.

*Below: Remains of seating substructure at the amphitheatre at Arles dating from the late 1st century AD.*

# ROMANO-BRITISH CITIES

*Above: Unearthed in Southwark in 2002, this plaque is inscribed with the name Londinium and dedicated to the god Mars. It is the oldest evidence of London's Roman name.*

*Below: This vivid mosaic of a horse is typical of the colourful decorations of the Roman baths at Bath.*

Pre-Roman Britain had no cities in the Graeco-Roman sense and few cities apparently survived the Roman withdrawal of *c.* AD407. However, most Roman cities – London, York, Bath, Leicester, Chester, Winchester – later revived to show that the Romans had chosen their sites with typical acumen. Colchester, rather than London, was the Romans' first urban settlement and also their first British colony.

Two very different places, London, the great commercial centre that became the province's capital and Bath, the pleasure town, exemplify the Romano-British city.

### LONDON
At the lowest possible crossing point on the Thames, Londinium was the merchants' preferred site and an important port, whether or not there was a Celtic settlement there earlier (the name Lun is Celtic). During Boudicca's revolt in AD60, the Britons killed a reported 70,000 Romanized traders in London and St Albans so it must have already been very populous. Tacitus said that London was "Crowded with traders, a hive of commerce". By *c.* 100AD it had acquired a governor's palace, a military fort on the north-east of the city covering 11 acres (4.45 h), a bridge across the Thames – initially in wood, later rebuilt in stone – and the city had probably become the administrative capital.

London retained its role as capital of Britannia Superior after the province was subdivided *c.* AD200. When Constantius I recovered Britain for the empire in AD296 from the rebel Allectus, London's citizens were so overjoyed by Constantius' troops' timely arrival to rescue them from Allectus' pillaging Frankish mercenaries that they hailed him as "Restorer of the eternal light". In the 4th century AD London received the title *Augusta*, indicating continued high status. Written records are few, however, and subsequent rebuilding has destroyed most of the archaeological remains.

One building was exceptional: London's basilica, beneath modern Gracechurch Street. The largest in the empire north of the Alps, comparable to a cathedral in scale and grandeur, it must have overwhelmed the north side of London's forum. A modest basilica had been erected under Domitian (ruled AD81–96) but when Hadrian visited Britain in AD122 – and ordered his wall built across northern England – it was massively reconstructed. (A coin of his reign has been found in its mortar.) The new building's main hall was around 49ft (192m) long, 115ft wide (35m) and about 89ft (27m) high. With triple aisles, it probably had apses at either end and statues such as the famous bronze bust of the emperor found in the Thames, but none have survived *in situ*. Refurbished in the 3rd century, it was demolished for unknown reasons in the 4th century AD.

*Right: The Roman baths at Bath, where hot water bubbles out of the earth. Although other areas of the baths are still roofed, this section is now open to the sky.*

One of the few Roman buildings now in the open is the temple to Mithras near the Mansion House. Built *c.* 200AD, it was about 60ft (19m) long, divided into a nave and two aisles by a row of columns, with an apse at one end. Later, other cult images, including Minerva, Serapis and Dionysus were added. These are among the finest found in Britain and make the temple almost a pantheon.

London's walls probably date from the reign of Caracalla (AD211–17) because a coin of his reign has been found in one section. They enclose an area of about 330 acres (132ha). Today, with few changes, these walls, which are about 3 miles (4.8km) long, mark the line and base of the medieval city walls and the boundaries of the City of London, although the street plan has changed. In the 330s AD, a wall reusing masonry and bits of sculpture was built along the Thames for the first time. After Count Theodosius' restoration of authority in Britain in AD367, London's walls were strengthened with projecting polygonal bastions incorporating not just old building materials but even tombs. By then, the city's population must have fallen from its 2nd-century peak of 35–40,000 people.

## A ROMAN SPA TOWN

The Celts had worshipped the goddess Sulis at the place where hot waters bubble out of the ground at 125°F (46.5°C). The Romans, identifying her with their Minerva, developed Aquae Sulis ("the waters of Sulis", Bath) as a religious sanctuary and fashionable spa. The spring was given a stone pool to create a head of water. This supplied what became a remarkable bath complex, part of which has recently been restored. At its centre was the Great Bath, a lead-lined swimming-pool with a wooden roof, later under a vault, with other smaller baths

with heated water to the west. North of the spring a temple to Sulis/Minerva was built in a colonnaded courtyard. It had four Composite-style columns on a base about 29ft (9m) wide. The gap between the columns was twice their diameter of 2.6ft (0.8m), an unusual ratio that was also found in the Temple of Fortuna Virilis in Rome. The columns supported an entablature containing a relief of a Medusa-like male head in a shield carried by flanking winged Victories. There is a Celtic air to these carvings, in contrast to the distinctly Roman temple itself.

The baths were obviously successful and the complex continued to be extended into the 4th century AD, when the temple may have acquired flanking chapels. All the Roman ruins now lie about 20ft (6m) below street level.

*Below: Bust of Hadrian, in whose reign (AD117–38) London gained an immense new basilica.*

# ROMAN ARTS AND SOCIETY

For centuries, Rome eclipsed all other cities. Its vast population, enriched by the taxes and tribute of the empire, sucked in raw materials, goods and human beings, many of them slaves, both from around the Mediterranean and from further afield. In order to supply Rome, traders explored new routes across the known world, bringing exotic goods back to the city. Fleets of huge ships set sail annually from Egypt, Spain and Africa with vital cargoes of grain and olive oil to feed the city, while agents roamed the empire's fringe to find the wild beasts whose violent deaths would amuse the Roman populace.

The urban life that developed in Rome after 150BC anticipated some aspects of modern city life, with its tall blocks of apartments, mass entertainments, high crime rates and problems with water supply and sewage disposal. However, Rome also offered opportunities that attracted free men to settle there, with its theatres, temples, libraries and lecture rooms and popular entertainments such as the arena or the baths.

Rome was a city of many gods and cults, which were often officially welcomed. Despite the numerous artworks adorning the city – it was joked Rome had more statues than living inhabitants – Roman culture was predominantly literate. A knowledge of both Greek and Latin was essential for any aspiring educated man. Women too could often read and, although barred from public life, played a greater role in Rome than in some comparable cultures. All these splendours were made possible by slavery, but slavery took many forms and lacked any hint of a colour bar. This allowed freed slaves to become citizens and to rise in what was, in some ways, a meritocratic civilization.

*Left: Roman pragmatism, shown in the census-taking scribe, is depicted in Greek style on the Altar of Domitius Ahenobarbus, c.100BC.*

# CHAPTER VII

# LITERATURE

The story of Latin literature begins with two great comic playwrights, Plautus and Terence, and the epic poet Ennius *c.* 200BC. Latin as a language survived the end of the West Roman empire in AD476 and continued to be used up to the 1960s by the Catholic church, which in the early Middle Ages had had a near monopoly on literacy. Latin remained the language of much science and diplomacy until the late 17th century in western Europe – Isaac Newton, a Protestant Englishman, wrote most of his scientific works in Latin.

Considered of central importance in education into the mid-20th century, Latin is still admired for its clarity and brevity and is useful for medicine, natural science and law. Ignoring the fall of Rome, poets carried on writing in Latin through the Middle Ages, and the language enjoyed a classicizing revival during the Renaissance (1400–1600) in western countries.

The great pioneers of Latin literature, especially the writers of its golden age (*c.* 70BC–AD14), were conscious of their debt to Greek literature, with seven brilliant centuries of achievement behind it. Ultimately the Greeks inspired rather than crushed their Roman followers. Roman poets such as Virgil, Horace and Ovid and prose writers such as Cicero created a classical style comparable to that of Greek writers. For the Roman empire was an empire of letters as well as of arms; literacy being relatively widespread. Sadly much Latin literature has perished, hand-copied books and scrolls being few and fragile.

*Left: View of Tivoli with Rome in the distance, painted by Gaspard Poussin in the 17th century. Tivoli was a favourite retreat of writers and emperors such as Horace and Hadrian.*

# THE FIRST ROMAN WRITERS

*Above: A portrait of Menander, the Athenian comedian who so influenced Roman playwrights.*

*Below: The theatre at Pompeii, built in the 2nd century BC, long before Rome had a permanent theatre. Its original plan followed Greek models in having a narrow stage front, but it was later remodelled by the Romans.*

Latin literature got off to a flying start with Plautus, a comic genius who knew how to entertain still relatively simple Romans with hilarious slapstick comedies. Terence wrote less rumbustiously and with less success for a possibly more select audience. Enough survives to give us a good idea of both their works, but only fragments remain of the work of their great contemporary, Rome's first epic poet, Ennius. All three adapted Greek originals for Roman audiences.

## PLAUTUS *c.* 254–184BC

Born to poor parents in Umbria, Plautus worked as a stage carpenter among other jobs and only started to write plays in middle age. He then became Rome's most successful adapter of Greek "new comedy". (This was derived from the work of the Athenian Menander, who had lived 100 years before, and of other Greeks whose works have been lost.) Plautus reputedly wrote 130 plays, of which 21 survive. Written in verse, like Greek comedies, they usually involve characters with Greek names in Greek cities. However, Plautus was mainly concerned with getting laughs from his audience, so he sacrificed consistency or subtlety of character for jokes and puns, far easier to accomplish in Latin than Greek.

Plautus often replaced spoken dialogue with songs accompanied by pipe music or with *cantica*, duets or solo arias, producing what might be called Roman comic opera or musical comedy. The result was an earthier, cruder comedy than that of Menander, and proved immensely popular and influential. Shakespeare and Molière, the French 17th-century playwright, were indebted to him in their plays such as *The Comedy of Errors* or *L'Avare*, while comic opera, pantomime and television sitcoms today are Plautus' distant but direct heirs.

Performed at first in makeshift wooden theatres, his comedies were, like the Greeks', usually linked with religious festivals, but as time went by they came to be seen as entertainment. In a typical early play *Aulularia* (*The Pot of Gold*), Euclio, a

poor elderly Athenian, discovers a hoard of gold and becomes obsessively suspicious of his daughter's suitor, who he fears is after it. All ends happily, however, after various alarms. In *Captivi* (*The Prisoners*) an old Greek, Hegio, buys prisoners of war, hoping to exchange one for his captured son. Two such prisoners, master and slave, secretly swap identities. The master is freed to negotiate the return of Hegio's son and the slave is finally revealed as Hegio's other son, kidnapped in childhood. In one of Plautus' most famous plays, *Bacchides* (*The Bacchis Sisters*), a dishonest slave called Chrysalus (Goldfinger) dominates the action, scheming to defraud his master, as he proudly tells the audience. Confusion is increased by two prostitutes who are both called Bacchis. Cunning slaves, desperate young lovers and miserly, jealous old men are among Plautus' stock characters.

### TERENCE *c.* 195–159BC

Born in North Africa and brought to Rome as a slave, Terence (Publius Terentius Afer) gained his education, his freedom and his entrée to aristocratic circles through his talents and good looks. Closer to the Greek model than Plautus', Terence's plays are concerned with love affairs and complications arising from ignorance or misunderstandings. Only one play, *Eunuchus* (*The Eunuch*) enjoyed popular success, because he added broad comedy to it. Normally, Terence retained the original Greek irony, translating Attic (Athenian) Greek into elegant, pure Latin that lacked Plautus' verbal exuberance. The resulting plays, six of which survive, found little favour with still unsophisticated Roman audiences but became part of the classical canon. Terence bitterly attacked the gladiators, tight-rope walkers and others who proved more popular than his plays but was himself criticized by literary men for cannibalizing different Greek plays to make his own. Although he died young during a visit to Greece, his influence on later European comedy of manners was huge.

### ENNIUS 239–169BC

Called the father of Latin poetry, Ennius was actually born to a Greek family in Calabria. (Southern Italy was then known as Magna Graecia, greater Greece, being deeply Hellenized.) After serving with the Roman army in Sardinia, Ennius came to Rome with Cato the Elder *c.* 204BC and ultimately gained Roman citizenship.

Ennius began writing epic poetry late in life, dying impoverished but confident of posthumous fame, as he claimed to be a reincarnation of Homer, the great Greek poet. Unfortunately, only fragments of his work survive, but they reveal his versatility, for he wrote tragedies, comedies, satires and other works. His greatest work was his *Annals*, a poetic history of Rome from Aeneas' flight from Troy to his own day. The work extended to 20,000 lines, written in the smooth-flowing Homeric hexameter (a verse line of six metrical feet) he introduced from Greek.

Ennius' few surviving lines, which are quoted by later writers such as Virgil, mingle high Greek heroism with Roman alliteration and love of puns. Although later sometimes mocked for clumsiness, Ennius was the first to show that Latin poetry could achieve epic greatness by adopting Greek classical forms.

*Above: Scene from a comedy by Plautus, the first and always the most popular Roman playwright. His fame spread around the empire, as this 3rd century AD mosaic from Sousse in Africa shows.*

*Below: A portrait of Ennius, the first Roman epic poet who came to see himself as a reincarnation of Homer. Ennius also wrote tragedies and comedies for the stage.*

# AUGUSTUS' POETS LAUREATE

*Above: Scene from the Prima Porta statue showing Augustus' diplomatic victory in 19BC when Parthia returned Roman legionary standards, a victory which Horace duly praised as effective poet laureate.*

*Below: A mosaic shows the poet Virgil writing* The Aeneid *between the muses Clio (history) and Melpomene (tragedy). Virgil's epic became popular across the empire.*

Although neither Virgil nor Horace sought the role, both became, in effect, poets laureate for Augustus. Although very different – Virgil introspective, moody, Horace urbane, if keenly aware of life's sorrows and joys – both wrote supremely classical verse.

## VIRGIL 70–19BC

Perhaps the greatest of all Roman poets, Virgil (Publius Vergilius Maro) was born near Mantua, in Cisalpine Gaul, which was by then almost fully Roman. His parents were only modest farmers, but Virgi was well educated and became closely involved in imperial affairs. He lived through civil wars that wrecked the Republic – there were wars in 16 of the 51 years of his life – and lost his farm in the chaos following the Battle of Philippi.

However, it was returned to him after an appeal to Octavian and he died rich, leaving 10 million sesterces. Such experiences deepened the longing for peace which permeates his poetry.

Virgil's first work, *The Eclogues*, written before 37BC, is set in an idealized Arcadia, influenced by Theocritus (310–250BC). It depicts shepherds' lives and loves but also refers to recent troubles, such as farmers' arbitrary evictions. *Eclogue IV* contains a passage in which the Sybil, Rome's oracle, foretells the birth of a divine child who will restore the golden age. *Jam redit et virgo, redeunt Saturnia regna…* ("Now the Virgin returns, the reign of Saturn returns …"). Actually praising the Julian family, this was interpreted by Christians as a prediction of the birth of Christ.

Virgil was now given substantial properties by Maecenas, who acted as patron for many poets under Augustus. His next work, *The Georgics*, appeared in 29BC. Its praise of Italian farm life – echoing Hesiod's *Work and Days* of *c.* 700BC – marvellously evokes the beauties of the Italian landscape but is of limited use as a farming manual. Pressed to write an epic about the emperor, Virgil instead responded with *The Aeneid*.

This work relates the legendary adventures of Aeneas, the Trojan prince who fled burning Troy to found Lavinium, Rome's legendary precursor. As the Julians claimed descent from Aeneas, this was subtle flattery. Aeneas is no bloodthirsty hero but an upright man who hates – yet excels at – fighting. His betrayal of Dido, queen of Carthage, appears shabby but he is driven by his destiny to abandon her. (Dido despairingly kills herself.) Virgil, who died before he completed his epic, wanted it destroyed, but after Augustus published it, it became accepted as Virgil's masterpiece, vital to Rome's self-image.

While rivalling Homer's *Iliad* in scope and grandeur, the *Aeneid* takes no delight in war. Instead it stresses Rome's responsibilities as ruler. *Hae tibi erunt artes, pacisque imponere morem/ Parcere subjectis et debellare superbos* ("These shall be your skills: to impose peace, spare the conquered and overthrow the mighty").

The epic starts majestically:
*Arma virumque cano, Trojae qui primus*
*abo oris*
"Arms and the man I sing, who, forced
    by fate
And haughty Juno's unrelenting hate
Expelled and exiled, left the shore.
Long labours both by sea and land
    he bore."

> (translated by John Dryden)

### HORACE 65–8BC

The son of a freedman (ex-slave) who had prospered enough to pay for his education in Athens, Horace (Quintus Horatius Flaccus) fought on the wrong Republican side at the Battle of Philippi in 42BC. Returning unhurt but penniless to Italy, he was introduced to Maecenas' circle by Virgil *c.* 37BC, later becoming a sincere supporter of the Augustan settlement. Maecenas gave him a small farm in the Sabine Hills at Tivoli near Rome. There Horace built a villa which he celebrated in his poems, but he was also a sociable man of the world.

Horace's *Satires* (*c.* 35BC) contain little satire in today's sense but praise Maecenas, a friend as well as patron, and include a tribute to his father, in lively, colloquial Latin. Celebrating peace after Actium (31BC), Horace produced the *Epodes* (lyric poems). Inspired by Archilochus (*c.* 640BC), they deal mostly with love and politics but also praise rural life: *Beatus ille, qui procul negotiis…* ("Happy the man who far from business, ploughs again his ancestral lands").

The poor reception for his first book of *Odes* in 23BC upset him, but they contain his finest poetry. They celebrate the return of spring: *Diffugere nives: redeunt jam gramina campis/Arboribusque comae…*

("The snows have fled. The grass returns already to the meadows, and leaves to the trees"); the joys of drinking: *Nunc est bibendum* ("Now's the time to drink!") and the passing of youth: *Ehue fugace, Postume, Postume/Labuntur anni, nec pietas moram…*("Alas, Postumus, Postumus, the years slide swiftly away and piety will not fend off wrinkles, old age or death…"). He ends triumphantly, proclaiming artistic immortality: *Exegi monumentum aere perennius* ("I have created a work longer-lasting than bronze…").

Horace had no successor as poet laureate, but some poems speak as freshly today as ever: *Dum loquimur, fugeret invida/Aetas: carpe diem, quam minimum credula postero.* ("While we talk, hateful time runs on. Seize the fruits of today, never rely on the future.")

*Above: A mural from Pompeii showing a wounded Aeneas being tended by a doctor.*

*Below: Virgil reading* The Aeneid *to Augustus, as painted by Ingres, c. 1812.*

# CATULLUS AND THE ELEGIAC POETS

*Above: The Venus de Milo, one of the most famous portrayals of the goddess of love in antiquity. Venus was a deity of overwhelming importance to the elegiac poets, whose poems deal primarily with affairs of the heart and of lust.*

*Below: Catullus, the supreme Latin poet of love, fancifully depicted reading a poem, in a painting by Stepan Bakalovich in 1885. In reality, Catullus was passionate but hardly romantic like this.*

The last decades of the Republic and first years of the Empire (Principate) saw huge political and social changes in Roman life that inspired the *Neoterici* (New Poets) to experiment radically. Greek models gave Catullus, then Propertius and Tibullus, the means by which to create new, more direct and moving forms of Latin poetry. (The description of these poets' work as Elegiac refers to their hexameter/pentameter metre. It does not mean that they wrote funereally!)

### CATULLUS 84–54BC

Born at Verona, Catullus (Gaius Valerius Catullus) was a leader of the *Neoterici*, or New Poets. His father was rich enough to entertain Julius Caesar but Catullus had no interest in politics. He owned a villa on Lake Garda, whose beauties he praised, but spent most of his short life in Rome and most of his energies on literature and love. In Rome he fell in love with Clodia, called Lesbia in his poems, who was probably the sister of Clodius Pulcher – Cicero's enemy – and Catullus'

social superior. Lesbia/Clodia became his obsession, adored then reviled in 25 brilliant, brief poems. For poetic models Catullus looked back to polished Alexandrians such as Callimachus (*c.* 320–240BC) and to Sappho (*c.* 600BC), perhaps the greatest woman poet, who wrote on love's bitter-sweet joys and torments. Catullus' poetry, mingling passion, urbanity and awareness of life's transience, raised colloquial Latin to new heights.

*Amemus mea Lesbia atque vivemus/ Rumoresque senum severiorum.* "Let us live and love my Lesbia, and ignore all old men's censorious talk", begins one poem addressed to her, which continues, "We, when our brief day is done, must sleep in everlasting night". He goes on to urge her in vivid, demotic Latin, *Da mi basia mille, deinde centum /Dein mille altera, dein secunda centum.* "Give me a thousand kisses, then a hundred, then another thousand and a second hundred".

Unlike most Greek poets, Catullus was writing about an individual woman at a time when aristocratic women in Rome were enjoying novel freedom and could appreciate – or reject – such admiration. Clodia seems to have rejected him, so Catullus later wrote angrily, *Odi et amo*, "I hate and I love" and described Lesbia "Giving herself to the sons of Remus", (becoming a common prostitute).

Catullus could also write in other ways. He lyrically mocked Lesbia's dead sparrow, for example: *Lugete, o Veneres Cupidenesque…* "Mourn, you Venuses and Cupids, and all men of true feeling. My lady's sparrow is dead". He also savagely lampooned his contemporaries.

Although what won Catullus contemporary renown were long mythological poems such as *Peleus and Thetis*, he was indisputably one the world's greatest lyric love poets.

## PROPERTIUS *c.* 54–16BC

Son of an equestrian (knight) of Perugia, Propertius (Sextus Propertius) probably had a legal training in Rome as a young man. In Rome he became friends with Virgil and Ovid and then with Maecenas, who gave him a house on the fashionable Equiline Hill. Propertius, however, had little interest in political life and refused Maecenas' request to write an epic about Augustus. Instead, his poems concentrate on his love life, especially his relationship with Cynthia.

Cynthia seems to have been either a high-class courtesan or a widow of independent mind and wealth. She used both to torment Propertius – or so his poems imply, depicting him in a grovelling role that was novelly demeaning for a Roman knight. His first book of poems was dedicated to, and about, Cynthia. *Non ego nunc tristes vereor mea Cynthia, Manes/Nec moro extremo debita fata rogo* … "I don't fear death's sad kingdom, Cynthia, nor resent being doomed to the funeral pyre at the last, as I have a fear that is harder than death itself – that I may no longer be loved by you when I die". Propertius' affair with Cynthia started in *c.* 30BC and lasted about five years, during which time his passion cooled as Cynthia was often unfaithful to him. For solace from love's torment Propertius turned not to nature – he was very metropolitan – but to art. He talked knowledgeably about classical Greek painters such as Apelles and some of his poems apparently describe scenes from extant wall-paintings.

## TIBULLUS *c.* 50–19BC

Handsome and wealthy, the son of an equestrian, Tibullus (Albius Tibullus) differed from Propertius in his love for the countryside. His first poems describe an idyllic existence far from city cares. However, Tibullus resembled Propertius in that he too was in thrall to a mistress. Delia – another pseudonym – had little time for such bucolic joys and clearly had the upper hand in their relationship. Her successor in Tibullus' affection was the even more demanding and ominously named Nemesis. Tibullus also fell in love with a boy, Marathus, who spurned him but used him to help pursue a girl. Tibullus dwells masochistically on his suffering in this love triangle. It is uncertain how much of the three extant books in Tibullus' name is really his own poetry.

## MAECENAS THE PATRON

The greatest literary patron of the Roman empire under Augustus, Maecenas claimed descent from Etruscan kings. One of the young Octavian's key ministers, he was renowned for discovering promising poets. Virgil and Horace were protégés who repaid his support with great poetry praising the new regime. Maecenas himself reputedly had luxurious, even decadent tastes, as surviving fragments of his own poetry suggest, affronting Augustus' official restoration of Roman *virtus*. Maecenas lost official favour well before his death in 8BC, but his name lives on as the archetypal patron.

*Above: The* Surrender of Briseis, *from the House of the Tragic Poet at Pompeii. Briseis was a slave girl in* The Iliad *who Achilles, bitterly jealous, had to hand over to Agamemnon. Catullus wrote on the subject with typical bittersweet passion.*

*Below: A view of Lake Garda in northern Italy, Catullus' birthplace, whose beauties he was the first to praise.*

# OVID AND LATER SILVER AGE POETS

*Above: An amber figurine of Cupid and Psyche from the 1st century AD. Ovid's poetry delighted in such myths.*

*Below: Ovid's grandest and most celebrated work, the* Metamorphoses, *had a huge impact on later artists and writers. This grand depiction of the myth of Cupid and Psyche was painted by the Renaissance artist Raphael (or his studio) in 1518–19.*

With Ovid, Latin poetry finally attained an elegance, lyricism and wit to rival that of any Greek. His unfading popularity down the ages is partly due to these characteristics, partly to his fantastical invention and partly to his sophisticated eroticism – the last finally led to banishment by Augustus. After Ovid, there was a hiatus in Latin poetry, then two poets of the "silver age" emerged, who attempted with mixed success to emulate the poets of the golden age.

### OVID 43BC–c. AD18

Born to an equestrian Italian family, Ovid (Publius Ovidius Naso) finished his education with the customary grand tour of Greece before settling in Rome. His first book of poems was the very successful *Amores* (*Loves*). He began writing the first book of the first edition c. 25BC, publishing the other four books over the next decade. (The surviving edition dates from

c. 3BC.) In his early books Ovid parodied the elegiac poets' love sickness but soon Ovid himself emerged as a fervent if light-hearted lover. Addressed to Corinna – who, unlike the lovers of earlier poets, was probably not an actual mistress, but a composite figure – the *Amores* depict amorous adventures among the more openly frivolous Roman upper classes. In the *Amores*, as in subsequent works, Ovid used myths not for deep psychological resonance but decoratively, to describe a woman's legs for example. If Horace tended to treat love as a light-hearted game from which the poet remains wisely detached, Ovid treated love as the only game worth playing. The title of Ovid's *Ars Amatoria* (*The Art of Love*) mimicks Horace's *Ars Poetica*.

Ovid's longest and most lastingly famous work was the *Metamorphoses*, 15 books of mythology which are epic in scale and by turn bewitching, moving, erotic

or witty. At the other end of the scale from Virgil's solemn myth-making, its underlying theme – that everything changes form – included serious comments among its erotica, such as *Video meliora, proboque;/Detrioria sequor* ("I see the better way and approve it, but follow the worse") and *Tempus edax rerum* ("Time, the devourer of all things").

### OVID'S EXILE AND DEATH

While many Romans laughed with Ovid, one important Roman was not amused: the ageing emperor. Always annoyed by upper-class promiscuity, Augustus particularly disliked his grand-daughter Julia's behaviour, exiling her for immorality suddenly in AD8. Ovid, caught up in the scandal, was exiled to Tomis on the Black Sea, a cold, uncivilized, remote area, now in Bulgaria, then Rome's Siberia. Augustus and his successor Tiberius stonily ignored the poet's piteous pleas to be allowed to return, and Ovid died in exile among a people he found barbarous.

In his last decade Ovid wrote *Tristia* (*Melancholia*) and *Epistulae ex Ponto* (*Black Sea Letters*). The lonely tedium of exile is conveyed by lines such as *Gutta cavat lapidem, consumitur anulus usu* ("Dripping water hollows out a stone, a ring is worn away by use"). However, his fame suffered no eclipse. He was revered throughout the Middle Ages and a bowdlerized version of his works called *Ovid Moralisé* (*Ovid the Moralist*) was circulated widely. The first great poet in English, Geoffrey Chaucer (1340–1400) wrote of "Venus' clerk, Ovid, that hath sown wonder-wide the great god of Love's name". Ovid's fame continued to grow during the Renaissance and after, with many translations or adaptations especially of the *Metamorphoses*.

### SILVER AGE POETS

After Ovid's death no significant poet emerged for 40 years until Lucan (Marcus Annaeus Lucan; AD39–65). Born in Spain, a nephew of the philosopher Seneca, Lucan was studying Stoic philosophy in Athens when Nero called him to Rome in AD60. For a short while he enjoyed imperial favour, being made a *quaestor* (magistrate), before he became involved in the Piso conspiracy of aristocrats with Republican sentiments against the despotic emperor. It cost him his life.

Lucan's great work was his uncompleted epic *Pharsalia*, which deals with Rome's civil wars of the 1st century BC. He begins with an address to his fellow citizens, not the usual invocation of the Muse: *Quis furor, o cives, quae tanta licentia ferri?* ("What was this madness, citizens, this great orgy of slaughter?"). The epic lacks a hero – Julius Caesar is portrayed as villainous and his rival Pompey is not wholly admirable either. Instead it focuses on the internecine bloodshed that wrecked the Republic. Lucan's poem abounds in epigrams, paradoxes and biting wit, with over 100 grand speeches. However, it can be argued that his characters are over-simplifed, his style is sometimes monotonous and that at times Lucan's work degenerates into sentimentality.

Statius (Publius Papinius Statius; AD45–96) was an epic poet who also felt driven to emulate Virgil. His chief work, his *Thebaid*, took him a decade to write. Published in AD92, it dealt with the same Greek legends about Oedipus' curse on Thebesand its traumatic consequences that the Athenian dramatist Aeschylus had written about 500 years before. Statius' style is too highly polished and suggests that, like Lucan, he had talent rather than genius. Such legendary heroics were increasingly seen as dated anyway.

*Below: Apollo and Daphne, sculpted by Bernini in 1622. The beautiful myth of the transformation of Daphne into a myrtle was wittily retold by Ovid in his* Metamorphoses.

# GREAT PROSE WRITERS

*Above: Marcus Tullius Cicero, the great orator, lawyer, statesman and man of letters. Although seldom an original thinker, Cicero translated major works of Greek philosophy into Latin, summarizing their arguments brilliantly. His superbly readable* Letters *inspired generations with their humane and liberal outlook.*

Rome was a nation of orators schooled in the art of high rhetoric. To match this, Roman writers created prose of unsurpassed power, clarity, pithiness and at times majesty. While there were cogent earlier writers such as Cato the Elder (234–149BC), only in the 1st century BC did Latin prose began to achieve its full, formal splendours, as befitted the language of the new rulers of the world.

### CICERO 106–43BC

Marcus Tullius Cicero, statesman and lawyer, wrote on many subjects from astronomy to art and education and in so doing almost invented philosophy in Latin. Caesar, Cicero's political opponent and not modest about his own feats, said that Cicero's was "A greater achievement, expanding the boundaries of Rome's culture, than those of its empire".

Much of Cicero's work, including 900 letters, has survived. This is unusual but hardly accidental: it survived because it was admired and copied. To the critic Quintilian (AD30–c. 100) Cicero was "The name not of a man but of eloquence itself". Cicero's philosophy also deeply affected Augustine, the Christian writer.

Cicero made some of the most brilliant political and legal speeches in Roman history, such as that against Verres, the corrupt ex-governor of Sicily in 70BC, which drove Verres into exile. However, his career as a writer really flowered later during his enforced absence from politics when Caesar dominated Rome (49–44BC). Starting with two minor works of political philosophy *De republica* and *De legibus* (*On the State* and *On the Laws*), he went on to produce *The Paradoxes*

*of the Stoics*, a rhetorical masterpiece in which he argued both sides of a debate (he had studied in Athens under the Sceptics). In 45BC Cicero outlined a plan to "give my fellow citizens a guide to the noblest form of learning" (philosophy). He wrote twelve books over the next two years most – following Plato – in the form of dialogues covering the main schools of ancient philosophy. *De finibus* (*Concerning Ends*) is typical of his brilliant summary of earlier Greek thinkers, notably the Stoics, and is expressed eloquently and clearly in Latin.

Cicero seldom propounded fixed philosophical viewpoints, nor did he claim to be original in his thinking. Instead, however, he established the rendering of basic Greek philosophical terms into Latin – terms such as *qualitas, moralis, beatitudo* for "quality, moral, happiness" – that remain in use today.

In *Scipio's Dream*, Cicero also outlined current geocentric views on the nature of the universe. His letters reveal more about urbane, cultured upper-class Roman life in the late Republic than any others and are profoundly admired even today for their style and humanity.

*Right: Bust of Seneca, Roman statesman, playwright and philosopher. He was Nero's tutor and adviser before being forced to kill himself.*

## SENECA 4BC–AD65

A Stoic philosopher, tutor and then minister to the young Nero, a successful if at times unscrupulous businessman, Seneca (Lucius Annaeus Seneca) was also a noted essayist and Rome's greatest tragic playwright.

Seneca's nine plays all deal with Greek legends and have titles such as *Oedipus*, *Hercules* and *Medea*. They are "closet tragedies", intended to be read aloud at small, aristocratic gatherings rather than performed in large Roman theatres.

Although Seneca's dramas hardly bear comparison with their prototypes in classical Athens, they proved very influential later, inspiring Shakespeare and other Renaissance dramatists. His *Epistulae Morales* (*Moral Letters*), 124 brief sermons in letter form dealing with subjects from vegetarianism to the humane treatment of slaves, were equally influential. He also wrote longer essays such as *De clementia* (*On Mercy*).

Seneca was eventually forced to kill himself by Nero after he had been implicated in the Piso conspiracy to assassinate the emperor.

## PLINY THE ELDER AD23–79

Pliny (Gaius Plinius Secundus) was a successful Roman administrator of the equestrian order as well as a writer of a boundless, indeed reckless, curiosity that finally killed him. Although he also wrote a history of the German wars, the work which has survived is his *Natural History*. This consists of 37 volumes that represent an encyclopaedia of Graeco-Roman knowledge of the universe, humanity, animals, trees, birds and plants, while also covering in detail medicine and the arts. Edward Gibbon later described it as "An immense register of the discoveries, the arts and the errors of mankind", for Pliny sometimes seems credulous to modern eyes. As commander of the fleet at Misenum near Naples during Vesuvius' eruption in AD79, he tried without success to investigate it and to organize relief efforts but was probably asphyxiated on shore by volcanic gases.

## PLINY THE YOUNGER AD61–c. 112

The studious nephew of the elder Pliny who wisely stayed behind at Misenum while his uncle sailed off with the fleet, Pliny the Younger (Gaius Plinius Caecilius Secundus) was tutored by Quintilian.

Pliny had a successful senatorial career, and he finally became a consul under Trajan in AD100. He thanked the emperor for this in his *Panegyricus*, which reveals a talent for fulsome flattery. Far livelier are his letters, many of them written for publication, which give a vivid picture of their age from a cultured noble's viewpoint. His letters to Trajan, written when he was the conscientious if somewhat flustered governor of Bithynia (in north Asia Minor) are also revealing. They cover topics from local fire brigades to the proper way to treat alarming new sects such as the Christians. Pliny the Younger probably died in office.

*Above: Using mud to cure skin complaints, as recommended by Pliny the Elder, in a book of 1481.*

*Below: The oldest extant manuscript of Pliny the Younger's Letters, dating from the early 6th century AD.*

# NOVELISTS AND SATIRISTS

*Right: The dreamlike, lyrical quality of Apuleius'* The Golden Ass *is echoed in this mosaic from Asia Minor of the 3rd century* AD. *It illustrates the myth of Cupid and Psyche, which forms the core of the book.*

*Below: Martial had the whole Flavian dynasty as his patrons, including an unlikely patron in the dour and despotic emperor Domitian (below), chiefly because he only attacked men who had prospered under Nero.*

After the heroic age of Roman literature, writers turned increasingly to satire in prose or verse – Juvenal's biting wit effectively created satire in its modern sense – or to novels that were satirical, romantic or both. However, prose fiction was considered a very low literary form.

## PETRONIUS (d. AD66)

One of Latin literature's most colourful figures, Petronius (Gaius Petronius Arbiter) was a Roman aristocrat about whom little is known. According to Tacitus, writing decades later, "His days were passed in sleep, his nights in the business and pleasures of life. The reputation that most men win through energy he gained through sloth. Yet as governor of Bithynia and later as consul, he showed himself highly competent". One of Nero's courtiers, Petronius was implicated in the Piso conspiracy and committed suicide – but not before he had recorded all Nero's vices and sent off the list and smashed a precious vase he knew the emperor wanted. His one surviving book – unmentioned by the historian – is his *Satyricon*, a sprawling picaresque novel about some insatiably bisexual adventurers, devoid of morals if not of intelligence, who wander around the Greek cities of southern Italy. They all have Greek names – Encolpion the cultured but depraved narrator, his faithless boyfriend Giton, Ascyltos his rival – following Roman theatrical custom. The most remarkable figure is that of Trimalchio, the multimillionaire freedman (ex-slave) whose gross vulgarity dominates many passages. Petronius was better at catching "street Latin", everyday language, than any writer since Plautus. He records but does not judge – not even the clause of Trimalchio's will which stipulates that all his legatees eat a bit of his corpse before they can inherit. The novel, of which only Books XV and XVI survive, was long considered obscene.

## APULEIUS (b. *c.* AD127)

Born in North Africa and educated at Carthage and Athens, Apuleius (Lucius Apuleius) lectured and travelled extensively. He also wrote the only Latin novel to survive complete, *The Golden Ass*. This relates in eleven books the amorous and comic incidents which lead Lucius, a sorcerer's apprentice, to be transformed into a donkey. The rest of the work recounts his varied adventures and misadventures in this form until his final restoration to human shape by the goddess Isis. The longest of these episodes, which takes up about a fifth of the book, is the tale of Cupid (Greek Eros) and Psyche. Parts of this tale, and even more the closing section's vision of Isis, are described with a true religious intensity which is unusually revealing of the depth of pagan devotion to the gods, especially in such an essentially light-hearted work. Although Apuleius may have derived his tale from the Greek poet Lucian's *Metamorphoses*, he wrote a strange, poetic, beautiful and original form of Latin.

## MARTIAL (AD40–*c.* 104)

Probably the greatest master of the epigram – a short, sometimes very short, poem with a sting in its tail – Martial (Marcus Valerius Martialis) was born in Spain but spent most of his adult life in Rome. Some 1,500 of his poems survive. Probably helped by his compatriot Seneca at first, he came to know people close to the emperor Domitian, in whose reign (AD81–96) he enjoyed his greatest success. Martial can be human, even genial when writing about children or pets, although at other times his work is blatantly pornographic. An early poem, *Liber Spectaculorum* of AD81, celebrated the opening of the Colosseum but he got into his stride with the *Xenia* and *Aphoreta*, which were written between the mid-80s AD and AD97, when he retired to Spain. Martial's dismissive two-liner "On a Critic" is typically pithy: *Versiculos in me narratur scribere Cinna/Non scribit, cuius carmina nemo legit.* ("Cinna is said to write versicles against me. A man whose poems nobody reads cannot be called a writer.")

## JUVENAL (*c.* AD60–*c.* 130)

The greatest Roman satirist and the first poet to devote himself to satire in our sense, Juvenal (Decimus Junius Juvenalis) came from a well-off family

and held local magistracies. He then fell foul of the emperor Domitian and may have been banished to Egypt before returning to a life of embittered poverty in Rome. His situation improved later under Hadrian and he ended his life in modest comfort, with a small country estate as well as his Roman residence.

Juvenal's early experiences helped shape the jaundiced view he gives of Roman life in which *probitas laudatur et alget* ("Honesty is praised and starves"). His 16 *Satires* were published in 5 books between AD110 and 130. In the first he declared his *saeva indignatio* (fierce indignation) at Roman corruption and vulgarity, but his prudent intention was to attack mainly those who had flourished under Domitian. He lambasted the aristocracy's bad habits – venality, parsimony, sexual voracity – in his first book. *Satire VI* contains a 700-line-long diatribe against women. Markedly misogynistic, it attacks female vanity and virtue. Later satires attack life in the megalopolis more generally: *duas tantum res anxius optat/panem et circuses* ("The populace longs for just two things: bread and circus games").

*Left: Manuscript from the 15th century with a page of Juvenal's satires. The first great poet who can be considered wholly satirical, Juvenal's devastating honesty proved inspirational to later Western satirists.*

*Below: Juvenal savaged women for wearing too much jewellery in a way that could be markedly misogynistic, so setting an unfortunate example for some later satirists. This mummy portrait of a woman is from Egypt, c. AD120.*

# LATE ROMAN WRITERS

*Above: The Moselle, whose vineyards and slopes Ausonius praised in his longest and most famous poem, Mosella.*

*Below: St Augustine grew up in the still-thriving province of Africa, whose splendid town life is revealed by these extensive 3rd-century mosaics from Carthage.*

The decline of the empire did not see the end of Latin literature, which continued even after Rome's final political collapse in AD476.

### AUSONIUS (*c.* AD310–95)
A native of Bordeaux, at whose university he both studied and lectured, Ausonius (Decimus Magnus Ausonius) was a prolific if uneven poet. A summons to the imperial court at Trier to be tutor to the young emperor Gratian led to his meteoric rise: he became governor of Gaul, then Africa and in AD379 consul. After Gratian's murder in AD383, he returned to his native Bordeaux. Letters to his friend St Paulinus of Nola reveal the widening gap between pagans and Christians – Ausonius was basically a pagan. Ausonius' most famous poem, which is lyrical if unoriginal, sings the praise of the beauties of the Moselle valley that he had seen around Trier.

### PERVIGILIUM VENERIS (*c.* AD350)
Both the author and date of this beautiful poem are unknown. The title means "Venus' Vigil" and the poem celebrates in 93 haunting, romantic lines the eve of the spring festival of Venus in rural Sicily; the upsurge of new life in flowers, animals and humanity. It has as its refrain *Cras amet quis nunquam amavit…*("Tomorrow let them love who have never loved; and let those who have loved love tomorrow. Spring is new, spring full of song, the springtime of the world is reborn.") Its language forms a link between classical and medieval Latin, while its content makes it a swansong of paganism.

### ST AUGUSTINE (AD354–430)
One of the great Church fathers, whose writings are fundamental to both Protestantism and Catholicism, Augustine is also an important figure in both literature and philosophy.

Born in Tagaste, North Africa, his mother was a devout Christian but his father only a reluctant convert. The young Augustine, tormented by sexual urges yet drawn to philosophy, joined the Manicheans, who believed the whole physical world was ruled by the devil. Augustine began teaching in Carthage in AD371 and had a 12-year-long relationship with a woman who bore his son. He only returned to Christianity in AD385 after his move to Rome and a mystical experience in a garden when he heard the voice of God. Intellectually he was influenced both by the teachings of Ambrose, Archbishop of Milan, and by Plotinus, the Neoplatonist whose pagan mysticism Augustine fused with Christianity.

Augustine now began writing the books that make him among the most eloquent of theologians: *Against the Academics, On the Greatness of the Soul, On Free Will* and *Against Faustus the Manichean.* In AD396

*Right: The Wheel of Fortune shown in this 15th-century manuscript was one of Boethius' main ideas, inspired by life and death.*

he became bishop of Hippo, an African city. He preached to the local people in lively demotic Latin, while writing a more formal classical Latin for his literary peers. His *Confessions*, his literary masterpiece of *c.* AD400, shows an honest, even agonized self-scrutiny unmatched until the 18th century. "Oh Lord make me chaste but not yet!" is its most famous line.

Augustine aggressively propounded orthodox Catholic beliefs against heretics such as the Donatists – who believed that only sinless priests should serve Mass – and Pelagius, a Romano-Briton who believed in human perfectibility. In *On Grace and Free Will*, he argued that every human was damned to hell unless God through his grace saved us from our sins. This gloomy doctrine suggested damnation for the majority.

Another pivotal work was *The City of God*. This was written after the Visigoths sacked Rome in AD410 to rebut pagan charges that Rome's desertion of its old gods was to blame. Augustine essentially held that the kingdom of God was not of this world, although we ourselves have to live in it. Such beliefs were needed, for Augustine died as the Vandals – barbarians who deserved their infamy – besieged the city of Hippo.

## NAMATIANUS (fl. AD404–16)

One of the last important non-Christian Roman poets, Namatianus (Claudius Rutilius Namatianus) came from Toulouse. Despite his paganism, Namatianus became Prefect of Rome under the (Christian) emperor Honorius.

Although he left Rome in AD416 soon after its sack by the Visigoths, Namatianus' parting poem expresses undimmed confidence in Rome's eternal glory. *Exaudi, regina tui pulcherrima mundi/Inter sidereos Roma recepta polos…* ("Listen, most beautiful queen of the world you have made your own. O Rome

received into the starry heavens/Listen, O mother of gods and men.") There were to be no further such pagan panegyrics of the Eternal City.

## BOETHIUS (*c.* AD480–526)

Although he was a Christian, Boethius (Amicus Manlius Severinus Boethius) never mentioned Christianity in his work. He came from an old aristocratic family, became consul in AD510 and then chief minister to Theodoric, king of the Ostrogoths, who was ruling Italy remarkably well. Boethius was implicated, probably unjustly, in a conspiracy against the king and sentenced to death. While in prison awaiting execution, he wrote *The Consolation of Philosophy* in a mixture of verse and prose. In this work, the most popular philosophical book in Western Europe for 1,000 years, Boethius drew on Platonist, Neoplatonist and Stoic ideas. He also provided much general intellectual knowledge that proved invaluable in the Middle Ages in a clear, classical Latin. He was the last such writer.

*Below: This ancient Roman statue and the Pervigilium Veneris are both beautiful invocations to Venus.*

# LITERATURE AND LITERACY

Literacy was relatively widespread in the cities of the Roman empire, at least in the sense of being able to read and write the odd inscription, if not to read major pieces of literature. Despite the lack of a formal education system, especially beyond the primary level, for all but the children of a small elite – even they relied heavily on private tutors – it seems that many people in towns and cities were at least semi-literate, as the abundant graffiti and marks on potsherds (pottery fragments) or walls testify. These ordinary citizens were, however, only a minority of the empire's inhabitants. At least 80 per cent of the population were peasants.

A certain degree of literacy was essential for advancement in public life and very useful elsewhere, not just in the households of great nobles or in the imperial bureaucracy that very gradually grew out of the emperor's own household.

In the absence of printing technology, literate slaves and later monks painstakingly (and sometimes inaccurately) copied manuscripts. Cheap, convenient writing writing materials were also lacking. The two rival materials papyrus and parchment were both very expensive. (The Chinese are credited with inventing paper which was later adopted by Europe.) Instead, Romans had wax tablets, which were used and reused. While many citizens

*Above: A wall painting from Pompeii shows a young woman, once thought to be the Greek poet Sappho, pausing for thought.*

of the empire may have been literate, fewer probably had access to much literature. Few would have been able to read the Latin classics regularly or easily, for books or scrolls were very expensive in real terms. While papyrus fragments of Virgil's *Aeneid* found on Hadrian's Wall show that some knowledge of the classical canon was widespread, scrolls or books remained relatively few and much-cherished, lent only with caution even to close friends. Symmachus, the wealthy, cultured late 4th century AD Roman aristocrat, offered a would-be historian of Gaul his copy of Caesar's *Gallic Wars* only as a special favour.

### ANCIENT LIBRARIES

Culture in the Graeco-Roman world remained overwhelmingly oral and declamation in public was the commonest means by which new books were published. (Traditionally, even the fully literate read everything aloud, though some historians now doubt this.) Both public and private libraries of any size were so few as to be noteworthy. In Pompeii, so far only one villa, the Villa

*Above: A 1st-century AD portrait from Pompeii shows the young Roman magistrate Terentius Nero and his wife. The image of the young couple pensively clutching writing materials reveals that women as well as men could read and write.*

*Below: Typical writing materials – a wooden tablet with three panels, a bronze inkwell and a stylus – from the 1st century AD. Papyrus, then the best writing material, was too expensive for most people for everyday use.*

of the Papyri, has been found to contain a significant number of scrolls. Although carbonized, they are slowly being deciphered. The emperor Gordianus III (AD238–44) reputedly had 60,000 tomes in his own library. This suggests a distinctly cultured emperor and was unusual enough to merit recording at the time.

The greatest library of the ancient world at Alexandria had around 500,000 volumes. Athens also had renowned public libraries. In the 2nd century AD, Rome reputedly had 39 libraries, although few if any of these were lending libraries. (The library behind Trajan's Basilica was divided into Greek and Latin sections.) Unlike public baths, aqueducts or amphitheatres, public libraries were not an automatic or even usual attribute of the typical Roman city. Ultimately, when urban life almost collapsed in the 5th and 6th centuries AD, monastic libraries became the chief repositories of Roman manuscripts. However, most Latin literature did not survive at all.

## PAPYRUS v. PARCHMENT

The commonest way of writing in the Roman world before *c.* AD250 was on papyrus, made from the papyrus plant that grows abundantly only on the banks of the Nile. (Tiny amounts grow elsewhere, such as Syracuse, but this did not affect Egypt's monopoly, which also sustained its high price.) Papyrus was manufactured into scrolls up 25ft (8m) long. Unrolling such scrolls while reading was difficult – a slave's help was useful – and they were easily torn. More expensive than even the best paper today, papyrus was also more fragile and less durable.

The Romans did not use clay tablets for literary works, although bureaucratic records on clay tablets survive in some abundance from Egyptian and a few Mesopotamian sites. Parchment, made from animal hides and far tougher than papyrus, was first made in the Hellenistic kingdom of Pergamum (Asia Minor). By the 1st century BC parchment sheets tied together with thongs were being used for commercial records. A century later, parchment was being used for literary texts as a *codex*, initially for cheaper editions. By AD200 this format was starting to replace papyrus scrolls.

The advent of Christianity in the 4th century AD accelerated this process. It was easier to find and read a passage from the Bible from a *codex* than a scroll and codices were also suited to legal documents. (Hence our term codex.) However, papyrus continued to be used until the Arab conquest of the Mediterranean in the 7th century AD finally cut Western Europe off from supplies in Egypt.

# CHAPTER VIII

# THE ARTS

If Roman art was heavily indebted to the Greeks, it soon developed its own characteristics, especially in portraiture and in reliefs commemorating particular historic events. Among opposed artistic currents are those of native *veristic* (realistic) art versus idealised Greek art and metropolitan versus provincial. The art of classical Greece long epitomized perfection to Rome's ruling class (and to many artists) and was much copied. Augustus in particular employed classical art in the service of the state.

Sculpture has generally survived better than painting, in part because of its sheer quantity. In the 4th century AD it was claimed that the city of Rome contained as many statues as it did people. This was an exaggeration – there were perhaps 700,000 Romans – but contemporary surveys record 154 gold or ivory, 22 equestrian and 3,785 bronze statues. Few bronzes survive as valuable metal statues were melted down. Marble statues still intact have lost their paint, giving an unduly marmoreal impression today. Inevitably, these sculptures mostly depict the rich and powerful.

Fortunately for posterity, the eruption of Vesuvius in AD79 preserved the wall paintings of more ordinary houses in Pompeii and Herculaneum. Other murals unearthed from Nero's palace display imperial taste in the mid-1st century AD. Art became flamboyant under the Flavians, then came a Greek revival under Hadrian. By *c.* AD330, the long tradition of classical realism was giving way to the more stylized art that we call Byzantine.

*Left: The arrival of Io in Egypt, a painting from the 1st century AD, shows Roman wall-painting in its prime, almost three-dimensionally realistic but also romantically poetic.*

# THE ETRUSCANS AND THE EARLY REPUBLIC

*Above: The Apollo of Veii of c. 500BC, a terracotta masterpiece of Etruscan sculpture, shows Greek influence interpreted by Italian craftsmen. The enigmatic archaic smile is typical of statues of the time.*

Little distinctively Roman art survives from the city's first centuries, when Rome was much influenced by its neighbours, the Etruscans. The latter, it is now accepted, were an indigenous Italian people like the Romans, not newcomers from Asia Minor as ancient legends suggest. In the 6th century BC they established a confederacy of 12 cities across central Italy. Their cultural influence extended south to the Bay of Naples and dominated Rome well after the traditional expulsion of King Tarquinius in 509BC that led to the founding of the Republic.

## ETRUSCAN VIVACITY

While the Etruscans were wealthy, Rome itself probably became economically poorer in the 5th century BC. The Etruscans were induced by the Greek vases they imported to copy Greek legends as well as styles, but they did so with novel vigour and colour. Most of their statues were made of brightly painted terracotta (baked earth) rather than the marble and stone which were so abundant in Greece. The Etruscans were also formidable bronze smiths. Roman art was for a time little more than a variant of Etruscan and the artists themselves were probably often Etruscan.

Etruscan vivacity is manifest in the Apollo of Veii, taken from the temple of the Etruscan city that Rome captured in 396BC. Dating from *c.* 500BC, this life-size terracotta statue shows the god striding forward in a long flowing robe with an enigmatic "archaic" smile. The contrast with the still static *kouroi* (naked male figures) of contemporary Greek archaic art is marked but the Etruscans lacked the idealizing drive that was about to create Greek classical art. Although the Etruscan Apollo is walking, the upper part of his clothed body shows no real sign of movement, suggesting that the sculptor had not studied the nude body as the Greeks did. The statue, whose colours faintly survive, is the grandest of the terracotta statues that adorned the roofs of most Etruscan and

*Right: The Wounded Chimaera of Arezzo, c. 380BC. This mythical creature, which bristles with almost electric menace, represents the peak of Etruscan bronze casting.*

early Roman temples. A fine sarcophagus, from *c.* 500BC, which depicts the terracotta figures of a couple reclining connubially on top of their coffin, also comes from Veii. Later the Etruscans began to portray individuals more realistically, as in the limestone and stucco Urn of Arnth Velimnas from the Tomb of the Volumni in Perugia of *c.* 150BC. Arnth Velimnas is depicted with a paunch.

Probably the earliest statue in Rome itself is the Capitoline Wolf, a bronze dating from *c.* 500BC whose pointed teeth and jutting ribs still radiate feral savagery. The statue illustrates the myth of Rome's foundation, when a she-wolf suckled the abandoned divine twins Romulus and Remus. It could be the statue referred to by Cicero that was struck by lightning on the Capitoline, although the figures of the twins are Renaissance additions or replacements. Even more aggressive is the Wounded Chimaera from Arezzo of *c.* 380BC, a creature that in myth breathed fire and here bristles with electric menace. Both are superb examples of the early bronze working skills developed in Italy.

Roman artists also created fine busts or statues of prominent men, always a vital art in Rome. Unlike the Greeks, Roman artists normally concentrated on depicting the face, which from the start they portrayed more realistically. The finest surviving such statue from the earlier Republic is the so-called Brutus, once thought to portray the Roman noble who, according to legend, helped to expel the last Etruscan king. The bronze is now thought to date from *c.* 300BC, two centuries later, but it catches the determination, intelligence and dignity of a noble Roman. There is a thin-lipped grimness about the figure which is appropriate to the men who would lead Rome through the long trials of the Punic Wars.

Work such as this shows Greek influence creatively mediated by Italic veristic (realistic) traditions. This would become less possible after Rome's conquest of the rich Hellenistic world led highly skilled Greek artists to flood into the city.

*Above: The Ambush of Troilus by Achilles, from Tarquinia, is typical of c. 540BC. It shows the Etruscans' awareness of Greek myths and style but interprets both in their own distinctive manner.*

## ETRUSCAN TOMB PAINTING

The Etruscans' superb tomb paintings are interesting as little painting has survived from the ancient world outside Egypt. (According to Pliny the Elder, Fabius Pictor (Fabius the Painter) painted superb battle scenes inside the Temple of Salus in *c.* 300BC, but these are now lost.)

The Etruscan *Ambush of Troilus by Achilles* from the Tomb of the Bulls from Tarquinia in southern Tuscany illustrates a scene from Homer's *Iliad*. It reveals Etruscan knowledge of Greek culture and myth as early as 540BC. The technique used is dark silhouettes for most people and distinct outlines for Troilus' horse, the lions and the blocks of the fountain.

Another delightful tomb painting is that from the Tomb of Hunting and Fishing of the same period. It depicts birds and boys climbing rocks and diving.

From the Tomb of Orcus in the 4th century BC comes the profile of a beautiful woman called Velia, crowned with leaves and with her hair hanging loose. Greek classicism is evident here, but again mediated by Etruscan taste. All this is very far from the art trumpeting military or dynastic glories that was to become the Roman norm.

*Above: The so-called Brutus, a fine bronze statue from c. 300BC, shows Greek influences in its style but is very Roman in its subject matter: a dignified Roman nobleman of the sort who would soon have to face the threat of Hannibal.*

# ART IN THE LATER REPUBLIC: 211–31BC

*Above: A fantasy city painted with almost perfect perspective in the bedroom of a villa at Boscoreale near Pompeii in the 1st century* BC.

*Below: The reliefs from the Temple of Neptune in Rome (formerly called the Altar of Domitius Ahenobarbus) mingle Greek style and Roman subject matter in a way very typical of the time, c. 100*BC.

In 211BC the Roman general Marcellus captured and sacked Syracuse, the great Greek metropolis of the West, bringing home art treasures that bedazzled the Romans. "Before this Rome knew nothing of these exquisite refined things… rather it was full of barbaric weapons and bloody spoils of war", wrote Plutarch 300 years later. He was exaggerating but in the following decades Greek artworks indeed poured into Rome as its armies returned triumphant from the eastern Mediterranean. Corinth fell to Roman arms in 146BC and the sophisticated kingdom of Pergamum was bequeathed peacefully in 133BC.

**ADAPTING GREEK STYLE**

With the artworks came Hellenistic artists whose impact was for a time overwhelming (although the native veristic tradition of portraiture survived only marginally modified). Demand for Greek artworks among Roman nobles became so insatiable that artists began copying them in the often repetitive Neo-Attic style. Unlike their Greek originals, many such copies have survived.

Greek influence from southern Italy appears in the simple, elegant Ionic *volutes* (scrolls) of the Sarcophagus of Lucius Cornelius Scipio c. 200BC. The first relief depicting a Roman historical event is the marble frieze of the monument to Aemilius Paullus at Delphi in Greece, which was erected after his victory at Pydna in 168BC. It features a specific event from the battle – a bolting riderless horse – in a way that is typically Roman although Greek artists sculpted it. Paullus brought back to Rome the Athenian painter Metrodoros, one among many imported Greek artists.

The famous reliefs in marble from the Temple of Neptune in Rome (once called the Altar of Domitius Ahenobarbus) of *c.* 100BC mingle Greek and Roman motifs. Three sides depict the usual mythological scenes – the wedding of Amphitrite and Neptune for example – with typical Hellenistic flair, but the fourth shows a mundane scene of Roman census-taking. This is handled more awkwardly as the unknown artist(s) struggled to adapt Greek style to Roman demands for commemorative works. It is possible that this last side was added to an existing altar.

A less happy adaptation of Greek styles was the practice of putting Roman portrait heads on to idealized Greek statues. The so-called Pseudo-athlete, in which the head of an Italian businessman of *c.* 80BC tops the heroic torso of a Greek athlete, is typical. The middle-aged Roman has

the head of a clearly older man and a well muscled torso with drapery around the hips. Equally ridiculous was the way some Roman magnates allowed themselves to be portrayed as Hellenistic god-kings in emulation of Alexander the Great. Pompey, hailed as a god on his victorious march through the Hellenistic East (66–62BC), was portrayed with an Alexander-style quiff that sits like a wig above his middle-aged Roman features.

Balancing this uncritical importation of things Greek was the veristic style favoured by more conservative Romans who had no taste for fancy foreign art and who preferred styles that reflected older Republican virtues. Instead, they favoured an almost excessively realistic portraiture style that emphasizes every wrinkle and furrow, such as the "Republican portraits" from the mid-1st century. These portraits may have been taken from the death masks many Romans kept in their homes for the worship of ancestors.

### POMPEIIAN ART: THE FIRST STYLES

The small but wealthy cities of Pompeii and Herculaneum in Campania, near Naples, were very open to Greek influences. They have the best preserved Roman mosaics and wall-paintings, although similar paintings have been found in Rome itself. The consecutive decorative styles of wall painting have been labelled the First, Second, Third and Fourth Pompeian styles. The First Pompeian style emerged in the 2nd century BC. Generally simple, it used plaster moulded and painted to look like coloured marble or stone.

The Second Pompeian Style that developed after 80BC was more interesting. It used realistically painted architectural features to create almost three-dimensional effects. The Villa of Oplontis, which belonged to Poppaea, Nero's second wife, boasts a remarkable vista – a colonnade behind a peacock and theatrical mask – that approaches true trompe l'oeil. The bedroom of the villa at Boscoreale has murals that show gardens or fantastic buildings that never existed

except in the unknown artist's imagination. The aptly named Villa of the Mysteries, however, shows rituals from a real Dionysiac mystery cult, with life-size figures that seem to stand or move on painted ledges in real space. This copies Greek *megalography* (large-scale figure painting). In a house on the Esquiline Hill in Rome, wall paintings of *c.* 50BC illustrate scenes from the *Odyssey* that use atmospheric perspective to increase the illusion of distance in the dream-like landscapes.

Mosaics, made by pressing small stones and pieces of glass or marble into a soft mortar bedding, were used widely by the Romans but had been used in the Hellenistic world too. The renowned Alexander Mosaic from the House of the Faun in Pompeii probably copies a Greek painting done by Philoxenos of *c.* 300BC. It may have been imported from Greece in the 1st century BC, but it is more likely that it was the craftsman who was imported. About 17 by 9ft (5.2 by 2.7m), it creates illusory real space to depict the drama of the Battle of Issus (333BC), when Alexander almost captured the Persian king Darius II.

*Above: In the Villa at Oplontis near Pompeii, which belonged to the empress Poppaea, the illusionism of the Second Pompeian Style, c. 50BC, is fully manifested, with the pillars receding dramatically into the distance.*

*Below: A fresco from the Hall of the Mysteries, in the Villa of the Mysteries at Pompeii, showing an initiate to the Dionysian cult weeping.*

*Above: A cameo showing an ageless Augustus in dignified profile. Such images had strong propaganda purposes, as the medieval emperor Lothair realized when he incorporated it in his crown.*

*Below: A sacro-idyllic landscape of the type which first emerged in the Third Pompeian Style. Supposedly depicting country shrines, in fact they offered the artists opportunities to create imaginary landscapes of a type not seen again until the Renaissance.*

# AUGUSTUS AND THE CLASSICAL REVIVAL: 31BC–AD64

After defeating his rival Mark Antony at Actium in 31BC, Augustus (as Octavian was known after 27BC) declared a policy of *restitutio rei publicae*. This meant a return to stable, constitutional, above all peaceful government. Art, architecture and literature were all enrolled in a highly successful propaganda campaign to proclaim the advent of a golden age after a century of civil strife.

## EMBODYING ROMAN *VIRTUS*

Augustus looked back to the art of classical Athens at its 5th century BC peak for an authority, perfection and calm that appealed to him both personally and politically. (He did not of course emulate Athenian democracy, but Rome had never been truly democratic.) The result, which marked the first classical revival, was far more original than most Neo-Attic art had been, for Augustus used Athenian forms for most un-Athenian ends: his portrayal as the supreme embodiment of Roman *virtus*, the archetypal Roman virtue of courage, excellence, piety and strength.

*Virtus* is very obvious in the statue of the Prima Porta Augustus (so-called after the villa where it was found, which had once belonged to the empress Livia). Possibly a copy of a lost bronze, it dates from *c.* 20BC, and was originally painted with lifelike colours.

A still youthful-looking Augustus is shown, larger than life, as a triumphant *imperator* (emperor/general) in ceremonial armour. On his breastplate, personifications of the sky, Caelus, and of the sun, Sol, at the top are balanced by the figure of Tellus, the earth, reclining at the bottom. Around them are other deities, including Diana and Apollo. Between them Augustus is shown receiving the legionary standards lost at the battle of Carrhae in 53BC from a baggy-trousered Parthian. This refers to a recent diplomatic triumph (20–19BC) and links the mythical and the political. At Augustus' feet a cupid emphasizes the claimed descent of his family, the Julians, from Venus through her son Aeneas, while the dolphin the cupid rides recalls his naval

victory at Actium. The whole statue is therefore loaded with political significance. Augustus' stance is modelled on the nude *Doryphoros* (spear-carrier), a statue by the great Athenian sculptor Polyclitus of *c*. 450BC.

Another, less idealized statue shows Augustus with his toga over his head in the role of a priest (he became Pontifex Maximus, supreme priest, in 12BC). Augustus is, as always depicted as boyishly youthful but here he is also solemnly pious. His features are typically classical – smooth skin, regular features, sharp-edged nose and brow – suggesting calm, benign authority. The same classical dignity pervades the bust of his grand-daughter Agrippina, wife and then widow of Germanicus, the popular general whom Tiberius allegedly harassed. There is a strong facial resemblance to her grandfather in a bust of *c*. AD30.

The Gemma Augusta, a cameo showing the dead and deified Augustus passing power to his successor Tiberius from *c*. AD20, perpetuates this fine classicism. However, later statues of the Julio-Claudians, such as that depicting the ungainly emperor Claudius as Jupiter, are less successful.

Perhaps the greatest achievement of Augustan sculptors was the Ara Pacis Augusti (Altar of Augustan Peace). Constructed between 13 and 9BC and dedicated on the empress Livia's birthday, it is set in a walled enclosure with its main decorations on the outer walls. These are about 34ft long by 38ft wide (10.5 by 11.6m). Their message is that Augustus has restored peace, piety and prosperity and their form is sublimely classical. A sculptural panel on the east side portrays a personification the earth Tellus (or of Italia or Peace), with fruits and babies on her lap to symbolize fertility, flanked by two female figures symbolizing the oceans and rivers. The inspiration came from a Greek 5th-century relief, the Stele of Hegesos. Similarly, the famous frieze of the Panathenaic Procession from the Parthenon in Athens probably inspired the imperial procession on the side walls of the altar. Here Augustus is portrayed as *pater patriae* (father of his country). He takes centre stage without overwhelming his friends and family, including the empress Livia. Small boys, his grandsons, clutch at the grown-ups' hands, adding a homely touch. This reveals the Principate at its height, dignified yet family-minded. Another relief shows Aeneas, renowned for his piety, sacrificing to the *penates*, the household gods that he had brought from Troy.

## WALL PAINTINGS

The Second Pompeian Style continued after 31BC. Livia's house on the Palatine is decorated with marvellous murals of gardens, while another house, now beneath the Villa Farnesina, had walls painted with remarkable trompe l'oeil to resemble a picture gallery. Outline paintings, such as one from this villa showing a woman pouring perfume, recall classical Greek art's sublime simplicity.

The succeeding Third Pompeian Style, which emerged at the end of the 1st century BC, was less solidly illusionistic. It treated walls as flat surfaces rather than as windows. Painted columns became slimmer, holding up delicate ornamental pediments. This style also saw the first emergence of "sacro-idyllic landscapes", romanticized misty landscapes centred supposedly on a shrine or temple but in reality rejoicing in vistas dotted with bridges, rocks and shepherds' huts, with mountains in the vague distance. While perhaps influenced by Hellenistic precursors, these are among the finest and earliest of European landscapes.

*Above: Official Augustan art looked back to classical Athenian precedents in works such as the Ara Pacis Augusti (the Altar of Peace of Augustus) finished 9BC. Tellus, the personified earth, has fruit and babies on her lap and is flanked by rivers.*

*Right: The Prima Porta statue of Augustus c. 20BC, a copy of a lost bronze. The ever-youthful emperor is in symbolic armour proclaiming the Parthian victory, while the Cupid at his feet hints at descent from Venus. All is nobly classical.*

# THE ROMAN ZENITH:
## FROM NERO TO TRAJAN AD64–117

*Right: A gouache copy of one of the now-faded wall paintings discovered in Nero's Domus Aurea, illustrating the elegant Fourth Pompeian Style which once decorated it. Architectural elements are colourfully mixed with the illusionistic Second Style.*

*Below: The playboy-emperor and would-be artist Nero, unflatteringly portrayed with curled hair and a double chin although still in his twenties.*

In AD64 the great fire that destroyed most of Rome also allowed Nero, now unrestrained by his old tutor Seneca and his first Praetorian Prefect Burrus, to give free rein to his far from classical tastes. Although Nero was deposed four years later and his final successor Vespasian favoured a more popular art, the fifty years following the fire saw Roman art flourish as never before. Hellenistic influences were finally absorbed and the empire's wealth allowed a dynamic, almost baroque yet Roman style to emerge. The eruption of Vesuvius, from the archaeologist's viewpoint, provided a blessed preservative.

The murals of Nero's Domus Aurea (Golden Palace), which were fresh when rediscovered by Renaissance artists – Raphael crawled down into the "grottoes" to admire them – have sadly faded but still give a good example of the Fourth Pompeian Style. This continues the Third Style but reverts also to more solid, illusionistic architectural elements of the Second Style in a fanciful manner.

### THE FOURTH POMPEIAN STYLE
In Pompeii, superb examples of the Fourth style come from the House of the Vettii brothers – probably merchants – which was rebuilt after a major earthquake in AD62. Copies of famous Greek paintings of legends – the death of King Pentheus, the baby Hercules strangling snakes – were incorporated as painted panels within wall decorations. The painting of Achilles and Briseis, a scene from the *Iliad*, in the House of the Tragic Poet is also impressive. Achilles smoulders

with half-suppressed wrath as his favourite slave-girl Briseis is led away for King Agamemnon's pleasure. Other Pompeian paintings treat everyday subjects and reveal that local artists could paint diverse subjects with equal skill. This window on to life in antiquity closed in August AD79.

## NERO'S SUCCESSORS

Sculpture and relief carvings remained the favoured forms of official art, prominently displayed in cities across the empire. Along with each emperor's coins, they carried the imperial image and official messages, although the effects may not have always been exactly what their imperial propagators envisaged. The statues and coins of Nero (ruled AD54–68) reveal more of his character – part debauched buffoon, part genuine aspiring artist, very seldom competent emperor – than he probably realized, with fleshy double chin and grandiose laurel crowns to proclaim his "victories" in the Olympic Games where he carried off every prize.

The busts and coins of his successor Vespasian, already 60 and a fine general when he gained the throne, are very different. Bald, unbeautiful but earthily humorous – on his deathbed he joked, "I think I must be becoming a god", referring to an emperor's customary posthumous deification – his features are shown in a revived veristic style.

Titus, Vespasian's handsome, young and prodigal son and heir, trumpeted his triumph over the Jews whose revolt he had crushed with flamboyant reliefs on his arch. The nearest figures in the imperial entourage, which include Titus himself in his four-horsed chariot with a winged Victory behind him, stand out in such high relief they are nearly in the round. These contrast with the lesser figures modelled in low relief but all, as usual in imperial art of this period, create the illusion of being in real space.

Under Trajan (ruled AD98–117), perhaps the most popular of emperors, Rome approached its zenith. His great column in Rome, erected in AD113

behind his Basilica, carries a brilliant spiral with some 2,500 figures showing his victory over the Dacians. Its scenes provide vivid (if not always wholly accurate) snapshots of the Roman army in action as it crossed rivers, stormed forts and tended its wounded. Panels from the Arch of Trajan erected at Benevento AD114–17 in southern Italy show the humanitarian ruler distributing food to poor children and presiding over the construction of a new port near Ostia, all facets of a great ruler.

## THE PLEBEIAN TRADITION

Not all surviving Roman art is imperial or aristocratic. The Tomb of the Haterii of *c.* AD100 was commissioned by a non-aristocratic Roman family, who were probably successful builders. Here attention is lavished on details of the building, a family mausoleum under construction. A disregard for perspective and a delight in rich, almost fussy ornamentation shows that this sort of popular art remained blithely unconcerned with the nobility's favoured classical naturalism and idealism.

*Above: The native Italian veristic tradition was revived for this bust of Vespasian, the emperor who came from small-town Italy. It shows him as realistically bald and elderly, but wryly humorous.*

*Below: A scene from the Tomb of the Haterii, probably erected for a family of rich builders c. AD90, shows a taste for rich ornamentation far removed from upper-class ideals of naturalism.*

# HADRIAN AND THE GREEK REVIVAL: AD117–285

*Above: The statue of Marcus Aurelius, the only surviving bronze equestrian statue from antiquity, AD164–6.*

*Below: Along with the multicoloured mosaics, the 2nd century AD saw very fine black-and-white mosaics, such as this floor at Ostia.*

Although the emperor Hadrian displayed architectural radicalism in the Pantheon in Rome and in his villa at Tivoli, he was conservative in his choice of artworks, favouring a return to classical or even earlier Greek styles. This second Classical Revival derived not just from his personal tastes, for the century saw the emergence of what is termed the Second Sophistic. This attempted to revive some aspects of classical Greek life – cities even began debating political issues of the 5th century BC – as Greek provinces finally regained some of their prosperity and self-confidence after the devastation wrought by Rome's conquest and civil strife.

## ART AT HADRIAN'S VILLA

At Tivoli, 20 miles (32km) from Rome, Hadrian filled his villa complex with numerous statues, mostly reproductions of famous Greek or Egyptian works, to remind him of his travels. His decorators also created superb mosaics such as that showing a battle between centaurs and wild beasts based on a Greek work by Zeuxis of *c.* 400BC. On his travels Hadrian fell in love with Antinous, a beautiful youth of royal birth from Bithynia, who accompanied him until he was drowned in the Nile in AD130. To commemorate him, the grief-stricken emperor founded a city on the Nile (besides more enduring foundations such as Hadrianopolis, now Edirne in Turkey) and "set up statues of him, or rather cult images, throughout the entire inhabited world", according to the historian Dio Cassius. Greek artists made statues showing Antinous as Apollo, Bacchus, Hermes and Osiris. If his body is truly Hellenic, he often has a most unclassical pout.

The Baths of Neptune in Ostia at the Tiber's mouth had a fine mosaic floor in black and white. Completed in AD139, it showed mythical sea-creatures – tritons, hippocamps, nereids – circling around the sea-god. The lack of colour brings out the fine draughtsmanship and this style remained popular into the 4th century.

Far to the north a remarkable fresco has been found in Southwark, across the Thames from Roman London, dating from *c.* AD150. It used very expensive pigments – gold leaf and cinnabar – to revive or perpetuate the Third Pompeian Style. Slender pillars supporting delicate pediments provide evidence that Roman wealth and sophistication had reached even this remote province.

One of the greatest of all Roman artworks is the sole surviving Roman equestrian bronze statue of Marcus Aurelius – preserved because it was thought to depict Constantine, the first Christian emperor – which was erected AD164–6. The philosopher-emperor is shown in heavy tunic and cloak as a general, his arm raised as if addressing a crowd, but his features retain a thoughtful, nobly compassionate air.

*Above: The debauched megalomania of Commodus, shown dressed as Hercules, is wonderfully conveyed in this decadent bust.*

A different, world-weary tone dominates the column of Marcus Aurelius of AD180–92, where the horrors of war are vividly portrayed. In comical contrast, the full-size naked portrait of Lucius Verus reveals the vanity of Marcus' idle co-emperor. The bust of Commodus, Marcus' worthless heir, dressed as Hercules with lionskin and club, is another masterly portrait, revealing the debauched megalomania of the last of the Antonines.

### SEVERAN ART

A new art began to emerge with the succeeding dynasty, the Severans (AD193–233). This partly rejected Graeco-Roman classicism for a more stylized art. However, the two approaches long co-existed (as the classical and veristic traditions had for centuries) and often mixed. There is a florid exuberance about the busts of Septimius Severus (first of the dynasty), whose elaborately curled beard and hairstyle sit oddly with the ruthless face of a general who destroyed two rivals to gain the throne. The busts

of the following period are increasingly in the veristic tradition and that of the brutal emperor Caracalla (ruled AD211–17) is almost alarmingly realistic. Most of his successors, such as Maximinus Thrax or Trebonianus Gallus, cultivated this thuggish look as the empire disintegrated into chaos. Only the emperor Gallienus (ruled AD253–68) reverted to a noble, spiritual air. This was well-suited to a ruler who patronized the unworldly philosopher Plotinus and lost much of the empire.

### SARCOPHAGI

One art form that developed steadily even in troubled times was the sarcophagus. This reflected the growing trend towards inhumation (burial) rather than cremation from Hadrian's reign on, and provided great opportunities for Attic (Greek) sculptors. In the 2nd century AD, these sarcophagi have fine classical carvings, often of Greek legends unconnected with the deceased's life. Typical is the sarcophagus of AD190 showing the scene from the *Iliad* of the corpse of prince Hector being dragged around the walls of Troy. Others combine myth with personal touches, such as the sarcophagus from AD250 showing a couple reclining together in death on the lid and legendary scenes from Achilles at the court of Lycomedes round the sides.

A rival to the Attic school of sarcophagi sculptors was the Asiatic school. Here too mythological scenes in a classical style decorated the sides of sarcophagi, but columns divide the scenes. A particularly elaborate example is dated *c*. AD180. Now in Melfi Cathedral in southern Italy, although its original occupant was pagan, it has *aediculae* (pavilions) on all four sides with mythological figures in each and a door at one end. The deceased's carved image reclines on top. Such pagan funeral imagery continued well into the Christian empire.

*Right: Hadrian's beautiful lover Antinous, who died mysteriously in the Nile, was portrayed in many different poses.*

*Above: Under the new African dynasty started by Septimius Severus in AD193, new forms of less classical art emerged, often more stylized but not wholly displacing classicism.*

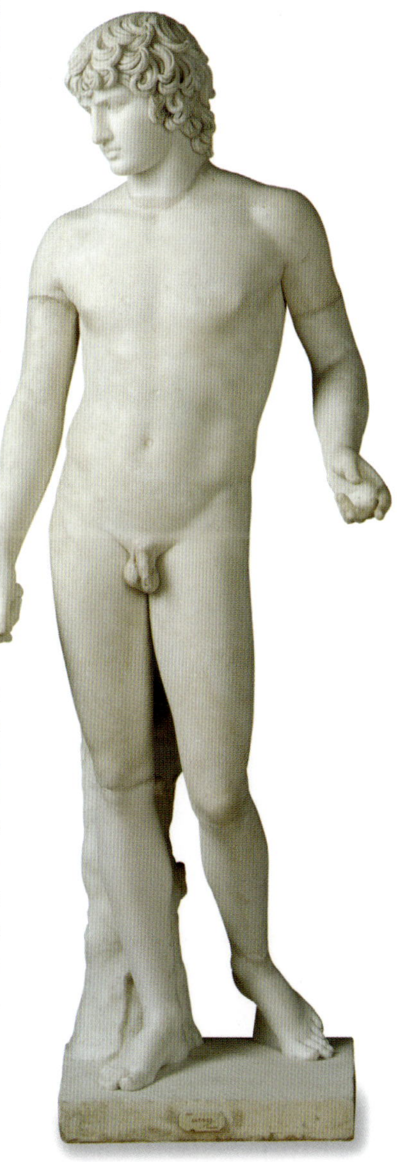

# ART OF THE LATER EMPIRE:
## AD285–535

With the advent of Diocletian in AD284, the troubled empire entered a new, more stable but more politically restricted era. Roman art reflected this as earlier trends away from classical idealism and its accompanying naturalism intensified. Instead, there emerged an art that aimed at creating overwhelmingly imposing images of imperial power, turned inward away from a collapsing natural world. This makes later Roman art effectively a bridge to that of the Byzantine and medieval world.

### THE STYLE OF POWER

Diocletian and his successors tried to exalt the imperial throne so far above its subjects that none would dare to challenge it. While this aim had limited success politically, it had huge repercussions aesthetically. The statues of the tetrarchs (four co-rulers) embracing in St Mark's, Venice, of *c.* AD305 reveal the new order's grim determination and also the tetrarchs' astonishing lack of individuality – their features are almost interchangeable. However, the real power of the new style is seen best in the giant head and hands of Constantine, all that remain of a colossal seated statue of the emperor that once stared down on observers in the Basilica Nova in Rome. The head alone is 8ft 6in (2.6m) high and the whole statue intact would have risen 30ft (9m). The huge eyes gaze out blankly yet all-seeingly on the subjects dwarfed below. The aquiline nose and clean-shaven jaw – Constantine was the first beardless emperor since Trajan – reinforce the feeling of sheer power which emanates from this superb piece of propaganda.

Less startlingly original was the Arch of Constantine. This partly reused Trajanic, Hadrianic and Antonine material but also has some new friezes. On two of these, panels showing Constantine delivering an oration or distributing gifts to the Roman people, the emperor stares out in grandiose isolation while his courtiers, lined up stiffly, gaze adoringly up towards him. The contrast with the classical realism of the two purloined Hadrianic roundels is striking. The change cannot be attributed simply to a decline in craftsmanship but must reflect a preference, emerging even before Constantine became Christian, for an art that was more hieratic and oppressive and less realistic and humanist than earlier official art. Man had ceased to be "the measure of all things", as he had been in classical Greece and Augustan Rome and now humbly genuflected before awesomely distant imperial – or divine – majesty. All the earlier panels are re-worked so that the emperor looks like Constantine. As a result he sometimes has a very small head.

Later imperial monuments such as the base of the Obelisk of Theodosius I in Constantinople (Istanbul) of AD390–3 take yet further this process of magnifying imperial glory while reducing subjects to mere ciphers. The emperor is shown standing behind the imperial pavilion's

*Above: The grim determination of the four tetrarchs (co-rulers) is graphically revealed in this unusual statue of c. AD305, now built into St Mark's, Venice, but originally from Constantinople.*

*Below: Constantine I favoured an art that overwhelmed the onlooker in its size and majesty. This head, once part of a huge statue, is 8ft 6in (2.6m) high.*

railing with a wreath in his hand, while beside and below him his courtiers, reduced to rows of anonymous heads, gaze out full-frontally. (Severe weathering has probably accentuated this impression of impersonality.)

Better preserved is the superb silver dish some 2ft 5in (73.6cm) in diameter made in AD388 which shows Theodosius with his co-emperors Valentinian II and Arcadius, his son, all holding orbs to symbolize power. The co-emperors are portrayed smaller to indicate their lesser power. Theodosius is presenting something to an official, who is shown far smaller, befitting a man of lower status. Such symbolism marks a clean break with naturalistic classicism.

The most beautiful examples of Late Roman/Byzantine imperial art come from Ravenna, reconquered by the Latin-speaking but Eastern emperor Justinian (AD527–65). The mosaics at San Vitale which show him staring out, flanked by clergy and soldiers, are Byzantine in their full-frontal two-dimensionality against a flat gold background, although traces of classicism remain in their individually identifiable features.

Ravenna's mosaics mark the final transition to post-Roman medieval art, for the wars to regain Italy from the Goths wrecked the last of Roman civilization more thoroughly than the Goths could.

## CLASSICAL SURVIVALS

Although the now Christian imperial court preferred the new unnaturalistic art for propaganda purposes, many educated pagan Romans long continued to favour some form of classical art. The Symmachus family, one of Rome's grandest noble families, commissioned ivory diptychs (two-leaved panels) in *c.* AD390. These depict pagan priestesses before a shrine to Bacchus and Jupiter in a style that consciously aimed to revive something of Augustan classicism.

In Britain, where villa life flourished in the first half of the 4th century AD, the superb mosaic, the Woodchester Great Pavement of *c.* AD350, shows Orpheus charming the beasts amid geometric patterns that recall a carpet. A similar subject is treated more naturalistically in the Littlecote villa near Hungerford of *c.* AD360. Even more dramatic is the Mildenhall Treasure, a superb silver dish about 2ft (61cm) in diameter that was buried around AD360 for safekeeping. It shows scenes of bacchic revelry with maenads and satyrs that in both spirit and form recall a far earlier art.

In Sicily, the remarkable mosaics depicting hunting and bathing from the Piazza Armerina villa of *c.* AD310–30 glow with truly pagan vitality, although their style has moved away from classicism to a less naturalistic if still vivid art.

*Above: This 6th-century AD mosaic from Sant'Apollinare Nuovo in Ravenna of the Three Magi (Wise Men) is a marvellous example of Byzantine art.*

*Below: The joyful, exuberant colours of the mosaics of the Piazza Armerina Villa in Sicily show that, even in the early 4th century AD, not all art was concerned with depicting grim power.*

# FURNITURE

*Above: A fresco of the 1st century BC showing a Roman banquet with the typical small, portable tripod table that was then common. These were usually richly decorated.*

*Below: A bronze Roman couch or bed probably from the 1st century AD. It would have had cushions and covers and a mattress of wooden slats and might have been used both for dining and for sleeping.*

Roman furniture was rather sparse but often also surprisingly elegant and comfortable. It certainly surpassed anything Western Europe was to know again for the next thousand years.

As with so much else, there was a marked Greek or Hellenistic influence on much Roman furniture design. Furniture for all but the poorest was always decorated in some way, for minimalism was never a virtue in Roman eyes. Excavations at Pompeii and Herculaneum have been invaluable for revealing well-preserved examples of furniture from the late Republican and early Imperial periods (100BC–AD79). The styles greatly influenced Neoclassical European furniture of the late 18th and early 19th centuries. However, it is unlikely that Roman furniture design changed radically in the three centuries that followed the eruption of Vesuvius.

## TABLES AND SEATING

The Romans seem to have used five different types of table. These were all of Greek origin and made of bronze or marble as much as wood. The tables could be rectangular with three or four legs, or round with three legs. These were often zoomorphic in form, with lions' paws or griffins' legs or even with legs formed with ithyphallic satyrs. Small bronze tripod tables with rims to prevent things falling off – very useful on uneven floors – were particularly popular. So, too, were square stone or marble tables with a single central leg. The latter design was particularly common in courtyards or gardens, where they might be fixed, but most other furniture could be moved around. Portable charcoal braziers, the chief source of heating in private houses around the Mediterranean, were an exception. (Hypocaust central heating remained a very rare, expensive luxury in private houses and was only used in certain parts of the house.) A particularly fine example of a bronze tripod brazier dates from the late 1st century BC. A masterpiece of Roman metalwork, its elaborate sphinxes reveal the brief fashion for things Egyptian following the victory at Actium in 31BC and the annexation of Egypt.

Couches were made mainly of wood. A rectangular frame held the mattress, which was supported by leather straps, webbing or wooden slats to make a firm bed. There seems to have been little difference between the couches used for dining and beds proper – in many houses the two were probably interchangeable. Traces of couches with leather sides and backs that may have had cushions have also been discovered. Headboards sometimes had ornaments in the form of bronze or brass animal heads and could be inlaid with ivory, silver or tortoiseshell. A couch with a relief of bones has been partially restored and is displayed in the Fitzwilliam Museum, Cambridge.

The Romans had many different types of seating. Benches were generally considered poor people's seating and were made of wood or stone. Elaborate chairs, sometimes with arms and back supports, are shown in Roman sculptures and paintings. Heavy, ceremonial chairs with solid

sides were used for official occasions. There is a carving from Trier of what looks like an armchair made of wicker in which a teacher sits instructing his students and a bronze-sheathed wooden chair leg has been found at Pompeii. Stools were widely used. A *sella curulis* (folding stool) with curving crossed legs was used by magistrates on official occasions. They were also used domestically; a relief from Ostia shows a woman seated under a tree on such a stool and Pompeii has produced a fine bronze-legged example. Thrones are usually shown with footstools.

## CUPBOARDS AND LAMPS

Roman cupboards, cabinets and chests were generally similar to modern ones. A remarkably fine wooden cupboard cum shrine has been found in Herculaneum. The shrine at the top takes the form of a little temple, with finely carved Corinthian colonnettes (mini-columns) at its corners, and housed the statues of the household gods, the Lares and Penates. The cupboard below contained glassware and ornaments.

Discoveries at Herculaneum have shown that many rooms had wooden shutters or partitions that have normally left no archaeological record. These could be elaborate, folding, multi-panelled affairs with doors in them. External shutters were made of solid wood. It is clear from literature, painting and sculpture that large curtains would also have been used to divide rooms, but none have survived.

## LAMPS

Roman houses were lit by lamps which burned olive oil. These ranged from very simple earthenware dishes to elaborate bronze stands. The simplest of these bronze lamp stands was a slender fluted column that rested on three animal paws and was topped by some form of calyx (flower top). Far more complicated were those with four or more arms, shaped either like branches or in the form of *volutes* (scroll-like ornaments). A particularly resplendent example

comes from the House of Diomedes at Pompeii. Dating from just before AD79, the lampstand rests on a platform decorated with a figure of a satyr riding a panther. The feet of the base are shaped like animal's paws.

*Above: A woman seated at her toilette in a wicker armchair from near Trier in Gaul, 4th century AD. A servant holds a mirror in front of her.*

*Above: An elaborate Roman strong box for money and other valuables. Decorated with classical motifs and very fine lion legs, it probably dates from the 4th century AD.*

# CHAPTER IX

# RELIGION AND MYTHOLOGY

The Romans had many gods and, like most other polytheists, normally accepted those of other peoples. Most Greek gods were identified with Roman ones early on but, as Rome's power spread east, stranger gods found followers in the multiracial city: Cybele from Asia Minor, Isis and Sarapis from Egypt, Mithras from the Persian world. Their cults, which offered initiates mystical experiences and usually promised salvation after death, appealed especially to poorer people in the empire. In contrast, the official religion of the Roman establishment was essentially pragmatic and utilitarian. Worship involved precise rituals to ensure that the gods brought victory in battle or that they saved Rome from plague.

From Augustus' time on, the worship of the emperor, whose *genius* or divinity was linked with Roma Dea, the goddess of Rome, was encouraged. This imperial cult helped to unite the disparate empire and was vigorously enforced in the troubled 3rd century AD. The Jews were exempt because of the antiquity of their religion, but Christians suffered for their refusal to worship the emperor. Christianity's final triumph was due chiefly to its promotion by Constantine after AD312. But, as the Roman empire became Christian, Christianity in turn became imperially Roman.

*Left: A scene thought to show the mystery rites of Bacchus (Dionysus) in a mural from the Villa of the Mysteries, Pompeii, c. 60–50BC. Note the goatlike ears of the left-hand figures.*

# THE CAPITOLINE GODS

*Above: The goddess Minerva, third of the Capitoline triad, from Souedia in Syria. Less obviously Roman than the other two, this patron of doctors and craftsmen was revered for her wisdom and widely worshipped.*

*Right: Thetis appealing to Jupiter in a painting by Ingres, 1811. The assimilation of such Greek deities into the Roman pantheon happened very early in Rome's history.*

The gods of early Rome were not initially anthropomorphic but, after 250BC, under increasing Greek influence, they soon acquired human characteristics. They were given mythical fixed forms like the 12 Greek Olympian gods by the poet Ennius. However, although myth and religion intertwined, religious fervour was not appropriate to the worship of Rome's state gods. Instead, punctilious performance of the rites was all-important.

Rome did not have a separate priestly caste or profession, although there were four priestly colleges by the late Republic. The *pontifices* were pre-eminent, while the *augures* divined the gods' will by observing the flight of birds or animals' entrails. Important Romans performed priestly duties as required, pulling their togas over their heads to indicate sacerdotal functions. The emperors from Augustus on became *pontifex maximus*, supreme priest, a title the Pope inherited.

The sacrifice of animals was central to the gods' worship. The animal entrails were examined for omens, an Etruscan habit which the Romans perpetuated. The best portions of the sacrifice were burnt as offerings to the gods and the priests and worshippers would eat the rest. Offerings of flowers or cakes were acceptable from poorer people and for lesser endeavours.

The temple of a pagan god was its house, not a place where worshippers gathered for collective rites. These rites were normally performed outside the temple. On special occasions the statue of the deity might be paraded through the streets, a custom still performed with Catholic statues on feast days. Jupiter, his wife Juno and his daughter Minerva, who sprang from his head fully grown and fully armed, formed the central Capitoline triad. However, Mars, the war god, was equally important.

## JUPITER

The king of the gods, equated with Zeus (though lacking the Greek god's colourful sex life or touchy temper), Jupiter was a sky god associated with thunder, lightning, rainfall and storms. He used to warn men and punished them with his three thunder bolts when required. The first he could discharge as a warning whenever he wanted; the second, also a premonitory bolt, could be hurled with the agreement of the 12 other gods, his *complices*. The last, destroying bolt could only be unleashed by the god with the consent of the *superiores*, the hidden superior gods.

At first the god of a rustic Rome, Jupiter Elicius (Who Brings Forth) was concerned with farming, but as Rome's power grew, so did his. Called Jupiter Imperator (Supreme General), Invictus (Unconquered) and Triumphator, his highest title was Jupiter Optimus Maximus (Best and Greatest).

In his temple on the Capitoline, Jupiter was portrayed majestically, bearded, with an eagle on a sceptre and thunderbolts. Long the supreme god of the Roman

state, senators declared war under his aegis and triumphant generals would donate a gold crown and part of their booty to him. The *Ludi Romani*, the chief games, were celebrated in his honour.

The Temple of Jupiter on the Capitoline Hill, which was built under the kings and rebuilt many times, was the grandest in the city of Rome. The rise of the cult of Sol Invictus (Unconquered Sun) eclipsed Jupiter's primacy in the 3rd century, but Diocletian (ruled AD284–305) revived Jupiter's glory, calling himself and his soldiers *Joviani*. Finally, the Christians adopted Jupiter's title of Optimus Maximus for their own god.

### JUNO

The consort and sister of Jupiter, equated with the Greek goddess Hera, Juno was the supreme goddess of the Roman state and of very ancient origins. A statue of Juno was taken from the captured Etruscan city of Veii in 394BC and installed in Rome in a form of religious annexation, but she had been worshipped in Rome long before. A temple to her was built on the Esquiline Hill in 735BC.

As Juno Lucetia she was a goddess of light, a moon goddess. Traditionally shown with a peacock and sceptre as *regina coeli*, queen of heaven, her sacred geese on the Capitol warned the Romans of a night attack by the Gauls during their sack of Rome in 390BC. She was also the mother of Mars, although not by Jupiter but by union with a magic flower. Above all, Juno embodied the virtues of Roman matronhood, which were much respected in the Republic. As Juno Lucina she was goddess of childbirth and fertility – the Sabine women prayed to her after their rape by Romulus and his gang. As Juno Pronuba she presided over marriage and as Populonia she encouraged the Romans to multiply. The month of June is named after her.

### MINERVA

Although identified with Athene, patron goddess of Athens and daughter of Zeus, Minerva was originally the Etruscan goddess Menrfa or Menarva (associated with an owl) and the least Roman of the Capitoline triad. At first the goddess of commerce, industry and education, she later became a warrior-goddess, depicted with helmet, shield and armour. Later still she also became the patron goddess of doctors, musicians and craftsmen and, in a typical example of Roman assimilation, was equated with the local goddess of Bath's hot springs, Sulis, in Britain. Her festival was celebrated in the Quinquatrus with Mars at the spring equinox.

*Above: Mars, the helmeted god of war, was a deity of central importance to the all-conquering Romans.*

*Below: Apollo, god of music, poetry, medicine and science, shown with his lyre, was a Roman import from Greece who was fully assimilated into the state religion by Augustus.*

## MARS

The war god Mars was perhaps the most truly Roman of the city's gods and his cult was more important to Rome even than Jupiter's. At first he was a rustic deity living in fields and forests, called Silvanus. Later, Ceres and Liber, deities of wheat and wine, took over these agricultural roles but Mars' chief festival was always celebrated at the Quinquatrus at the spring equinox in the month that bears his name.

Born almost parthenogenetically from Juno's mystical union with a fantastic flower, he was identified with Ares but was a nobler and more dignified figure than the often irascible Greek god. At Rome he had a *sacrarium* (shrine) on the Palatine, where his 12 sacred spears were kept. His grandest temple in Rome was that built by Augustus to him as Mars Ultor, Mars the Avenger, to celebrate victory over Julius Caesar's assassins.

The Romans built temples to him across the empire, in which he was generally portrayed bearded with helmet and armour. Sacrifices were made to him by generals before they set out for battle and after their victory he received his share of booty.

On the battlefield he might appear accompanied by Pavor and Pallor (terror and paleness) which he inflicted on Rome's enemies, while his other two companions, Honos and Virtus, filled Roman soldiers with honour and courage. In the Romance languages Tuesday (Martes, Martedi, Mardi) is named after Mars.

## APOLLO

The archetypal Greek god of poetry, medicine, music and science, Apollo had no Roman equivalent but was imported into the city in the 5th century BC to ward off plague. The dictator Camillus promised Apollo a tenth of the spoils from the Etruscan city of Veii, which Rome captured in 396BC, for Apollo was honoured also by the Etruscans.

Apollo was the son of Zeus (but not of Jupiter) and the titaness Leto. His twin sister was Artemis/Diana. Born on the island of Delos, Apollo slew the dragon Python at only four days old. Renamed as Delphi, the spot where the slaying took place later became the site of his oracle, the most sacred in the Greek world. Called Phoebus (brilliant), Apollo was a god of light and was later sometimes identified with the sun. Augustus built a fine temple near his house on the Palatine to the god whose lucid virtues he tried to propagate and many more were built across the empire.

## DIANA

The goddess of the hunt and of the moon, later equated with Artemis and so Apollo's twin, Diana was the patron goddess of wild beasts. She was also associated with the moon, especially the harvest moon, for she was a fertility goddess. In her great temple at Ephesus in Asia Minor she was shown as many-breasted.

Diana undoubtedly had a savage temper. When Actaeon the hunter chanced upon her bathing with her nymphs, she angrily changed him into a stag and he was then killed by his own dogs. At Rome Diana was worshipped as a goddess

of childbirth in a temple on the Aventine founded in the 6th century BC. Her greatest shrine was on the shores of Lake Nemi north of Rome, where her priest was traditionally an escaped slave. To win this priesthood he had to kill his predecessor in single combat, after which he had to patrol the lake's forested shores looking out for potential successors.

## SATURN

An ancient agricultural god whose name was connected with *satur* (literally: stuffed), Saturn was identified with the Greek god Cronus. Expelled from heaven by Jupiter, Saturn was held to have ruled Italy during its golden age before the invention of iron and war. Saturday is named after Saturn.

Saturn's annual festival, the Saturnalia, which took place between the 17th and 23rd of December, saw an orgy of merriment when all rules were relaxed, the Lord of Misrule governed, masters waited upon their slaves and huge public banquets were eaten in the open. Saturn's temple in the Forum Romanum housed the public treasury and the standards of legions not actually campaigning. It was also a very early shrine of the Republic dating from *c.* 494BC.

## VESTA AND THE VESTAL VIRGINS

Vesta was goddess of the domestic hearth and sown fields. She was linked with the Greek goddess Hestia, a notably chaste goddess. In Rome she was served by six patrician girls who were chosen by lot at the age of six. They were required to serve for 30 years from the age of ten in the special Atrium Vestae, the House of the Vestals next to the circular Temple of Vesta in the Forum Romanum. After that time they were free to marry, although few did, as they were considered too old. The Vestal Virgins were, however, much respected. Their main duty was to keep the goddess' sacred flame burning, and their chief restriction was their vow of chastity. Any Vestal Virgin who broke this vow faced whipping to death or burial alive. Apparently only 20 Vestals broke their vows in over a thousand years.

# VENUS, VULCAN AND OTHER GODS

The Romans adopted gods and goddesses from many different civilizations. Venus, for example, filled a huge gap in the Roman pantheon, which was notably lacking in amorous or beautiful deities, and Vulcan was identified with the Greek god Hephaestus.

### VENUS

Originally a minor Italian nature goddess associated with spring, in the 3rd century BC Venus became identified with Aphrodite, the daughter of Zeus/Jupiter and supremely beautiful Greek goddess of love. Venus had many shrines, including a Greek shrine on Mount Eryx in Sicily and another in Pompeii. Her fame grew when Julius Caesar, claiming divine ancestry for the Julian family, ordered the building of the temple of Venus Genetrix in 46BC.

According to Homer, Aphrodite/ Venus was the mother of Aeneas, the Trojan prince. The fragmentary Roman legends that Virgil transformed into the *Aeneid* state that Aeneas had fled burning Troy to found Lavinium, the precursor of Rome. As the Julio-Claudian emperors claimed descent through Aeneas, Venus was linked with Rome's imperial destiny. Hadrian dedicated a huge double temple to Venus and Roma Dea in AD135.

Imperial propaganda did not reduce the allure of the sweet-natured goddess. Born from the sea's foam, she was wafted ashore naked on a shell by gentle zephyrs, to land at Paphos in Cyprus, where the Horae, the attendant hours, were waiting to clothe her and usher her into the presence of the gods. All were overwhelmed by her. Both Mars and Mercury had affairs with her as erotic chaos broke out on Mount Olympus, the gods' home. Finally Juno and Minerva, furiously jealous, competed in a beauty parade with her to see which goddess Paris would pick. The Trojan prince chose Venus and from the other goddesses' undying enmity arose the Trojan war. Aeneas was born of Venus' affair with the Trojan Anchises,

*Above: Venus by the forge of Vulcan, the blacksmith god to whom the goddess of love was improbably married – although not for long.*

*Below: The birth of Venus and her passage ashore on a seashell, depicted on a fresco in Pompeii.*

but she herself was no warrior-goddess and relied upon her charms, rather than strength. Doves were sacred to her, as was the evening star, the planet Venus. Lucretius started his great philosophical poem *De rerum natura* (*About the Nature of Things*) with a passionate invocation to Venus: *Aeneadum genetrix, hominum divumque voluptas, alma Venus* ("Mother of Aeneas, delight of gods and men, kindly Venus"). Catullus and other poets constantly invoked her and she remains the most enduringly appealing of all Graeco-Roman deities.

## VULCAN

The ugly blacksmith god Vulcan was the polar opposite of the graceful goddess of love. Under the name Volcanus he was an ancient Latin deity, an original protector of Rome and consort of Juno.

After Jupiter displaced him, Vulcan concentrated on working in the hot bowels of the Earth: the Romans placed his divine smithy both inside Mount Etna and on the volcanic Aeolian islands. Vulcan was lamed after being thrown from Mount Olympus for interfering in a quarrel between his parents Jupiter and Juno. Falling into the sea, he was rescued by nymphs and there learnt his metal-working trade, creating a marvellous gold throne that glued Juno to it when she sat down. To obtain her release, the gods had to agree to allow him to marry Venus. Their marriage was not made in heaven, however, for Venus, repelled by the dirty smith, had an affair with Mars. Vulcan angrily threw a metal net over the adulterous couple as they slept, trapping them for the other gods' mirth.

## JANUS

One of the very few Roman gods without a Greek counterpart, Janus was an ancient and popular Italic god, his cult traditionally established by Romulus.

Janus was the god of all doorways and public gates through which roads passed. His emblems were his keys and the *virga* (stick) that porters used to drive intruders

away. Janus was most famous for being *Janus bifrons*, two-faced, so that he could see people coming and going. Because he was the god of new beginnings, the first month of the year, January, was named after him, and the first day of each month was sacred to him. In the Forum Romanum his temple had gates that were opened in time of war and – far more rarely – closed in times of peace.

## LARES AND PENATES

The domestic gods Lares and Penates, the guardian spirits of the household, were also typically Roman deities. Each Roman house traditionally had one *lar* (the word was originally Etruscan, meaning prince) and two *penates*, whose names derived from *penus*, larder.

The *lar* was invoked on all important family occasions such as marriages and funerals. A bride crossing the threshold of her new household made an offering to the house's *lar*, whose image was always decorated at festival times. There was also a *lar* of the crossroads.

The *penates* oversaw the family supply of food and drink and their altar was the hearth, which they shared with Vesta. On the Ara Pacis, Aeneas is shown sacrificing to the *penates*.

*Left: Vulcan's forge, a 2nd-century AD mosaic from Dougga in North Africa. The god of all metal workers, clever but unlovely, Vulcan had his forge either beneath Mt Etna in Sicily or in the Aeolian islands just to the north.*

*Below: The two-headed god of the crossroads, Janus was unusual in that he was a completely Roman deity. His ancient worship, traditionally started by Romulus, was very popular throughout Italy.*

# EMPEROR WORSHIP AND THE GODDESS ROMA

Since the reign of Alexander the Great (336–323BC), the Greeks had hailed as gods kings or generals whom they wished to honour or appease. The step from superhuman hero to demi-god or god was a short one in a world filled with gods. When Roman generals succeeded Alexander's successors as arbiters of the eastern Mediterranean, Greeks began treating them, too, as divine, starting with Flaminius in 196BC. Many cities set up altars to the deity Roma Dea, the goddess Rome. Mark Antony, who ruled the East from 42–31BC, was hailed as an avatar of Dionysus/Bacchus in Greek cities in Asia Minor and in Egypt, where he sat enthroned beside Cleopatra dressed as Isis. This did not help his reputation among the Romans, however. Augustus' supporters said that Antony had gone native and lost his Roman *virtus*.

## THE IMPERIAL CULT

Augustus dealt pragmatically with the desire of many of his non-Roman subjects to worship him in his turn. He allowed altars or temples to his *genius* (guardian spirit) or *numen* (divinity) to be erected across the provinces. In Aphrodisias in southern Asia Minor, a large *Sebasteion* (temple to Augustus) was built by prominent local individuals and served by priests recruited from local aristocrats. Cities competed with each other to offer the emperor honours and sacred hymns were composed to him at Pergamum. More deliberately, Augustus built a small temple on the Athenian acropolis to Augustus and the goddess Roma combined, underlining Rome's divinely sanctioned power in the heart of Greece.

In Egypt, where Augustus was the heir to the divine pharaohs and Ptolemies, his worship presented no problems. At the other end of the empire in Gaul, a Great Altar to Augustus and Roma was set up at Lyons (Lugdunum), Gaul's largest city. Representatives of the three Gallic provinces came every year to demonstrate their devotion to Rome and the emperor. Many Romanized Gallic nobles happily contributed to such cults, which demonstrated their new status in the empire. At Colchester (Camulodunum) in the new province of Britain, a temple to Claudius the god was established but proved less popular. It was burnt down in Boudicca's revolt of AD60. However, this reaction was uncommon.

In contrast, the Roman nobility, whose support Augustus needed to run the empire, regarded any presumption of divinity by the emperor as an outrage tantamount to tyranny, and he had to tread carefully. During his lifetime, Augustus was still only *princeps* (first citizen). Although he prominently advertised himself as *divi filius*, son of a god, he never allowed anyone to call him a god in Rome or to build a temple to him in Italy.

It was different with the dead, however. Julius Caesar was deified posthumously and a temple was built to him. On his death Augustus was also declared a god by the Senate, his soul soaring into heaven in the form of an eagle released from his burning pyre. Most popular emperors were subsequently deified, although rulers found odious by the Senate – Tiberius, Caligula, Nero, Domitian, Commodus – were denied this honour. Antoninus Pius (ruled AD138–61) had to threaten to abdicate before the Senate would deify Hadrian, a superb ruler but one who had not got on with the Senate. Later Septimius Severus deified the megalomaniac Commodus to link his family with the Antonines.

Wiser emperors – Augustus, Trajan, Marcus Aurelius – accepted these encomia reluctantly, but by the 3rd century emperors were assuming divine attributes

*Above: Augustus with his toga pulled up over his head to indicate that he is acting as a priest. He took the title Pontifex Maximus (Highest Priest) but never let himself be worshipped as a god in Rome or Italy while he was alive. He was only deified at his death.*

during their lifetime and some, especially those who had inherited the throne, let this worship go their heads. Caligula (ruled AD37–41) was one of the maddest, addressing Jupiter's statue on the Capitoline as an equal. Nero saw himself as an incarnation of the sungod Helios, and Domitian insisted on being called *dominus et deus* (Lord and God). Commodus even wanted to rename Rome after himself. However, most educated people knew that the emperor was not literally divine and throwing incense on the altar to the emperor and Roma required no religious commitment. It was merely indicative of a general patriotic loyalty.

## PERSECUTION

Not all the peoples of the empire could accept this, however. The Jews, spread around the Mediterranean even before Titus destroyed the Temple in Jerusalem in AD70, regarded emperor worship as an abomination. The Romans respected the Jewish religion for its antiquity and dignity (although they found it puzzling) and exempted Jews from emperor worship. When Caligula tried to have his statue installed in the Holy of Holies in the temple in Jerusalem, he almost triggered an uprising, but this was an exception.

The Christians, who were recognized as a sect distinct from the Jews by AD64, were not exempted in the same way and so were intermittently persecuted. However, as the correspondence between the emperor Trajan and Pliny the Younger, governor of Bithynia, reveals, the Romans did not usually seek out Christians to persecute. It was only during the crises of the 3rd century AD, when Rome's rulers appealed to every god in heaven to aid the stricken empire, that Christians were harshly persecuted for risking the gods' wrath. Even then, only the most stubborn – or devout – experienced martyrdom.

*Above: Base of the Column of Antoninus Pius (AD138–61), showing the apotheosis of Faustina, his wife, and also of himself.*

*Above: Gold coin showing the head of the deified Claudius. Even the undignified Claudius was worshipped in Britain during his lifetime and became a god after his death.*

# BACCHUS AND CYBELE

The official Roman gods were vital to the maintenance of Rome's political fortunes and of family life. However, they lacked the mystical appeal of the new gods and mystery cults from the East which promised immortality to those initiated into their secret rites. The Senate, alarmed that secret devotions might lead adherents to neglect their social and political duties, initially tried to restrict them.

## BACCHUS

The Romans had their own cheerful rustic wine god, Liber Pater, whose festival they celebrated in March. However, Bacchus, identified with the Greek Dionysus, the most dangerous god in the Greek pantheon, was very different.

Born to Semele, a Theban princess, son of Jupiter, the young Bacchus overcame the jealous goddess Juno's varied attempts to kill him. (His mother was blasted by lightning and he himself was chopped up by Titans and cooked in a cauldron.)

Resurrected by Jupiter, Bacchus was educated partly by nymphs and led a procession of satyrs, muses and maenads in a chariot drawn by tigers or panthers. He was famed for spreading the cult of wine and his intoxicated festivals.

Bacchus married the abandoned Cretan princess Ariadne on Naxos and drove the mother of King Pentheus of Thebes (who had imprisoned him) so mad that she blindly tore her son to pieces. In classical Greece, Bacchus as Dionysus was recognized as the official god of drama. His spring festival was noted both for the plays staged under his auspices and for the ecstatic excesses of the maenads, his female followers.

Later, Bacchus' cult spread wider and became secretive. In 186BC the Roman Senate ordered the suppression of most altars to the god throughout Italy after the "Bacchanalian incident", details of which remain obscure. The cult, which had entered Rome via the Greek cities of southern Italy, went underground for a time until, wiser than King Pentheus, the Romans accepted Bacchus' worship.

The remarkable murals of the Villa of Mysteries at Pompeii show a woman being whipped and then comforted while a winged *daemon* (spirit) looks on. The murals probably depict an initiation scene from this mysterious cult, which was especially popular with women.

## CYBELE, THE *MAGNA MATER*

Few cults less suited to the dignified Roman Republic could be imagined than the orgiastic worship of Cybele, the *Magna Mater* (Great Mother). A Phrygian fertility goddess , she was worshipped on mountain tops and underground. Her son Attis emasculated himself in ecstatic devotion to her in an act her followers repeated in public in gory rituals. All her priests were eunuchs, something no

*Above: Bacchantes dancing with a whip and cymbals from the House of the Mysteries, Pompeii.*

*Below: The so-called Temple of Bacchus (Dionysus), the god of wine and ecstasy, at Baalbek, Lebanon.*

Roman citizen could be and retain his citizenship. However, in the darkest days of the war against Hannibal, the Romans consulted the Sibylline Books. These predicted that Italy would only be freed if the "Idaean mother of Pessinus" was brought to Rome. The Romans understood this to refer to Cybele and set about bringing her cult to Rome. It arrived in the form of a black stone, possibly a meteorite, in 204BC, just as Hannibal was about to leave Italy.

Installed in 191BC in her own temple on the Palatine, the *Magna Mater* had a special band of eunuch priests (*galli*) to serve her, and her festival, the Megalensia, was held annually from the 5th to 10th April, with religious processions, games and theatrical performances in the Circus Maximus. Although a Roman magistrate presided over the ceremonies, the *galli*, dressed in bright-coloured robes stained with blood from their self-flagellation, offended Roman sensibilities, for Roman citizens were forbidden to be priests. Finally the open-minded emperor Claudius (ruled AD41–54) incorporated her cult into the official Roman pantheon.

### THE PYTHAGOREANS

Pythagoras (*c.* 570–500BC) was the great mystic among mathematicians. One of the leading early Greek Presocratic philosophers, traditionally he was the first man to call himself a philosopher.

Little definite is known about Pythagoras' life or teaching, but he reputedly believed in metempsychosis, the transmigration of souls, whereby human souls are reincarnated in animals or plants according to their past lives. He also advocated strict vegetarianism and forbade the eating of beans because they caused the breaking of wind, which he held to contain the human soul.

Pythagoras moved from his native island of Samos to southern Italy, where he established a school at Crotona. There he taught a select few mathematics, astronomy and music. He also taught a secret political programme that allowed the Pythagoreans to wield real power for some years in several western Greek cities before they were eventually expelled and driven underground.

Under the Romans their beliefs revived. Nigidius Figulus, a praetor in 58BC, was a Neopythagorean as, apparently, was Apollonius of Tyana *c.* AD200. A tiny underground basilica by the Porta Maggiore in Rome, discovered by chance in 1917 and decorated with exquisite mythological scenes about the love and death of the Greek poet Sappho, is probably Neopythagorean. The cult clearly had to remain half-secret, however. One likely member, Statilius Taurus, was condemned in AD53 for practising "magic arts". In fact the Neopythagoreans were the most intellectual of the mystery cults.

*Above: A 3rd-century AD mosaic showing the triumph of Bacchus over the Indians in his tiger-drawn chariot. The Romans adopted the worship and myths of Dionysus, the Greek god of drama, whom they called Bacchus.*

*Right: A eunuch priest of Cybele, the Great Mother goddess. Her worship was imported into Rome in 204BC.*

# NEW GODS FROM THE EAST

For the Romans as for the Greeks, the traditional gods of pharaonic Egypt, such as the jackal-headed Anubis, seemed absurdly zoomorphic, suited only for Egyptian peasants. Nonetheless, the antiquity and mystery of the land impressed Western rulers from Alexander the Great on and two deities emerged from Egypt that spread around the Roman empire as far north-west as Britain: Isis and Sarapis.

*Above: Statue of Tiber, the god of the river. It was found at the sanctuary of Isis and Sarapis in the Campus Martius, where Caligula had built a temple to the two Egyptian deities.*

*Below: A 2nd-century AD relief from Alexandria in Egypt showing the bearded Sarapis seated between the goddesses Demeter and Venus (Aphrodite). His worship was more usually associated with that of Isis.*

## ISIS

The greatest goddess of Egypt in Hellenistic and Roman times, Isis was of great antiquity. Originally she had been simply a local goddess of the Delta. According to much-embroidered myth, she was the consort and sister of Osiris and mother of the hawk god Horus. When Set, their evil brother, murdered Osiris, she wandered the earth to find her husband's dismembered body, mourning as she went. The legend reveals that she was originally a fertility goddess connected with the natural cycle of death and rebirth, like Cybele and many other goddesses. Under the Greek-speaking Ptolemies, who ruled Egypt 323–30BC, she was Hellenized and her role expanded into that of a cosmic saviour. Aspects of her cult then acquired genuine spiritual and ethical elements that Apuleius later voiced most lyrically in his novel *The Golden Ass* of *c.* AD150.

As her worship spread around the Mediterranean from its origins in Alexandria, Isis became known as Stella Maris (Star of the Sea), the divine protector of sailors and fishermen. In Rome, spectacular annual festivals in her honour celebrated the start of the sailing season on 5th March with *navigium Isidis* (the Relapse of the Ship) and its completion in the autumn.

Isis' strongest appeal initially was to women, freedmen and slaves; old-fashioned Romans such as Augustus and Tiberius disapproved of her. The emperor Caligula (ruled AD37–41) was a devotee, however, and encouraged the building of a temple to her and her co-Egyptian deity Sarapis in the Campus Martius in Rome. Pompeii boasted a fine temple of Isis, the earliest one in Italy, as did many other cities across the empire, especially those involved with foreign trade such as Ostia. These temples had heavily Egyptian decorations to stress their exotic appeal, but the cult itself seems to have been uplifting rather than orgiastic. A mural from Herculaneum shows very solemn-looking priests and worshippers conducting ceremonies. In the final section of *The Golden Ass*, Apuleius waxed lyrical about how Isis appeared to him in a dream, saying "I am the first of heavenly beings, mother of the gods, I am Minerva, Venus, Diana… the Universal Mother, mistress of the elements, primeval child of time…queen of the dead, queen also of the immortals".

The worship of Isis continued to grow through the 3rd century and even survived early Christian persecutions; her great temple at Philae in Egypt was only

*Right: The worship of Isis, the great goddess of Egypt, was very popular. The rites were dignified if mysterious, as this fresco from Herculaneum shows.*

finally closed in the 6th century. Some aspects of her cult, including her blue robe and the title Stella Maris, were taken over by the cult of the Virgin Mary.

### SARAPIS

Sarapis was a wholly syncretic deity, invented under the Ptolemies who conflated Osiris, Isis' consort, with the sacred Apis bulls. The resulting god, Osorapis, or Sarapis, then became identified with the dynasty and with Zeus/Jupiter.

Worshipped in Alexandria as a bearded man, Sarapis was seen by the Greeks as a healing god, similar to Asclepius, the Greek healing god who was introduced to Rome in 291BC. Sick people went to his temple to be cured through divine dreams in a process called incubation.

Meanwhile, and supposedly connected with this but in reality perpetuating a far older cult, Egyptian priests continued to worship Apis at Memphis.

Vespasian (ruled AD69–79) titled himself the new Sarapis when he launched his victorious bid for the imperial throne in Alexandria in AD69. Later Caracalla (ruled AD211–17) built an impressive Serapeum on the Quirinal Hill in Rome.

### THE SIBYL

At several desperate moments in its history, the Sibyl and the Sibylline books were of crucial importance to Rome. Traditionally, the Sibyl, a priestess of Apollo from Cumae, a Greek colony near Naples, offered to sell King Tarquin nine books of prophecy in the 6th century BC. King Tarquin refused twice to buy them, baulking at the price. Each time he refused, the priestess threw three of the books into the fire and doubled the price of the remainder. Tarquin eventually capitulated and bought the last three, which were then kept in the Capitol. The books were consulted by the Senate in

emergencies about which foreign gods to import. An outbreak of plague led to the introduction of the worship of Apollo in 431BC. The books were also thought to contain prophecies and some Christians later maintained that they foretold the birth of Christ. They were all lost in the invasions of the 5th century AD.

*Right: A wayfarer consults the Sibyl. Originally a priestess of Apollo from Greek Cumae, she became central to Rome's religious practices.*

# CULT OF THE SUN

The Graeco-Roman pantheon was essentially anthropomorphic and did not deify natural phenomena. However, the Greeks worshipped the sun god Helios just as the Romans worshipped Sol Indiges. Worship of Sol Invictus, the Unconquered Sun, was at times linked to the worship of Mithras.

## MITHRAS

Possibly Indo-Iranian in origin, Mithras became an archetypal saviour deity for the Romans, a precursor and rival to Christianity. First appearing in Rome in the 1st century BC, Mithras was usually portrayed in Persian clothes wearing a Phrygian cap (from Asia Minor), killing the bull of cosmic darkness.

There were strong astrological associations to the cult of Mithras. Aion (impersonal time) sometimes appeared as a lion-headed deity beside him on carvings and the evil scorpion was depicted being crushed. Mithras offered his worshippers redemption from the otherwise inexorable fate revealed by astrology. Mithraism's hierarchy mirrored that of the Roman army, of which most of its adherents were members, and initiation into his worship came in grades. Each congregation was composed of *fratres* (brothers) and *patres* (fathers) – titles the Christians later copied – who promised to support each other.

The final initiation rite may have required the neophyte to lie in a pit while the blood of a freshly sacrificed bull showered down on him but, as with other mystery rites, the exact details of Mithraic rites are unknown. The cult was spread around the empire mainly by the army, but it also appealed to unmilitary types such as merchants of Ostia, where 15 *mithraea* (shrines) have been found, and to the emperor Nero. Ever interested in novelties, Nero appeared dressed as Mithras when investing Tiridates as king of Armenia in a grand ceremony at Rome in AD66. In the 2nd century AD, Hadrian and Commodus were initiated as emperors and so, reputedly, was Julian,

*Above: The 3rd-century* AD *Altar to Mithras in the mithraeum of the Circus Maximus in Rome. Most shrines to this god were underground, like this one. Only the initiated were able to watch the rites whose secrets are now lost.*

*Right: One of the most attractive aspects of Mithraism was its practice of mutual support, which rivalled Christianity's. Here a mystical banquet sanctifies the solidarity of his worshippers.*

the last pagan emperor (ruled AD361–3) who ordered the building of a *mithraeum* in Constantinople, the new capital. There was an underground *mithraeum* in London, whose ruins are almost the only Roman buildings which survive in the open in the city. An obvious limitation to the spread of Mithraism was its restriction to men. Mithras' cult vanished with the fall of the Western empire in the 5th century AD.

## THE UNCONQUERED SUN

During the imperial period there was a growing tendency among the intellectual to look for a unifying divine force behind the empire's plethora of deities. This is implied in the dedication of the emperor Hadrian's greatest temple, the Pantheon, to *all* the gods.

Sol Invictus, the Unconquered Sun, was first mentioned in the 2nd century AD and the emperor Septimius Severus added a radiant solar nimbus to his imperial attributes around the same time. His son Caracalla, who extended Roman citizenship to (almost) all free inhabitants of the empire in AD212, unwittingly furthered such syncretic attempts to unite the gods in the *pax deorum*, the harmony of the heavens. (Caracalla was concerned chiefly with extending the death duties which were paid only by Roman citizens.)

The solar cult took a giant step forward in the reign of Elagabalus (ruled AD218–22), the juvenile high priest of the sun god Baal in Emesa. His orgiastic worship of his Syrian deity, aimed at making Baal superior to all Rome's gods and said to involve human sacrifices and mass homosexual orgies, proved too much for Romans. After his assassination his successor Alexander Severus carefully restored the older gods.

Alexander reputedly had images of many saviours in his private chapel, including Orpheus, the legendary poet, Apollonius of Tyana, a recent pagan magus, Abraham and Christ. Yet in the subsequent catastrophic decades, when the empire almost foundered amid endless civil wars, barbarian invasions and

massive economic disruption, people yearned for a simpler, universal god. Among these, Sol Invictus, immediately visible as an object of adoration and the obvious bringer of light to all men, incorruptible and perfectly round, had the strongest appeal. The emperor Aurelian (ruled AD270–5), who regained Gaul and the Eastern provinces for the empire and built Rome's new walls, also built a fine circular temple to Sol Invictus in Rome. With a special new priestly college, Sol Invictus was now made the primary object of official imperial worship in Rome and across the empire and 25th December, the dedication day of the temple, was made a public holiday. Christmas was later deliberately moved to that date.

The tetrarch Constantius Chlorus (ruled AD293–306) also worshipped the Unconquered Sun as did Constantine I in his early years, until the Edict of Milan in AD313, when he and his co-emperor Licinius proclaimed tolerance for all religions. Even in AD324, after his final victory over Licinius, Constantine was still issuing coins bearing images of Sol Invictus and in Constantinople he erected a statue of himself with a crown of solar rays. Although this reflected political caution vis-à-vis his overwhelmingly pagan subjects, it also shows the solar cult was not just an imperial preference.

*Above: A reconstruction of a Mithraic temple showing Mithras slaying the bull of cosmic darkness. The most popular saviour god among the legions, Mithras was also worshipped by civilians, but his cult excluded women.*

*Below: Head of the sun god Helios or Sol Invictus. The Romans were slow to worship the impersonal sun, but 3rd-century AD crises led Aurelian to institute an official cult of the sun to help unite the empire.*

# CHRISTIANITY: TRIBULATION TO TRIUMPH

*Above: A head of Constantine I hints at the colossal arrogance of the first emperor to actively promote Christianity.*

*Below: The Apostles Peter and Paul from an early 4th-century AD Roman bas-relief. St Peter's, Rome, was one of the first great basilicas.*

In *c*. AD33 Jesus, an obscure but probably heterodox Jewish preacher, was put to death on the reluctant orders of the governor of Judaea, Pontius Pilate. The event had no impact on the Roman empire, although Jesus' followers claimed to have seen him alive soon after and began preaching his resurrection, first to Jewish communities around the Mediterranean and then, under the forceful guidance of Paul of Tarsus, to the wider Greek and Latin-speaking world.

## A NEW RELIGION

Initially considered a form of Judaism by the Romans, Christianity was recognized as a distinct sect in AD64 after the great fire of Rome, which the people blamed Nero for starting. The Christians made useful scapegoats for the emperor, who had some rounded up, coated with pitch and set alight. Even Roman audiences

found this hard to stomach and such mass persecutions were long the exception. The Christians were not popular, however. Tacitus, writing *c*. AD100, called them "haters of the human race". Like many Romans he misunderstood Christianity's doctrines and saw the eucharist as an orgy involving cannibalism.

Christianity first appealed mainly to women and slaves and so attracted official suspicion. However, letters between Trajan and Pliny the Younger, *c*. AD110, show the emperor restraining would-be persecutors, insisting that Christians be given fair trials and forbidding anonymous letters of accusation. Hadrian restated this approach in AD122.

Although mobs seem to have enjoyed tormenting this helpless minority, Christianity continued to expand and the Christian church's cellular structure proved supportive in a way unmatched by any other cult. Christianity also appealed to intellectuals (such as St Clement) and to the illiterate alike.

What Christians believed did not worry most pagans; it was what they openly refused to accept that caused problems, especially when the empire was in crisis. By refusing even to sacrifice incense to Roma and the imperial *genius* (spirit), Christians were offending the *pax deorum*, the gods' united protection that the empire desperately needed. This led to imperially sponsored persecutions, from the brief attack under Decius (AD251) to the Great Persecution launched by Diocletian and Galerius in AD303.

Not only priests but ordinary believers were now hunted out. Diocletian himself was no fanatic – he had a Christian wife – nor were many of his officials. Transcripts of AD303 show the governor of Egypt urging his Christian prisoners to reconsider their decision the next day. Many Christians did abjure, but Christian

*martyrs* (witnesses) went to their deaths with impressive confidence in the life to come, finally convincing Galerius and many others that persecution was pointless. In AD311 Galerius rescinded his edicts and asked Christians, too, to pray for the empire.

## CONSTANTINE'S CONVERSION

Traditionally Constantine had a dream the night before his victory at the Milvian Bridge in AD312 which led him to put Christian insignia on his army's standards, so guaranteeing him victory. Afterwards, he noticeably failed to climb the Capitol to make the usual offerings to Jupiter.

While the Edict of Milan in AD313 granted toleration to all religions, Constantine attended the Council of Bishops at Arles in AD314 and the more important Council of Nicaea in AD325. At both, he vainly strove to reconcile warring factions, for Christians, upon ceasing to be persecuted themselves, now began persecuting each other.

Further victories confirmed Constantine in his belief that he was protected by the Christian god. However, he continued to employ pagans and for a time himself observed pagan rituals, even permitting the restoration of old temples in Byzantium after he made it his capital.

Such moves were common sense, as perhaps 95 per cent of his court, army and empire were non-Christian. Nonetheless, he tried to restrict public pagan sacrifices and exempted the Christian clergy from onerous public duties where possible.

Constantine also had material reasons for favouring Christianity. The pagan temples whose despoliation he started were filled not just with centuries of great artworks, many covered with gold and ivory, but had also been used as safe deposits by locals in the absence of reliable banks. Constantine's looting of old treasures – comparable in scale perhaps to Henry VIII's dissolution of the monasteries – helped to pay for his huge building programme. This included not only

his many secular works – in Rome and Constantinople – but also vast numbers of churches, including Old St Peter's and St John Lateran in Rome.

When Constantine died in AD337 (he was buried in the Church of the Apostles in Constantinople), his successors continued his Christianizing policies. The notable but brief exception of Julian's two-year reign revived pagan hopes but failed to shake the slowly emerging Christian establishment.

Imperial toleration of paganism, which was always reluctant, vanished in the later 4th century AD. In AD386 the fervently Christian emperor Theodosius I ordered the removal of the statue of the goddess Victory from the Senate House in Rome, despite the impassioned protestations of Symmachus, a pagan, that "So great a mystery could not be approached by one path alone".

With the disasters of the 5th century AD, most Romans in the West turned in despair to Christianity, whose kingdom was not of this world. However, in the East paganism survived in substantial pockets into the 6th century AD.

*Above: The disciples pictured in the catacombs of St Callistus in Rome. Christians may have worshipped in the catacombs and were buried there, but they did not live there.*

*Below: This mosaic from the 5th-century AD Mausoleum of Galla Placidia in Ravenna shows St Lawrence the Martyr as a deacon carrying a cross. Martyrs were much revered.*

# SPORT AND GAMES

Games, especially gladiatorial combats and chariot races, are among the most famous, even notorious, aspects of life in ancient Rome. Many Roman cities built amphitheatres. The Colosseum in Rome was the largest such arena in the Roman world, but gladiatorial games were first staged in the Forum Romanum and beast displays in the Circus Maximus, which could accommodate possibly six times as many spectators as the Colosseum.

The games required expensively trained professionals, most of whom were slaves, and did not necessarily involve the killing of the human combatants. Although the chariot races staged in the Circus Maximus in Rome were indisputably expensive and dangerous, the arenas of less well-developed provinces such as Britain may have seen far more sporting contests and military tattoos than gladiator fights.

The Circus and the Colosseum were also the venues for *venationes*, wild beast hunts and games which, along with public executions, were much relished by audiences. Roman theatre, in contrast, saw mimes, dances and the Roman *pantomimus* – an entertainment which often involved real violence – grow in popularity during the empire.

Physical fitness was long thought desirable in Rome, where men were liable for arduous military service in the Republic. Exercise grounds were later laid out in Rome and other cities.

*Left: A wild beast hunt in a 4th-century AD mosaic. These* venationes *(wild beast hunts) rivalled gladiatorial displays in their popularity.*

# GLADIATORIAL COMBATS

*Above: A terracotta oil lamp from the 1st century AD, showing gladiators in combat. Gladiatorial combats were popular decorative themes.*

*Below: A Retiarius (right) and a Secutor (left) depicted on a mosaic from a Roman villa in Negra de Valpolicella, Italy.*

Gladiatorial combats were funerary in origin, hence their name *numera* (rewards, sacrifices). The spirits of the dead were thought to appreciate human blood, so captives or slaves were set to fight each other to death at aristocratic funerals.

The first recorded gladiatorial show in Rome was staged in 264BC, when three pairs of gladiators fought to the death in the Forum Boarium (Cattle Market) for the funeral of Marcus Iunius Brutus. Over the next 200 years, Roman nobles competed to put on ever more lavish shows. In 65BC, Julius Caesar displayed 250 pairs of gladiators at funeral games for his father – who had died 20 years before.

This extravagance, which the Senate tried to limit, was an attempt to win votes, for, as Juvenal later noted, *duas tantem res anxius optat, panem et circenses* ("The mob cares only for bread and circuses"). Finally the emperor became the main, often sole, provider of games for Rome's frequent public holidays, while in other cities local magnates continued to provide gorily expensive games involving gladiators and wild animals. Games were often staged as part of ceremonies to do with the imperial cult in the provinces or with triumphs in Rome under the emperors.

At first, gladiators were recruited from among slaves, condemned criminals or war captives. Later, as supplies of these groups dwindled, some free men volunteered for a fixed, usually three- or five-year term. Some slaves were sold off for training as gladiators by owners who wanted to punish them, until Hadrian forbade the practice in the 2nd century AD.

A successful gladiator might hope to earn his *rudis* (wooden sword) of liberty, after three years in the arena and to make enough money from gifts to retire in comfort before he was killed.

**SCHOOLS FOR GLADIATORS**

Gladiatorial training was always arduous and often brutal. Petronius recorded the oath of obedience that the *tiro* (novice gladiator) swore to his *lanista* (trainer), "We solemnly swear to obey the *lanista* in everything. To endure burning, imprisonment, flogging and even death by the sword". Although discipline was savage, the food was good and accommodation not bad by contemporary standards.

Novice gladiators learned how to fight with wooden swords and wicker shields, feinting at the *palus* (wooden post) before progressing to real but padded weapons in a way that paralleled military training. *Lanistae* were used in the later 2nd century BC to train soldiers and in emergencies, such as the Marcomanni invasions of AD167, gladiators could be enrolled into the army, receiving their freedom in return. As it took several years to train a skilled gladiator, they did not usually fight to the death.

Training schools for gladiators were established across Italy and then the Western parts of the empire. In Rome, about 2,000 gladiators, along with doctors, armourers and trainers, lived in one of four *ludi* (schools), of which the biggest was the Ludus Magnus, located just 60 yards east of the Colosseum. Probably started under Domitian (ruled AD81–96), its construction was completed under Hadrian 30 years later. It was an imposing building of brick-faced concrete with a central courtyard surrounded by porticoes. Occupying much of this courtyard was an arena large enough to accommodate 3,000 spectators, where gladiators practised. The Ludus Magnus was connected with the Colosseum by an underground tunnel.

To the south of the Ludus Magnus and much the same size was the Ludus Matutinus, where *venatores*, wild beast fighters, were trained. These schools were considered so central to Rome's well-being that they were eventually run by the state. The emperors appointed Praetorian Prefects to recruit and supervise the training of new gladiators.

### TYPES OF GLADIATOR

By the early imperial period there were a number of different types of gladiator, who were usually identified by their equipment and fighting tactics.

The Samnite or *hoplomachus* was originally a light-armed fighter, who was not necessarily a Samnite but who fought like one. He became progressively more heavily armed and armoured until he was called a *hoplomachus*, like a Greek heavy infantryman. He now wore a large-crested helmet with thigh-length greaves and carried a large rectangular shield and a stabbing sword (the *gladius hispaniensis*), much like a legionary.

The Thracian gladiator emerged in the 2nd century BC when Rome first encountered this warlike part of the Balkans. He was armed with a small round or square shield and two thigh-length greaves and carried a *sica*, a typical curved weapon from the Danube.

The Gaul was at first lightly armed, with a long flat shield and a cut and thrust sword about 2ft (60cm) long. By the end of the Republic he too had gained a helmet and a slashing sword. He then became better known as a *murmillo*, from the Greek fish *murmillon* which adorned his helmet.

The Secutor, the traditional opponent of the net-wielding Retiarius (literally sword man), was among the most recognizable of gladiators, for he had a unique egg-shaped helmet with a metal crest but no brim. He bore the legionary's *scutum* (rectangular shield) and stabbing sword and had a laminated *manicae* (arm-guard).

The Retiarius was armed with a *rete* (net) and trident and had defensive armour only on his left arm and shoulder. He normally fought one of the more heavily-armed gladiators. Technically, the Retiarius was not a gladiator since he did not have a sword.

There are records of women gladiators, who fought each other and wild beasts, but they were less common and in AD200 were banned altogether.

*Below: A typically ornate gladiator's bronze helmet from Pompeii, 1st century AD. Gladiators always dressed to impress.*

*Below: This swordsman, probably a* hoplomachos *or* murmillo, *seems to have just finished off a Retiarius, a trident-wielding netman, who is lying beside him.*

# THE GREAT GAMES

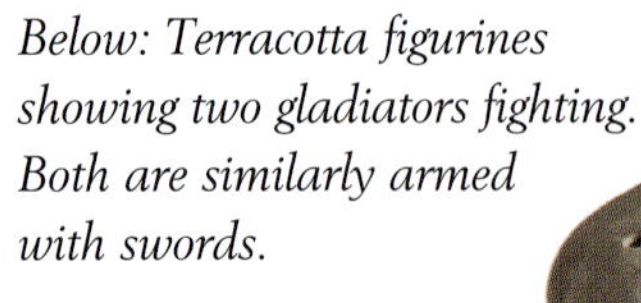

*Above: Gladiatorial combats continued into the 4th century AD, as this mosaic shows. Here a heavily armoured gladiator is shown with a dead Retiarius.*

By the time of the late Republic and early empire huge numbers of gladiators were assembled and wounded or killed for special celebrations. For example, the games that marked the inauguration of the Amphitheatrum Flavium, or Colosseum, in AD80, reputedly lasted 100 days.

## THE CONDUCT OF THE GAMES

Such games opened with a procession of gladiators, who had had a special dinner (the *libera cena*) in public the night before, although not all may have been feeling hungry. To rousing music from a band in the arena – consisting typically of a water organ, horn blowers and trumpeters – they marched around the arena two abreast in full costume, with purple and gold embroideries if they could afford it. When they reached the *pulvinar* (imperial box), they raised their right hands and cried out, *Ave, Caesar! Morituri te salutant!* ("Hail Caesar, those about to die salute you!")

The gladiators were then paired off by lot. Different types of gladiator were pitted against each other; a nimble Retiarius against a heavier Secutor, for example. Often the *lanista* was present less as a

referee than to goad them on with whips and cries of *Iugula! Verbera!* ("Kill! Strike!"), cries which the crowd echoed. Bets were placed and the fight lasted until one combatant was either badly wounded or surrendered. Then trumpets sounded and the wounded man appealed for *missio* (reprieve). The games' sponsor – in Rome normally the emperor – then turned to the spectators. If they thought the gladiator had fought well, they cried *Mitte* ("Let him go"). If the emperor agreed, he would "press his thumb" – a Latin phrase whose precise meaning is unknown but which is interpreted in Hollywood films as raising his thumb. Otherwise, an attendant dressed as Charon, a figure from the underworld, approached with a mallet to finish off the defeated gladiator, whose corpse was dragged through the Porta Libitina (Gate of Execution) with hooks.

The bloodied sand was then replaced while the victor pranced around the arena receiving gifts from spectators and perhaps the palm of success. More rarely he won the wooden foil of freedom. Graffiti from Pompeii, which had the earliest permanent amphitheatre, record various gladiators' fates: "Pugnax, a Thracian of the Neronian *ludus* with three fights to his credit, victorious; Murrans, a *murmillo* of the Neronian *ludus* with three fights to his credit, killed… Atticus, a Thracian with 14 fights, killed".

## STAGED SEA BATTLES

Sea fights with small galleys (*naumachiae*) were also staged. At his triumph in 46BC, Julius Caesar had an artificial lake dug in the Campus Martius (just outside the city) and a battle enacted. These battles were very realistic. Galleys were propelled by slaves who fought

*Below: Terracotta figurines showing two gladiators fighting. Both are similarly armed with swords.*

ferociously. Augustus had a special *naumachia* or artificial lake dug in Trastevere across the Tiber, with its own aqueduct. Here in 2BC he staged a lavish re-enactment of Athens' great victory over the Persians at Salamis in 480BC.

For the inauguration of the works to drain Lake Fucinus under Claudius, a *naumachia* involving 19,000 men took place on the lake. It almost ended in farce when Claudius returned the traditional gladiators' salute, "Hail Caesar, those about to die salute you!" with the quip, "Or not, as the case may be". This so annoyed the gladiators that they downed swords and had to be coaxed back to fight. Nero used Augustus' *naumachia* for varied nocturnal frolics but after that it seems to have fallen into decay. The Colosseum may have been partly flooded for *naumachiae* later.

Most Romans accepted and some even defended gladiatorial shows. Cicero asserted they taught Roman audiences contempt for pain and death, while Pliny the Younger maintained that watching such massacres, in which even criminals and slaves showed a love of glory, would make Romans courageous.

A few emperors, such as Marcus Aurelius, who openly dealt with his correspondence in the arena rather than watching the games, tried to interest the Roman populace in *lusiones*, mock games without bloodshed, but were unsuccessful. Claudius, who watched the fights eagerly and spared no wounded Retiarius, was more typically Roman. Expense led to the decline of the games after the 3rd century AD.

### SPARTACUS THE REBEL

The most famous gladiator of them all, who challenged and threatened to overthrow Roman power, Spartacus took his name from the Greek city of Sparta, although he probably came from Thrace. Trained at the Capua *ludus*, he started his revolt there in 73BC, leading the gladiators out from their barracks, then freeing agricultural slaves to form an army many

thousands strong. Reputedly, Spartacus had once served as a Roman soldier, which explains how he managed to defeat hastily conscripted armies sent against him.

For a time Spartacus controlled much of southern Italy. Finally Crassus, the richest man in Rome, was given command. Decimating his legions (killing one man in ten) to restore order, and with the help of Pompey arriving belatedly from Spain, he cornered and destroyed Spartacus' army in 71BC. Along the Via Appia from Rome to Capua 7,000 rebels were crucified in ghastly but effective warning. There were no more such revolts.

*Above: An orchestra, sometimes with a woman playing the water organ, often accompanied the games, as in this mosaic from Zliten, near Lepcis Magna, Africa.*

*Below: In this 4th-century AD mosaic, found on the Via Appia, just outside Rome, gladiatorial combat is carefully controlled by the* lanistae, *the trainers. Strict rules governed most combats.*

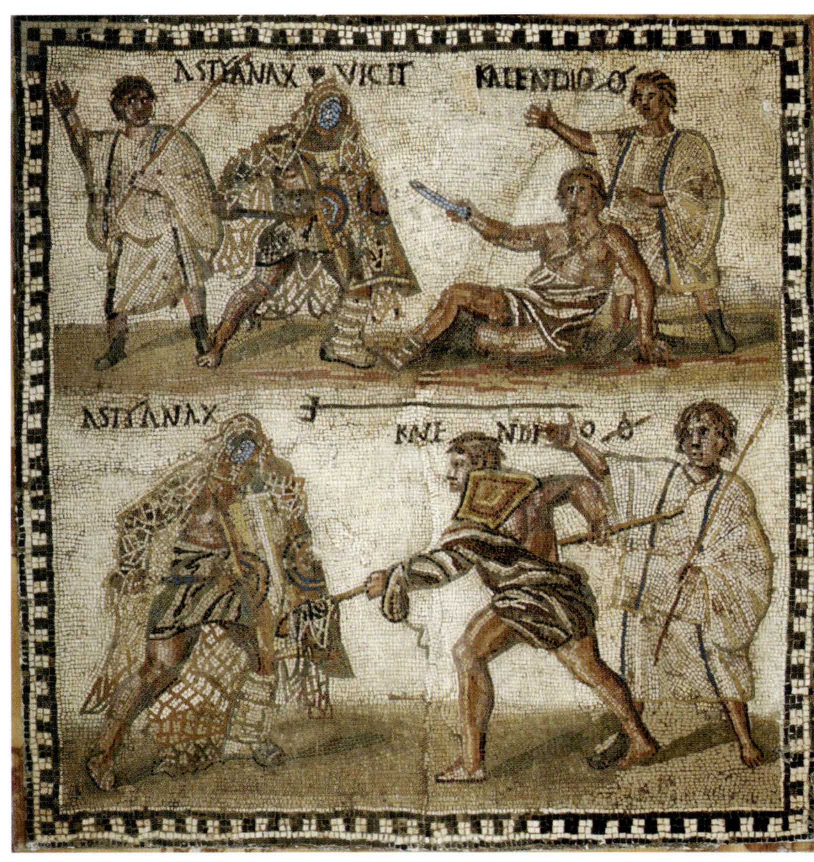

# WILD BEAST GAMES

*Above: A bestiarius (animal fighter) is thrown into the air by a bull in this 3rd-century AD funerary stone from Africa. Fighting wild beasts could be very dangerous.*

*Below: A lion fight in the Circus Maximus in Rome in the 1st century AD. The lion on the right seems to have already killed a man, but is about to be speared himself. On the left a lioness leaps to savage an armed man.*

Parallel to the gladiators' fights were the *venationes*, the wild beast games, which were if anything an even larger business. The *venatores* (huntsmen) and the *bestiarii* (animal fighters) had their own *ludus*, the Ludus Matutinus (so-called because the beast displays were usually staged in the morning), although they never enjoyed the same prestige as gladiators.

*Venationes* provided the Roman urban populace with a glimpse of the often dangerous hunting – for wild boar among other animals – that the emperor himself enjoyed in the country proper. However, they became almost as ruinously expensive as the *munera*.

The first *venationes* or hunting displays started innocuously enough: a hundred elephants that had been captured from the Carthaginians in 251BC were forced to perform tricks. However, in the 2nd century BC more violent displays developed. By 99BC, full-scale fights between elephants were being staged in the Circus Maximus. Marcus Scaurus, who reportedly built a luxurious if temporary amphitheatre of marble and glass in 58BC, imported

150 leopards along with a hippopotamus and five crocodiles for his games. Increasingly bloody *venationes* were hosted from then on.

Caesar had 600 lions, 400 other great cats and 20 elephants in his triumphant *venatio*. Titus surpassed this, killing 5,000 animals on one day to inaugurate the Colosseum in AD80. Trajan had 2,246 wild beasts slaughtered in just one of his many *munera*. The poet Martial mentions more innocent circus turns, including teams of panthers obediently drawing chariots and elephants kneeling to trace Latin phrases in the sand with their trunks. The populace wanted blood, however, and to satisfy it the Romans pitted bears against water buffalos, panthers against leopards, lions against tigers and bulls against rhinoceroses. (The latter were normally victorious, tossing great bulls into the air like balls.)

The *venatores*, armed with spears, bows, daggers and firebrands and sometimes assisted by hunting dogs, fought animals in the arena. Trees and shrubs were placed in the arena to create the illusion of a forest in which the *venatores* hunted and killed the doomed animals. The Romans were no more sentimental about killing animals than about killing humans and viewed the *venationes* as a re-affirmation of their dominance over nature.

Criminals were sometimes executed by the *damnatio ad bestias* (thrown unarmed or with rudimentary weapons into the arena to face wild animals or gladiators). War captives were another source of arena fodder. Under Claudius, captive Britons were slaughtered in the arena in AD47. Titus had Jewish captives killed in games after the Jewish War (AD66–70) and Constantine I had Frankish captives thrown into the ring in Trier in AD308 to celebrate his victory over them. At the other extreme, one or two debauched

emperors, including Nero and Commodus, personally took part in the games. Commodus actually performed in the arena, shooting hundreds of ostriches to demonstrate his *virtus* (courage), but Nero forced senators and equestrians to fight (though not kill) in the arena themselves. Young Roman nobles under the empire sometimes stepped into the arena to fight as amateurs to exhibit their *virtus*, but gladiators on the whole never escaped their low status. Although a few became celebrities, no gladiator ever held high office, although some were used as bodyguards or assassins.

## CATASTROPHIC EFFECTS

The Romans imported exotic wild beasts from all over the empire and at times from well beyond their frontiers. In the first millennium BC, great cats such as lions, panthers and tigers still roamed freely in western Asia; in 51BC Cicero's brother, who was governor of Cilicia, was asked to supply panthers from Asia. There were hippopotami and crocodiles on the banks of the Nile and elephants and ostriches could be found north of the Sahara. This rich fauna was devastated over the centuries, as a highly efficient system of capturing and transporting them was established to satisfy audiences in Rome and in other great cities around the empire. By the 4th century AD it was becoming increasingly hard to find animals to satisfy the demands of the arena. Almost none of these great animals, with the exception of a few lions in the Rif Mountains of Morocco, are to be found north of the Sahara or west of India today.

*Above: A Roman fresco from the amphitheatre of Mérida in Spain showing a venator (huntsman) facing a lion with only a spear. Animal games were popular in cities all round the empire.*

*Below: Arena substructures, possibly a lion pit, in the amphitheatre of Thysdrus (El Djem), Africa, built c. AD230.*

# AT THE CIRCUS: CHARIOT RACES

*Above: Chariot races in the Circus Maximus, Rome, with the* spina *in the centre.*

*Below: A* quadriga *chariot from a 3rd-century AD mosaic. Only one man rode a chariot.*

Although they had different origins, the *ludi circenses* (circus games) were the *munera*'s greatest rival attraction. Racing with chariots generally took place in the Circus Maximus (the biggest circus). The arena was well-named since it was truly vast, over 660yds (600m) long and 220yds (200m) wide, sited in a natural hollow between the Aventine and Palatine Hills. Progressively adorned, it was given its final form under Trajan, who turned it into a massive structure with three marble-faced arcades built up on vaults. It is estimated it could seat up to 300,000 people, about a third of the city's population.

## THE RUNNING OF THE RACES

All drivers belonged to one of four *factiones* (teams) in the imperial period: the Whites, the Reds, the Blues and the Greens. These were sizeable companies or corporations, each with its own stables and team of trainers, coaches, saddlers, vets, blacksmiths and grooms sited in the Ninth Region of the City near the present Palazzo Farnese.

The *factio* normally supported by the people was the Greens, while the Senate supported the Blues. Huge bets were placed on each team or rider. The number of races held per day was 12 under Augustus, but under Caligula – who was almost literally mad about the games – this was doubled and 24 races a day became the standard. Each lasted 7 laps of 620yds (568m), run anti-clockwise around the central *spina* (masonry rib). This was decorated with seven metallic eggs, seven bronze dolphins and other statues. At each end of the *spina* were the *metae* (turning posts).

Most races were for *quadrigae*, four-horse teams. Two-, three-, six-, eight- and even rarely ten-horse teams (*decemiuges*) were known, but the last was normally reserved for egomaniacs like Nero who drove one while collecting every prize at the Olympic Games in AD67. Only the inner pair of horses actually pulled the chariot. The outer pair were only loosely attached by a *junis* (trace), but they were vital to the chariot's stability. Racing chariots were mere boxes, given a little stability only by their driver's weight.

Charioteers wore short sleeveless tunics and leather helmets, and carried knives to cut themselves free from the leads tied round their waists if there was a collision. As up to 12 *quadrigae* chariots could compete in the circus, collisions were common occurrences.

Before a race started, each of the chariots was placed in one of the *carceres* (starting gates). Above them a magistrate presided over the games. When he gave the signal, by dropping a white napkin into the circus, a trumpet sounded, a

spring mechanism opened the gates and the chariots were off. Each charioteer strove to attain the best inner position on the left, but fine judgement was crucial. If his chariot wheel so much as touched the *spina*'s stone kerb, it could shatter, wrecking his own and probably others' chariots in the crash. However, if his chariot swung out too far, it risked losing the advantage of the inner position.

As each lap was completed, one of the eggs on the *spina* was lowered to keep count. The last lap was the most excitingly dangerous of all. The winner was greeted with ecstatic applause and given a victor's palm or gold crown and neck chains. To placate the losers among the spectators – and many poorer Romans gambled madly – donations of money would be thrown to the audience and free meals provided afterwards.

As well as the races, there were exhibitions of trick-riding and other less dangerous gymnastic sports. The Circus Maximus also staged wild beast shows.

## FAMOUS CHARIOTEERS

Although almost all charioteers were slaves or ex-slaves – and so scarcely higher in Rome's social hierarchy than gladiators – a few became very famous and very rich, both from gifts they received from magistrates and other rich men and also from the fantastic wages they could command from their *factio* for their loyalty.

Supreme among these star charioteers was Gaius Apuleius Diocles, who competed 4,257 times and won 1,462 victories. He wisely retired in AD150 – with a fortune of 35 million sesterces – to a life of quiet philanthropy at Pozzuoli.

Others in the races' heyday – the later 1st and early 2nd centuries AD – also did extremely well. They were known as *milliari* not because they were millionaires – although they often were – but because they had competed more than 1,000 times in the races. Among these *milliari* were Pompeius Musclosus, who competed 3,559 times, and Scorpus, who completed 2,048 races before he was killed.

Chariot-racing, unlike gladiatorial combat, was not banned by the newly Christian rulers of the empire. Indeed, a hippodrome (circus) in the new capital of Constantinople was built right next to the imperial palace in direct emulation of Rome. The bitter rivalry that existed between the Blues and Greens (the other *factiones* were ultimately subsumed) also continued into the 6th century AD and caused the *Nike* (victory) riots in AD529 that almost drove the emperor Justinian from his throne.

*Above: Chariot-racing was popular in the provinces too, as this 2nd century AD mosaic from Lyons, then Gaul's greatest city, shows.*

*Below: A charioteer from the Circus Maximus, Rome, in the 1st century AD. Horses were occasionally raced individually by jockeys as well as being used to pull chariots.*

# AT THE THEATRE: FARCE, MIME AND PANTOMIME

*Above: Two actors wearing masks, from a 1st century AD relief. Roman actors normally wore masks both for comedy and for tragedy.*

*Below: A 1st-century AD fresco of a tragic actor. This copies a Greek 4th century BC original, revealing Roman links with Greek drama.*

Other entertainments the Romans enjoyed were *ludi scaenici* (theatrical performances), performed in the impressive theatres found in almost every city across the empire. These still often splendid buildings give a misleading impression of the importance of theatre, especially of tragedy, to the Romans, however.

In the Roman world, theatre never had the central role that it had in the cities of classical and Hellenistic Greece (500–100BC). This was partly due to the rival attractions of circus and arena which shaped public tastes. Traditional plays without music or dancing were supplemented by musicals accompanied by dancing, spectacular performances, mimes and *pantomimus*. In these lavish displays, spoken dialogue took a distant second place after extravagant special effects.

## THE ORIGINS OF ROMAN THEATRE

Roman theatre emerged in the 4th century BC with broad comedy and farce, the *Phlyakes* and the Atellan farces and was performed mainly in southern Italy. The actors wore grotesque masks and padded costumes suiting their stock characters, who had ludicrous names such as Bucco and Maccus (both fools) or Dosennus and Manducus (greedy buffoons). As the play's titles also reveal – *The Pig, The Sow, The Inspector of Morality* – this was unsubtle, rustic humour, with satire directed not at the ruling class – who would have reacted strongly – but at ordinary people.

Rhinthon of Tarento, a Greek city in southern Italy, was one of the most popular playwrights but there was much ad-libbing and many plays were not written down until much later. Farce was the dominant note, forever loved by Italian audiences.

In the 2nd century BC, Plautus and Terence raised the level of comedy. Their plays, concerned with love and its problems, were inspired by the Greek New Comedy, which lacked the satirical bite of Aristophanes and Old Comedy and so was politically acceptable. Only 21 of the 130 comedies attributed to Plautus survive, but his work and that of Terence remained popular with Roman audiences for centuries. However, the Roman comic repertory expanded only slightly later.

Roman poets such as Ennius (239–169BC) also wrote tragedies, but none has survived. However, tragedy was never very popular with Roman audiences. This was partly due to the huge size of many theatres. (The Theatre of Pompey in Rome seated an audience of around 29,000 and the Theatre of Marcellus seated around 14,000.) Such vast structures were not well-suited to plays that required the audience to concentrate carefully on spoken dialogue, no matter how good

their acoustics. It was more importantly due to the fact that Roman audiences were generally less well-educated than those of classical Greece and to their wish to be entertained and amused rather than intellectually taxed. Seneca's melodramatic tragedies, so influential in later European theatre, were probably never performed in public at all but reserved for private readings.

## BRUTAL THRILLS

Perhaps the fundamental reason why Roman audiences turned away from even the broadest situation comedy lay in their increasing attraction, even addiction to the brutal thrills provided by the amphitheatre and circus.

However, the Romans resourcefully found other uses for their theatres. These involved dance or balletic performances, mime and pantomime. The last was a truly Roman invention, consisting of masked dancers miming a story, which was often based on, or a burlesque of, myth. The first great *pantomimus* (He Who Mimes Everything) was Pylades in Augustus' reign, an actor of great skill who performed most of the action accompanied by music. His performances were so popular that they literally caused riots.

The earlier Roman stage had no actresses and women's roles had been taken by men, as in Greece. Women now appeared on stage, not wearing heavy masks but elaborately made up to add to their appeal. In some later mimes actresses stripped off completely. This was especially useful for enacting mythical scenes such as the rape of Pasiphae, the Cretan queen who became so enamoured of a bull she had a special wooden cow built in which to receive him. (The resulting child was the half-bull, the Minotaur.)

At times, executions in the plot, such as that of *Laureolus*, were literally carried out on criminals. *Laureolus*, who was crucified, remained very popular with Roman audiences for two centuries, as did the *Death of Hercules*, which involved the immolation of a criminal on a pyre.

There is no evidence that these "plays" were staged in the theatre, although they were certainly staged in the Colosseum in AD80. Some theatres in the Eastern half of the empire, where purpose-built amphitheatres were rare, were adapted to stage gladiatorial combats or wild beast displays, even in Athens itself. The citizens of the supposedly more civilized east seem to have got over their initial revulsion, although the first gladiatorial games performed in Antioch reportedly caused a riot.

Actors were considered scarcely better than charioteers or gladiators socially. It was thought demeaning for a Roman citizen to act at all, such things being better left to half-Greek freedmen.

When Nero performed in public theatres, sometimes taking female roles, he deeply shocked all Roman opinion, not just among the nobility. The Christian emperors finally put an end to such entertainments because of their religious associations, which St Augustine found particularly immoral.

*Above: Broadest comedy was what most pleased Roman audiences. Buffoonish comic actors such as this one, with his clown-like mask, from a 1st century AD mosaic at Pompeii, were much loved.*

*Below: Elaborate masks such as this one, depicted on a floor mosaic, covered the faces of all actors except some women in later productions, who even reputedly sometimes stripped.*

# GAMES AND EXERCISES

*Above: Caracalla built (AD 211–17) enormous public baths that included palaestrae (exercise areas).*

*Below: Roman aspiration to Greek athleticism is exemplified by this statue of c. 100BC, in which a Roman head is stuck on a Greek body.*

The Romans regarded keeping fit as a vital part of a citizen's personal regime, but they never fostered a cult of athletics in the way that the Greeks did. Their lack of enthusiasm for nudity was the inverse of the Greeks' near mania for depicting heroic nudity, from soldiers on funerary monuments to stark naked gods, wearing only a helmet. Combined with the ingrained Roman sense of *dignitas*, this meant that no athlete became a civic hero as had happened so often in Greece. However, *mens sana in corpore sano* ("A healthy body and a healthy mind"), as Juvenal put in one of his less satirical satires, was a Roman motto as much as a Greek ideal.

Although ordinary Roman life involved at least a modicum of daily exercise for everyone, rich Romans, unlike their counterparts in classical Greece, appear to have suffered from some of the diseases of affluence, possibly because they were such very enthusiastic gourmands.

From the later Republic on, Rome was a crowded city notably lacking in public spaces. To counter this, Marcus Agrippa, Augustus' chief minister, built *palaestrae* (exercise grounds or gyms) in the open land of the Campus Martius just west of the old Servian walls where the very first legions

*Above: Boxing, shown in this 3rd century AD mosaic from Africa, was a popular participatory sport.*

had mustered. Later *palaestrae* were generally attached to the great public baths, so that athletes could bathe after their exercises. At Trajan's Baths, built AD104–9, a corporation or club of athletes was based in the large open-air *palaestra* on the Baths' west side. It flourished for more than 200 years up to the mid-4th century AD. There seems to have been a similar corporation in the Baths of Caracalla, which were built just over a century later.

Wrestling was a popular sport and wrestlers used to smear themselves with *ceroma*, a lotion composed of oil and wax which made the skin more supple. Women also wrestled occasionally, thereby offending the moralistic Juvenal. Dumbbells were popular with men and women as was rolling a metal hoop and running.

## BALL GAMES

The Romans had many kinds of ball game. These included the *trigon*, in which three players formed a triangle and tossed the ball back and forth between them; a sort of tennis played with the palm of the hand for a racquet; and the *harpastum*, in which contestants had to catch the sand-filled ball as it flew between players. For all these games except wrestling, a short tunic was worn, for the Romans generally did not like to exercise naked as the Greeks did.

## PUBLIC GAMES

None of these simple sports could rival the races or gladiatorial games in popularity, but there were repeated attempts under Nero and Domitian in Rome to enthuse the populace about athletic displays derived from Greek models. This was partly, no doubt, because they were cheaper as well as more edifying to stage than *munera* or *ludi*.

Athletics displays were popular as interval entertainment in the circus, and continued to be important in the Greek part of the Roman empire. Augustus, following the precedents of some earlier philhellenes such as Pompey, founded the Actiaca, games to commemorate his victory at Actium, in which he encouraged young Roman nobles to participate in Greek-style games. He had only fleeting success, however, for the Actiaca is not recorded after AD16 (only two years after the emperor's death).

True to his philhellenism, Nero tried to revive these contests with his Neronia, which were intended to be regular festivals with both athletic and poetic competitions. The senatorial nobility participated in the first but shunned the second, probably because they feared competing directly against the emperor.

It was Domitian (ruled AD81–96), normally considered among the more dourly despotic of emperors, who finally established a cycle of athletic games which endured. In AD86 he set up the *Agon Capitolinus* (Capitoline Games), with prizes for racing on foot, boxing, discus-throwing and javelin-throwing, as well as for eloquence, Latin and Greek poetry and music. He built the Circus Agonalis, now the Piazza Navona, for the

sporting events and an Odeum on Monte Giordano and the Campus Martius for the cultural contests. The poet Martial sang the praises of the winners. The games survived Domitian's assassination and continued into the 4th century AD. This was partly because they recurred only once every four years, but also because they were aimed at relatively small, select audiences. The Odeum could seat no more than about 5,000 people and the stadium only about 15,000. These were small numbers compared to the crowds in the Colosseum and the Circus Maximus.

Unlike theatres and amphitheatres, these games were not widely copied around the Western empire. In Greece itself the Olympic Games continued to be staged, although the Roman nobility chose not to compete. Theodosius banned them by AD393.

*Above: Two wrestlers in a gymnasium are shown in this relief from the tomb of Caecilia Metella. Wrestling was a hugely popular sport. Wrestlers would smear themselves all over with* ceroma, *an oil and wax lotion to make it harder for their opponents to grip them.*

*Left: A sculpture of a Hellenistic athlete, signed by Agasias of Ephesus and dated to c. 100BC. Such fine imported artworks helped shape Roman attitudes to physical beauty.*

# CHAPTER XI

# SCIENCE, TECHNOLOGY AND THE ECONOMY

The Romans, famously pragmatic, were not speculative scientists in the Greek mould, but in the prosperous centuries of the Pax Romana (Roman peace) neither science nor technology stood still. Most scientists were polymaths, interested in many fields. Strabo was a philosopher and historian as well as a famed geographer, while Ptolemy wrote on music and mechanics. Practical matters were not neglected, although they were under-recorded by writers concerned with more prestigious subjects. Water power was exploited more thoroughly, new forms of concrete and glass were developed and ships became far larger. Agriculture, too, made incremental advances and better olive presses were introduced. One revolutionary idea was developed for a tantalizing instant only to be abandoned: Hero's steam engine.

Despite the Romans' complete ignorance of economic theory, there was an immense boom in trade both within and beyond the empire, with new routes reaching as far as India and even China. Massive amounts of wheat and olive oil were shipped across the Mediterranean from Egypt and North Africa. Intercontinental trade on such a massive scale would not recur before the 17th century.

*Left: A Roman soldier kills Archimedes, the Greek scientist, during the siege of Syracuse. Fortunately such disasters were exceptional, for Greek science flourished under Roman rule.*

# STRABO AND GRAECO-ROMAN GEOGRAPHY

Alexander the Great's conquests as far as northwest India (356–323BC) led to a vast expansion of Greek geographical and scientific knowledge. There followed the golden age of Greek science of the following centuries. This knowledge was collated by Alexander's heirs, especially the Ptolemies of Egypt (322–30BC), who used their vast wealth to turn their museum and library at Alexandria into the greatest scholarly and scientific centre of the ancient world.

### A NEW GEOGRAPHY

When Roman power spread – around the Mediterranean, east as far as the Caspian and the Gulf, then north towards the Baltic and Britain – so Roman interest in, and need for, such knowledge grew.

Lucullus and Pompey, the Roman generals who in the last decades of the Republic conquered Eastern kingdoms such as Syria and Pontus, inherited these monarchies' cultural assets and pretensions. Lucullus set up a fine library at Rome with the intellectual spoils of his victories and it was to Rome, the new world ruler, that Greek philosophers and polymaths such as Posidonius (135–50BC) came, teaching rich Roman students and even a few Greeks. Foremost among the Greek students was Strabo.

Strabo (64BC–*c.* AD21) came from the aristocracy of his native town of Amaseia in northern Asia Minor. Rich and well-connected, he made friends with the Roman nobility, spending long periods in Rome whose government and institutions he admired almost uncritically. "Never before has the world enjoyed such perfect peace and prosperity…cities and peoples united in a single empire, under one government," he enthused. He came to see his work as a two-way bridge between Greek culture and learning and Roman government and authority. Roman power would facilitate the extension of Greek knowledge, while Greek thinking and culture would complement and underpin Roman arms.

Strabo's learning was openly derived from the works of his great predecessors, especially Eratosthenes (275–194BC) – an Athenian who settled in Alexandria to become one of the city's brilliant polymaths – and Posidonius. He wrote in Greek, then the language of almost all scientific thought across the Mediterranean. His first work, a history in 47 books, has vanished completely but he went on to write 17 books on geography which he published in 7BC. These have mostly survived. For Strabo, geography encompassed history, folklore and mythology as well as astronomy and geometry. So, when talking about Palestine and the Jews, he briefly mentions Moses; when discussing Tarento, he notes its legendary and its historical links with its mother city, Sparta.

Strabo accepted the then commonly held view that the Earth was a perfect (immobile) sphere, with all the (known) continents, Europe, Asia and Africa,

*Above: Inscribed with many languages, the walls of the Bibliotheca Alexandrina rise in a modern recreation of Alexandria's great library.*

*Below: The flooding of the Nile was among the mysteries that perennially fascinated Graeco-Roman geographers.*

*Left: A map of the Roman Empire and its neighbours AD212. As Roman power spread outwards, around the Mediterranean and into northern Europe, Graeco-Roman geographical knowledge grew with it.*

forming a single mass surrounded by the encircling waters of Oceanus, a belief as old as Homer. In his first two books he gave reasonably accurate latitudes and longitudes for the cities, oceans and countries he described, ranging from Spain to Assyria (Iraq), from Britain to Ethiopia. He then described each country and people's beliefs and customs.

Strabo seems to have travelled extensively himself, although his description of Armenia suggests that he had a rather credulous acceptance of local beliefs. "Armenia also has huge lakes, one being the Mantiane which, translated, means 'Blue'. It is the largest salt water lake after Lake Mareotis (in Egypt), it is said, extending to Atropatia, and it also has salt works. Another is Arsene, also called Thopitis. It contains soda that cleans and restores clothes, but this ingredient makes the water undrinkable. The Tigris flows through this lake after rising from the mountain country near the Niphates. Because of its swiftness, its current remains unmixed with the lake. Hence its name Tigris, which in Median (Iranian) means arrow."

(*Geography*, Book V.12)

## THE ROMAN CONTRIBUTION

Although no later writer under the Roman empire rivalled Strabo in scope and information, he did have successors among writers in Latin, a language still regarded as unsuited for scholarship by many Greek-speakers. For example, Lucius Junius Columella, a Roman of equestrian status from Cadiz who seems to have served as a tribune in the army, wrote a book about geography and agriculture – the two topics were not then distinct – around AD50.

Much the most significant later such writer, however, was Pliny the Elder (AD23–79), an intellectually omnivorous if often undiscriminating writer. In his encyclopaedic works, especially his *Naturalis historia* (*Natural History*) Pliny showed himself the heir of Strabo. He claimed to have recorded 20,000 noteworthy facts about life on earth in its 37 books.

In Books III to VI, Pliny deals with geography and later volumes cover his views on biology and botany. His views, like those of many Latin writers, came to be regarded as almost papally infallible in the Middle Ages.

*Below: Roman merchants often ventured beyond the empire's boundaries, but John O'Groats, at Britain's northernmost tip, was Ultima Thule, the furthest land known before the encircling ocean.*

# ASTRONOMY

*Below: The Farnese Atlas, a Roman statue showing the mythical titan who sustained the Earth on his shoulders. Myth and science intermingled in ancient astronomy.*

The greatest astronomers of the ancient world were all Greek, although Cicero gave a poetic version in Latin of current cosmogonies in *Scipio's Dream* around 45BC. In the Roman empire Alexandria remained the centre of astronomical science.

Its most brilliant figure was Ptolemy (Claudius Ptolemaus) who wrote in the middle of the 2nd century AD. Ptolemy's work, however, was merely the culmination of a tradition going back six centuries that combined often meticulous observations with daring speculation.

Without any form of telescope, all ancient astronomers had to rely solely on what could be discerned of the universe with the naked eye. This inevitably shaped their views. Greek astronomical theories originated with the early Ionian thinkers of the 6th century BC such as Thales, who predicted the solar eclipse of 585BC, and his reputed pupil Anaximander, but during the classical period (480–320BC) astronomy languished. With the establishment of the great library at Alexandria *c.* 300BC, astronomy was revived as a more systematic science.

About 275BC, one especially daring astronomer, Aristarchus of Samos, had suggested that, "The fixed stars and the sun stay motionless and the Earth moves in a circle about the sun", but his ideas were almost universally rejected for what were at the time very cogent reasons. (If the Earth rotated around the sun, centrifugal forces would spin everything off the Earth's surface while the "fixed stars" would have to be unbelievably distant to remain fixed in our view of the sky.)

More typical was Eratosthenes who calculated the Earth's circumference with remarkable accuracy (to within 4 per cent) about 225BC. Hipparchus of Nicaea, probably the finest Hellenistic astronomer, invented varied optical aids a century later, drew up star maps and discovered the precession of the equinoxes, while noting a *nova* (new star).

**PTOLEMY'S GRAND COMPILATION**
Ptolemy inherited, summarized and consolidated these achievements. He wrote books on mathematics, optics – based on his own experiments in refraction and reflection – and geography. However, his great achievement was his *Grand Compilation*, better known by its Arabic name the *Almagest*, which indicates its amalgamated nature.

Developing Hipparchus' system, Ptolemy provided a detailed mathematical theory to describe the movements of the sun and moon and of the five planets known without a telescope: Mercury, Venus, Mars, Jupiter and Saturn. His system, which was based on his own precise astronomical observations, perfected the geocentric theory of the universe, ingeniously detailing the epicycles and regressive motions needed to make the "wandering planets" fit such a system.

Ptolemy also wrote a book on music, *Harmonics*. This describes several musical instruments but is chiefly concerned with mathematically perfect harmony – an idea

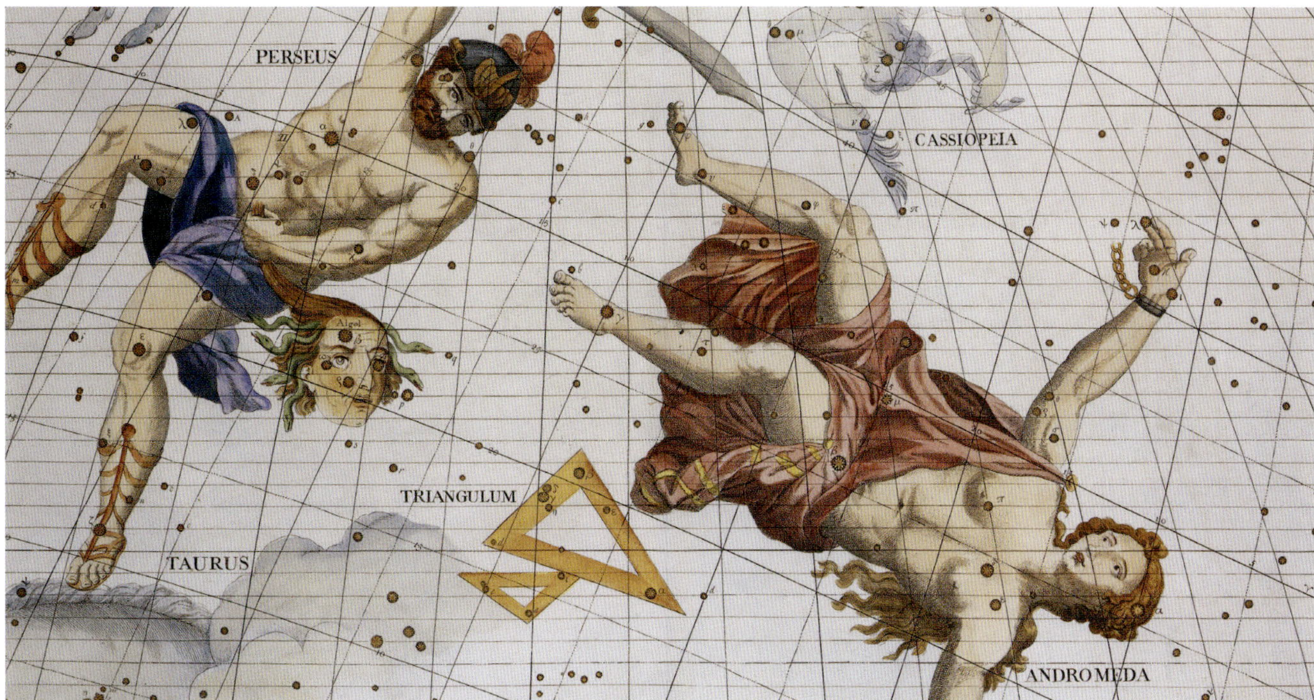



first developed by the mystical philosophers Pythagoras and Plato. He believed that such harmony underpinned the universe and linked it with the human soul. One section is headed, "How the interrelations of the planets are to be compared with those of musical notes.".

Such an apparently workable but mystical view of the cosmos proved hugely influential over the next 1,400 years, both in the Christian and Islamic worlds. Shakespeare was still under its sway in 1598 when he wrote the famous passage in *The Merchant of Venice*, which gives perhaps the most lyrical exposition of the geocentric universe. "Look how the floor of heaven is thick inlaid with patines of bright gold/There's not the smallest orb which thou beholdest/ but in this motion like an angel sings/still choiring to the young-eyed cherubins./ Such harmony is in immortal souls."

### A DANGEROUS SCIENCE

Astrology was one of the Romans' many cultural imports from the Hellenistic East The Romans were very superstitious and heeded soothsayers and other diviners, including *haruspices*, who read

the future in the entrails of sacrificed animals. Accepted almost universally by intelligent people, astrology was a deadly serious business in the Roman empire.

Astrology's basic premises fitted what was then known of the universe and Ptolemy himself related astrology to his own cosmogony. (The five known planets were increasingly identified with their corresponding gods.)

Augustus and his friend Agrippa, young men in 44BC, consulted the astrologer Theogenes at Apollonia in Greece – he predicted amazing futures for both – while Augustus' gloomy successor Tiberius kept his own astrologer Thrasyllus, who established an observatory at Capri. As astrologers were thought to be able to forecast precisely the hour of an emperor's death, it became a crime under the more paranoid Caesars to consult one on such a sensitive subject.

The despotic Domitian had the astrologer Ascletario put to death to confound his prediction that his corpse would be torn to pieces by wild dogs – in vain, for it was – but he entirely believed astrological predictions of the exact hour and manner of his death in AD96.

*Above: The Constellation of Perseus and Andromeda, painted by James Thornhill in 1725. The Greeks and Romans viewed the stars' patterns anthropomorphically.*

*Below: The Ptolemaic system postulated that the Earth lay immobile at the centre of the universe, with the planets and stars circling it in sometimes very complicated epicycles.*

# WATER MILLS

*Above: A fresco from Alexandria showing oxen turning a mill. Such animal-powered mills were very common but not nearly as powerful as water mills.*

*Below: The remains of a giant water wheel of the Roman era near Cordoba, Spain. Water power was used in Spanish mines for pumping out water and for sluicing rock faces clean of debris.*

Among the most enduringly useful innovations that spread around the Mediterranean under the Pax Romana were water mills. They seem to have originated in western Asia and to have been known, if scarcely used, in Greece by the 4th century BC. Traditionally first seen by the Romans in Armenia during their wars against Mithradates of Pontus (89–66BC), they were taken up only slowly at first, probably because of the abundance of slaves in the late Republic and early empire (c. 100BC–100AD). However, as the empire ceased to expand so rapidly, supplies of cheap slaves dwindled and water power was exploited to supplement animal and human muscle power for the first time in Western history. It has been calculated that while a slave-operated mill could grind only 15lbs (7kg) of grain per hour and a mule-powered mill about 60lbs (28kg), a typical water mill could grind 330lbs (150kg) per hour. However, as such technological developments were not thought especially interesting or prestigious, they were seldom mentioned by writers or rulers and we have to rely on archaeological evidence which is only now emerging. Who supplied the finance for the larger projects remains unknown, but the state probably played a major role. Windmills do not appear to have been used by the Romans.

## THE USES OF WATER POWER

The Romans used water power not only for grinding corn but also for pumping water, especially out of mines, for sawing wood, raising hammers in iron works and washing out mineral deposits. In Spain, whose mines employed thousands of slaves to produce much of the empire's gold and silver, huge reservoirs were built above the workings at Rio Tinto with sluices at one end. When the reservoirs had been filled via aqueducts, the sluices were suddenly opened and a great surge of water washed over the exposed seams to carry away the soil. Sophisticated water-powered pumps were also used to pump out mines, where flooding was a perennial problem.

One of the largest water mill complexes so far discovered was at Barbegal near Arles in southern Gaul. Supplied by a branch of the main Arles aqueduct, 16 mill wheels were set in pairs down a steep slope which dropped about 80ft (23m). This complex probably dates from around AD200 and was involved in supplying the city with its daily bread. It is thought to have ground about 660lbs (300kg) of flour an hour – enough to supply a large proportion of the population of Arles. Only ruins of this industrial-sized complex remain. At the other end of the empire, a Roman-era mill, its huge wheel repaired many times, still turns slowly but proudly at Hama in Syria. However, most mills of the Roman period have long since vanished, leaving no visible remains.

## WATER MILLS IN ROME

The first known water mills in ancient Rome were situated on the slopes of the Janiculum Hill. They were powered by the waters falling from the Aqua Traiana, the aqueduct built by the emperor Trajan early in the 2nd century AD. Probably early in the 3rd century AD, a complex of water mills was built in the standard brick-faced concrete across the aqueduct. Parts of the site have recently been excavated, although much remains concealed under nearby streets.

Two mill races branched off the Aqua Traiana and ran parallel to it before rejoining it. There were either three or four mill wheels in the northern mill race and one larger one in the southern mill race.

Mills like these ground Rome's wheat into flour, a necessity as the *annona* (wheat dole) was from the late 2nd century AD normally distributed in the form of baked bread rather than wheat. This particular mill complex seems to have survived the political catastrophes of the 5th century AD. In AD537, Rome was easily captured by the Byzantine general Belisarius and then besieged by the Ostrogoths under Totila, who were trying to regain the city they had ruled for 40 years. When the Goths cut off the city's water supply by breaking down the aqueducts, they also cut off Rome's supply of bread. Ingeniously, Belisarius circumvented the problem by floating water mills placed in boats at a sheltered spot on the Tiber near the island. (The Tiber itself supplied water, along with the city's wells, to the much-reduced population.) The floating mills managed to grind wheat into flour for the populace, according to the Byzantine historian Procopius, who accompanied Belisarius for a time on his military campaigns.

The use of the aqueducts for powering water mills outlasted that of supplying the baths, institutions of which the Christian clergy, by then dominant in the city, disapproved. Water mills for grinding corn lined the Tiber until the late 19th century.

*Above: Roman water wheels at Hama in Syria, still turning slowly but effectively after nearly 2,000 years in use. Water mills were built across the empire wherever there was demand and a suitable river.*

*Below: The emperor Trajan (AD98–117), whose Aqua Traiana aqueduct came to supply water power for Rome's mills.*

# STEAM ENGINES

*Above: Hero of Alexandria, whose many inventions included the world's first steam engine.*

*Below: Hero, like most scientific polymaths of the Roman empire, had a very practical side, describing in his Metrica ways of measuring land and cubic capacity and in his Stereometrica ways of measuring volumes.*

The scientific curiosity and technological experiment of the Roman empire is exemplified by the career of one of the most remarkable inventors of antiquity, Hero of Alexandria, who lived in the 1st century AD. Hero was another gifted Hellenistic polymath – his mention of the solar eclipse of AD62 reveals that his interests included astronomy – but his chief fame is as the author of *Pneumatica*, which lists his varied inventions. Among these are mechanisms which use steam to produce a rotary motion.

This mechanism, which was almost certainly the world's first steam turbine, was more thermodynamically efficient than the piston engines that powered the early industrial revolution and anticipated the steam turbine of Charles Parsons by 1,800 years. Unlike the British engineer's invention, however, Hero's device remained little more than a toy.

## HERO'S INVENTIONS

Hero mentioned more than 80 different devices in his main works, *Treatise on Hydraulics*, *Treatise on Pneumatics* and *Treatise on Mechanics* (the last preserved only in an Arabic translation). In these, he described the fundamentals of hydraulics, pneumatics and mechanics as well as many applications, including drinking fountains, self-trimming lanterns, self-filling wine goblets and temple doors that were opened by heat which caused the metal hinges to expand.

The *Treatise on Mechanics* dealt with utilitarian devices such as cranes, hoists (lifts) and presses, while another book, *Metrica*, outlined geometrical methods of measuring land, weights and cubic capacity, including that of the pyramids.

In *Stereometrica* Hero gave highly practical advice on how to measure the contents of *amphorae* (jars) and ships' cargoes. More fancifully, in *Automatapoetica* Hero described two mechanized puppet theatres which he had constructed. In these, miniaturized versions of *The Bacchae*, along with other classical Greek tragedies, were staged. His book on clocks, sundials and other chronometers, *Dioptra*, has sadly been lost.

The inventions which have made Hero lastingly famous were his steam engines. One simply used escaping steam to make a ball jump in the air. The other, more sophisticated version was the *aelopile*. This consisted of a large sealed metal cauldron beneath a hollow metal sphere. Steam from the cauldron's boiling water was forced into the sphere, from which its only way of escape was via two small hooked pipes attached to the top and between which it could rotate freely. As pressure built up inside the sphere, the steam made the sphere rotate swiftly on its axis. This delighted onlookers but most scholars now think it did no more.

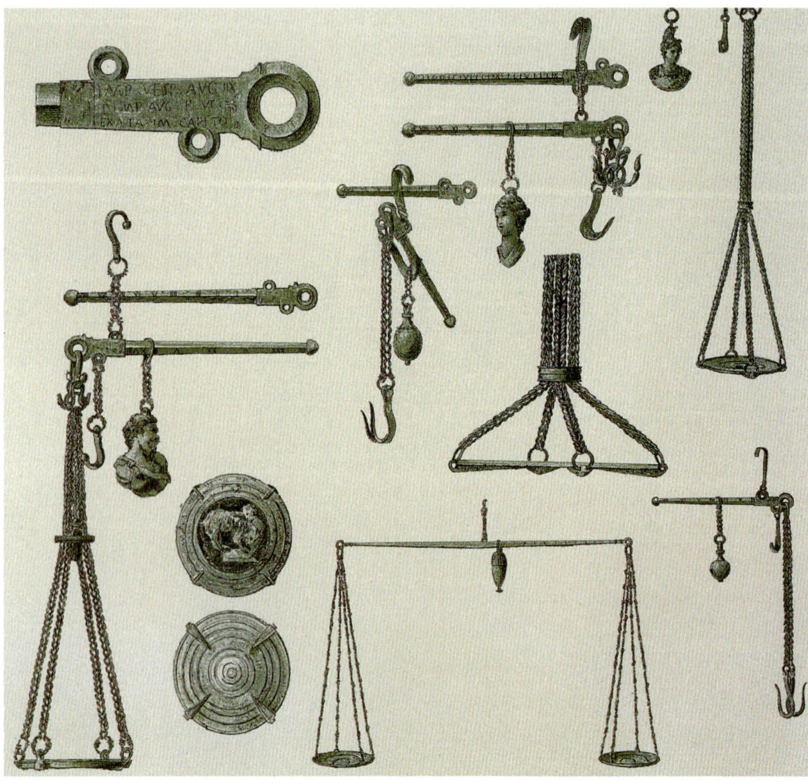

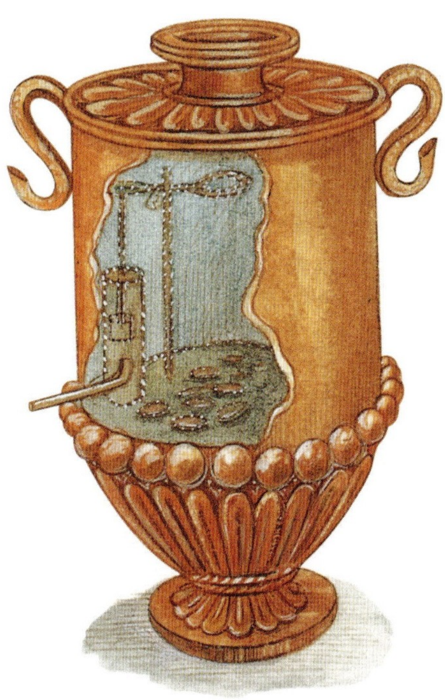

*Above: Among Hero's many ingenious contraptions was a water dispenser that refilled itself automatically, a useful if hardly world-transforming device.*

An intriguing but unsupported legend endures that a vastly scaled-up version of Hero's steam engine was constructed to help lift the fuel up to the top of Alexandria's 400ft (122m) *pharos* (light-house). This would have made a real contribution to the city's economy. Whatever the case, Hero the steam-engine maker certainly had no successors and his invention died with him.

### INVENTIONS SQUANDERED?
Some writers have seen the Roman empire's failure to develop and exploit Hero's steam invention during the period of its peaceful prosperity as a crushing indictment of Roman – and by extension of Greek – attitudes to manual work in general and to technology in particular. Marxists, among others, have blamed it on the prevalence of slavery, which made the Graeco-Roman elite unwilling to dirty their hands with practical work. In support of this argument, they quote the 2nd-century AD Greek biographer

Plutarch's accounts of Archimedes, the great mathematician and inventor of the 3rd century BC. "Considering the business of mechanics and all utilitarian arts…fit for vulgar craftsmen, he [Archimedes] turned his attention only to things where the beautiful and extraordinary are not mixed with the necessary."

This passage simply reflects the attitudes of Plutarch, a Greek nobleman who shared the prejudices of his caste – views which were still powerful even in the industrializing Europe of the 19th century – but they were not necessarily those of polymath scientists like Archimedes, who invented his famous water-lifting screw, or of Hero, who discussed many practical topics. Real technical and economic factors prevented the development and exploitation of Hero's steam devices.

### MATERIAL LIMITATIONS
The ancient Mediterranean world, unlike Britain, Germany and the USA in the 19th century, did not have accessible, abundant supplies of the coal which was to fuel the first two centuries of the industrial age. Even wood was in increasingly short supply by Hero's time, as demand for timber and charcoal led to deforestation. The ancient world's metallurgy, too, was far less advanced than that of Britain around 1800, although Hero had developed the necessary valves and pistons for his steam machines. Most critically, the Greeks and Romans never discovered how to use coal in iron-making. All these factors would have prevented widespread adoption of Hero's devices even if the emperors themselves had supported him. Nonetheless, it remains true that, for the ancient world, entertainment was always the priority, and Hero's spinning automata remained in that category.

*Below: Hero not only invented the world's first steam engine but he designed it in the form of a turbine, a sphere with two pipes exiting in opposite directions heated over a fire, far more efficient than pistons. Whether this remained only a toy, or whether it was scaled up to supply the great* pharos, *remains unknown.*

# MEDICAL PRINCIPLES AND PRACTICE

Medicine was another field dominated by Greek or Hellenized figures, but it was under Roman auspices, in the imperial capital, that the last great Greek physicians, including Dioscorides and Galen, worked and wrote. The Romans greatly appreciated Greek medical skills. Julius Caesar granted Roman citizenship to any Greek doctors who settled and worked in Rome.

In the 1st century AD, Dioscorides, who came from the Greek city of Anazarbus in Asia Minor, settled in Rome. He had probably served with the Roman army as a doctor and he thrived under the emperors Claudius and Nero (ruled AD41–68). Dioscorides was a brilliant botanist and his book *On Medical Materials* describes plants from many places across the empire, and as far beyond its frontiers as India, that could be used for drugs.

Soranus, who came from Ephesus, spent much of his successful career in Rome in the mid-1st century AD. His *Gynaecology* was the only ancient medical text that was wholly concerned with women's health. He was an emi-nent surgeon and won the title *princeps medicorum* (First Among Doctors). A typical polymath, Soranus also wrote on philosophy and language.

**THE IDEAL PHYSICIAN**

Considered the greatest Greek doctor since Hippocrates (*c.* 460–380BC), Galen (*c.* AD129–200) summarized the whole Greek medical tradition. He was born in Asia Minor in Pergamum, where he seems to have started his career tending wounded gladiators. He studied anatomy at Alexandria's famous schools before settling in Rome *c.* AD162 to pursue a dual career as a practising physician and a medical writer. In the first role, he mostly attended the rich and mighty. He became the personal physician of the emperor Marcus Aurelius, the emperor's son Commodus and the wife of the former consul Flavius Boethus. Reputedly, Galen fled the city when it was ravaged by a plague brought back by troops victorious in the East in AD166, but his career and reputation clearly revived on his return.

Galen generally accepted Hippocrates' views that four "humours" control the human condition, both physically and mentally: blood, phlegm, black bile and yellow bile. A person who was ill probably had an imbalance in these humours and treatment was required to return the balance to normal. This might include bleeding, enemas or induced vomiting. Never a revolutionary, Galen incorporated these ideas – which for millennia were almost universally accepted – with more recent Hellenistic research to create his grand synthesis.

In his early days, Galen lectured and dissected in public, normally using pigs' corpses. (Human dissection was not practised by the Romans, although Hellenistic doctors had long been

*Above: Funerary stele of Sempronio Hilario, a 1st-century AD Roman doctor.*

*Below: A woman giving birth using a birthing chair. Soranus of Ephesus wrote* Gynaecology, *the one book devoted to women's health.*

doing dissections in private.) Following contemporary customs, Galen used these anatomical exhibitions to prove pre-conceived theories, rather than discover new and possibly disconcerting facts. Nonetheless, he was one of antiquity's greatest anatomists. He was also a true physician, taking a holistic view of medicine and of human health.

Galen's works have survived unusually intact – they now make up about ten per cent of all extant classical Greek literature – and deal with many subjects. One is called *The Ideal Physician is Also a Philosopher*, a title which perhaps reflected his own ambitions. Galen aimed above all to establish medicine as an exact yet humane science. He always stressed the importance of exercise, a balanced diet, general hygiene and baths.

Galen acquired such immense authority in his own lifetime and subsequently that all ensuing ages, until at least the 17th century, followed his advice – often blindly. Oribasius, the personal physician of the emperor Julian 200 years later, when told by his master to "Collect all the main writings of the best physicians", started with Galen's summaries on the uncontentious grounds that Galen was the best doctor of them all.

### KNOWN BY REPUTATION

There were no medical boards or recognized qualifications for doctors in the Roman empire. Reputation, therefore, was vitally important to a successful doctor. This in turn depended partly on luck, partly on skill and partly on a good bedside manner. Doctors were urged to be dignified but smart in their appearance and to give poor people free treatment. Greek and Roman doctors had almost no effective drugs, although they used a variety of herbal remedies and may have had opium. They therefore laid great emphasis upon listening to their patients.

*Asclepieia*, shrines dedicated to Asclepius, the god of medicine, received the sick overnight. Patients would sleep in the sacred precincts and there have healing dreams in which Asclepius might

appear and take away their illness. One of the best-preserved of these shrines is at Pergamum. Surgery, in an age without anaesthetics, was only performed when absolutely essential and speed was crucial to avoid death through shock. Medical instruments recovered from Pompeii include probes, catheters, forceps, chisels, scalpels and needles.

*Above: A young boy is examined by a doctor in this 1st century BC relief with a Greek inscription.*

*Below: Building in the Sanctuary of Asclepius, Pergamum, where the sick may have slept, hoping to be cured by the healing god.*

# PERILS OF URBAN LIFE: PLAGUES, FLOOD AND FIRE

*Above: The Tiber, which flows through Rome, was a turbulent, unpredictable river, prone to sudden floods that could sweep across the city.*

*Below: Plague, graphically personified in this painting by Elie Delaunay of 1869, ravaged Rome repeatedly from AD166 onwards and added to the perils of urban life.*

For most people in the world's first cosmopolis, life could be dangerous, unpleasant and short. Public health was probably far better in the empire's smaller towns, but they and the countryside supplied Rome with the stream of immigrants needed to maintain and expand the metropolitan population. Smallpox is the most likely culprit for the plague that ravaged Rome from AD166 for several years and that may have killed 300,000 people (nearly a third of Rome's population). However, epidemics were only the most dramatic of the endemic health problems that dogged the rich and poor inhabitants of ancient Rome.

## MALARIA

The worst of these endemic health problems was probably malaria. As Galen dryly commented, doctors practising in Rome had no need to consult the writings of Hippocrates for descriptions of semitertian fever (a stage of malaria among adults), because its symptoms could be observed any day in the city. However, malaria was not recognized as such and the link with the disease-bearing mosquito was unsuspected. Run-off water from the seven hills, overflows from the constantly running public fountains and water-basins and stagnant residue left by the Tiber's frequent floods created ideal breeding grounds for mosquitoes.

Cicero and Livy praised the healthy hills of Rome, where the nobility and later the court lived in spacious houses, in contrast with the low-lying parts of the city, where the large majority of the population lived in often cramped *insulae* (apartment blocks). However, even the rich found it advisable to quit Rome in late summer when malaria was at its most rampant, leaving the poor to their uncertain fates.

No figures are known for Roman malaria deaths, but extrapolation from other parts of Italy similarly afflicted until recently, reveals that mortality rates as high as 60 per cent in the 20–50 age group may have been common.

Malaria would also have increased the mortality rates for pulmonary diseases such as pneumonia, bronchitis and asthma. All are likely to have been as common in Rome as in other cities whose populations approached the million mark before modern medicine.

However, Rome added further unique problems. Although the abundant fresh waters brought in by its aqueducts helped reduce waterborne diseases such as dysentery and typhoid – scourges of metropolitan life until the 20th century – other Roman habits would actually have spread them. People with bowel infections, for example, were urged to bathe their exposed anuses in the public bathwater that other people then bathed

in! Communal as well as private brushes were used instead of paper in public lavatories, another effective way of spreading germs. Further, while the rich few suffered from overeating, many Roman people were chronically malnourished, despite the grain dole. (This was later supplemented by free olive oil, wine and even sometimes pork, but a typical Roman's diet must have left him or her with vitamin deficiencies and this would have further undermined resistance to disease.)

**FLOODS AND FIRES**
The Tiber provided a useful waterway down to the sea and up into central Italy, but it was a swift, sometimes violent river, prone to dramatic flooding as the snows on the Apennine mountains melted. There were floods nearly every year and major floods in 193BC, when the lower parts of the city were inundated and many buildings collapsed.

As the growing city spread on to the low land in the great bend of the river about the Campus Martius, its inhabitants became yet more vulnerable. In 23BC the Pons Sublicius was swept away – for the second time in 40 years – and for three days the city was better navigated by boat than on foot. Hadrian, among other emperors, tried to improve the embankment walls, but in AD217 floods poured through the Forum Romanum in the heart of the city, sweeping away many startled citizens.

Even worse were the dangers from fire. The *insulae*, blocks of flats up to seven storeys high which housed most of the population, were often jerry-built and prone to collapse (although their construction did improve after the great fire of AD64). Heated by moveable charcoal stoves, lit by smoky oil lamps and built mostly of timber before AD64, they were also extremely flammable. Crassus, one of the late Republic's richest and most powerful men, famously boosted his fortunes by turning up at the site of a fire and buying the still-smouldering site cheap from its stunned owner.

Augustus created a corps of *vigiles*, nightwatchmen/firemen, but they had only limited success. The fire of AD64, which totally destroyed three of Rome's 14 districts, gave rise to Nero's subsequent sensible building regulations. *Insulae* were to have terraces for fire fighting, buildings were to be faced in fired brick and there was to be a minimum distance between them. However even this failed to prevent fire recurring. In AD192 Rome was so devastated by fire that the (half-mad) emperor Commodus proposed to rename the reconstructed city after himself, a project his assassination prevented. The Curia (Senate House) was later destroyed by fire and rebuilt under Diocletian.

*Above: The great fire of AD64, here depicted by the 18th-century painter Robert Hubert, was one of the most devastating and also the best documented of the recurrent fires that the inflammable cosmopolis experienced.*

# TRADE, SHIPS AND NAVIGATION

As Rome grew, it sucked in ever more products from across the globe, establishing new patterns of supply and demand. Although merchant ships had criss-crossed the Mediterranean for millennia, early in the 2nd century AD trade grew to a peak under Roman rule that was not to be reached again for more than a thousand years. This growth is confirmed by the increase in the number of shipwrecks found along major trade routes – such as that past the Aeolian Islands north of Sicily, where many ships bound for Rome sought clearly inadequate shelter from storms – and by the huge numbers of *amphorae* found, the clay jars in which loose liquid substances such as oil, fish paste and wine were transported to Rome.

*Below: A woman grocer from Ostia, Rome's great river port, is depicted standing at a trestle table selling fruit and vegetables stored in wicker baskets. The capital city of Rome traded in goods of all sorts.*

## THE MERCHANT CLASS

Members of the senatorial order, Rome's wealthiest class, were banned by the *lex Claudia* of 218BC from owning sizeable ships – those that could carry more than 300 *amphorae* – for commerce was considered debasing. However, some senators probably traded through proxies. Other classes did so openly, the equestrians (knights) particularly benefiting from the boom in trade during the late Republic. So did the numerous *mercatores, navigatores* and *negotiatores* (merchants, ship owners and businessmen) who were often not Roman citizens but freedmen.

Emperors, anxious to keep the Roman populace supplied with essential wheat and oil, offered incentives to ship owners. Claudius, for example, promised privileges to anyone owning a ship with a capacity of at least 10,000 *modii* (about 70 tons) who used it to supply Rome with wheat for six years. These ranged from citizenship for non-citizens to exemptions from taxes and burdens such as the *lex Poppaea* which penalized childless couples.

However, most merchants preferred to invest their money in land, which offered security and prestige, rather than found mercantile dynasties. In the 2nd century BC, Cato the Elder voiced the opinions of many Romans for a long time to come when he wrote, "The trader I regard as energetic man, bent on making money; but his is a dangerous career, liable to disaster".

Nonetheless, goods flowed in to Rome, and to other cities and between provinces. Wheat for the million mouths of the metropolis came first from Sicily and Sardinia and then from Egypt and Africa; olive oil came from Spain and Africa; gold and silver from Spain and Dacia; ivory from Egypt and Africa; papyrus and linen from Egypt; textiles and jewels from Syria, and from beyond it silk and spices. Wine, honey and marble came from Greece

and Asia Minor; wool, wheat, wine and pottery from Gaul; tin, wool and lead from Britain; copper from Cyprus and wild animals and timber from Mauretania (Morocco). In the earlier empire Italy produced much wine and pottery and always produced fruit and vegetables. Such a list is far from exhaustive.

## SHIPS AND SHIPPING

The *pharoi* (lighthouses) the Romans built around their empire as far north as Dover show the importance they attached to shipping, which was preferred to slow, laborious land transport over longer distances. On the few rivers that were truly navigable, such as the Rhône, regular barge services connected cities like Lyons with the coast, but sea trade was far more important.

As piracy had been almost eliminated under the empire, sea travel might appear to have been relatively safe, but in fact perils abounded, despite the astonishing size of some merchant ships.

The ship that was used by Claudius as the base for the lighthouse of his new harbour near Ostia was vast. About 340ft (104m) long and 64ft (20.3m) wide, with six decks and displacing 7,400 tons, it required a crew of 700–800 men. Pliny the Elder recorded that its main mast was so massive it could only be spanned by four

men linking arms and it had a ballast of 800 tons of lentils. This may have been the largest vessel built in antiquity – possibly the largest wooden ship ever, specially made to carry an obelisk from Egypt to Rome – but there may have been other large cargo ships of 3,000 tons ferrying wheat or oil. Galleys, which were highly expensive to crew, were seldom used for cargo.

Although remarkably large, these sailing ships remained technically simple. They generally had only one main mast in the centre with one or two sails and smaller masts at the bow and stern. They never evolved the complex rigging and sails of 17th-century warships or merchantmen. They continued to rely on steering-oars and did not develop rudders like ships of the later Middle Ages.

These lumbering monsters were probably never very seaworthy or manoeuvrable, as they were unable to tack easily with their crude sails. St Paul's famous shipwreck on Malta was not that exceptional. Roman navigators also lacked compasses, sextants and other aids, relying instead on landmarks and the stars in the night sky to determine their position. Fortunately both were often visible in the clear Mediterranean.

*Above: A mosaic from Sousse, Tunisia of the 3rd century AD shows a cargo of iron being unloaded from a ship. Heavy goods such as this almost always went by sea, sea transport being generally far cheaper than land transport.*

*Below: Galley-type ships like this wine-barge from Neumagen on the Moselle, from a 3rd-century AD funerary monument, were used on the larger rivers such as the Rhine, Tiber and Moselle. At sea sailing ships were the norm.*

# PASSAGES TO INDIA

*Above: A cloth merchant presents a client with a length of fabric in a relief from a Christian sarcophagus from Trier of the 4th century AD. Textiles were often traded over long distances.*

*Below: A harbour scene in a fresco from Pompeii gives a vivid impression of the commercial bustle of a Roman port in the 1st century AD.*

Trade grew within the empire but did not stop at the empire's limits. In 116BC a sea captain in the service of the Ptolemy rulers of Egypt discovered the sea-route to India from the Red Sea port of Berenice. Using the monsoon winds that blow across the Indian Ocean, he set sail eastwards in July and returned blown by the reverse winds in December. The routes east were outlined in the *Periplus Maris Erythraei*, a handbook for sailors of the 1st century AD. Greek navigators had by then mostly replaced the Arabs who had once monopolized trade with India.

After Egypt passed into Roman control in 30BC, the lucrative trade grew even faster. From India and other parts of Asia, especially Felix Arabia (the Yemen), came spices, nard, incense, unguents, jewels, cotton textiles and ivory; in return went Roman pottery, glassware, gold and silver. This trade could be fantastically profitable. One consignment alone might be worth three million sesterces and a good-sized ship could carry many consignments. The Greek orator Aelius Aristides (AD117–89) was only slightly exaggerating when he noted that, "Cargoes from India and even from Felix Arabia (the Yemen) can be seen so abundantly as to make one think that in those countries the trees will have been stripped bare and their inhabitants, if they need anything, must come and beg us for a share of their own produce".

Conservative Romans like Seneca muttered about the debilitating effects of such luxury, and Pliny the Elder worried about the adverse economic effect of the outflow of gold and silver to pay for imports – 100 million sesterces a year, he claimed. However, finds of pottery and other artefacts made in the empire along the coasts of western India suggest that Rome's eastbound merchants often exported the empire's products too. The imperial coffers would have profited by the *portorium*, import/export duties levied at 2½ per cent.

## THE SILK ROAD

The Indian Ocean was not the only great trade route to the East. Caravans went east across the Syrian desert via the great merchant city of Palmyra – which provided and charged for "protection" and use of its water resources – or down through Mesopotamia, most of which was normally outside Roman control, via the great emporium of Seleucia-on-Tigris, to the Gulf. Spasinochorax at the head of the Gulf seems to have been semi-independent under the Parthian kings, like Palmyra under the Romans. Its great port, which was briefly captured by Trajan in AD116, had regular connections with India and Sri Lanka.

Another route, going entirely by land, struck north across the Iranian plateau to link up with the legendary Silk Road. This is a misleading title, for this was no pan-Asian highway but several different

routes taken by camel caravans through central Asia to the western outposts of imperial China. The first Silk Road route was traditionally if unintentionally pioneered by Zhang Qian, an official sent by the Han emperors of China in 135BC to discover and import large horses for the Chinese army. Zhang ultimately succeeded in his mission, although it took him ten years. Traders ventured in his wake, bringing silk west, among other luxury goods, often in stages through the Kushan kingdom in central Asia and via Iran to Syria. Some caravans may have turned south into India, their goods reaching Egypt by sea.

Whatever the route, silk remained an expensive luxury for Romans. Cleopatra VII, last Ptolemy monarch of Egypt and Mark Antony's famous lover, wore silks from China. Such sensual clothing was portrayed as a sign of dangerous decadence by Antony's opponent Octavian, although rich women in Rome soon began wearing silk too. (Sericulture remained a jealously guarded Chinese monopoly until in the 6th century AD, some Byzantine monks under orders from the emperor Justinian managed to smuggle silk worms out of China and inaugurate the Byzantine silk industry.) There were only rare direct contacts between the two distant giants. Chinese envoys arrived in Antioch during the reign of Marcus Aurelius (AD161–80) whom they called Marc-Antun, reputedly mistaking the Syrian metropolis for the imperial capital.

### TRADE WITH THE BARBARIANS

Not all trade went east, however. The barbarians to the north traded as well as fought with Rome. Amber had long been imported from the Baltic but Germania – between the Rhine and Vistula rivers – became an increasingly important source of furs, hides, leather, honey and above all, as the empire matured, of slaves.

Scythia (the south Russian and Ukrainian steppe) was another important source of hides, furs and honey. It was also for a long time a major exporter of

grain, helping to feed the cities of Greece. Unfortunately, the migratory chaos of the 3rd and 4th centuries AD disrupted grain-growing in the area just when Constantine's new capital on the Bosphorus would have welcomed it. The problem was dealt with by diverting wheat from Egypt bound for Rome to feed the city of Constantinople.

To the south, the Sahara Desert formed a barrier nearly as effective as the Atlantic for the Romans, who seldom rode camels. Rome had few contacts with sub-Saharan Africa except in Egypt, but there were some routes across the Sahara, and Africa north of the Sahara was still fertile enough to provide wild animals for the circus.

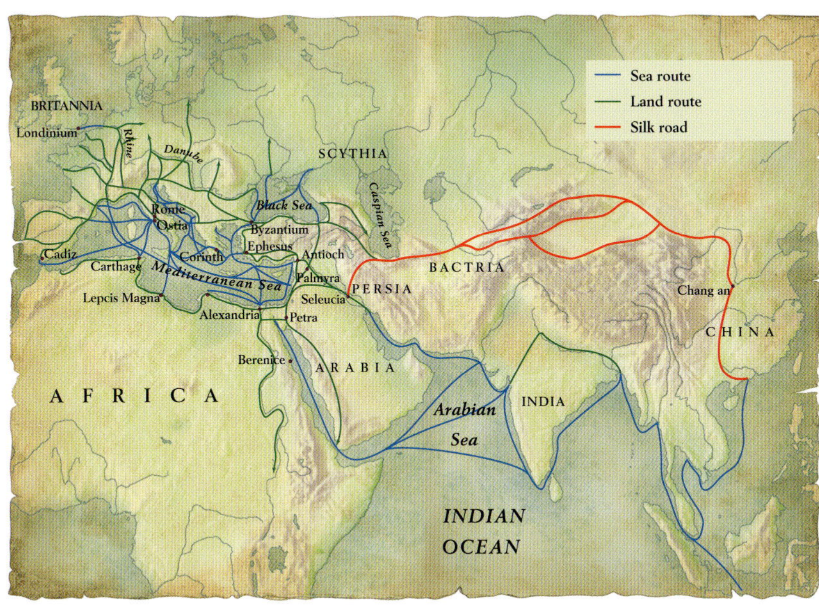


*Above: The famous Silk Road from China across central Asia to the Mediterranean ports was eclipsed in economic importance by the sea routes to India via the Red Sea or the Gulf.*

*Below: A stele showing ship-building in Ravenna, one of the empire's main naval bases.*

# FARMING

*Above: Taking manure to the fields, from a cycle showing the country months in Gaul c. AD200.*

*Below: Vineyard workers, from a mosaic at Cherchel, Algeria, c. AD100. Wine was produced around the empire.*

The great majority of the empire's population (at least 85 per cent at Rome's economic zenith *c.* AD100) always lived and worked on the land. This rural dominance formed the constant background to urban life in the ancient world and farming was always the basis of the Roman economy. Farming, or at least living off the rents and profits from estates, was also considered the most respectable form of existence by the ruling classes.

All senators had to possess land worth at least one million sesterces and most owned far more. Poets such as Virgil and Tibullus praised an idealized rural life that in practice must have been very tough for all but wealthy landowners taking a break from metropolitan cares. However, upper-class Romans were not being entirely hypocritical when they praised country life, for many did take an interest in their estates.

From the 2nd century BC, writers such as Cato the Censor in *De re rustica* (About Rural Matters) gave other landowners advice on how best to profit from their lands in Italy, where *latifundia* (large slave-worked estates) seem to have become common. Cato considered farms as small as 100 jugera (62 acres) as viable but most estates were larger. All such estates strove to be self-sufficient not just in basic foodstuffs but also in carts, tools, harnesses and even in labourers' clothes. The owner should "be inclined to sell and disinclined to buy". Large landowners, however, could afford the outlay of 724 sesterces required for an olive press in Pompeii, for example, while smaller farmers could not.

## REPUBLIC OF FARMERS

Traditionally, early Rome was a republic of robust independent farmers, tending perhaps tiny plots but still able to buy their own armour and so rank as Roman legionaries. The influx of slaves and wealth following the Punic and Macedonian Wars of 264–168BC, coupled with the long periods that the Roman soldier-farmer was away from his farm, led large landowners to buy up or simply take over neglected farms, where slaves replaced the doughty Roman peasant.

This view, propagated by the land-reformer Tiberius Gracchus in 133BC among others, painted a dismal picture of an Italy devoured by rapacious great landlords dispossessing little farmers. It is only part of the picture, however. While there certainly were huge new ranches worked by hundreds of slaves, the sort of farm Cato envisaged would have had only about a dozen slaves. Their efforts would have been supplemented by seasonal

free labourers working side by side. Another group, the *coloni* (tenant farmers) remained important, as the letters of Pliny the Younger, who made a point of listening to all his tenant farmers' complaints, attest. A few small independent farmers survived alongside their powerful neighbours well into the empire.

Some large estates came to specialize in viticulture, which needed semi-skilled workers; in sheep rearing, which required little labour of any type; and some near Rome in market gardening.

The phenomenal growth of Rome (and other cities) expanded demand, but expanding supply was more difficult. Marginal land in Italy and other well-settled areas could be taken into cultivation but this might make only a marginal difference. Those working such land even in meteorologically good years might consume most of its meagre crop.

In newly conquered Britain parts of the Cambridgeshire fens were drained to grow cereals that were exported to feed the army on the Rhine in the 4th century AD, while in Africa careful planting of olive trees and the collection of every drop of rain allowed agriculture to advance into what had been arid savannah. Southern and central Spain also saw a great expansion of grain and olive cultivation. All these products could also be exported, but Roman wealth created no agricultural revolution. The commonest way to increase farm production was simply to work labourers, whether free or servile, harder.

## FARMING TOOLS AND TECHNIQUES

The Romans had good farming tools on a small scale but failed to exploit other technological possibilities. A Roman farmworker would have had excellent axes, spades, sickles, scythes, saws, shears and forks. The multi-purpose vine-dresser's knife, *falx vinotoria*, which was developed from the billhook, has never really been surpassed for its purpose. On a larger scale, the Romans at times used the wheeled plough, which

was Gallic in origin and could turn heavier soils easily, a wheeled threshing-machine with spiked axles called the *plostellum poenicum* and possibly of Carthaginian origin, and two types of reaping machine.

These tools were known and used in Gaul and Britain but they do not seem to have spread round the empire, partly because the Romans remained limited to oxen as draught animals for ploughs and carts. They had failed to develop a form of harness for horses that would allow the animal to draw heavy loads without half-strangling itself. Horses in antiquity therefore only pulled light ceremonial or racing chariots, not carriages, wagons or ploughs.

Farmers normally let some of their arable land lie fallow every other year, to allow it to recover its fertility. This was essential but limited production and illustrates one restriction on Roman power at its most fundamental: it could not easily grow more food.

*Above: Oxen being used to plough fields in a mosaic from Cherchel, Algeria, c. AD100. Africa became Rome's chief source of grain and olive oil.*

*Below: Ploughing with oxen, from a sarcophagus of the 2nd century AD. Oxen were the main draught animals.*

# CHAPTER XII

# PEOPLE OF ROME

The citizens of Rome of all social classes often showed a preference for *otium*, leisure, over *negotium*, or business of any sort, whether this was governing the empire or running a shop. The cities built or expanded in the centuries of the Roman peace reflected the belief common at the time that the good life was one spent enjoying the amenities of urban life: the baths, theatre, circus, amphitheatre, forum, libraries and the social rounds of dinner parties for those who could afford them.

Most people in the empire in fact lived not in cities of any size but in the country, yet urban life still set the overall tone. Complementing life in the public sphere, the Romans had a strong sense of family and – at least among those who could afford it – of their ancestors.

The position of Roman women, although they were barred from public life, was better in some ways than in comparable cultures, possibly no worse than it was in Britain before the late 19th century. Slavery, a notorious part of the Roman world, was a far more mixed affair than might be assumed. Many slaves were freed and sometimes prospered in business or other work and their sons were later able to hold public office.

Before the triumph of Christianity, the Romans displayed typically level-headed pragmatism about sex, being at times bawdy, at times romantic.

*Left: A frieze on the Ara Pacis (Altar of Peace) dedicated in 9BC, showing Tellus (Earth) or Italy, surrounded by symbols of the fertility and harmony restored by Augustus.*

# MARRIAGE, DIVORCE AND THE POWER OF THE FATHER

*Above: A father reclining at ease among his family, a relief from a child's sarcophagus of the 3rd century AD illustrating a Roman paterfamilias' power at its most benign. The Romans were markedly family-minded, even among the nobility.*

*Below: A plan of Rome showing the imperial metropolis at its prime c. AD200. Rome was never a city of grand boulevards or avenues but rather a city of densely packed buildings. filled with political and family intrigue.*

Like the Greeks but unlike the early Jews or the Persians, the Romans were always monogamous. The extended family was central to Roman law and society and especially to the real workings of its informal political system.

Although Roman marriage had as its explicit goal the production and rearing of children, among the great political families of the late Republic and empire political motives often dictated unions. Caesar's daughter Julia was married to the much older Pompey to help seal the First Triumvirate in 60BC; Octavia, Octavian's sister, had to marry Mark Antony in an unsuccessful bid to keep the Second Triumvirate together 20 years later, and Tiberius was forced to divorce his adored first wife Vipsania and marry Augustus' only child Julia instead, in a marriage that proved a most disastrous mismatch. Financial motives also played a major role in most noble marriages. However, this did not mean that all were unhappy. Augustus (when still Octavian) married Livia for love rather than politics (she happily divorced her first husband) and despite his later frequent infidelities, theirs was a happy marriage.

Divorce had become common at least among the nobility by the end of the Republic, although for less exalted people, where personal feelings possibly counted for more, it remained more unusual, although devoid of any stigma. In divorces, children normally remained in their father's custody. However, judging by the feelings expressed on memorials, many ordinary Romans were devoted to their spouses.

### THE *PATERFAMILIAS*

The theoretical powers of the father in the early Republic were unbounded. A *paterfamilias* (male head of the household with no living father or grandfather) held *paterpotestas*, powers of life and death over all family members, including his slaves and most of his freedmen. In theory, a father could beat his son although the latter might be middle-aged and hold high office. Family courts dominated by the *paterfamilias* could even hand out death sentences, though these became so rare as to be almost legendary. The *paterfamilias* nonetheless retained the key right to accept – or occasionally reject, if the baby was deformed or of dubious paternity – every newborn child laid at his feet.

Such was the prestige linked to being a *paterfamilias* that senators were hailed as *conscripti patres* (conscripted fathers) and one of the proudest titles held by Caesar and Augustus in turn was *pater patriae* (Father of His Country).

The dependents of a *paterfamilias* could number hundreds for a great household – and later for the *familia Caesaris*, the imperial family, thousands. However, Roman politics in the Republic and the early Principate depended crucially on these extended households for governing

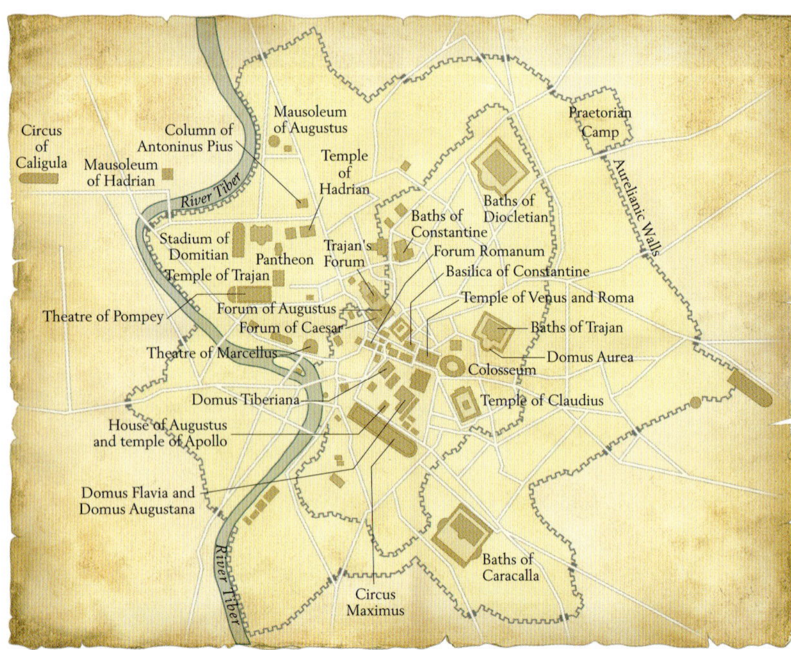

the empire, with slaves or freedmen effectively taking on the role of civil servants. In practice, these vastly extended and powerful dynasties were balanced by more numerous nuclear families, composed just of parents and children. When a *paterfamilias* died – and not many lived long enough to torment their grown-up children for long – his estate had by law to be divided equally among all his surviving children, for primogeniture (in which the first born inherits all) was unknown. Because Roman mortality rates were so high, especially among women giving birth, many people found themselves marrying several times without divorce.

## MARRIAGE CUSTOMS

Among the upper classes in Rome, marriages were often arranged for dynastic reasons, but the comedies of Plautus (among others) demonstrate that love was as important for the Romans as for anyone else. Paternal consent was needed, however, for the first informal engagement. This was followed by a banquet at which the man, who was normally about ten years older than the woman, gave his fiancée a large present and the future father-in-law promised a dowry in return.

On the day of the wedding – June was a popular month – the bridegroom arrived early in the morning at the house of the bride with his friends. The matron of honour joined the couple's right hands ceremonially in the *dextrarum iunctio*, an animal was sacrificed and the marriage contract was signed. The groom paid for the reception, which included food, dancing and music. Augustus became alarmed at the increasing extravagance of wedding ceremonies and introduced a sumptuary law to limit the cost of a marriage to 1,000 sesterces. This proved ineffectual.

The bride wore a prescribed hemless tunic-style dress (*tunica recta*) tied at the waist by a woollen girdle (*cingulum herculeum*), with a saffron-coloured cloak over it and an orange veil (*flammeum*). Her hair was dressed in an old-fashioned style, with strands parted using an iron

spearhead. In the wedding procession after the banquet, all the guests escorted the bride to her new home.

The bride herself had three young boys to attend her: one held her left hand, one her right hand and the third carried a torch before her that had been lit at the hearth of her own home. As she approached the bridegroom's house, the torch was thrown away. According to old beliefs, whoever caught the torch was assured a long life.

Upon reaching the bridegroom's house, the bride performed a set of symbolic acts. She smeared the doorposts with oil and then covered them with wool, and ritually touched the hearth fire and water inside the house. She was then helped to prepare for her wedding night by women who had only been married once. Most girls, at least among the nobility, were virgins for their first marriage.

*Above: Portrait, possibly of an engaged couple, with a cupid between them, from a fresco in a villa at Stabiae destroyed by Vesuvius in AD79.*

*Below: Detail of a marriage ceremony from a votive altar of the 3rd century AD, showing a couple formally linking hands.*

# ROMAN WOMEN

*Above: A young woman wearing a wreath of leaves from Herculaneum, c. 10BC.*

Women in Rome were barred from playing any role in public life, whether in war or in peace. There were no women consuls, generals, senators or emperors. In this exclusion Rome was in tune with classical Greek precedents but not with the Hellenistic world, where queens such as Cleopatra in Egypt ruled as acknowledged sovereigns. High-ranking women could hope to be powers behind the throne, like Augustus' wife Livia or Nero's mother Agrippina, but they could never assume imperial power in their own right.

In Rome, women were regarded as unfit for that supreme test of Roman *virtus*, military service (which was indisputably arduous). Further, women's voices were thought to lack the carrying power to make themselves easily heard in public places such as the Forum. Oratory was vital to Roman political life even after the end of the Republic.

## DOMESTIC POWER

Traditionally women remained always *in manu* (under a man's control), first their father's or guardian's and then their husband's. However, even as early as the 3rd century BC such constrictions were being evaded by marriage contracts that specified the dowry the woman could take back with her if the marriage ended in divorce or death. Divorce could be initiated by either party without formality, although aristocratic marriages with political implications remained more complicated.

*Left: Cornelia, mother of the Gracchi brothers, who held the first known literary salon in Rome.*

A Roman *matron* (married woman) ran the household, controlling the domestic slaves and holding the keys of the house. By the age of 25 she could normally manage any property that she had inherited independently, which made her better placed than women in early Victorian Britain. When her husband was away, a wife took control of family affairs. Domestic duties, such as looking after the children and the household, traditionally included making clothes for the family even for wealthy women. *Lanam fecit* (she made wool) was a common tribute to a deceased wife. However, by the later Republic women were joining men at dinner, that central event in convivial Roman life, where they acted as hostesses. This was in marked contrast to their seclusion in Greece, as Cornelius Nepos, the first extant Latin biographer, noted. Although girls received less in the way of formal education than their brothers, by the 2nd century BC many upper-class Roman women were literate, as is shown by the life of Cornelia Gracchus.

## INCREASING FREEDOM

Cornelia, daughter of the great Scipio Africanus who had defeated Hannibal, was among the first newly independent women (although scarcely liberated in the modern sense). She married Tiberius Cornelius Gracchus and among her progeny were the famous if ill-starred reformers Tiberius and Gaius Gracchus.

Cornelia took control of her six sons' education – a task traditionally reserved for the *paterfamilias* – and selected the finest Greek tutors for them. She was the first woman known to have held a literary salon in Rome where poets, philosophers and politicians gathered. As a widow she was so widely admired that Ptolemy VII, the Hellenistic king of Egypt, asked (unsuccessfully) for her

*Left: A mother breast-feeding her child in a vivid fresco from Pompeii. The maternal role was inevitably considered women's chief occupation, although aristocratic women in fact had relatively few children by the late Republic.*

hand in marriage. Although she was later content to be known as "the mother of the Gracchi", Cornelia deserves fame in her own right as a pioneer of women's independence. By the 1st century BC, other women were enjoying considerable freedom. The married aristocratic woman, who Catullus addressed as Lesbia and passionately loved, clearly had enough independence to have affairs.

Augustus tried to restrict women's freedom in his restoration of public morality. This re-emphasized gender differences, in deliberate contrast to the perceived immorality of the late Republic and to Cleopatra's "Eastern" court which had allegedly corrupted Anthony. Augustus even banished his daughter Julia and her daughter (also called Julia) for sexual immorality. Here he applied his own laws, for under the *Lex Julia* of 18BC, adultery had become a serious crime, at least for women, who could be banished, lose half their dowry and be prohibited from remarrying. Women now went to the public baths at different times to the men and were restricted to high seats in the theatre and amphitheatre. (They continued to sit with men in the Circus, however, and Ovid recommended the Circus as a good place for young men and women to meet and flirt.)

## WORKING WOMEN

Most women could never be empresses or wives of great politicians, but some still made their way in a male-dominated world. A few managed to be accepted as doctors – there is a funerary inscription in Latin for a female doctor, Asyllia Polla, from Roman Carthage – although later women seem to have been excluded from practising medicine for a time. As no formal medical body existed to regulate doctors, this may have reflected changes in the social climate.

Some women worked as bakers, pharmacists – another then unregulated profession – and shopkeepers, either with or without their husbands. There was only one woman Latin poet of note, Sulpicia, niece of an important politician *c.* 20BC, and almost no opportunities for women to make their voices heard in public life.

*Below: A relief showing a woman pharmacist in her shop. Pharmacy, like medicine, was a totally unregulated profession and so one which women could enter and where they could, with luck and industry, prosper.*

*Above: Children play with walnuts in a relief from Ostia of the 2nd century AD, then a thriving harbour city.*

*Below: Sculpture of a sleeping child. Very high rates of infant mortality meant that few children lived to adulthood.*

# CHILDREN: EDUCATION AND UPBRINGING

In the 2nd century BC, Cato the Censor boasted, perhaps untruthfully, that he had taught his sons everything from reading to swimming but, over time, education in richer households passed from the hands of fathers to professionals, slaves and free, as Rome filled with well-educated Greeks. However, Roman education remained generally unsystematic and for girls was almost non-existent beyond a basic level which was normally taught at home.

## AN AD HOC EDUCATION SYSTEM

Primary schools, which were mostly private and which only some Romans attended, taught the three basic subjects of reading, writing and arithmetic. Most teaching took place in porticoes or similar public areas such as the great *exedrae* (recesses) of Trajan's Forum.

Teaching was mostly a matter of learning texts by rote, with underpaid teachers beating lessons into boys. Among wealthier families, a *paedagogus*, a slave-tutor who was usually Greek-speaking, took care of the education of boys. Supposedly his pupil's master, he was in reality his slave and accompanied him everywhere.

Relatively few pupils progressed to secondary education where a *grammaticus*, again often a Greek-speaker, taught Latin and especially Greek literature. The poet Virgil was grateful that his parents, who were only moderately prosperous provincial farmers from the Po Valley, had given him a good education in Milan and Rome rather than at the local school full of "centurion's sons with their satchels".

Although emperors such as Trajan established chairs for lecturers paid by the public purse in Rome, there were only sporadic attempts to establish an educational system across the empire. Hadrian, for example, tried to encourage primary schooling in remote parts of the empire by offering tax concessions to school masters willing to teach in the villages of the mining region of Vipasca in Lusitania. Even fewer students went on to higher education, where a *rhetor* taught the vital art of public speaking. The Senate at first actually discouraged the spread of higher education in case it undermined its own monopoly on power.

After being taught by a *grammaticus*, some young Roman nobles went to one of the acknowledged Greek centres of cultural excellence to learn not only rhetoric but philosophy. Athens was long acknowledged as the greatest of these but it always lacked a proper university in the modern or even medieval sense, for private lecturers competed openly for students.

Marseilles' enduring Greek character in the 1st century AD made it a centre of learning. The mother of Agricola, who became a great general, sent him there to complete his education. Later, a few Western cities such as Bordeaux acquired universities, but their prestige never rivalled that of medieval Bologna or Oxford or contemporary Harvard.

## THE LANGUAGE OF LEARNING

Latin was the language of most of Italy and later of the Western provinces, but not of every inhabitant of polyglot Rome, let alone of the empire. Greek was also very widely spoken. Almost all cities in the Eastern half of the empire, and most in Sicily and southern Italy, were at least partly Greek-speaking, while until *c.* 50BC Latin literature hardly compared with Greek.

For a long time, the majority of Romans acknowledged, with varying degrees of reluctance, the supremacy of classical Greece in the cultural field, while considering contemporary Greeks their political and social inferiors. So important was a fluent knowledge of Greek to

an educated Roman thought to be that the Roman rhetorician Quintillian (*c.* AD35–100) suggested that upper class boys should learn Greek *before* they learnt Latin. Quintillian, who wrote on education, was given a salary by the emperor Vespasian. As tutor to Domitian's nephews, he soon became the acknowledged head of the teaching profession in Rome, so his views were hardly those of an outsider.

Latin remained, however, the language of the army, the administration and the law. In the 4th century AD, a school teaching law in Latin was actually established in Beirut in a long-Hellenized part of Syria. Although many Greeks must have known a little Latin in order to deal with officials and soldiers, they hardly mentioned it. One exception was Ammianus (*c.* AD330–94), a native of Antioch who learnt Latin to write stirring histories of the Persian wars in the mid-4th century in a style that was modelled on Tacitus and Livy. Apuleius, the Latin-speaking author of *The Golden Ass*, makes his central character a Greek-speaker who (comically) apologizes for his poor Latin.

## COMING OF AGE

Between the ages of 14 and 19, usually at the age of 17, the Roman male came of age, putting on a new white *toga virilis* to mark his status as a full citizen. He then went to the *Tabularium* (Records Office) with his family to be officially enrolled, after which a family banquet was held in his honour. High infant mortality meant that many children died long before this age, however. In the Republic, young male citizens were liable for military service.

*Above: A 4th-century AD class from Gaul, showing a teacher, flanked by pupils, all in fine, probably wickerwork armchairs, while a late arrival tries to apologize. The students are reading from papyrus scrolls.*

*Below: A woman baths a child in a mosaic of the 3rd century AD from the House of Theseus in Paphos, Cyprus.*

# SLAVES AND FREEDMEN

*Above: A slave serves wine in a bas-relief of the 2nd century* AD *in Rome.*

*Below: A mural from Pompeii showing two young women and a younger girl attended by a slave hairdresser. Rich Roman women usually had many domestic slaves to look after their every need.*

The traditional view of the wealth and power of the Roman empire existing only through the sweated efforts of wretched slaves can be very misleading. The truth is more complicated, for the relative status of "slave" and "free" might appear strange to modern eyes.

### THE STATUS OF SLAVES

A Roman nobleman might have a Greek-speaking slave as his secretary or clerk, another as a librarian or tutor to his children and another as bailiff or overseer of his land. These were often positions of importance and responsibility and some-times of real if limited power. As Romans prided themselves on *manumission* – formally freeing worthy slaves – and as other slaves could at times save enough money from doing work on their own to buy their freedom, the number of freedmen, especially in Rome itself, was large.

A few, like the gross Trimalchio – a fictional but half-plausible character from Petronius' novel *Satyricon* (*c.* AD64) – became multi-millionaires. Others, like Narcissus and Pallas, the emperor Claudius' principal secretar-ies, indeed rose to become some of the most powerful men in the empire, although their influence over the malleable emperor was resented by the Roman aristocracy. Freedmen's sons could hope to rise to be magistrates, while freedmen themselves often became priests in a local cult in the provinces.

Slavery in ancient Rome was therefore radically different from its last manifesta-tions in the Western world, when millions of enslaved Africans remained slaves just because of their colour. Most slaves who flooded into Rome as it conquered the Mediterranean world in the years after 260BC would have looked broadly similar to the Romans themselves, with darkish hair and olive skin. Those from the Eastern cities were often at least as educated and cultured as their Roman masters, some-times more so. As the empire developed, less sophisticated Germanic tribes from across the Rhine and the Danube became the chief source of slaves and there was no more such cultural enrichment. The Romans always snobbishly disdained everything about the Germans except their fighting qual-ities (despite Tacitus' seeming praise for the Germans' love of primitive free-dom). There are few depictions of black Africans in Roman art, which suggests that the Romans had only a few slaves from sub-Saharan Africa.

Precise figures are lacking, but prob-ably nearly a third of the population of Italy in the 1st century AD were slaves, while at that time about half Rome's own population may have consisted of slaves and freedmen. A proposal in the Senate in the 1st century AD that all slaves

*Left: Making a will: a funerary stele for man and wife from the 1st century AD, showing a slave with a counting tablet on the left. Slaves were sometimes given their freedom by their masters in such wills. This was a strong inducement to good behaviour.*

should wear a uniform to identify them was rejected when it was realized that this would reveal how numerous they were. Across the whole empire, however, the proportion of slaves to non-slaves was close to 10 per cent. Slavery probably peaked at the end of the Republic and the beginning of the empire and then very slowly began to decline, as the wars of easy conquest petered out. Such wars were the chief source of slaves, although piracy, kidnappings and abduction of foundlings, along with *verna*, the children of slaves born in the household, provided other major sources, as did trade with peoples beyond the empire.

### THE GROWTH OF SLAVERY

Slavery had always existed in Rome as in almost every ancient society. The Twelve Tables of the Law of 451–450BC stipulated that Romans were only to be sold into slavery "across the Tiber" (outside Rome). A common form of early slavery was the *nexus*, in which a Roman citizen who had become indebted lost his freedom to his creditors. Debt bondage was abolished by the *Lex Poetelia* of 326BC.

Soon after, Rome began the series of wars of conquests that provided it for a time with seemingly inexhaustible supplies of unfree labour. About 11,000 Samnite war captives were reportedly enslaved after their final defeat in 290BC. But the fleets the Romans raised to fight the First Punic War in 260BC were rowed mostly by free men – usually citizens of the lower property classes – as were most later fleets of galleys. A perennial disadvantage of owning slaves was that they needed feeding all year round even when not working. War galleys, for example, spent more than half the year ashore.

In 167BC, the systematic destruction of the kingdom of the cities of Epirus (north-west Greece) reputedly brought 150,000 slaves as war captives to Rome, probably helping to raise the intellectual tone of the whole city. Less accomplished, and so cheaper, were the 65,000 Sardinian slaves put up for sale in 177BC. The slave markets must at times have faced gluts. Cato the Censor noted with disgust about this time that pretty slave boys were fetching higher prices in the slave market than sturdy ploughmen, reflecting supply and demand. In the 1st century BC, Strabo estimated that the great port at Delos in the Cyclades was capable of handling 10,000 slaves a day (although this was a maximum, not a norm). Strabo also noted that slaves were one of Britain's main exports. Gallic chieftains reputedly sold a slave for a single amphora of Italian wine. Slaves were among the main booty of Caesar's Gallic wars (58–51BC) soon afterwards.

*Below: A slave bringing in food for a banquet, from a mosaic from Roman Carthage of the 3rd century AD. The more attractive or intelligent slave could hope for such domestic service. Those lacking such charms often ended up in the mines or on farms.*

# ASPECTS OF SLAVERY

By the end of the Republic, owning a slave or two was as common even for quite ordinary Romans as owning a car is today, and scarcely more reprehensible. Often such slaves would do domestic duties or work on the farm or in the family business alongside free hired labourers, and they could be hard to tell apart from poor citizens. In contrast, great nobles could have hundreds of slaves around them in their houses and possibly thousands more working their *latifundiae* (great estates).

## THE WORK OF SLAVES

Slaves performed many different tasks in the Roman world and so did not form a single economic or social class. Their jobs and their social status differed greatly, ranging from the highly educated Greeks whose intellectual powers were appreciated by Roman nobles who exploited them as secretaries, librarians, tutors or clerks – Epictetus the philosopher being the outstanding example – via attractive young girls and boys who were sexually exploited, to those at the very bottom of the servile scale. These last, lacking beauty, intelligence or any other notable qualities, could find themselves condemned to crushing work on the land or in the mines.

*Above: The mines of Las Medulas in Spain where many slaves were worked to premature deaths.*

*Left: A slave being freed, showing his progress from prostrate subjection to shaking his ex-master's hand.*

Many farm and mining slaves were appallingly treated. Pliny the Younger talks of chain-gangs of agricultural slaves who had "speaking" iron collars forged around their necks. These collars, as uncomfortable as they were demeaning, requested the finder to return the slave to its rightful owner like a dog. Even worse were conditions in the mines where slaves worked alongside criminals. Although tiny quantities of coal were mined in Roman Britain, these were for the most part metal mines. Some of the largest and most profitable mines were imperial property. The copper mines in Cyprus and gold, silver and lead mines in Spain were huge. The biggest industrial undertakings in the whole empire, they employed many thousands of slaves who were worked to early deaths underground.

Elsewhere, in the fertile province of Africa for example, even large estates seem to have been worked mostly by free tenant farmers. In much of the empire free seasonal labour supplemented slaves at busy times like the harvest. Slavery therefore, while part of Roman culture, was not always fundamental to agriculture but it was to quarries and mines.

## REVOLT AND REBELLION

Unsurprisingly, slaves sometimes revolted. In Sicily, where huge *latifundiae* worked by slaves were established early on, slave revolts in 135–132BC and again in 104–100BC threatened Roman control of the island.

In the second revolt, a Greek-speaking slave calling himself Antiochus briefly established control over almost all Sicily. Spartacus' gladiators' revolt of 73–71BC attracted many other slaves far closer to Rome. In the troubled 3rd century AD, much of central Gaul was for years in the hands of the *Bagaudae* (literally, brigands), who even set up their own courts.

Household slaves very seldom turned on their masters. The case of the senator Larcius Macedo, who was attacked by his domestic slaves *c.* 100AD, was shocking to his contemporaries precisely because it was so exceptional.

### MANUMISSION

Something which impressed Greek visitors to Rome was the ceremony of *manumission*, in which Roman slave owners gave particularly favoured slaves their freedom. This often formed part of the owner's will.

With freedom normally came admission for the newly liberated to Roman citizenship. However, as *manumission* was granted through *paterpotestas*, the power of the head of the family, freedmen were normally considered bound to their former owners by ties of gratitude, taking their names and joining their patron's *clientalia*, network of retainers. Obviously, *manumission* was less significant for a small builder or blacksmith who only manumitted one or two exhausted slaves in his will, than for a noble who grandly freed many slaves. The promise of manumission must have helped to encourage good behaviour among slaves.

Although there were no famous abolitionists of slavery in the ancient world, the Greek philosopher Aristotle (384–322BC) did not consider slaves inherently inferior to free citizens and both the Stoics and Epicureans considered slaves capable of philosophy. For Christians, even the most degraded of slaves had immortal souls, an important part of their religion's early appeal, but richer Christians owned slaves like everyone else.

Every slave owner retained power of life and death over his human property, although more humane emperors tried to mitigate abuses of this power. Augustus saved the life of a slave boy whose irascible master, Vedius Pollio, had wanted to feed him to the lampreys for breaking a precious glass; and Claudius banned the

practice of masters reclaiming sick slaves left to die on the island in the Tiber, saying that if slaves recovered their health they also recovered their liberty. Domitian forbade the castration of slave boys for sexual purposes (although slaves still had no defence against their owners' sexual demands) and Hadrian stopped slave owners handing their slaves over to the gladiatorial schools as a punishment and made executing slaves dependent on the approval of the prefect of the *Vigiles* (night watchmen).

Slavery, if waning in importance, as an institution, survived both the gradual conversion of the empire to Christianity in the 4th century AD and the end of the West Roman empire in the 5th century AD.

*Above: Relief from the theatre of Sabratha, showing a scene of a slave rebuked by his master, c. AD180.*

*Above: Claudius, an emperor who tried to limit the mistreatment of slaves.*

# BUSINESS AND COMMERCE

Like most aristocracies, the Roman nobility liked to advertise the fact that they could enjoy a life of leisure as well as their riches. In the later empire, senators were excluded from politics and the army although many still had their large estates to run. *Otium cum dignitate* (cultured, dignified leisure) was always their motto.

## HARD WORK

Earlier, the senatorial order had been closely involved in public affairs during both the Republic and Principate. This is well illustrated by the careers of two men who lived near the empire's apogee: Pliny the Younger, who died *c.* AD112, probably in office as proconsul of Bithynia, after a career as a soldier, lawyer and a consul; and Sextus Julius Frontinus, who died at the age of 70 in AD100 while still the highly effective *curator aquarum* (controller of Rome's water supply) after a career as a consul, soldier and imperial administrator. Conscientious emperors – and most emperors were conscientious if not brilliant rulers – were often also grossly overworked.

At the other end of the social scale, the poorest among the free laboured until exhausted for a pittance. The supposedly pampered populace of Rome, although given *panem et circuses* (free bread and circuses), had to find other means to pay Rome's notoriously high rents. Many did odd labouring jobs, among which portering the huge quantities of food the capital demanded must have been one of the most important, along with working on construction. However, most Romans tried to divide their day clearly into *negotium* (literally: "not leisure", or business) and *otium* (leisure) – the latter having the real appeal.

Although winters in Rome can be chilly and wet, life for men was lived in the open as much as possible or at least in the shelter of porticoes, principally those surrounding the Forum Romanum, and the adjacent imperial fora. The Forum Romanum, at the heart of Roman public life, was also initially the site of the food markets, but these were moved out closer to the Tiber to the Forum Boarium (Cattle Market) and Forum Holitorium (Vegetable Market). This segregation of the messier aspects of commercial life from the ceremonial and social happened in other cities, such as Pompeii and Pozzuoli, and Lepcis Magna and Timgad in Africa, for Romans wanted to make each Forum a splendidly adorned centre of civic pride. In the Forum Romanum male citizens, supposedly all dressed in togas, would meet to discuss matters and renew their ties of mutual obligation. Women remained at home.

## THE WORKING DAY

Business of many kinds, of which commercial business in the modern sense was only a part, occupied the first part of the day. This began early, often at first light. Although the Romans had numerous

*Above: A Roman sundial from Utica in Africa. The Romans, who lacked mechanical clocks, relied on sundials, hourglasses and waterclocks to tell the time.*

*Below: A Roman relief depicting a vendor of pillows, furniture coverings and textiles. Many poorer Romans found underpaid work in such small-scale service industries.*

public holidays, they did not have a specific day of the week as a day of rest as Sunday is today for many of us. However, the hours of their day, delimited chiefly by sundials, varied according to the time of year, both the hours and the day being far longer in summer. The Romans relied on sundials and water clocks copied from the Hellenistic world. Men working in particular trades, most of which had their own guilds, went out to work. The building trade was one of the most important in Rome up to the 3rd century AD, but there were also guilds of butchers, fishmongers and bakers, all of which held regular dinners.

In the morning every patron, who might be a powerful noble but who might also be considerably lower down the social and political ladder, would meet some of his *clientalia*, his retainers or supporters. Almost every citizen in Rome was tied by bonds of *obsequium*, mutual obligation, from the poorest man without work to great nobles. Only the emperor had no one above him. Clients were expected to vote for their patrons in return for the occasional gift, which often included daily *sportula* (small gifts of free food), as well as more substantial occasional gifts such

as a new toga for appearing in public, support in legal or social problems and financial aid at times. Later, after elections of magistrates were abolished in AD14, clients were still expected to accompany their patron on his rounds through the city, perform little tasks for him and add to his general glory. Juvenal attacked the way each morning Rome's streets filled with clients hurrying to pay their respects in the *domus* (house) of their patron.

*Above: The Forum Romanum in the 4th century AD, seen from the area of the House of the Vestal Virgins.*

*Below: A bas relief of the 2nd century AD showing a butcher hacking meat in his shop in Ostia. Many Romans were small shop-keepers.*

# LEISURE AND HOLIDAYS

*Above: Gambling in bars and other public places was a common Roman pastime. These dice players are from a north African mosaic of the 3rd century AD.*

*Below: A wealthy Roman woman going to the baths accompanied by her servants, from a mosaic at Piazza Armerina, Sicily, of the 4th century AD. Women usually had different bathing times to those of men.*

By midday, most Romans would have been up for six hours or more and would have hoped to have accomplished their *negotium* (business) – on days when business could be conducted at all. There were numerous *dies nefasti*, days of ill omen when judgements could not be made and when public assemblies could not be held.

## DAYS OF ILL OMEN

On the many such inauspicious days the Romans celebrated religious rites such as the *Ludi Apollinares* dating from 208BC which ran from 6–13 July, or the *Ludi Victoriae Caesaris* which commemorated Caesar's military conquest of Gaul from 20–30 July.

The purpose of these displays was not to encourage mass idleness and drain the public coffers but to celebrate the power of the Roman people and honour the appropriate gods. The latter included deified former emperors. By the reign of Claudius (AD41–54) 159 days a year were *dies nefasti*. He and subsequent wise emperors such as Vespasian tried to reduce the number. Marcus Aurelius restored the business year to 230 days.

## LEISURED AFTERNOONS

Even on *dies fasti* (when judgements could be made), the Forum emptied of citizens conducting business as the afternoon wore on. Most drifted off in search of entertainment in the warmest part of the day. One important event for the poorer citizens – who formed the majority of Rome's inhabitants – was the monthly distribution of the *annona*, the grain ration, which was handed out at the Porticus Minucia. By AD200 this came in the form of baked bread and was later supplemented by wine, oil and pork.

Far more spectacular were the gladiatorial games, the races at the circus and performances at the theatre which diverted the Roman people. As these huge public structures could contain much of the city's population – the Circus Maximus could seat about 300,000 people, the Colosseum and the Theatre of Pompey about 50,000 people each – this was truly mass entertainment.

The other enormous draw was the public baths. There were 170 in Rome by 33BC and 856 by AD400, but by the 4th century AD the small establishments had long been eclipsed by the 11 huge imperial baths, the *thermae*, that were some of the grandest Roman buildings. Starting relatively modestly with the Baths of Agrippa of 25BC, these assumed majestic form with the Baths of Trajan, which opened in AD109. The even larger *thermae* that followed in the next two centuries – the Baths of Caracalla, Diocletian and Constantine – expanded the same concept, which was copied in the provinces.

Lavishly designed and decorated, these complexes combined the functions of gyms, health centres, swimming pools, libraries, restaurants, meeting places and bordellos. Romans in cities around the empire would spend leisurely afternoon

hours exercising in the *palaestra*, bathing in the *caldarium, tepidarium* and *frigidarium* (respectively the hot, warm and cold baths), swimming in the open-air *natatio* (swimming pool), walking in the gardens, relaxing, and enjoying relationships of varying degrees of intimacy with other bathers. Some women joined men at the baths. But as there were designated hours for women, it was probably only women of ill-repute who bathed with the men. When early Christians fulminated against the amount of time wasted sinfully at the baths, they were attacking less physical cleanliness – although Christian ascetics frowned upon washing, preferring to mortify their dirty flesh – than this openly sybaritic aspect of Roman life.

## SHOPS AND BARS

Almost all of Rome's *tabernae* (shops) were small and specialized. They consisted of one room, often at the ground level of an *insula* (apartment block), with a wooden or masonry counter across the entrance that was closed off at night by shutters. They normally had a mezzanine floor above. Most *tabernae* lined the narrow streets. Bakers would have grain storage space, mills and baking ovens at the back of the shop. One shop in Ostia has murals of its goods behind the counter, such as grapes and olives. Another depicted on a terracotta plaque shows a poultry shop with baskets of eggs on the counter. A few jewellers and shops selling luxury goods remained in the Forum Romanum. Domitian tried to clear the streets of the clutter of shops, with limited success. However, complexes of shops were developed early at Terracina, and Livy mentions an early specialized food market near the Forum Romanum. Much the most splendid complex of markets and offices was Trajan's Market, rising above Trajan's Forum. This is thought to have offered covered shopping inside one of Rome's most remarkable buildings.

Rome and other cities also had plenty of bars where men could drop in for a quick drink or a snack. Some were tiny,

little more than holes in the wall, but others, such as that found in the House of Amphitrite in Herculaneum, had seating with *amphorae* stacked in wooden wall racks. Romans liked to gamble as well as drink in such bars, while snacking on olives, bread, seafood and sausages. There were also modest restaurants, such as that found in the Via di Diana in Ostia. This had shelves and counters lined with second-hand marble and simple tables.

*Above: A tavern in the Via dell'Abbondanza in Pompeii, with* amphorae *stacked behind the bar.*

*Below: Interior of a tavern at Ostia, 1st century* AD. *Most taverns were just for drinking but this one had a table and bench and may have served snacks or even full meals.*

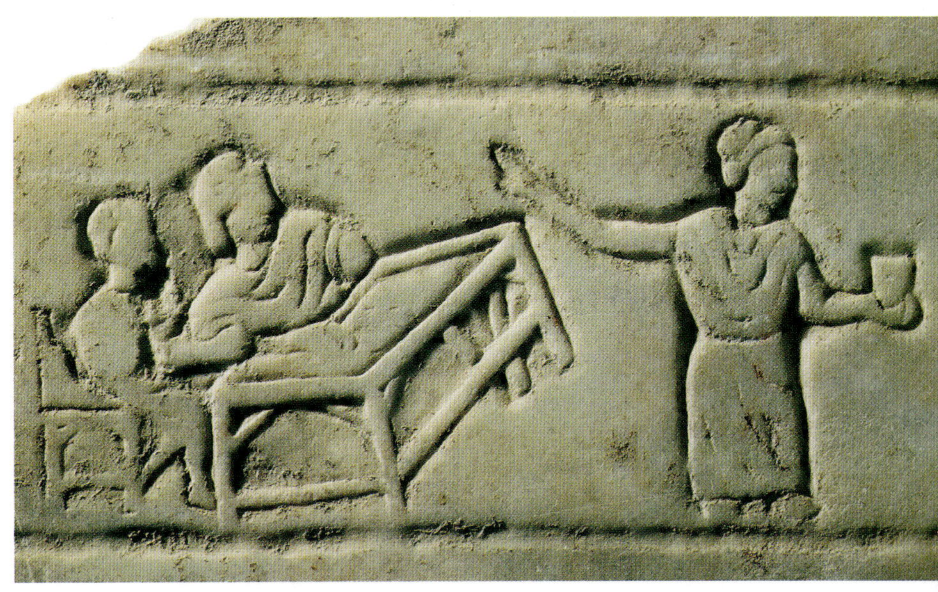

# DINNER PARTIES

Towards evening, after their lengthy baths, Romans headed home for the meal that was usually the social highlight of the day: *cena*, dinner. This was eaten around the eighth hour in winter or ninth hour in summer, which is about 4–6 p.m. in modern terms, for the Roman day varied according to the season. Originally there had been three daily meals but by the late Republic the first two, *ientaculum* and *prandium*, seem to have become little more than snacks, eaten without formality or even a table. The *cena* was the great meal of the day, sometimes the occasion of excessive gourmandizing but more usually of modest meals, to which the Romans came bathed, in clean clothes if they had them.

### THE DINING ROOM

All Romans who could afford it liked to dine reclining on *triclinia* (couches which ran on three sides of a table), set around a table, which gave the *triclinium* (dining room) its name. Covered with cushions and mattresses, these couches were sometimes built into the walls to save space. Others could be elaborately decorated and gilded. By the 2nd century BC women ate reclining alongside men. Only children and favoured slaves sat on stools or chairs at the end of the *triclinium*, a position which was considered undignified. Cato the Younger, one of Caesar's staunchest opponents, vowed never to eat reclining as long as Caesar's tyranny lasted, an extreme of self-denial more admired than imitated. (Cato committed suicide.) Some dining rooms were windowless, lit by oil lamps, but decorated with fine murals and mosaics. However, in country villas, *triclinia* could take advantage of the view seen through colonnades.

The couches were arranged around a table, one side of which was left free for service. The most honoured couch was opposite the empty side of the table and on each couch the most privileged position was that by the *fulcrum* or head of the couch. A *nomenclator* (usher) announced the guests and showed them their place on the couch, after they had removed their shoes. If more than nine people were to dine, other *triclinia* had to be brought in, twelve places being the usual maximum.

### EATING AND DRINKING

*Ministratores* (waiters) now brought in dishes and bowls. Diners had knives, toothpicks and several spoons, but as the Romans did not have forks, they ate mainly with their hands. They washed their hands frequently throughout the meal from bowls brought round by slaves. Every guest had his or her own napkin but some brought their own napkins with them which they filled with *apophoreta* (titbits) to take home. This was considered perfectly acceptable.

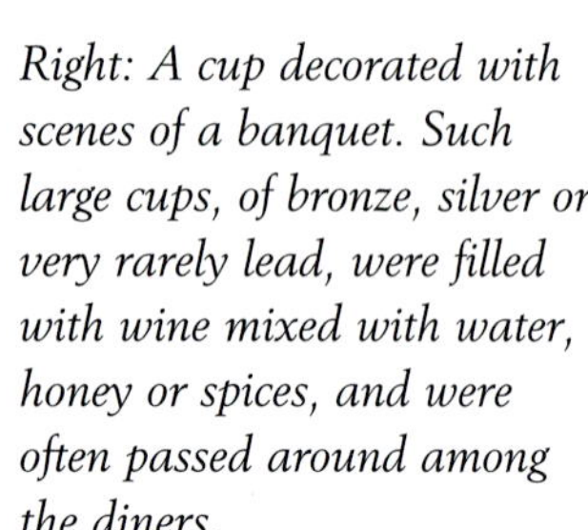

*Above: A young servant girl, probably a slave, carrying a dish of food, from a fresco in the Villa of the Mysteries, Pompeii c. 60BC.*

*Right: A cup decorated with scenes of a banquet. Such large cups, of bronze, silver or very rarely lead, were filled with wine mixed with water, honey or spices, and were often passed around among the diners.*

A grand *cena* could be formidable, an occasion for ostentatious display by the rich. Seven courses were not uncommon: a *gustatio* or hors d'oeuvre, three entrées, two roasts and a dessert. Juvenal *c.* AD120 described, "Huge lobsters garnished with asparagus…mullet from Corsica… goose's liver, a capon as big as a house, a piping hot boar…truffles and delicious mushrooms". Such descriptions might seem wildly exaggerated if not reiterated by the Greek historian Herodian 100 years later and by Macrobius, governor of Africa, in AD410. Juvenal also attacked hosts who kept the best dishes and wines for themselves and important guests, while giving "black meal" to the less important.

The Romans drank correspondingly. A first libation started the meal. *Mulsus* (honeyed wine) followed the first course and slaves went round refilling the *cratera* (mixing bowl), for wine was diluted with water. The proportion of water to wine could be low but generally it was somewhere in the region of 4:1.

After dinner there might be *acommissatio*, a drinking match in which diners had to empty their cups in one go. Dancers, clowns and striptease provided entertainment at some dinner parties, which could sometimes turn into orgies. Belching after such meals was perfectly acceptable and the emperor Claudius, who loved his food, considered an edict authorizing other emissions. But only the greediest diners vomited up their meal into pots held by slaves or on to the fine mosaic floors.

Only the length of such dinners tempered such excess, for they could go on for hours. Nero and his short-lived successor Vitellius, a noted gourmand, often stayed eating and drinking until after midnight, which was thought gross. Juvenal attacked those who "went to bed with the rise of Lucifer, the morning star, at an hour when our generals in the past would be moving their standards and camp".

Against such gourmandizing should be set the frugality of both Plinys. Pliny the Elder rose from the table when it was still light in summer and after only the

first hour of night in the winter, while his nephew praised "elegant but frugal meals". He accepted a dinner invitation once from Catilius Severus on the condition that "You treat me frugally and our table abounds only with philosophical conversation". Much more typical of most Roman meals than Neronian banquets was the dinner organized by the Funeral College in Rome for its members in AD133 at which each guest was given simply a loaf of bread, four sardines and an *amphora* of wine.

*Above: A banquet in Carthage, depicted on a mosaic of the 4th century AD. The diners appear to be sitting up, perhaps to view the performers.*

*Below: This banquet scene from Ancona in eastern Italy shows the classic pattern of diners reclining on triclinia arranged around three sides of a table, the fourth side being left free for servants.*

# FOOD FOR RICH AND POOR

*Above: Bread being sold at a bakery in Pompeii, a fresco of the 1st century AD. Note the flattened, circular shape of the baker's loaves.*

Two things stand out about Roman attitudes towards food in general. The first is that they were almost omnivorous. "If it moves or grows, cook it and eat it" could have been their motto, for they lacked religious or sentimental dietary taboos (except against cannibalism, and they did not eat dogs or cats). A large type of dormouse was specially bred for eating and most song birds were considered fair game, or were bred in captivity. This catholic approach led to dishes of great variety and increasing complexity and richness on the tables of the rich in Rome and other great cities.

The other salient point is that meat was expensive and most people ate a simple diet, based on cereals, olive oil and vegetables with quite a lot of wine, and modest amounts of meat – principally pork, seldom beef or chicken – and seafood. Slaves and paupers ate often rancid cereals as a gruel or porridge and suffered chronic malnutrition, as modern analysis of skeletons at Pompeii has shown.

## THE CHANGING DIET OF ROME

The early Roman diet was simple, based on cereals, olive oil and locally grown vegetables. Later orators used to praise the ancient frugality of Curius Dentatus, who "gathered his scanty vegetables and cooked them himself in his little stove". This moderation did not long survive Rome's rise to wealth and power.

From 200BC on, Rome could no longer be supplied locally and soon foreign wars led to imports of entirely new foods. Lucullus, the great late Republican general, for example, introduced the cherry to Rome from Asia Minor. However, most of the bulk of the food sucked into Rome remained the essential supplies of wheat, which came from Egypt, Africa and Sicily, and olive oil which came from Africa and Spain.

There were many other dishes but, as the Romans had no refrigeration, most perishable foods tended to be produced and eaten locally. Martial's *Epigrams* list

*Right: From 200BC on, Rome began to import food, metals, textiles and other goods from a growing range of countries around the Mediterranean both for their luxuries and as staple necessities.*

the many foods available for those who could afford them at the end of the 1st century AD. Pork came from Gaul, cured meats from Spain, spices from Asia, wines and fruits – including apples, pears, figs, grapes, melons and plums – from vineyards and orchards in Italy, along with asparagus (a favourite of Augustus), olives, beans, lentils, radishes, peas, pumpkins, lettuce and cabbages.

Seafood in all its variety was much prized in an empire centred on the sea. Red mullet and shellfish, especially lobster, were delicacies, but oysters were not a luxury and were transported inland along the roads, even in Britain, to be eaten by travellers. From the edges of the Sahara in Africa came pomegranates and dates, and fresh game came from the woods of Italy. Most dishes were cooked in sauces flavoured with spices from the East such as pepper. Perhaps the most characteristic Roman flavouring was *garum*. This was made from fish guts, salted and placed in tanks in the sun until they had gained sufficient potency to be used to flavour dishes – a process that could take four to six weeks.

By the 1st century AD Roman cuisine in all its sometimes overwhelming intricacy is revealed – albeit in caricatured form – in the great banquet that Trimalchio gave in the *Satyricon*, where the chef could create '"a fish out of a sow's belly, a wood pigeon out of bacon, a turtledove out of ham". Dormice "sprinkled with honey and poppy seed" made an amazing hors d'oeuvre and a boar stuffed with live thrushes that flew out as it was being carved made an eye-catching main roast. Although such absurdly complex courses must have been rare, Roman cooks delighted in concocting dishes that were unusual. However, as the still-life murals of bread, fruit and game from Pompeii suggest, most families would normally have eaten far more simply. Sausages, meat pies and cubes of roasted meat were popular, along with fruits both fresh and dried and buns filled with both savoury and sweet things. Honey was the universal sweetener.

### WHAT THE ROMANS LACKED

Ancient Romans did not have citrus fruits such as oranges or grapefruit, nor rice, sugar, apricots, coffee, pheasant or peaches, all of which were introduced by the Arabs to Europe during the Middle Ages. They did not have tomatoes, potatoes, corn, peanuts, guinea fowl, red and green (bell) peppers, chocolate and turkey, which came to Europe from Central or North America in the 16th century.

The Romans did not drink tea, which was still a Chinese secret, and they scarcely ate butter, for it apparently seldom occurred to them to store surplus milk in this way. In fact, they did not eat much in the way of dairy products apart from cheese. Their diet approximated to the modern ideal of the Mediterranean diet.

*Above: A still life showing fruit, nuts and a water jug from the House of the Stags at Herculaneum, 1st century AD. This fresco illustrates what the well-to-do Roman mainly ate better than some more elaborate written menus.*

*Below: Seafood of many types was much-prized by the Romans, both rich and also the poor if they lived near the sea. Lobster and mullet were thought delicacies. The Mediterranean in those unpolluted days still teemed with abundant marine life.*

# WINE AND VINEYARDS

*Above: The Romans had over 50 distinct varieties of grapes, but most of their wine was red.*

Wine played a hugely important role in Roman life, for they had no tea, chocolate or coffee, nor soft drinks nor spirits. They hardly drank beer from the middle Republic on – they knew of it but considered it fit mainly for Germans, although beer was drunk by Roman soldiers on Hadrian's Wall. Romans drank wine, an estimated 100 million litres a year in Rome alone at its peak, most of which came from outside central Italy. For the undernourished majority, wine was an important food, a source of minerals, vitamins (including, we now know, vital anti-oxidants) and sugars. Slaves drank water with a little thin wine.

## ROMAN VITICULTURE

The Greeks had long grown wine in southern Italy, from where viticulture spread north to central Italy. Etruria was thought to produce some of Rome's best wines, such as Graviscanum, Caeres or Tiburtinum, but the especially renowned Falernian wine came from just north of Naples. Most famous vineyards were not far from the coast, as sea transport was so much cheaper than land transport. Greek wine was also highly regarded by the Romans, although it may not have tasted like Greek wines today. Spain later became another major wine exporter. Wine transported long distances in pinewood barrels may have acquired a resinous tang like modern retsina, but the Romans do not seem to have objected as they added various flavourings to their wine when they mixed them.

As trade around the empire boomed in the three centuries after 100BC, wine-growing spread to new regions. The Greek cities of southern Gaul, especially Marseilles, had always grown wine and under the Romans viticulture reached northern Gaul. In AD71 Pliny the Elder noted that vineyards already existed around Bordeaux but he knew little about their wines and they remained obscure. The warmer and drier Rhône valley was more promising territory for a viticulture based on Mediterranean methods and grape varieties. Trier, surrounded by sun-trapping vineyards hanging from the steep slopes above the river Moselle, may have produced wine as early as the 2nd century AD. However, evidence of its flourishing vineyards comes only from the second half of the 4th century AD,

*Left: Pressing grapes in a winery from St Romain en Gal, France, c. AD200. Vine-growing was introduced into southern France by the Greeks.*

in a famous poem by the imperial tutor, governor and poet Ausonius, supported by archaeological evidence in the form of wine presses in the Moselle valley at Piesport. The Moselle flowing past Trier, the Western empire's capital at the time, reminded Ausonius of his native Bordeaux, where vineyards lined the river Garonne. He described wealthy villas with their smoking chimneys, boatmen exchanging jocular insults with men working among the vines, fish playing in the river and, in a famous passage, the hills mirrored in the Moselle's waters.

*What colour paints the river shallows, when*
  *Hesperus has brought the shades of evening.*
*The Moselle is dyed with the green of her*
  *hills; their tops quiver*
*In the ripples, vine leaves tremble from afar*
*And the grape clusters swell even in the*
  *clear stream.*

The most informative Roman author on viticultural matters was Lucius Junius Columella in the 1st century AD. In *De re Rustica* (*About Rural Matters*) he wrote about many aspects of farming beside vineyards, but he did discuss different grape varieties and how to balance quantity against quality. He listed more than 50 grape varieties and praised a native Italian variety called the Amminean.

The Romans sometimes used to trail vines along elms and other trees such as poplars for support, and it has been suggested that the traditional English elm (now almost extinct) was first imported into Britain by Romans for such purposes.

Bacchus, the wine god, was an important deity to the Romans and libations, the pouring out of wine in honour of a god, were a common sacramental use of wine. The last of a particularly good wine was sometimes thrown on the

floor as an offering to the gods. Later, as the empire slowly became Christian, the frequent use of wine in the Eucharist again encouraged the spread of viticulture into northern Europe, for wine remained expensive to transport long distances until Bordeaux began shipping its wines north in the 12th century.

## VINTAGES AND WINE STORAGE

Although the Romans may not have had completely airtight corks (they used lead as an extra sealant) they did develop glass bottles besides traditional pottery *amphorae* for better wines. These were marked with a distinguishing *pittacium* (label) stating their vintage. The Romans apparently kept certain of their finest wines for a remarkably long time. Horace when in his middle-age wrote of drinking a vintage older than himself, and the most famous vintage, that dating from the consulate of Opimius in 121BC, was reputedly kept for 125 years. However, most Roman wines were drunk young when they were sharp, even rough, and strong. The Romans never drank their wine neat, but diluted it usually with drinking water, sometimes with seawater, or they would sweeten the wine with honey. Roman wines at times could possibly have tasted a little like sangria.

*Above: Late 2nd-century* AD *bottle and drinking glass from the mosaic pavement of a* triclinium *(dining room) at Thysdrus, El Djem.*

*Right: Although the Romans drank wine regularly, being seen drunk in public as in this Hellenistic statue of an old woman was considered a disgraceful condition and was not the norm.*

# ROME THE GREAT CONSUMER

*Above: The symbols of grain merchants in a mosaic set in the street leading to the market in Ostia, Rome's great harbour town, c. AD100.*

*Below: Amphorae (earthenware jars) for transporting and storing oil and wine came in a variety of shapes and sizes, but under the empire their shapes were increasingly standardized. These amphorae come from a sunken ship.*

One of the chief concerns of those governing Rome, from the later Republic until the end of the ancient city in the 6th century AD, was supplying it with essential foods. Other large cities imported grain, but Rome's demands eclipsed all others.

### WHEAT, WINE AND OIL

Since Clodius started the free distribution to male citizens over the age of ten of five *modii* per month of grain (880lbs/400kg per person of grain annually) in 58BC, rulers who failed to provide the *annona* (dole) faced riots. The emperor Claudius (AD41–54) was pelted with stale crusts by a hungry crowd after a poor harvest and storms delayed the grain fleets.

Claudius' response was to build a giant artificial harbour north of Ostia at Portus, which Trajan improved with an inland basin 60 years later. Grain, mainly wheat, and olive oil were the staples of the Roman diet, but olive oil also lit the city's countless oil lamps and was lavishly used for personal hygiene, in place of soap. Wine was almost the only drink available.

Wheat, wine and oil were therefore needed in unprecedented quantities – about 400,000 tons per year of foodstuffs, of which 240,000 tons were wheat. (Meat, seafood, fruit and vegetables, supplementary to these dietary basics, are less easily estimated, although early in the 3rd century AD Septimius Severus added oil, and in AD275 Aurelian pork and wine, to the *annona*, but by then the city's population was beginning to fall.)

The great mound rising beside the Tiber in Rome known as Monte Testaccio is made of pieces of broken *amphorae* (earthenware jars). Rising 112ft (34m), it has a circumference of 3,200ft (1km) and contains fragments of at least 53 million *amphorae*. The majority once held olive oil shipped from Spain in the years AD140–250. Africa was another large source of oil. Most *amphorae* came in a variety of standardized sizes. They were designed to be neatly stacked in ships' holds. They were usually broken up after being emptied because their interiors absorbed oil which went rancid, although a few were later used to lighten architectural vaults.

About 1,000 shiploads of wheat were needed for Rome each year, as the average merchant ship carried about 240 tons. Inclusion of the shipping needed for the estimated 100 million litres (22 million gallons) of wine and 20 million litres (4 million gallons) of oil would boost this total to at least 1,700 ships a year arriving at Rome's ports – excluding those lost.

Most ships arrived in the sailing season, which lasted 100–120 days a year. The Romans never developed state-controlled fleets but relied on private contractors, whom they encouraged in various ways. After the bread riots Claudius offered anyone who used a ship holding at least 10,000 *modii* (70 tons) to supply Rome, privileges ranging from citizenship for non-citizens to exemptions from various taxes.

Emperors from Augustus on appointed officials such as the *praefectus annonae* (wheat dole prefect), who soon acquired assistants. By AD200, the *sub-praefectus annonae* (wheat dole subprefect), was paid 100,000 sesterces, a large salary reflecting his importance. However, grain supplies always remained precariously dependent on the caprices of harvests and of storms at sea. A serious grain shortage in AD190 caused riots which the emperor Commodus only defused by having Cleander, his favourite minister, executed as a scapegoat.

### HAULAGE AND STORAGE

When the food reached Rome's ports of Pozzuoli, Ostia or Portus it had to be unloaded, dragged up the river and stored. Grain and oil had to be rowed or hauled the 20 miles (32km) up the Tiber from the port in smaller boats or barges in a journey that took two to three days.

Four types of boat were used: the *scaphae*, *lintres* and *lenunculi*, all rowing boats, and the *codicariae*, specialized boats used to transport goods from Ostia and Portus up river to Rome. These had oars and lowerable masts but were often rowed or hauled, less often by slaves than by free but poor casual labourers. Although they had to be hauled upstream, they could

be rowed or sailed downstream. The Romans did not use horses for haulage, as they never developed suitable horse collars. The boat haulers, known as *helciarii*, used to chant rhythmically as they trudged along pulling their heavy vessels up stream towards the city. They even had their own guild. Upon arrival in Rome, the grain, oil and wine were stored in *horrea*, specially built warehouses by the Tiber such as those below the Aventine Hill in the region called Marmorata (so-called because this is where the marble coming into Rome was unloaded).

Some *horrea* were immense: the Horrea Galbana, for example, had 140 rooms on the ground floor alone and covered about 5 acres (2ha). These multistorey warehouses were massively built, with walls at least 2ft (60cm) thick. They had small external windows and massive doors to preserve their valuable contents from thieves. Inside they had large internal windows, both between rooms and opening on to courtyards, to provide plentiful ventilation to keep the grain dry. For the same reason they normally had raised floors. The floors also stopped rodent activity and provided circulation of air to prevent the spontaneous combustion of overheated grain. Much grain was lost to rodents nonetheless.

*Above: Free labourers or slaves haul a barge full of wine barrels up a river, probably the Rhône, since the relief is from Avignon. The Romans could not use horses for such work as they did not have the right type of horsecollar.*

*Below: Many warehouses were monumental structures boasting fine architectural features, such as this grand gateway of the Horrea Epagathania in Ostia, whose pediment and pillars are worthy of a public building.*

# TUNICS AND TOGAS

*Below: This Roman magistrate from Asia Minor in the 5th century AD wears similar clothes to those worn 500 years before.*

It is striking how little fashions changed from the late Republic to the end of the Western empire 600 years later. A senator from Cicero's day might have looked rather oddly dressed four centuries later but he would not have seemed to be wearing fancy dress. The same could not be said today. The very slowly changing nature of Roman fashion, however, is more typical of most societies around the world than the increasingly rapid sartorial changes of recent centuries. Clothes generally denoted status in the Roman world and, while definitions of social status changed gradually, fashions were never dictated by designers, nor did individuals dress solely according to their own whims. Although the odd dandy like Caesar wore his toga with particularly wide sleeves, the Romans were generally rather puritanical about what citizens should wear, adhering to a simplicity that can be called classical.

## TYPES OF FABRIC

The basic Roman garment for all classes was the *tunicum*, a simple tunic made of wool or, less commonly, linen. Cotton was rare for a long time and silk was always a luxury item imported from furthest Asia. Although the use of silk increased steadily, for a long time it was thought utterly effeminate for men. (Caligula caused a scandal by appearing once in gaudy silk robes.) However, under the Principate it became increasingly common for richer women. Finally, in the grandiose courts of the later empire (after AD284) most courtiers wore elaborate silk robes. Wool, undyed

*Above: A Roman wearing a* pallium *(cloak) over his tunic from Sicily, 4th century AD. Only richer citizens could afford a* pallium.

for poor people and white for richer citizens, remained the commonest material, however. The *tunicum* was made of two pieces of cloth sewn together, usually untailored so that the surplus produced short sleeves, with a belt around the waist. Slaves, labourers and the very poor wore almost nothing else, but richer citizens often wore a *pallium* or Greek-style cloak over their longer *tunicum*. It is possible that some Romans wore a *licium*, a loin cloth, as underwear.

Formal dress for male Roman citizens consisted of the toga, a large semicircular piece of woollen cloth about 9ft (2.7m) long worn draped over one shoulder to leave the other bare and almost reaching the ankles. Exactly how this was put on has been tentatively reconstructed. A toga was certainly a cumbersome, heavy garment, which citizens liked to discard as soon as possible but which emperors repeatedly tried to make citizens wear in public as late as the reign of Commodus

(AD180–92). In the evenings a *synthesis*, a comfortable compromise between a toga and a tunic, was often worn for dining on a couch. Senators were distinguished from ordinary citizens by the *laticlava*, a broad purple stripe running down their tunics, while equestrians had a narrower stripe, the *angusticlava*. Emperors wore the most purple, so "being raised to the purple" came to mean becoming emperor.

Hooded cloaks, *paenulae*, could be worn over the tunic or toga in bad weather but hats were generally unknown apart from straw hats worn informally against the sun. In bad weather part of the toga could be pulled over the head for protection, as it was for priestly roles. Trousers were known to the Romans but were long considered barbarous garments – worn by Persians and Germans – and were only adopted partially at the end of the empire, in a sign for conservatives of general decay. Clerical dress in the Catholic and Episcopalian or Lutheran churches, with its long, superimposed robes, still perpetuates old Roman dress. In the later empire, heavy military-style belts were worn by bureaucrats as well as soldiers, revealing the general militarization of Roman government.

### WOMEN'S WEAR

Roman women also wore long loose tunics. These, called *stolae*, were often in bright colours and of fine material, such as good linen, cotton or silk. Underneath they often wore a *strophium*, a leather band that served as a simple bra. Over their *stola* went a rectangular woollen mantle, the *palla*, which was draped over the left shoulder, across the back and under the right arm. Prostitutes and convicted adulteresses wore female togas, the former often wearing transparent silks.

Women's dress also seems to have changed remarkably little over the centuries, although brooches – buttons were unknown to the Romans – became progressively more elaborate, as did jewellery generally.

### FOOTWEAR

The basic Roman footwear was the sandal in varying shapes. The *solea* was a form of basic sandal of a type still worn by some Catholic monks, with the sole attached to the instep by straps. *Crepidae* were sandals secured by a strap passing through eyelets, while *calcei* were leather half boots with crossed laces. In the army soldiers wore *caligae*, hobnailed boots that laced up round the ankle. (*Caligula*, Little Boots, was the nickname of the emperor Gaius, who grew up in the camp of his father Germanicus.) The Romans increasingly wore *fasciae*, a form of puttee, around the feet and lower legs, in northern parts of the empire and in winter. Women wore either sandals or soft leather shoes, but high heels were unknown. Socks were sometimes worn.

*Right: A pair of leather sandals from Egypt of the 3rd century AD. Sandals were the standard footwear across areas around the Mediterranean.*

*Above: As these women conversing on a mural from Pompeii c. AD70 show, Roman women wore long, loose brightly-coloured stolae (tunics) of linen, cotton or silk. Their fashions changed only very slowly over the centuries.*

# HAIRSTYLES AND COSMETICS

*Above: The curly beard and hair of the 2nd century AD as sported by Lucius Verus.*

*Below: Women's hairstyles became very elaborate, then reverted to simpler styles with hair tied back and a middle parting, as in this Egyptian mummy portrait of the 4th century AD.*

Although Roman clothing changed very slowly, hairstyles and fashions in beards underwent remarkable developments that perhaps reveal something about wider changes in Roman society itself.

### BEARDED OR CLEAN-SHAVEN?

In the early Republic, according to tradition – such as the story about the Gauls pulling at the beards of elderly senators during the sack of Rome in 390BC – and in surviving portraits such as the so-called "Brutus", men had beards and short hair. The Romans always remained short-haired but by *c.* 150BC most Roman men were clean-shaven, possibly following Hellenistic styles. Fashion dictated that they remained so until after the death of Trajan in AD117. (A few soldiers had earlier had clipped beards and moustaches.)

Shaving was not, however, an easy or pain-free task for Romans, as they lacked both soap (for working up a lather) and high-quality steel for a clean shave. It was difficult and unusual even to try to shave oneself. Important Romans used to have barbers come to shave them in their houses and some, like Augustus, carried on their daily business at the same time. Ordinary Romans visited regularly but not always daily the *tonsor* (barber).

The barber's shop, the *tonstrina*, opened on to the street and was the place where men came to exchange news and gossip. Here they had their hair cut and their faces shaved, by a *novacula*, a blunt iron razor, by a form of poultice called *dropax*, made of several types of wax that depilated rather than shaved, or by *forcipes aduncae*, tweezers. The whole process was long and painful. Skilled barbers could make a lot of money; the unskilled made a painful mess of their customers' faces.

When Hadrian, either because he had a scar on his face that he wished to hide or because of his love of all things Greek, began wearing a beard after AD117, the fashion quickly spread and soon almost all Roman men sported beards. In the 4th century AD fashion changed again. Constantine always appears in his portraits clean-shaven, as do his sons. Julian, in emotive reaction against his Christian precursors, wore a beard like a Greek philosopher. Although Julian's successors were mostly clean-shaven, by the 6th century AD most men were bearded again.

While beards came and went, male hairstyles – with the flamboyant exception of Nero and some of his courtiers, who adopted *bouffant* big hair copying that of charioteers – remained short and generally plain until the 2nd century AD. They then became steadily more elaborate. Hadrian is shown with a head of curly hair and soon men adopted hairdos of really elaborate complexity. Lucius Verus, the idle co-emperor of Marcus Aurelius, had a tremendous head of curly hair, but so had the ascetic Marcus and the militaristic Septimius Severus, emperors who followed rather than set the style. Their intricate curls reflect the barbers' skills. The latter used combs or a *calamistrum*, a heated curling iron, and even dyed some customers' hair. In the catastrophe-ridden 3rd century AD, men's hair became short and plain again, as Gallienus' and Diocletian's respectively austere and grim busts attest.

## WOMEN'S COIFFURE

Hairstyles for women in the Republic were simple, with the hair drawn back from a central parting and gathered in a chignon at the nape of the neck. Under Augustus, women's hair was often braided and with Messalina, Claudius' notoriously unfaithful wife, high-piled hairstyles appeared. Under the Flavian emperors and Trajan (AD69–117) female hair became extremely complicated, with great masses of curls piled high on the head. Trajan's sister Marciana and his niece Matilda both dressed their hair in diadems, "high as towers", the product of long hours spent with their *ornatrix*, or hairdresser.

Imperious Roman women of the nobility were prone to lash out at any hairdresser who failed to please them – many were slaves – at least according to the poet Martial, who tells of "Lalage avenging with the mirror in which she had seen it [an unfortunate hairdo] and Plecusa falls, hit because of those unruly locks of hair". Juvenal mocked women whose "numerous tiers and storeys piled upon one another on the head" made them look taller than they really were. Later hairstyles were less elaborate. Wigs were occasionally used to disguise baldness.

## COSMETICS

In addition to her work as a hairdresser, an *ornatrix* also took care of wealthier women's makeup. Often lead-based – the Romans were not aware of the dangers of lead – the cosmetics were stored in glass phials or flagons and alabaster vases. Creams, perfumes and unguents were extensively used. Red for the lips and cheeks was made from ochre, a lichen-like plant called *ficus* or from molluscs. Eyeliner was made from soot or powders of antinomy, which was also used to thicken the eyebrows. Mirrors, an essential part of the daily toilette, were made of highly polished metal, for true mirrors of reflecting glass were unknown. Ovid, ever aware of the erotic side of life, advised women to bolt the door of their chamber when making themselves up for "[your beauty] lies stored in a hundred caskets". Women also adorned themselves with elaborate jewellery, including *armillae* (bracelets), *catellae* (trinkets) and *periscelides* (ankle circlets).

*Above: A woman pouring perfume into a flask from the Villa Farnesina, c. AD10.*

*Below: A casket containing a wealthy Roman woman's toilette items from Cumae.*

# EROTIC LOVE

*Above: Tombstone showing a brothel-keeper and customer. Prostitution was accepted and regulated in Rome.*

*Below: An erotic fresco from Pompeii. Many Romans enjoyed often fine erotic art such as this in private.*

The Roman reputation for widespread sexual debauchery is hardly merited. It derives more from Suetonius' racy portraits of the first 12 Caesars, reinforced by Hollywood films and discoveries of "shocking" pictures at Pompeii, than from the reality of life for most people in the Roman world, who seldom had the opportunity for sexual depravity. Most of them worked hard, married young and remained reasonably faithful. If there were no lethal sexually transmitted diseases to discourage promiscuity, there were no contraceptives to facilitate it either. Prostitution existed, was recognized but not revered (unlike in Babylon or parts of Syria), and was regulated. Prostitutes wore distinctive toga-style dresses.

However, if unworried by Christian fears of eternal damnation for extramarital sex, the Romans were very concerned with the maintenance of public dignity and social stability, both of which were based on the conventional family unit. Monogamy within marriage was always the ideal and female "virtue" (chastity) was much praised in the legends of early Rome. Lucretia, a noble Roman virgin killed herself rather than give in to the advances of the Etruscan tyrant Tarquinius. (Tarquinius was soon after expelled from Rome.) However, as with most pagan religions, minor fertility gods around the empire were honoured by sometimes ithyphallic statues, while statues of major deities, often half-naked, adorned public places. These can give ancient cities an unwarranted air of eroticism to modern eyes.

## SEXUAL MORALITY

Heterosexual romance and love were the main themes of many novels, plays and poetry, from the numerous plays of Plautus in the 2nd century BC to Longus' romantic novel *Daphnis and Chloe* 300 years later. Here the naivity of the peasant lovers is mocked. Apuleius, writing *The Golden Ass* at about the same time, caters to a more sophisticated audience, but he attributes bad faith and perversity to characters with Greek names.

In the late Republic there had been a marked loosening of sexual restrictions, at least among upper class Romans. Augustus tried to control this. The *Lex Julia* made adultery a criminal offence and he banished his own daughter, grand-daughter and the poet Ovid for sexual immorality. Augustus himself, however, had mistresses. Women, making use of their new freedoms, could choose or reject lovers, but women's own voices are seldom heard. That of Messalina, Claudius' notoriously promiscuous wife, is exceptional. Lesbianism presumably existed but escaped record because writers were men.

## HOMOSEXUALITY

The Romans had no specific word for male homosexuality, for they seldom thought in terms of predetermined sexual orientation but rather about public behaviour. While the Romans never idealized homosexuality as some upper-class Greeks had, they did not demonize it either, as Christians later did. Homosexuality was, however, often considered a Greek habit and, as with most things Greek, it seems to have become more widespread in the later Republic. Augustus typically tried to discourage it by legislation in his attempt to boost the birth rate among citizens. Petronius' *Satyricon* involved the adventures of characters – bisexuals of singular cynicism – with Greek names in the still Greek cities of southern Italy. However, Roman poets such as Tibullus and Horace also revealed homosexual sentiments.

There remained a strong sexist bias in Roman attitudes to homosexuality: men who took the passive or female role in such relations were despised and risked losing their citizenship – hence the force of stories circulated by his political enemies that Julius Caesar, when young, had been King Nicomedes of Bithynia's boyfriend. (Caesar later became a noted womanizer.) Emperors like Nero who allowed themselves to be penetrated – according to Suetonius Nero appeared dressed as the bride at his own mock-wedding – forfeited public respect. Public decorum was the key.

When the popular Titus became emperor in AD79, he put aside his harem of catamites along with his much-loved Jewish mistress the princess Berenice. (The latter was thought unacceptable because she was an exotic royal foreigner rather than because of any Roman anti-semitism.) Trajan took a harem of boys with him on campaign but, as he was even more popular than Titus, this was accepted, at least outside Rome. By contrast, Hadrian's prolonged mourning for his boyfriend Antinous, who drowned in the Nile, struck many as excessive and undignified for an emperor. Emperors such as Caligula in the 1st century AD and Elagabalus in the 3rd century AD behaved so outrageously in public – Elagabalus reputedly prostituted himself – that they were soon assassinated.

From the 3rd century AD on, attitudes towards sex began to change. If Christians were the only real ascetics – Origen castrated himself to avoid the temptations of a beautiful young female pupil – non-Christians too began to become more obviously restrained in their behaviour. Herodian's novel *The Ethiopian Story* of the 3rd century AD praises the fidelity of its two engaged young lovers so strongly that Christians later claimed him as a covert co-religionist, which he probably was not. However Neoplatonism, the dominant philosophy in the later empire, tended to regard the flesh as something to be transcended, an attitude dating back to Plato which now became increasingly common. On this point at least pagan and Christian could meet.

*Above: An erotic scene from a bedroom in the huge villa at Piazza Armerina, Sicily, c. AD320, shows that Roman enjoyment of carnal pleasure persisted into the later empire.*

*Below: The emperor Hadrian erected huge numbers of statues of Antinous, his beautiful young lover who drowned in the Nile. This one is in Lepcis Magna, Libya.*

# FUNERALS AND THE AFTERLIFE

*Above: The Mausoleum of Augustus in Rome, completed 28BC, housed the funerary urns of members of the imperial family and was once topped by cypress trees, a custom going back to the Etruscans.*

*Below: A women's funerary choir performing a ritual dance from a tomb in Ruvo of the 5th century BC. Greek beliefs and customs deeply influenced Rome's in this field as in many others.*

The pagan Romans never had a consistent or united view about what happened to them after death. Beliefs varied greatly, from the uncompromising materialism of Lucretius, the poetic adherent of Epicurus who believed that we simply become again our constituent atoms, to the far more common belief that some aspect of an individual might survive death, but probably not in a very agreeable way. Only with the Roman world's gradual conversion to Christianity in the 4th and 5th centuries AD did fixed beliefs in heaven and hell emerge.

## THE ROMAN AFTERLIFE

Before then, people generally took what seemed most attractive – or least incredible – from what has been called the "inherited conglomerate" of myths, legends and beliefs that was constantly added to over the centuries but never reformed or subtracted from. The original Roman mixture of Etruscan and Greek ideas, in which the first was initially the most significant, was later enriched by new religions such as the cults of Bacchus, Isis and Mithras, which promised their adherents salvation. There were as well as the secretive, mystical sects such as the Pythagoreans and Orphics, who apparently believed in metempsychosis (reincarnation as animals or even plants).

For most people in the Roman world, however, the afterlife was a gloomy place of shadows and sometimes of torment, hardly more cheerful than the Christian or Muslim ideas of hell, which they may well have influenced. (The early Jews had had little belief in life after death.) In Book VI of Virgil's *The Aeneid*, which soon became Rome's national epic, Aeneas visits Hades, the underworld, and there talks to the shade of his father Anchises, for he was a notably filial son. This is an obvious reference to Odysseus' not dissimilar experience in Homer's *Odyssey*, and apposite as Roman ideas of the underworld were influenced by the Greeks. However, the Roman view of Hades was perhaps even gloomier, following Etruscan beliefs.

According to the composite Graeco-Roman story, Hades, the shadowy underworld, was governed by Pluto, sometimes called Orcus, the god of wealth as well as death. The souls of the dead were carried off by *genii*, spirits, who could be good or evil. This kingdom had several entrances through caves on Earth, but to reach it the dead had to pass Cerberus, the many-headed hound who guarded its gates. They then crossed the River Styx by paying Charon, the boatman, an obol, who became identified with Charun, a sinister Etruscan god of the dead. Sometimes Rhadamynthus and Minos, legendary kings of Crete, would then judge the souls of the dead, most of whom were left in a fearful limbo. Only a few heroes or deified emperors were thought to escape to the Elysian fields. Another infernal deity was Dis Pater, whom the Romans feared and seldom worshipped openly.

Such dismal views of the afterworld frightened many ordinary people. Writers like Lucretius, Cicero and Seneca, all infused with different aspects of Greek

*Left: These Roman tombs in the Isola Sacra cemetery near Ostia, probably dating from the 2nd century AD, would have housed many members of the same family over the years. By then burial was becoming common.*

philosophy, tried in vain to reassure them. However, most Romans regarded life on Earth as the important thing, not as a mere trial before eternal life in heaven, as Christians were meant to do.

## TOMB TYPES

One of the laws of the famous Twelve Tables of 451BC forbade burial within the sacred *pomerium* (city boundary) so, as Rome grew, burial sites were pushed outward by the expansion of the city. Tombs and burials were traditionally located along the roads out of the city, at least for the wealthy, from the Forum Romanum and the Esquiline Hill to the Campus Martius, an early favourite location between the Servian Wall and the Tiber. Here Augustus built a mausoleum for his own family, but this area too was rapidly built over. Soon cemeteries began to line the roads leading out of Rome, especially the Via Appia to the south, where many fine tombs still stand.

Augustus' Mausoleum, started in 28BC, is typical in revealing marked Etruscan influences although the Greeks and Persians had also had *tumuli*: circular masonry drums topped by conical earth mounds, on which trees were often planted. Hadrian's great mausoleum across the Tiber, built *c*. AD135 to

house his own and the Antonine dynasty's remains, now the Castel Sant'Angelo, perpetuates something of the same tradition but with stronger Greek influences. An alternative type of tomb, probably derived from Hellenistic Syria, consisted of several superimposed columnar structures with either a pyramidal or a conical roof. Diocletian built an octagonal mausoleum for his body in his retirement palace at Split, while his successor Galerius erected an equally grand monument to himself. Built at Thessalonica a few years later in *c*. AD311, it is now a church.

*Below: Funeral relief of a woman from Rome, dating from the 2nd century AD but with a Greek inscription, indicating that the woman was Greek in origin and thereby demonstrating the cosmopolitan nature of Rome's population.*

*Above: Funerary banqueting scene on the urn of Julia Eleutherides (a Greek surname but Roman first name), from the 2nd century AD.*

*Below: Funerary relief showing mourners bearing the catafalque of a body in procession from Rome, 1st century AD. A banquet normally followed the cremation or burial.*

One of the most eye-catching of all tombs in Rome and still almost intact, is the "Pyramid of Cestius". Erected south of the city *c.* 20BC, near the later Porta Ostiensis and housing the remains of an important Roman noble, it recalls in its form the brief passion for Egyptiana that followed the annexation of that kingdom to the empire in 30BC. However, few later nobles outside the imperial family built on such a large scale. Probably the most unusual imperial tomb is Trajan's. The ashes of this popular emperor, who died in Tarsus in AD117 after the failure of his Parthian campaign, were placed inside his great column in the heart of Rome. A special senatorial decree overrode the ancient laws to permit the interment.

## OTHER TOMBS

Not all tombs were grandiose dynastic statements, for many ordinary inhabitants both of the capital and other cities wanted to perpetuate their names, partly as a protest against the anonymity of metropolitan life, partly because, with such doubts about immortality, they wanted to be remembered after their deaths. Both interiors and exteriors were richly decorated, to impress the living and provide a fitting *domus aeterna* (eternal home) for the dead. The Romans often buried grave goods to accompany the dead, with elaborate furnishings suggesting an almost Egyptian belief in the deceased's continued existence. A fine example of such decorations comes from the painted stucco vaulting of the Mausoleum of the Anicii of the 2nd century AD.

A flamboyant but non-aristocratic tomb has been preserved at the Porta Maggiore in the Aurelianic Wall. This is the Tomb of Eurysaces, a wealthy baker and freedman of the late 1st century BC. The circular openings in the tomb probably emulate baker's ovens. The tomb of the Haterii, a family of rich builders, is another fine example of a resplendent non-aristocratic tomb.

Poorer citizens might subscribe to a burial club that would arrange a decent funeral for them, while all but the very poorest had their graves marked by *amphorae* buried in the ground up to their necks. Many survive in the Isola Sacra cemetery near Ostia. The inscriptions on some tombs can be humorous: "Here in my tomb I drain my cup more greedily, because here I must sleep and here must stay for ever". However, more often they are simply poignant: "May the passer-by who has seen these flowers and read this epitaph say to himself: 'This flower is Flavia's body'".

## FUNERAL RITES

A funeral began with the laying out of the corpse for seven days so that friends and relatives could pay their last respects. There followed a funeral procession to the burial place where there was usually a funerary banquet, like a wake. The family would return regularly to the tomb during their mourning period, the first time only eight days later. They would continue to have commemorative picnics for long after. If the funeral was that of an

important person, the procession might wend its way to the Forum Romanum, where a funeral oration would be given. Originally these were reserved for men only, but by the 1st century AD exceptional women were also honoured in this way. Occasionally, as with the speech Mark Antony gave at Caesar's funeral, such speeches had political significance.

Cremation on a pyre in public was the usual form of disposing of bodies for most Romans up to *c.* AD100, when fashions began to change for reasons that are not entirely clear. The change seems to have begun among the upper classes – although the emperors themselves long continued the custom of cremation – and then spread down through the social hierarchy. Whether this can be connected with the slow changes in other attitudes is unknown. It certainly encouraged some splendid sarcophagi, but the mythological scenes carved on them seldom suggest any very powerful belief in an afterlife. Typical scenes show cavorting Tritons and Nereids, mermen and sea nymphs, as on a sarcophagus in the Louvre. Battle scenes were also very popular, usually showing the sack of Troy or some other well-known legend, but few suggest any specific religious belief.

Christian attitudes towards tombs and burial were very different. As they confidently expected the resurrection of the body, cremation was always out of the question. Bodies were buried, sometimes in Rome's catacombs by both pagans and Christians, especially the latter, for Christians often wanted to keep a low profile even when not trying to avoid persecution. There the Greek word for fish, *ichthys*, served as an acrostic for the words "Jesus Christ, God's Son [and] Saviour". When Constantine made Christianity the imperially favoured cult, Christian art and iconography developed. The finest surviving early such tomb is the Mausoleum of Santa Constanza, a circular building whose interior is graced by delightful paintings of birds and flowers with no obvious religious connotations.

### THE CULT OF THE ANCESTORS

Despite being in the underworld, the dead were strongly believed to haunt the living and therefore needed to be appeased – hence the origins of the gladiatorial games and their name *munera* (offerings). As the Christian writer Tertullian scathingly noted in *The Shows c.* AD200, "Men believed that the souls of the dead were propitiated by human blood". (Tertullian also disapproved of those tombs that invited the passing to drink to the deceased's memory.) *Mos maiorum*, the customs of our ancestors, always had a strong appeal to the Romans as an ideal, for Roman piety and dynastic pride were both connected with honouring the dead. The family death masks were kept prominently in the *domus*, normally in the atrium, and taken out and paraded through the streets on special occasions.

*Above: Hadrian giving the funeral oration of his wife Sabina in the Forum Romanum, 2nd century AD.*

*Below: Vault of Santa Constanza, Rome, the Mausoleum of Constantine's daughter Constantia.*

# INDEX

# ACKNOWLEDGEMENTS

This edition is published by
Lorenz Books, an imprint of
Anness Publishing Ltd
info@anness.com
www.lorenzbooks.com
www.annesspublishing.com

© Anness Publishing Ltd 2026

All rights reserved. No part of this
publication may be reproduced,
stored in a retrieval system, or
transmitted in any way or by any
means, electronic, mechanical,
photocopying, recording or
otherwise, without the prior
written permission of the
copyright holder.

A CIP catalogue record for
this book is available from
the British Library.

Publisher: Joanna Lorenz
Editorial Director: Helen Sudell
Editor: Joy Wotton
Designer: Nigel Partridge
Jacket Designer: Nigel Partridge
Illustrations and maps: Vanessa
   Card, Peter Bull Art Studio
Production Controller:
   Ben Worley

PUBLISHER'S NOTE
Although the information in this
book is believed to be accurate at
the time of going to press, neither
the authors nor the publisher can
accept any legal responsibility or
liability for any errors or omissions
that may have been made.

p.1. Terentius Nero and his wife,
a fresco from the ruins of Pompeii.
p. 2. The Arch of Titus, Rome.
p3. Mosaic portraying comedy and
tragedy masks. p. 4. *Left*: The Villa di
Poppaea, Oplontis. *Right*: View of the
Forum Romanum in the 19th century.
p. 5. *Left*: Mosaic of a wild beast fight.
*Right*: The Arrival of Io in Egypt, a fine
Roman wall-painting.

PICTURE ACKNOWLEDGEMENTS
**Ancient Art and Architecture
Collection**: 102b, 103b, 127b.
**Art Archive**: 228t, /Museo di Roma
Rome/Dagli Orti 4t, 42–3, /Galleria
Borghese Rome/Dagli Orti 5b, 182–3, /
Dagli Orti: 6b, 22tl, 24t, 37b, 40b, 49b,
51b, 70l and r, 71t, 72t, 92b, 96t, 98t
and b, 99b, 110b, 111t, 117b, 121b,
122t, 124t and b, 125t, 153b, 161b,
174b, 181b, 189b, 207b, 208t, 223b,
230b, 231t, 232t, 238t, 240tr, 245t,
246t, /Bardo Mus. Tunis/Dagli Orti
9t, 113t, 169t, 171t, 194tr, 211t, 230t,
233t, 237t, /Santa Costanza Rome/
Dagli Orti 9b, 249b, /Archaeological
Mus. Madrid/ Dagli Orti 13m, 190b, /
Bibliothèque des Arts Décoratifs Paris/
Dagli Orti 14–15, 128–9, 204b, 229t, /
Album J. Enrique Molina 16–17, 49t, /
Historical Picture Archive 19t, /Harper
Collins Publishers 22b, /Museo della
Civita Romana Rome/Dagli Orti 54b,
56t, 178b, 190t, 192t, 195tr, 207t, 211b,
212t, 222t, 224t, 225t, 226b, 233b,
244t, 248t and b, /Museo Capitolino
Rome/Dagli Orti 55b, 176b, 180t,
247b, 249t, /Private Collection/ Eileen
Tweedy 64, /Archaeological Mus.
Naples/Dagli Orti 87b, 108b, 109t,
135t, 145b, 177t and b, 185t, 193t,
219t, 220t, 221t, 224b, 234t, 235t,
241t, 243b, 244b, 246b, 256t, /Nicolas
Sapieha 91t, /Archaeological Museum
Istanbul/Dagli Orti 100t, 240bl, 242t,
/Diozesanmuseum Trier/Dagli Orti
119, /Ephesus Mus. Turkey/Dagli Orti
120t, /Archaeological Mus. Sousse
Tunisia/Dagli Orti 133t, /Musée du
Louvre Paris/Dagli Orti 136t, 176t,
184t, 195b, 215b, 218t, 225b, 242b, /
Museo Nazionale Terme Rome/Dagli Orti
138t, 162t, 188b, 191b, 219b, 243t, /
Biblioteca Nazionale Marciana Venice/

Dagli Orti 141t, /Provinciaal Mus.
G M Kam Nijmegen Netherlands /
Dagli Orti 146b, /Archaeological Mus.
Florence/ Dagli Orti 150b, /Cathedral
Treasury Aachen/Dagli Orti 154t, /Villa
of the Mysteries Pompeii/ Dagli Orti
164–5, 174t, /National Mus. Damascus
Syria/ Dagli Orti 166l, /Musée Granet
Aix-en-Provence /Dagli Orti 166br, /
Cathedral Mus. Ferrara/ Dagli Orti
171b, /Archaeological Mus. Ostia/
Dagli Orti 175b, 206b, 210, 231b, /
Museo Nazionale Romano Rome 179b,
/Museo Opitergino Oderzo Treviso /
Dagli Orti 184b, /Archaeological Mus.
Sfax/Dagli Orti 188t, /Archaeological
Mus. Merida/ Spain/ Dagli Orti 189t, /
Musée de la Civilisation Gallo-Romaine
Lyons /Dagli Orti 191t, /National
Archaeological Mus. Athens/ Dagli Orti
194b, /Archaeological Mus. Alexandria/
Dagli Orti 202t, /Museo Concordiese
Portogruaro/Dagli Orti 206t, /Musée
d'Orsay Paris/Dagli Orti 208b, /Museo
Nazionale Ravenna/Dagli Orti 213b, /
Musée des Antiquités St Germain
en Laye/ Dagli Orti 214t, 236b, /
Archaeological Mus. Cherchel Algeria/
Dagli Orti 214b, 215t, /Musée de Cluny
Paris/Dagli Orti 241b.
**Bridgeman Art Library**: 8t, 22tr, 25b,
29t, 53b, 76t, 114t, 130–1, 133b, 135b,
136b, 140tl, 143b, 145t, 155b, 173b.
**Corbis**: 11m, 47t, 65b, 160b, /Araldo de
Luca 1, 68b, 71b, 79b, 88b, 111b, 139,
140b, 146tl, 147t, 150t, 151b, 157t,
159tl and br, 163t and b, 167br, 172,
178t, 193b, 221b, 228b, 237b, /Mimmo
Jodice 5t, 6t, 76b, 77t, 86b, 87t, 90t, 91b,
96b, 97b, 106t, 108t, 132t, 137t, 146tr,
148–9, 153t, 154b, 168t and b, 170t and
b, 192b, 212b, 235b, 255, /Lawrence
Manning 7b, /Michael S. Yamashita
8b, 30t, 55t, 144t, /Sandro Vannini 10m,
10r, 112b, 151t, 198t, 222b, /Roger
Ressmeyer 12m, 104–5, 106t, /Andrea
Jemolo 18b, 46b, /Paul Almasy 20b,
125b, /Alinari Archives 21t, 29b, 53t,
158b, 185b, 186t, /Gustavo Tomisch
21b, /Carmen Redondo 23b, 26t, 82b, 83t,
/ML Sinibaldi 24b, /Angelo Hornak 25t,
36b, /Peter M Wilson 26b, /Bill Ross
27t, /Vittoriano Rastelli 27br, /Dennis
Marsico 28b, /Archivo Iconografico, S.A.
31b, 66t, 73t, 116b, 156b, 186b, 187b,
229b, 232b, 239t, /David Lees 31t,
138b, /Michael Nicholson 32–3, 117t,
122b, 203t, /Vince Streano 34b, /Hans
Georg Roth 35t, /Richard T. Nowitz
36t, /John Heseltine 41b, 65t, 199b, /
Ludovic Maisant 52t, /Roger Wood 54t,
59b, 86t, 95tl, 112t, 114b, 115b, 134b,
142t, 175t, 187t, 227t, 245b, /Yann
Arthus-Bertrand 58t, /Vanni Archive
59t, 63t, 67b, 89b, 101b, 107b, 110t,
132b, 144b, 239b, /Tony Brown/Eye
Ubiquitous 60t, /Ruggero Vanni 60b,
68t, 118t, 152b, /Freelance Consulting
Service 61t, /Bettmann 62b, 100b, 223t,
/Mark L. Stephenson 63b, /Paul Hardy
73b, /Massimo Listri 78b, 137b, 156t, /
Werner Forman 88t, 152t, 157b, 160t,
247t, /Macduff Everton 93t, 94, 95b, /
David Ball 97t, /Stapleton Collection
101t, 201t, /Nik Wheeler 102t, /
Stephanie Colasanti 116t, /Richard
Klune 118b, /Hanan Isachar 121t, /
Wolfgang Kaehler 123, /Reuters 126t,
147b, /Kevin Schafer 126b, /Benjamin
Rondel 127t, /Chris Hellier 142b, /
Philip Spruyt 143t, /Dave Bartruff
158t, /Gérard Degeorge 161t, /Origlia
Franco/Corbis Sygma 167t, /Charles and
Josette Lenars 169b, 181t, /Elio Ciol
180b, /Christel Gerstenberg 196–7, /
Enzo and Paolo Ragazzini 201b, /Roger
Antrobus 202b, /Franz-Marc Frei 216–17,
/X. Noticias 226t.
**Mary Evans Picture Library/Edwin
Wallace**: 204t
**Photo Scala, Florence**: /© 1990 18tl, 19b,
39, 51t, 56b, 61b, 66t, 69t, 72b, 95tr, 99t,
113b, 162b, 173t, 209, 238b, /© 1999
13l, 30b, /© 1990 Fondo Edifici di Culto
– Min. dell'Interno 50t, /© 1990/courtesy
of the Ministero Beni e Att. Culturali
11l, 20t, 23t, 44b, 48b, 62t, 74–5, 78t,
80t and b, 81t and b, 82t, 92t, 93b, 141b,
155t, 198b, /© 2003/Fotografica Foglia
4b, 84–5, 200, /© 2003 Luciano Romano
90b, /© 2003/HIP 103t, /© 1998 220b.